S.C.

Portrait of Stephen Crane painted by Corwin Knapp Linson in 1894; reproduced from the original in the possession of Clifton Waller Barrett.

STEPHEN CRANE: LETTERS Edited by

R. W. STALLMAN AND LILLIAN GILKES

With an Introduction by R. W. Stallman

NEW YORK UNIVERSITY PRESS

1 9 6 0

© 1960 by New York University
Library of Congress Catalog Card Number: 59–15192
Manufactured in the United States of America

DESIGN: Marshall Lee

Second Printing, 1970

To
WILSON FOLLETT
and
AMES W. WILLIAMS
and
VINCENT STARRETT

INTRODUCTION

1

"**I** GO through the world unexplained, I suppose," Stephen Crane wrote Nellie Crouse, one of the women he loved. To explain Crane is one purpose of this book. His letters and the correspondence about him explain him by details not subsumed or recreated within his works. The letter, rather than his literary style or works, *is* the man. Crane, it has been said, carried into his correspondence little of the glamour of his creative work. That is precisely as it should be: the one cannot very well compete with the other. Nevertheless, his letters are characterized by several points of resemblance to his creative works; for one thing, many of them are cryptic. Also, they are full of common sense, wisdom, and frequently humor.

His love letters to Lily Brandon Munroe and his cagey and secretive letters to Nellie Crouse are here brought together for the first time. From them, together with other letters such as Cora Taylor's about Stephen, a new Crane emerges quite different from the Crane portrayed by Thomas Beer in his *Stephen Crane* (1923).

Cora Taylor, with whom Crane lived as her husband during his last three years, appears in Beer's biography only peripherally (in two scant references); and Lily Brandon Munroe and Nellie Crouse, since their letters were unknown to Beer, are not mentioned at all. Although Beer knew far more about Cora Taylor than he gave out, he felt obliged for the sake of the Crane family not to divulge the truth about her, and, while rightly exonerating Crane from much of the irresponsible slander surrounding his name, he also deferred to them in silencing some of the truth about Crane lest it offend. It would appear then that Beer had to pay respects during the jazz age to that very same squeamish moral code which Crane in the nineties had rebelled against (although himself somewhat priggish and puritanical), and which Beer in his biography aimed to expose. His book, after all, is the biography not so much of an author as of an epoch, scored for its moral hypocrisy, in which Crane figures centrally as the maligned victim of scandal and calumny—a social study manipulated by an impressionist painter, a brilliant stylist.

Obviously Crane never expected his letters to be published, and no doubt he would register surprise to find that everything he once said or did, even to offhand remarks and trivial incidents, has the importance that this collection of his letters provides. By bringing Stephen Crane's letters together with Cora's, together with the letters of their recipients (Howells, Garland, Conrad, and others) and a selection of the correspondence dealing with the Cranes, a new perspective emerges; for this collection presents by the interrelationship of all these letters a pattern not known to any of its contributors. The contributors include many of the most important literary figures of Crane's time: Joseph Conrad, H. G. Wells, William Dean Howells, Hamlin Garland, Harold Frederic, Edward Garnett, and others.

Crane's letters disclose the many sides of his contradictory nature. He conceals from Willis Brooks Hawkins his true feeling about the banquet given him in Buffalo by the Society of the Philistines, and then, writing Nellie Crouse the same day, he declares it. His love for outdoor life is shown in the letters written while vacationing at a camp in northern Pennsylvania two months after his return from the West and just after reading the proofs of *The Red Badge of Courage*. This love is even more lyrically expressed in the letters written while he was reworking the manuscript of *George's Mother* at his brother's house in Hartwood, New York. And then, in conflict with his love for the outdoors, he expresses his fondness for sociability and city life in some letters preparing for poker games with Hawkins and friends, for meetings with members of the Lantern Club, and for the banquet of the Society of the Philistines. For Crane, experiencing life went hand in hand with writing about it; his compulsion to withdraw from it stands in conflict with his compulsion to experience it to the full. Ironically enough, even in the midst of retreating to the woods he is confronted by the forces of engagement versus withdrawal when six girls show up at the camp in Parker's Glen: "There are six girls in camp and it is with the greatest difficulty that I think coherently on any other subject" (Letter 79).

"I have lost all appetite for victory," Crane wrote Nellie Crouse not long after he had attained his goal through the publication of *The Red Badge of Courage:*

I will be glad if I can feel on my death-bed that my life has been just and kind according to my ability and that every particle of my little ridiculous stock of eloquence and wisdom has been applied for the benefit of my kind. From this moment to that deathbed may be a short time or a long one but at any rate it means a life of labor and sorrow. I do not confront it blithely. I confront it with desperate resolution. There is not even much hope in my attitude. I do not even expect to do good. But I expect to make a sincere, desperate, lonely battle to remain true to my conception of my life and the way it should be lived, and if this plan can accomplish anything, it shall be accomplished. It is not a fine prospect. I only speak of it to people in whose opinions I have faith. No woman has heard it until now.

(Letter 131.)

Long before Stephen Crane's *Love Letters to Nellie Crouse* appeared (1954), an admirer of Crane was permitted to read them but not to quote from them. In the *Chap Book* of May, 1930, Jerre G. Mangione summarized their importance: Crane "could not refer to his own life without suggesting a tense struggle going on within himself." It was the struggle "between uncompromising realities and deeply rooted ideals, one which filled Crane's soul with irony and despair." This characterizes everything Crane wrote. Not only his letters to Nellie Crouse, but all Crane's letters express this conflict. Furthermore, his poetry and fiction manifest the same conflict: the conflict between illusory theories or ideals, empty forms or abstractions, and the concrete facts of unpredictable reality. Ideals versus realities define the structure of ironies by which *The Red Badge of Courage* achieves its form. A correlation thus exists between the personal revelations Crane made in his letters and those in his creative works.

Artists are notoriously self-contradictory. They contradict themselves in their works by treating obversely the same theme. Katherine Mansfield, as she recorded in her *Journal*, thought life meaningless to her after her brother died. Something of the poignancy of her loss is rendered in "The Daughters of the Late Colonel." In "The Fly," on the contrary, she deals ruthlessly with the same theme, rendering its obverse side. Flaubert professed scorn of life, but nevertheless pictured life with sacred devotion in "A Simple Heart" and with passion in *Madame Bovary*. Authors make public pronouncements in their prefaces and then contradict in their letters what they have publicly professed. Conrad, who in his letters declared his detestation of life at sea, retired to land and wrote in contradiction of his bias some memoirs and works of fiction commemorating ships and sailors and life at sea. Crane, who sought adventures and believed that to write about life one must first experience it, created in *The Red Badge of Courage* the reality of war without himself having experienced it. It was the same for *Maggie: A Girl of the Streets,* the plot of which Crane invented. He did not know the Bowery intimately until after he had written at least one draft of his novel.

The hazard for critics lies in assuming that what the literary work means must be the same as what the author in his letters said he intended it to mean. Crane's intention in *Maggie: A Girl of the Streets* was "to show that environment is a tremendous thing in the world and frequently shapes lives regardless" (Letter 17). *Maggie: A Girl of the Streets* embodies unsuspected richnesses in its texture and structure, concealed significances not hinted at by the author's declared intention. It is not merely a sociological study; it is first of all a work of art. *The Red Badge of Courage* is not only what Crane said he intended it to be, "a psychological portrayal of fear"; it is that, but it is also a great deal more. The unwary reader needs only D. H. Lawrence's pointer to warn him: "Never trust the artist. Trust the tale." Conrad concealed from his public what his novels are really all about by planting in his Author's Notes bogus trade secrets about his literary aims; he would have you believe by his subtitle to *The Secret Agent* that this richly designed novel is nothing more than "A Simple Tale."

Crane was many-sided. He was humble and shy, but he was also arrogant and conceited. He was a gentleman and he was also a smart aleck and an irresponsible heel. On occasion an ornery cuss, he was also lovable. Whether you liked him or not meant nothing to him; to get to know him you made the first move, not he. Howells, Henry James, and Conrad liked him; Frank Norris, loathing him, wrote a satiric sketch in mockery of Crane as a war correspondent. Ford Madox Ford reports that Crane changed character a half-dozen times in a single day. He was a man of many moods, but the fact that he was many-sided is not to say that he was complicated. Very few artists are actually complicated enough to be interesting personalities. "It is the really complicated mind that writes Boswell's Journal."

Biographical matter serves to satisfy our curiosity about the author as a man—what kind of person was he? Crane's letters would not interest us except that it is Stephen Crane who wrote them. That is our justification for peeking, as it were, over his shoulder and reading what he never intended us to read. He must submit to our intrusion because he is Stephen Crane, one of America's most important literary artists. An author's letters correct our distorted views and mistaken prejudices about the man himself (Pope is one example); they serve to clear the air of cant. Although an author's letters frequently furnish some clues to understanding his works, the literary critic is concerned primarily with the works themselves. The author's pronouncements about his art, however interesting, remain critically irrelevant for establishing the validity of his works *as* works of art. Letters are no substitute for critical scrutiny, for it is only in the works themselves that the author's intention or formed meaning resides. Critical inquiry is, I think, a one-way traffic. It is directed away from personal documents to the works themselves.[1] Reverse the traffic and you are interpreting the works solely for a reconstruction of the author's biography, the literary works thus being returned to the history from which they came. What an author's letters disclose may reinforce the critic's interpretation of his works, or it may stand at odds with his interpretation. In either case such external evidence as provided by letters or notebooks is coincidental, supererogatory.

There is the artist writing literary works, and there is the man writing letters. They are two distinct selves, each of which is probably many-sided. Crane's letters open up certain sides of his nature not reflected in his literary works (as well as some characteristics identifiable there); they are filled largely with such residual stuff as incidents and emotions not made use of in his art, moods not relevant to the creative one, and so on.

The letters reveal the man. Crane's letters throw a vivid light on his character. They have use not only for the biographer but also for the critic, for they document Crane's views on art and the creative process; they re-establish and correct both the chronology of personal events and the composition dates of his works.

Crane, unlike his friend Henry James, revealed himself in his letters. Most of James's letters amount to no more than the "mere twaddle of graciousness." You rarely find James discussing in his letters his craftsmanship or the art of the novel—he left that for prefaces, essays, and reviews. The letters of Conrad, like those of Crane, express expediencies, emergencies, personal plights, prospects, and setbacks, the business of our daily routine. (Unfortunately, the Conrad letters having intrinsic value as revelations of his creative and critical mind were not the ones he addressed to Crane.) Crane was incapable, more so than Conrad, of writing the Jamesian twaddle. Not that letter writing was for James a perfunctory thing; on the contrary, it was for him a kind of challenge. His letters "drew on every side of his capacity and character, tested every possible element in his nature, animated his emotion and exer-

---

[1] Henry James regarded burned or unanswered letters as one more wedge toward forcing the biographer or critic to confront the literary work as a thing in itself.

cised his imagination in a way that casts a sharp light on his constitution as a creative talent." [2] James wrote letters as though he were writing fiction; they are frequently epistolary works of art. For Crane, on the contrary, letters have a business to exact—let's get it said in so many words. No style, no twaddle!

Crane was not a great letter writer; but then, he made no conscious effort to be one. He did not write letters with any megrim about posterity looking over his shoulder—as Henry James did. On the other hand, it is not true, as has been said, that Crane's scarce letters are often not interesting. Although many of them are routine and dull, taken as a whole, they are interesting as the record and signature of an artist, as reflections of an artist's many-mooded personality. Even his business notes to literary agents, particularly the collected Stephen and Cora letters to James B. Pinker, Crane's literary agent, evoke our interest by the pathos of his financial plight—how desperately the Cranes besiege Pinker for money, money, money. Again, all these letters are interesting, especially in their cumulative effect, because they provide a corrected perspective of his life and work. They show how feverishly he worked his bankrupt body against the clock.

II

Except for the popularizing influence of *The Red Badge of Courage* in its recent cinema version, the twentieth-century revival of Crane owes more to Beer than to any other source. Beer's importance must be granted, but to take issue with his book is inescapable, for its scholarship is found wanting. It is the same with John Berryman's *Stephen Crane* (1950). Nothing in Beer and Berryman is documented, and almost all of Beer's source-material has disappeared—letters unidentified and now lost. He kept no copies of them and, incredible too, in writing his book he kept no notes. Berryman pieced together the facts for new insights, mainly psychoanalytical ones, and sometimes filled in here and there the chronology; most of his facts, however, are drawn from Beer, though not identified as so drawn. Also, the facts in Berryman's version sometimes get ignored for the sake of his special thesis. It is Beer again, in style and theme and method. Nor is Beer reliable; the facts are frequently distorted, with gaps in the chronology disguised by tricks of camera, cinematic shadow work, and kaleidoscopic effects. Beer's stylized portrait gives equal weight to every detail, dramatizes every episode, and sentimentalizes. A new biography is needed.

---

[2] London *Times Literary Supplement:* September 20, 1957.

The letters in this collection chart the main events in Crane's career and thus provide the first documented chronology. While the chronology gets redefined, new chapters are added to the biography.

Crane's latest biographer did not have access to the Columbia University Library Crane Collection (hereafter referred to as the Butler Library Crane Collection) nor to the Clifton Waller Barrett Collection. He rests his conclusions nevertheless "heavily upon unpublished materials, including three extensive important sources which I am not permitted to cite" (Berryman, p. xiv). Some of this mysterious source material is, I surmise, included in the present volume of letters. The skittish nature of certain collectors and scholars makes for an impasse in determining how many letters not presented in this volume remain extant and in attempting to bring to light certain materials believed to exist. Melvin Schoberlin claims that he owns 600 letters, which means, I presume, that he holds photocopy of the Butler Library Crane Collection as well as others collections *Stephen Crane: Letters* draws upon. "He seldom wrote letters," says Beer, but Crane wrote several hundred letters—most of which are presented here.[3] It is difficult, if not impossible, to estimate Crane's total output in letters. But almost everything about Crane is complicated. There are contradictions in evidences and opinions about him, and even Crane as a person is very difficult to characterize. He resists certitude, and so does the chronology of his life. No American author confounds his biographer with so many incertitudes and debatable issues and gaps in his chronology as Crane; wherefore, while his editors lament his untimely death, they cast a sigh of relief that by his early death they are spared additional biographical difficulties. Enough!

III

If anyone is capable of editing letters, it would probably seem first of all to be the author himself, the man who wrote them; for who other than the original letter writer can possibly know more about them? If only he were at hand to explain such and such a reference, annotate his

---

[3] Writing to Thomas Beer in 1932, John Northern Hilliard claimed ownership of 150 Crane letters held in storage with some Crane-inscribed books. All this is untraced and presumably now lost. Hilliard's daughter says that she cannot recall any such library in her father's possession. Perhaps Hilliard was exaggerating his holdings; but who knows? Meanwhile it may be presumed that additional new Crane letters, not known to exist, will now and then continue to turn up.

own enigmatic phrasings, and say when it was that he wrote all these undated letters!

The letters in this book are ordered chronologically and by numbered sequence. (See List of Letters, pp. xxi–xxx.) Gaps in the chronology are frequent, and uncertainties remain for the dating of many letters. Assigning dates for undated letters has not been easy. Where the date or address remains in doubt, we indicate our uncertainty by a question mark within brackets. Where we feel rather certain about the date or address for letters lacking such specifications, we use brackets without the question mark.

Identification of correspondents is made by introductory notes linking the text of letters and preceding the group of letters having to do with the given correspondent. Identification is also made by footnotes when the correspondence is negligible in quantity or importance. Editorial notes also precede events having importance in Crane's life, the initial note introducing what subsequent correspondence pertains to that given occasion.

Repetitions in the text of Crane letters and inscriptions have been reproduced on the ground that we cannot shy from our obligation to reproduce faithfully all Crane letters known to exist. The very fact that he repeats himself verbatim from inscription to inscription or from letter to letter casts a lighted clue on Crane from the angle of his biographer's interest.

Although the full text of Crane letters is here reproduced except in instances where only fragments are available, some deletions have been made in the text of letters not by Crane, the deletions being indicated by ellipses. The majority of the letters printed here have been transcribed from photocopy of the originals. The largest exception is a set of typed copies of Stephen and Cora Crane letters to James Pinker belonging to the George Arents Crane Collection at Syracuse University Library. For this set of typed copies no originals are available. Other letters lacking originals include those taken from the texts already printed in periodicals or newspapers or books (mainly Beer's biography). Crane, at times, was careless in his spelling. At the risk of being charged with pedantry, we have preserved Crane's misspellings, while correcting such slips in letters of other correspondents.

IV

This collection had its beginning in the set of new Crane letters published in *Stephen Crane: An Omnibus* (1952), which presented the first collection of Crane letters (120 in all, 57 of which were printed there for the first time), and in new material about Cora and Stephen Crane prepared by Lillian Gilkes for her biography of Cora Crane (Indiana University Press, 1959). *Stephen Crane: Letters* presents all the Crane letters that are known to exist, together with all Crane inscriptions, a selection of Cora Crane letters, and a selection of letters by Stephen's friends writing about him after his death. Fifty-six Stephen Crane letters and inscriptions and fifty Cora Crane items are published here for the first time. The Appendix presents a selection of letters, mainly in recollection of Stephen Crane, some by well-known literary figures, others written by former friends of Crane's. All in all, 184 new letters and autographs are published for the first time. New letters and Crane manuscripts are scarce to come by.[4]

Every Crane letter possible to obtain has been gathered from individual collectors, libraries, and inaccessible periodicals and newspapers. The Conrad to Stephen and Cora letters, first published in the *Bookman* (1929), are here reproduced from the originals in the Butler Library Crane Collection; the *Bookman* text of these Conrad letters being corrected.

---

[4] Over a dozen new Crane manuscripts were brought to light in "Stephen Crane: Some New Stories," ed. R. W. Stallman, *Bulletin of the New York Public Library*, LX (1956) and LXI (1957). Five new Crane letters and an inscribed card have come to light since the present book began to go to press, and are now part of the Barrett Collection.

ACKNOWLEDGMENTS

Our debt is first of all to Alfred A. Knopf, Inc., as this book could not have been possible without Knopf's permission to publish all Stephen Crane letters, both letters reprinted and letters here published for the first time. The former category includes letters first published in *Stephen Crane: An Omnibus*, edited by R. W. Stallman (New York: Knopf, 1952; London: Heinemann, 1954); the Crane letters published in *Stephen Crane's Love Letters to Nellie Crouse*, edited by Edwin H. Cady and Lester G. Wells (Syracuse University Press, 1954); letters from the Berg Collection first published in "Stephen Crane's Letters to Ripley Hitchcock," edited by R. W. Stallman, *Bulletin of the New York Public Library*, LX (1956); the Crane letters reprinted from Thomas Beer's biography and from John Berryman's biography. For this permission to publish Crane letters, both reprints and new ones, we are particularly indebted to William Koshland of Alfred A. Knopf, Inc.

Our next largest debt is to Clifton Waller Barrett for providing us in photocopy the letters and inscriptions drawn from the Barrett Collection, together with the portrait of Stephen Crane reproduced in the frontispiece.[5] Our debt to Mr. Barrett is immeasurable. His Crane Collection, recently donated to the Alderman Library of the University of Virginia, includes the recently acquired H. B. Collamore Stephen Crane Collection.

Of the hundreds of letters in the Butler Library Crane Collection at Columbia University, letters addressed to or written about the

---

[5] The photograph was first printed in *Stephen Crane (1871–1900): An Exhibition of His Writings Held in the Columbia University Libraries, September 17–November 30, 1956*, arranged and described by Joan H. Baum (Columbia University Libraries, 1956).

Cranes, we have selected what seemed to us of importance or of relevant importance and interest. For permission to publish this material here for the first time (with occasional exceptions of printed items), we are indebted to Roland Baughman, Head of Special Collections at the Butler Library; also for kind co-operation in these details we are obliged to Miss Alice H. Bonnell, Assistant Librarian of Special Collections.

For permission to include Stephen Crane to Pinker letters and thirty-three Cora Crane to Pinker letters, we thank Lester G. Wells, Head of the Manuscript Division of Syracuse University Library; and for permission to republish Crane letters in *Stephen Crane's Love Letters to Nellie Crouse* (Syracuse University Press, 1954), and for other letters not by Stephen Crane in the same book, we thank Syracuse University Press.

The letters of William Dean Howells, belonging to the Butler Library Crane Collection, have been proofread and corrected for us by Mildred Howells. As noted in *American Literature* of November, 1957, these Howells letters were published in *American Literature* of January, 1957, without permission of the Howells' estate—the set of ten new Howells to Crane letters had been granted us for first publication in *Stephen Crane: Letters.* They are published here by the exclusive permission of W. W. Howells on behalf of the heirs of William Dean Howells and may not be reprinted without their permission.

The letters of Hamlin Garland are published by permission of Mrs. Constance Garland Doyle and Mrs. Isabel Garland Lord, to whom we express our thanks. Also, to Lloyd A. Arvidson, Curator of the American Literature Collection at the University of Southern California, who kindly aided us in clarifying certain questions about the Crane-Garland letters.

We thank also the trustees of the Joseph Conrad estate for permission to publish the Conrad letters, some of which are printed for the first time.

We are grateful to Miss Alice B. Beer for permission to publish for the first time letters from the papers of Thomas Beer.

We are also grateful to Dr. Edmund H. Crane and Miss Edith Crane for permission to publish for the first time letters by Edmund and William Crane.

We have a number of other obligations to discharge. For contributing letters by Crane or about him, most of which are reproduced for the first time, or for granting permission to publish, we thank the following: Ames W. Williams, Vincent Starrett, Gordon Ray, David Ericson, Odell S. Hathaway, Frederic M. Lawrence, Corwin Knapp Linson, Melvin H. Schoberlin, Eliott B. Hague, John D. Gordan, B. J. R. Stolper, David Garnett, Roger M. Frewen, Philip M. Barr, and Waring Jones, who offered us photocopy of a new Crane to Hilliard letter (also, Miss Helen Hilliard for permission to publish this and other Hilliard letters). We thank Frederick B. Smillie for the unpublished Crane to Dorothy Brandon letter and for photocopy of the Lily Brandon Munroe letters. For permission to publish the letter of Theodore Roosevelt we thank the Theodore Roosevelt estate and Herman Hagedorn, Director of the Theodore Roosevelt Association. We thank also the Bacheller estate for permission to publish three letters of Irving Bacheller; and Trinity College, Oxford, and A. P. Watt and Company for permission to publish a new letter of A. E. W. Mason.

Grateful acknowledgment is made to William A. Jackson of the Houghton Library at Harvard University for grant of some new Crane letters; to John D. Gordan, Curator of the Berg Collection at the New York Public Library; to Josiah K. Lilly for three Crane letters now in the Indiana University Library (reprinted from *Omnibus*); and to Robert F. Metzdorf, Curator of Manuscripts at Yale University Library. (Not included in this collection are nineteen a.l.s. Cora Crane to G. H. Perris letters in the Manuscript Division of Yale University Library.)

We also thank the librarians and curators of special collections at the Boston Public Library, Dartmouth College Library, the Public Library of Newark, the Rochester Public Library, the Buffalo Public Library, Lafayette College Library, The Library of Congress, the Huntington Library, the University of Illinois, and the University of Virginia.

We thank Dorothy Brewster for aiding us in research, and Carol Decker for loan of her manuscript of the catalogue she compiled of the Crane Collection at the Public Library of Newark, New Jersey. We are grateful indeed to Roberta Smith, Reference Librarian at the University of Connecticut, for her constant aid in matters of bibliographical research.

Among those to whom the editors owe a note of acknowledgment in gratitude for various kinds of assistance are Paul Revere Reynolds, Bruce Catton, L. C. Brown of J. M. Dent & Sons, Ltd., M. E. Grenander, Thomas Mabbott, the late Max Herzberg, and John S. Mayfield. Also Arnold Schwab, Lewis Leary, Daniel G. Hoffman, E. R. Hagemann, Edwin Cady, and Georges Remords of the University of Strasbourg. For permission to quote from Irving Bacheller's *Coming Up the Road* we are indebted to The Bobbs Merrill Company.

For final typescript of the manuscript we thank Mrs. Virginia Stallman; for preparatory drafts of the text of this book, Mrs. E. E. Hammerberg and Mrs. Edith Lapins of the English Department, University of Connecticut.

We also thank Felizia Seid for assistance in indexing the book, and Pauline Gelert for assistance in checking the Catalogue.

For grants-in-aid of research I thank the American Philosophical Society. I acknowledge also the grant of sabbatical leave (Spring, 1957) by the University of Connecticut.

Miss Gilkes edited the letters subsequent to November, 1897, when Cora Crane enters the picture, comprising roughly one-half of the text of the volume. Responsibility for the Introduction is mine.

R. W. STALLMAN

LIST OF LETTERS

---

† Hereafter the writer, where his name is not cited, is Stephen Crane.
* Items marked with an asterisk are inscriptions.

PART FIVE: 1900

A P P E N D I X

My wife and I like best to remember him riding to meet us at the gate of the park at Brede. Born master of his sincere impressions, he was also born horseman. He never appeared so happy or so much to advantage as on the back of a horse. . . . Those who have read his little tale "Horses" and the story of "The Open Boat," in the volume of that name, know with what fine understanding he loved horses and the sea. And his passage on this earth was like that of a horseman riding swiftly in the dawn of a day fated to be short and without sunshine.

JOSEPH CONRAD

1

1871 – 1893

STEPHEN CRANE, fourteenth child of the Reverend Jonathan Townley Crane and Mary Helen (Peck) Crane, was born in Newark, New Jersey, on November 1, 1871, and died on June 5, 1900, in his twenty-ninth year. Stephen's father died in Port Jervis, New York, in 1880, when Stephen was eight, and his mother died 1891. "My father died when I was seven years old," Stephen mistakenly wrote, and "My mother when I was nineteen." Mrs. Crane was the daughter of the Reverend George Peck, an eloquent Methodist minister and at one time editor of the *Christian Advocate*, the official organ of the Methodist Episcopal Church. She had had a university education, and she wanted Stephen to learn French. He learned no more than a schoolboy's grasp of French, which he exhibits when writing Corwin Knapp Linson from New Orleans in a letter of February 19, 1895 (No. 63). Nor had he a scholar's interest in classical literature, to which his Uncle Luther was devoted.

"Tell Stephen that I spent a half day recently with his Uncle Luther," William Howe Crane, attorney at Port Jervis, New York, wrote Cora (Stephen's presumptive wife) at Brede Place, Sussex, England. "I should have been extremely bored with the entertainment that the old man offered me, if I had not been interested in a little speculation of my own, as to how much Stephen owed to the Peck side of his make-up for his literary abilities. Uncle Luther read to me (and translated) extracts from the Greek poets and took down book after book from his shelves and read me little marked passages for the sole and only purpose of enjoying with me the literary beauties of his favorite authors. At times, the tears came into his eyes. He said, among other things, that 'The Open Boat' was worthy of being a book by itself. My point is that Uncle Luther lives among his books and has a very keen literary appreciation." (Letter of October 15, 1899.)

The Reverend Jonathan Townley Crane was born at Connecticut Farms, near Elizabeth, New Jersey, in 1819 and was graduated from Princeton in 1843. In 1848 Dr. Crane married Miss Mary Helen Peck. "Mrs. Crane, too, was an unusual woman, of broad culture and active far beyond the ordinary in all church work. She was much interested in the cause of temperance; also after her husband's death she wrote for some time for the New York *Tribune*." (Newark *Sunday Call*, May 3, 1896.)   Stephen's mother wrote articles for Methodist papers and reported Methodist meetings for the New York *Tribune* and the *Philadelphia Press*. On August 3, 1889, the *Tribune* published "Crowds at Ocean Grove," by Stephen Crane, then in his eighteenth year.

Stephen's father was a learned divine, a manuscript preacher, a noted wit, a man of broad scholarship and generous enthusiasm (as one of Crane's friends reports him), president of Pennington Seminary for nine years (1849–1858), and four times a member of the legislative body of the Methodist Episcopal Church; he was the presiding elder of the Methodist Episcopal Church in the Newark district. "He was a great, fine, simple mind," Stephen said of him in one of his letters (No. 125). Dr. Crane was a writer of wide appeal. He contributed to the *Methodist Quarterly Review* and the *Christian Advocate* and wrote treatises such as *The Right Way* and *Holiness the Birthright of All God's Children* (1874). From his mother's uncle, Bishop Jesse T. Peck, of New York (a founder of Syracuse University), Stephen inherited in 1881 an inscribed copy of Bishop Peck's *What Must I Do to be Saved?* (1858).

H. G. Wells said that Crane was "a New Englander of Puritan lineage," and Edward Garnett, the London *Academy* critic who befriended Crane in England, made the same mistake. The name of Crane occurs on almost every page of the records of Newark, New Jersey. Newark was founded in 1666, and Jasper Crane was among the founders and was chosen two years later to serve as one of the two magistrates of the community, "an office of extreme importance at that time." (From "Stephen Crane, Jerseyman," New York *Sun*, June 10, 1900.)

Crane's ancestors included several clergymen and soldiers. As one of Crane's friends was first to point out, "It is an interesting study in heredity to note the influence of these two professions in Mr. Crane's literary work, the one furnishing the basis of style, the other of incident." (Clarence Loomis Peaslee, *Monthly Illustrator*, 1896.)

Crane's father jotted down a note in 1879 which reads: "Held the Love Feast: many present, and an unusually melting time." Of the

Crane family, Agnes (one of Stephen's sisters), called it "such an oyster-like family."

Crane grew up in full rebellion against the family tradition, against the Methodist strain in it, and it is amusing to find him engaged in all the vices that his father preached against and wrote about in *The Arts of Intoxication,* a treatise against tobacco, opium, and alcohol—of which four thousand copies were sold by the 1870 edition—and in *Popular Amusements* (1864). Baseball, which Stephen preferred to books, his father prophesied was in decline because so many vices cluster about the ball ground. "In fact, so many vices are beginning to gather about the 'great national game,' as some foolishly term it, that every one connected with it seems to be regarded with a degree of suspicion." The stage, which his father thought immoral, Stephen aspired to by writing plays. Dr. Crane damned novels as the vice of the age. He listed four maxims in warning against the cursed vice of novel reading—No. 4: "If any harm results, Stop at once." Excessive novel reading creates an overgrowth of the passions, a "morbid love of excitement somewhat akin to the imperious thirst of the inebriate." Having given a set of rules in guidance of readers of novels, he recants at the end of this chapter and proposes to substitute in place of it "a rigid iron rule for the guidance of all, young and old, learned and unlearned: TOTAL ABSTINENCE FROM NOVEL READING HENCEFORTH AND FOREVER." Poor Stephen, cursed with the blight of smoking and drinking, not only read novels but wrote them.

❖ ❖ ❖

The letters in this section, beginning with the Reverend Jonathan Townley Crane's birth notice of his fourteenth child and Stephen Crane's earliest known letter (to Odell Hathaway, 1889?), span the period of Crane's schooling at Claverack College and then at Lafayette College and finally Syracuse University. They document Crane's early love affairs—first with Helen Trent, who was already betrothed; and then with Lily Brandon, who was already married. They record Crane's first encounter with the publishing world and with its influential editors and authors, such as Gilder, Garland, and Howells. They announce the birth of *Maggie: A Girl of the Streets* and *The Red Badge of Courage.* They trace, albeit with many gaps in the chronology, Crane's rise to maturity and artistic achievement.

❖ ❖ ❖

1. THE REVEREND JONATHAN TOWNLEY CRANE TO AN UNKNOWN RECIPIENT

[14 Mulberry Place, Newark, New Jersey] November 2, 1871

I was interrupted yesterday and did not send this to the Post Office. Mrs. Crane sends her regards. The new baby is a boy and we have named him Stephen for his ancestor who signed the Declaration.[1]

2. STEPHEN CRANE TO ODELL HATHAWAY [2]

Asbury Park [New Jersey]/Xmas morning [1889?]

Hello central:/hello:/ Give me tough Hathaway, Middletown   Well, old man, I hope you are having a merry, merry X'mas. I expect to stop up and see you as I promised but cant tell for sure yet. Johnnie wrote me that he was afraid he couldn't show up, but would try. I expect to go to P. J.[3] in a few days and on my way back will stop and see you I heard from Puzey and I also heard a voice from Mich. say he had not left my overcoat on the route. Write me here at A. P. Merry Xmas to you and all your friends. Yours sincerely   *Stephen Crane*

3. TO ODELL HATHAWAY

Asbury Park [4] [New Jersey]/Sunday, June 15, 1890

My dear "Tough"/ I thought I would enjoy writing to you today, as I am home with lots of friends, yet, longing for some of my old com-

---

[1] This Stephen Crane was of the third generation of Cranes. The first Stephen Crane to come to America arrived in Massachusetts from England in 1635. "His son Stephen Crane settled in Connecticut and the Stephen Crane of the third American generation settled in New Jersey on lands that now hold the cities of Newark and Elizabeth" (so Crane says in Letter 125).

[2] A classmate of Crane at Claverack College and Hudson River Institute, a coeducational and military college near Hudson, New York.

Stephen attended school at Asbury Park, 1882–1888, and from 1888 to 1890 he attended Pennington Seminary at Pennington, New Jersey, and then the Hudson River Institute at Claverack, New York. On September 12, 1890, he entered Lafayette College and completed one semester. He joined Delta Upsilon Fraternity.

[3] Port Jervis, New York, where William Crane, Stephen's brother, lived. Crane's schoolmates Johnnie, Puzey, and Mich have not been identified.

[4] The Crane family moved to Asbury Park in 1882, and there Townley, one of Stephen's brothers, operated a news-reporting agency, The New Jersey Coast News Bureau. Stephen reported "shore news" this summer for Townley's bureau, and the next summer he reported one of Hamlin Garland's lectures in American literature at the Seaside Assembly, published in

panions at Old Claverack. I am smoking a cigar after a 10.00 AM breakfast of roast pigeon and gooseberries yet I wish to God I was puffing on a cigarette butt after a 7.00 AM breakfast of dried-beef and oat meal at H.R.I. If you see Tuttle give him my kindest regards and tell him to write. Goodbye, old man, write to me. I dont forget my friends and you will always have my best wishes. Yours ever

Stephen Crane

4. TO ODELL HATHAWAY

[Lafayette College, September or October, 1890]

Dear Boys,/ I send you a piece of the banner we took away from the Sophemores [sic] last week. It dont look like much does it? Only an old rag, ain't it? But just remember I got a *black and blue nose*, a barked shin, skin off my hands and a lame shoulder, in the row you can appreciate it.[5] So, keep it, and when you look at it think of me scraping [sic] about twice a week over some old rag that says "Fresh '94" on it.

Stephen Crane

5. TO A CLAVERACK COLLEGE SCHOOLMATE

#170 East Hall   Lafayette College/[November ? 1890]

My dear boy,/ Your letter gladly recd. So you are not having a hell of a time at C. C.,[6] eh? Well, you had better have it now because, mark my words, you will always regret the day you leave old C.C. The fellows here raise more hell than any college in the country, yet I have still left a big slice of my heart up among the pumpkin seeds and farmers of Columbia Co. You asked me if I thought as much of Pete as ever. Well, I should think so, and a great deal more besides, and don't you forget it. We both may possibly come up on Thanksgiving and you fellows whom I still love as of old, must give us a jolly time. So long, old man, don't forget me even if I can't be at C.C. Yours, as ever

Stephen Crane

6. TO ODELL HATHAWAY

Delta Upsilon Chapter House [7]   Syracuse, N.Y./Jan. 9th. 1891

My dear Hathaway, Those pictures have not come yet and neither

---

the New York *Tribune*, August 18, 1891. "Garland Discussed at Avon-by-the-Sea" was reprinted in *Modern Language Notes*, January, 1955, in an article by Donald Pizer.

[5] This tug of war for the flag probably became the inspirational source of the contest between the enemy flag-bearers in *The Red Badge of Courage*.

[6] Claverack College and Hudson River Institute.

[7] Here, in the Delta Upsilon house, Crane wrote this spring a first draft

has any letters from the little crowd of tough devils who hang out in Sioux's [8] room. I ate like a fiend as soon as I got away from Claverack and am eating like a devil now, every chance I get. What has Harry had to say to you since I have been gone? Has he jumped on the mob any more? If he has, damn him. The ΔΥ Chapter here has got a dandy house valued at $20,000.00, situated on a high hill overlooking the entire city. I hope you may all come here sometime, although the fellows here *are* somewhat slow. Yet, . . . [*portion of letter missing*]. As I said before to Sioux there are certainly some dam pretty girls here, praised [*sic*] be to God. Not as nice as they as [*sic*] are in Newburgh, however. There is where the dandy girls are found. Gene has got an awful big belly on him, but he is the same old Gene as of old, good-natured, jolly and sociable. Travis still keeps his same military step that he once used with such success in H.R.I. Brusie is just such a chap that he was; hard, dry, cold and calculating . . . [*portion of letter missing*]. [This is a] dandy city at least and I expect to see some fun here.

---

of *Maggie: A Girl of the Streets*. Transferring from Lafayette College, Crane entered Syracuse University in January, 1891, and stayed until June. He played varsity baseball and received only one mark, an A in English literature, and, though he was not expelled, he was advised by the dean that since he was an indifferent scholar, it would not be wise to return the next term unless he intended to improve his scholarship.

"I did little work at school," Crane admitted in one of his letters [No. 137], "but confined my abilities, such as they were, to the diamond. Not that I disliked books, but the cut-and-dried curriculum of the college did not appeal to me. Humanity was a much more interesting study. When I ought to have been at recitations I was studying faces on the streets, and when I ought to have been studying my next day's lessons I was watching the trains roll in and out of the Central Station. So, you see, I had, first of all, to recover from college. I had to build up, so to speak."

On Crane's writing *Maggie* while at Syracuse University see Frank Noxon's letter (Appendix 24). The history of *Maggie* is given in the introduction to Bowery Tales in *Stephen Crane: An Omnibus*, ed. R. W. Stallman (Knopf 1952, Heinemann 1954), pp. 3 ff.

[8] Sioux was Earl T. Reeve, nicknamed the "Rushville Indian" by Crane because he came from Rushville, Indiana. Travis was Abram Lincoln Travis, Syracuse '94. He taught at Claverack College in 1894–1895 and established the Travis Classical School in Syracuse. Brusie—Sanford Brusie—became a Methodist clergyman. Noted in *Stephen Crane's Love Letters to Nellie Crouse*, ed. Edwin H. Cady and Lester G. Wells (Syracuse University Press, 1954), pp. 3–4.

The original of Crane's letter was quoted in part in the Syracuse University *Alumni News*, October, 1946.

Well here is where I must stop. Give my love to everyone in the old crowd and don't forget this poor devil. Yours always

Stephen Crane

❀   ❀   ❀

Helen Trent

A tall, darkly pretty girl, Helen Trent was already betrothed when Crane fell in love with her. The next summer he fell in love with a married woman, Lily Brandon Munroe. His affair with Miss Trent forms one strand of *The Third Violet* (as Wilson Follett was first to point out). Earlier, while at the Hudson River Institute, Crane was in love with Miss Harriet Mattison, a redhead; she died, and then there was a tall dark girl from Sioux City, and later another redhead, Jennie Pierce, whom he loved "madly" at seventeen. He said that if he ever met a woman with golden hair he would marry her. He found her at Jacksonville, Florida, in November, 1896—Cora Taylor, who lived with him as wife during his last years in England. Thomas Beer, Crane's first biographer (*Stephen Crane*, 1923), makes no mention of three women who played an important part in Crane's life: Lily Brandon and Nellie Crouse, who were pursued by Crane, and Amy Leslie, who seems to have been in love with Crane—at any rate she pursued him. Beer interviewed the middle-aged woman who had been Crane's beloved Miss Trent. Crane's opinions had shocked Miss Trent: "A Negro could be handsome, even without the 'classic profile' demanded by a world soaked in the art of Leighton and Poynter; American religion was 'mildewed'; he found Buddhism interesting; he saw no reason why a young actress with a cottage at Avon couldn't go swimming at dawn, when the beach was empty, without a bathsuit." Crane, nevertheless, did not approve of women who smoked, though on the other hand he approved of the Bowery. Miss Trent forbade him to go near the Bowery. "She had sung in charitable concerts there and it was a slum as vile as anything in Paris or Munich. It was not 'nice' of Crane to go there." So they argued; and Crane, on the rebound, mailed her a note from the ferry to Jersey City, presumably in September, 1891:

❀   ❀   ❀

7. TO HELEN TRENT

I shall come back tomorrow night and we can start all over again. Yours sincerely,   *Stephen Crane*

8. TO HELEN TRENT

[Lake View, N.J.] [9]   September 18, '91

Dear Miss Trent: I have found out something that you should know
at once and will be up this evening to tell you. Yours,   S. C.

9. TO HELEN TRENT

[September 19, 1891]

Your window was lighted all last night but they said you were not in.
I stood and looked at your window until a policeman came and made
me go away. But I came back and looked until my head was just a
sponge of lights. Please do not treat me like this. Nothing else counts
but that.

10. TO HELEN TRENT

[September 20, 1891]

You have the most beautiful arms I ever saw.[10] You never should have
to wear dresses with sleeves. If I could keep your arms nothing else
would count. It would not matter if there was nothing else to hope for
in the world or if there was no more world. In dreams, don't you ever
fall and fall but not be afraid of anything because somebody safe is
with you? I shall be here tomorrow. I must get back to Ed's house,
now.

11. TO ODELL HATHAWAY

Lake View, N.J./Feb. 10, 92

Dear old man: Are you dead? Why dont you write to a fellow? I
think you owe me a letter, you terrier. I received a letter from the

---

[9] Lake View was Edmund Crane's home; later he lived at Hartwood,
New York, a hamlet of Sullivan County, not far from Port Jervis, where William Crane lived. Lake View, then a suburb, is now part of Paterson, New
Jersey. Crane wrote the first draft of *The Red Badge of Courage* in the attic
at Edmund's house in the spring of 1893.

[10] This love note transposes into the poem in *The Black Riders*, No. X:

Should the wide world roll away,
Leaving black terror,
Limitless night,
Nor God, nor man, nor place to stand
Would be to me essential,
If thou and thy white arms were there,
And the fall to doom a long way.

Rushville Indian. He is well, and evidently happy. He says he is "going to be married to a girl whom" he "really loves." See?

I often think of you, old man, and wonder what has become of you and if you ever think of the old times at C.C. and remember your old friends.

Write to me, now, damn you. Yours always truly   *Stephen Crane*

12. TO ACTON DAVIES

[New York City, May 26, 1892]

Dear Acton: Please send me $5 by this bearer whose name is only Smith. Am going to Ed's at Lakeview [*sic*] and need some grub. Other wise I shall eat the front door, his baby and the cat.[11]   S. C.

13. TO THE MANAGER OF THE AMERICAN PRESS ASSOCIATION

Asbury Park, N.J./August 25 1892

My dear sir: I am going south and, also, west this fall and would like to know I could open up a special article trade with you.[12] I have written special articles for some years for the Tribune and other papers. Much of my work has been used by the various press associations, and I would like to deal directly with you if possible. Kindly let me know if it would be worth my while to send you copy for consideration. Yours very truly   *Stephen Crane*

14. TO LUCIUS L. BUTTON

Pendennis Club [13]/1064 Eastern Boulevard [New York City]
Lake View, N.J./Wednesday. [December 14, 1892]

My dear Button: I was glad to be made aware by your genial pen

---

[11] Stephen's family knew nothing of his privations. He told Karl Harriman in 1899: "I was foolishly proud back then. I hated to borrow money from my brothers who were not too well off. I borrowed too much which I have never paid back. The sane thing would have been simply to have lived with Will or Ed constantly and trusted to fortune for some luck in paying them back. They have never asked me for a cent and that hurts like hellfire" (from a letter of Thomas Beer, January 30, 1923).

[12] Crane did not go west until 1895, and then for the Bacheller-Johnson syndicate. He was always anticipating journeys. In 1894 he thought he should be going to Europe, but nothing came of his expectations. He went west to Texas and Mexico City in 1895; in 1896 he got to Washington, D.C., and later that year to Florida.

[13] Crane's nickname for the boardinghouse where he roomed in the fall and winter of 1892–1893, shared by some medical students, including

that the dragon is sad because I have escaped her. But if she be vindictive, I will have my revenge. I have had a dog given me. And I am seriously thinking of inflicting it on our admirable land-lady after Christmas. It is a mere little fox-terrier with a nose like a black bead and a pedigree as long as your arm. It evinces a profound tendency to raise the devil on all occasions, which it does, mostly, by tearing up gloves, and wading around in any butter plate, mince-pie, or cake which it may perceive at large. It also has a violent antipathy to larger dogs, cats, and all fowls of the air. Withal, it is a meek little thing when in human presence and keeps it's [*sic*] black, white and tan coat spotlessly clean. If I can prevail upon our dear, domestic tyrant to let me pay it's board, I shall certainly bring it down after Christmas. I adore dogs.[14] I think I shall be again at the Pendennis Club tomorrow night to see you fellows before you all hie away for Christmastide.

I am gratified that you remembered me by your note of this evening and, meanwhile, I remain, my dear boy, Yours always,

Stephen Crane

15. TO ODELL HATHAWAY

[Hartwood, Sullivan County, N.Y., 1893?]

Hello, you old devil. I was going through here[15] today on the Ontario & Western and thought I would drop you a line. How's things anyhow. You never answer a mans [*sic*] letters so thought you might be dead. Write to me at Hartwood Sullivan County, NY, or I'll come down and wipe you off the earth, the same as I used to at H. R. I. Yours as ever

Stephen Crane

❀   ❀   ❀

Maggie: A Girl of the Streets

Maggie: A Girl of the Streets: A Story of New York was published under the pseudonym of "Johnston Smith," at the author's own expense,

---

Frederic M. Lawrence, a fraternity brother of Crane, at Syracuse, and Lucius Lucine Button, later a physician at Rochester, N.Y.

[14] As is evidenced in the several dog stories Crane wrote, one of them published this year in the New York *Tribune*, July 24, 1892: "The Black Dog: A Night of Spectral Terror." Other dog stories include "Yellow Undersized Dog," Denver *Republican*, August 16, 1896, and "Dark Brown Dog," published posthumously in the *Cosmopolitan*, March, 1901.

[15] Middletown, N.Y., where Hathaway lived.

early in 1893. The publishers, a firm of religious and medical printers, got about $700 out of Crane and, to quote him, "did me the dirt." Beginning the writing at Syracuse University in the spring of 1891, and recasting it at Edmund Crane's home at Lake View in December ("I wrote it in two days before Christmas," Crane boasted to Wallis McHarg in January, 1892), he next revised it in March and, at Frederic Lawrence's boardinghouse—the so-called "Pendennis Club"—he made a fourth draft in the winter of 1892–1893. That March he had taken his manuscript to Richard Watson Gilder, who rejected it as too "cruel" for the *Century*.

Published in mustard-yellow covers, this paper-bound *Maggie*, priced at 50 cents, sold not at all. In 1930, however, this first edition was described as "the rarest in modern literature," an inscribed copy then fetching $3,700. Having given away about a hundred copies to friends (out of the 1,110 copies printed in 1893), and having used the remainder to kindle his boardinghouse stove, Crane himself possessed only one copy in 1896. The number of extant copies known to collectors was reported in 1937 to be fewer than thirty. In 1935 Mrs. Florence Crane Coughlan brought eleven copies for auction at the Anderson Galleries, to be sold at the rate of two each season thereafter, but most of these copies were chipped, torn, or stained. They had been stored in a wagon-house for twenty years and mice had nibbled them. There had been other copies too, but Mrs. Coughlan's two eldest sisters had burned them, "believing they were 'not nice.'"[16] *Maggie* remained unchristened until William Howe Crane, Stephen's brother, gave the book that name.

✿   ✿   ✿

16. TO THE LIBRARIAN OF CONGRESS

Pendennis Club/1064 Eastern Boulevard N.Y. [City]

[About January 18, 1893]

Librarian of Congress: Enclosed find a printed copy of the title page

---

[16] From Catalog 4175 of the American Art Association—Anderson Galleries (New York City), sale of April 24–25, 1935. As executor of Stephen's will, William Crane listed in his accounting twenty-seven copies of *Maggie* which he had not sold because he could then get no offer from any bookseller.

of a book [17] written by me, and one dollar, for which please send a copy of the record of the copyright which is applied for, to

Stephen Crane

17. TO HAMLIN GARLAND

[March ? 1893]

[Inscribed across the cover of a copy of *Maggie*] [18]

It is inevitable that you will be greatly shocked by this book but continue please with all possible courage to the end. For it tries to show that environment is a tremendous thing in the world and frequently shapes lives regardless. If one proves that theory one makes room in Heaven for all sorts of souls (notably an occasional street girl) who are not confidently expected to be there by many excellent people.

It is probable that the reader of this small thing may consider the Author to be a bad man, but, obviously, this is a matter of small consequence to   *The Author*

18. TO DR. LUCIUS L. BUTTON

[March, 1893?]

[Inscribed on a copy of *Maggie*]

It is inevitable that you will be greatly shocked by the book but continue, please, with all possible courage, to the end. For it tries to show that environment is a tremendous thing in the world and frequently shapes lives regardless. If one proves that theory one makes room in Heaven for all sorts of souls, notably an occasional street girl, who are not confidently expected to be there by many excellent people.

It is probable that the reader of this small thing may consider the author to be a bad man; but obviously that is a matter of small consequence to   *The Author*

---

[17] The book was *Maggie*, but it was copyrighted without the title *Maggie*. Crane's typewritten title page read simply: *A Girl of the Streets,/ A Story of New York.—By—/Stephen Crane*. The librarian received Crane's request for copyright on January 19.

[18] A note about this inscribed copy of *Maggie* in the holograph of Hamlin Garland reads: "The first copy Crane sent to me, probably about Oct. '92 H. G." Garland has misdated it, since *Maggie* was not published until early 1893. Crane repeated this inscription almost word for word in inscribing *Maggie* copies for Button (1893?) and Dixon (1895). He probably inscribed a batch of copies with this same message upon receiving the books from the printer in 1893 and had some remaining in 1895, at least the one he sent the Reverend Thomas Dixon early in 1895.

19. TO HOLMES BASSETT [19]

[March ? 1893]

[Inscribed on a copy of *Maggie*]

This work is a mudpuddle, I am told on the best authority. Wade in and have a swim.

20. TO MISS WORTZMANN [20]

[March, 1893?]

Miss Wortzmann. This story [21] will not edify or improve you and may not even interest you but I owe your papa $1.30 for tobacco. S. *Crane*

21. TO BRANDER MATTHEWS [22]

1064 Ave A. N.Y.C.[23]/March 21st, 93

My dear sir: By same mail I send you a very small book [24] which Mr. Hamlin Garland thinks will interest you. If you write me what you think of it, you would confer a great favor. Faithfully yours

Stephen Crane

❖   ❖   ❖

Hamlin Garland

Hamlin Garland, befriended by William Dean Howells when Garland first came east, himself befriended Crane by introducing his work to Howells and various editors. Crane first met Garland in June, 1891, when he reported Garland's lecture on American literature, "The Local Novel," at a summer school at Avon-by-the-Sea, Crane being then a youthful reporter for the New York *Tribune*.

---

[19] Bassett was an Englishman. "Met him in a whorehouse in New York when we were kids" (Crane in a letter to Sanford Bennett, August 29, 1899). Bassett, then in Ottawa, must have been surprised, on receiving *Maggie,* to discover that his friend was an author.

[20] Identity unknown.

[21] *Maggie.*

[22] Professor of English at Columbia University; a well-known critic. This holograph letter is in the Brander Matthews Collection in the Butler Library of Columbia University.

[23] This is the address of the Pendennis Club, but the street (formerly Eastern Boulevard) has been renamed Avenue A.

[24] *Maggie.* This letter and No. 23 provide evidence that *Maggie* was published in late February or March, 1893. In Ames W. Williams and Vincent Starrett, *Stephen Crane: A Bibliography* (1948), the publication date is given as "sometime between late February and May."

Thomas Beer in his *Stephen Crane* (1923) dates the occasion of Crane's visit with Richard Watson Gilder, editor of the *Century*, as March 23, 1892; but Garland never read the manuscript of *Maggie* and did not know about the novel until Crane sent him the printed book in March, 1893. The identity of the book's author was concealed under the pseudonym "Johnston Smith," whereupon Garland wrote Crane accusing him of being the author (cf. Garland, *Roadside Meetings* [1930], p. 131). He then sent Crane to Gilder with the manuscript to induce Gilder to publish *Maggie* in the *Century*. What Crane took him, however, was a different manuscript altogether.

✿   ✿   ✿

22. HAMLIN GARLAND TO RICHARD WATSON GILDER

[March 23, 1893?]

Dear Gilder: I want you to read a *great* M.S. of Stephen Crane's making. I think him an astonishing fellow. And have advised him to bring the M.S. to you. Yours sincerely   *Hamlin Garland*

This is not the MS spoken of. This is a different one.[25]

Stephen Crane

23. TO WILLIAM DEAN HOWELLS

1064 Ave A./March 28, 93

My dear Mr. Howells: I sent you a small book some weeks ago.[26] Mr. Garland had, I believe, spoken to you of it. Having recieved [*sic*] no reply I must decide then that you think it a wretched thing? Yours faithfully   *Stephen Crane*

---

[25] Crane wrote this in pencil across the bottom corner of Garland's holograph letter to Gilder. The manuscript was likely the first draft of *The Red Badge*. Gilder read *Maggie* in book form, not in manuscript, probably this same month (see Beer, *Hanna, Crane and the Mauve Decade*, pp. 272–73): "On his own admission, made in 1904, *this book* gave Richard Gilder a fearful shock. It seemed to him daring and filled with good touches but it was 'cruel.' There was no visible sentiment. These creatures of an environment had no tenderness and no restraint of action to excuse their callosity, and next day Gilder sat pointing out excessive adjectives and slaughtered infinitives to the shy boy, who finally cut him short with an untactful question: 'You mean that the story's too honest?' "

[26] *Maggie.* It was the literary creed of Howells and Hamlin Garland that influenced Crane to reconstruct *Maggie*, an influence that he acknowledged—"a certain re-adjustment of his point of view victoriously concluded some time in 1892" (see Letters 34, 80). Howells wrote an Appreciation of *Maggie* for Heinemann's 1896 edition.

24. WILLIAM DEAN HOWELLS TO STEPHEN CRANE

40 West 59th St.,/March 2e, 1893 [27]

Dear Mr. Crane: I have not yet had a moment to read the book you so kindly sent me. From the glance I was able to give it, I thought you were working in the right way. When I have read it, I will write you again. Yours sincerely,   *W. D. Howells*

25. TO MRS. ARMSTRONG [28]

[April 2, 1893]

Thank you very much for letting me keep these so long.[29] I have spent ten nights writing a story of the war on my own responsibility but I am not sure that my facts are real and the books won't tell me what I want to know so I must do it all over again, I guess.

26. TO WILLIAM DEAN HOWELLS

1064 Ave A. New York/April 8, 93

Dear Mr. Howells: I write to find if you could write me a letter to Mr. Godkin of the *Evening Post*.[30] I am about to apply to him for work. I

Corwin Knapp Linson in his *My Stephen Crane*, edited by Edwin H. Cady (Syracuse University Press, 1958), says that Crane's "Avenue A environment had furnished a background for *Maggie*, being near the river which held the Island with 'its gray ominous building,' but it had served its purpose, and his landlady was the genie who lifted him out of it." His landlady moved to 136 West 15th St., and with her went Crane.

[27] The "2e" is a typing error; the date must be March 28 or March 29, since obviously this is Howells' reply to Crane's letter of March 28.

[28] Formerly Miss Olive Brett, who, at Ocean Grove, New Jersey, in 1883, spanked young Stephen for burying her nephew in the sand (cf. Thomas Beer, *Stephen Crane* [1923]; in Beer, *Hanna, Crane, and the Mauve Decade* [1941], p. 243).

[29] The *Century's Battles and Leaders of the Civil War*. This note to Mrs. Armstrong, says Beer (p. 231), is "the birth notice" of *The Red Badge of Courage*. What Crane had then written was the first draft; the story as yet had no name. When Crane did give a title to the revised and expanded manuscript, he first called it "Private Fleming/His Various Battles." Later he wrote above this title (on MS LV) the final and symbolic title: "The Red Badge of Courage./An Episode of the American Civil War." On the original manuscripts of *The Red Badge of Courage* see *Omnibus* (1952), pp. 201–24.

[30] Edwin Lawrence Godkin was editor of the New York *Evening Post* and of the *Nation*, which he founded. During the Crimean War he had been correspondent of the London *Daily News*. On his retirement in 1899

would like to get it without badgering people for recommendations, but I know I cant.

However, I have humiliating misgivings that you never do such things. If so, please forget that I have asked you. Sincerely Yours

Stephen Crane

27. WILLIAM DEAN HOWELLS TO STEPHEN CRANE

40 West 59th St./April 8, 1893

Dear Mr. Crane: I write you instead of Mr. Godkin, and you can show him my letter, if you like, which I wrote you about your book. You know how well I think you handled that subject, and if I could not agree with you in all points of theory, I thoroughly respected your literary conscience, and admired your literary skill.

Personally I know nothing of you except what you told me in our pleasant interview.[31] But I suppose you can readily establish your respectability to Mr. Godkin. Yours sincerely,   *W. D. Howells*

❋   ❋   ❋

Lily Brandon Munroe

Crane first met Lily Brandon during the summer of 1892 while he was combing Asbury Park, New Jersey, for resort news for the New York *Tribune;* he met her at the Lake Avenue Hotel. She was with him during the parade of the Junior Order of United American Mechanics, a parade that Crane made famous by his corrosive account in the *Tribune* for August 21: "On the New Jersey Coast." [32] Crane lost his job because of it. But otherwise it was a happy summer for Stephen, squandering his meager income on ice cream at Day's for Lily, riding the merry-go-round with her, strolling the boardwalk and observing people. Crane despised the gossiping porch sitters at the hotels and delighted in shocking them.

---

the *Literary Digest* (December 23) said: "Mr. Godkin has probably aroused, in turn, as much animosity and as much intellectual admiration as any man in American journalism."

[31] This letter is important because it establishes the date of Crane's first meeting with Howells as approximately the first week of April.

[32] This article is reprinted in *Omnibus*, pp. 21–22, with an account of this incident, pp. 7–9. Crane's article in the *Tribune* cost Townley Crane his job, as well as Stephen's. The effect on Stephen was negligible, but losing his job seems to have turned Townley into a broken man.

Crane, on the other hand, was prudish.[33] He did not approve of the then "daring" bathing suits worn by women, and perhaps it was because of his influence that Lily Brandon never took to swimming in all her life. They used to dance, though he didn't care for it. Lily had a good voice, and sang well enough to attract admirers, a practice Crane discouraged. He was not a handsome man,[34] but he had remarkable almond-shaped eyes. Abjectly poor and undernourished (he ate little and seemed to resent others eating heartily), he smoked incessantly—a cigarette was always dangling from his lower lip—and he had a hacking cough even at that time.

One night after leaving Lily at her home in New York City, Crane stood watching her window in hope of seeing her pass to and fro; a storm had come up, and she had turned out the light he had asked her to burn. This incident recalls a similar occasion with Miss Trent (see Letter 9), when Crane, thinking she was at home, stood outside her lighted window waiting for her until a policeman made him go away. Although that romantic infatuation was not reciprocated, Lily was in love with Stephen,[35] but she was married and Stephen's future seemed not then exactly promising. Neither she nor Crane had then any thought that he might become famous. Still very fond of him, she remembered him in her later life as the most sincere and natural person she had ever known. Married, but not happily, to a geologist whom she later divorced, she was at Asbury Park that summer of 1892 with her mother-in-law, who was a suffragist. Crane was then rewriting *Maggie*, and he gave Lily one of the manuscripts, which her husband out of jealousy destroyed, together with some love letters and photographs. The one photograph that was saved, probably Crane's gift to Lily's younger sister, Dorothy, shows Stephen in the military uniform

---

[33] On Crane's prudery Beer reports (p. 360): "He was perpetually nervous when gentlewomen smoked before him and a man who would accept a woman's prolonged fidelity without offering her marriage was, in some way not explained, censorable." It is ironical that Crane lived unwed with the woman who was otherwise his devoted wife, Cora Taylor; they could not marry because Cora could not obtain a legal divorce from her husband.

[34] "Women invariably thought him handsome" (Beer, p. 279). Lily Brandon, however, saw him as not exactly handsome. He was also indifferent to dress; at times he would use his cuffs to jot down notes.

[35] John Berryman in *Stephen Crane* (1950), p. 45, remarks that the blonde and very handsome Lily felt no "special interest in her unkempt, dry, taciturn junior." But Crane was very much in love with Lily, and she with him. The notes here are recast from Mrs. Ames W. Williams' recorded notes taken after an interview with Lily Brandon, then Mrs. Smillie, for the transcript of which we are indebted to Ames W. Williams.

of the Hudson River Institute, 1888: he has braids looped around his chest, he has thick lips, and he has bangs!

Crane begged Lily to elope with him, and she considered his proposal seriously before declining. Her family was well to do and not eager for anything serious to happen between them; oddly enough, the Crane family was also opposed. Lily's father, a highly educated man and fluent in several languages, once rebuked Stephen while dining in New York City with him and Lily, when Stephen addressed some few words to him in French. "My daughter does not speak French, Mr. Crane." [36]

Stephen once told Lily that he should not live long; all he wanted was a few years of happiness. He was a troubled spirit, seeking a happiness that always seemed just beyond reach. He enjoyed most of all watching the surf with Lily, and he told her that whenever she saw the ocean she would think of him. She did.

What Crane's letters to Lily Brandon Munroe contradict is the superstition that he was incapable of any deep or lasting attachment to women, that his attitude toward them was ambivalent, or, on the other hand, that his only deep involvement was with Nellie Crouse. These letters to Lily Brandon Munroe are reproduced here in full for the first time (except for Letter 75).

❅   ❅   ❅

28. TO LILY BRANDON MUNROE [37]

1064 Ave. A. NYC [April, 1893]

Dearest L. B. I am sure that you have not concluded that I have ceased to remember. The three months which have passed have been months of very hard work to S. Crane. I was trying to see if I was worthy to have you think of me. And I have waited to find out.

Well, at least, I've done something. I wrote a book.[38] Up to the

---

[36] Beer (p. 328) has it that Crane did not read or speak French.

[37] Parts of this letter and of No. 29 were reprinted in *Omnibus* from *Stephen Crane*, by John Berryman (William Sloane Associates, 1950), p. 45. Berryman also used fragments of Letter 34, and Melvin H. Schoberlin reproduced about one-third of it in his Introduction to the *Sullivan County Sketches* (Syracuse University Press, 1949), p. 19. The complete text of these three letters to Lily Brandon Munroe is from the originals in the possession of Frederick B. Smillie.

[38] *Maggie.* Since Howells had not read *Maggie* all March, this letter must be dated for April, 1893, rather than for March (as Berryman has it, pp. 45, 52).

present time, I think I can say I am glad I did it. Hamlin Garland was the first to over-whelm me with all manner of extraordinary language. The book has made me a powerful friend in W. D. Howells. B. O. Flower [39] of the "*Arena*" has practically offered me the benefits of his publishing company for all that I may in future write. Albert Shaw of the "Review of Reviews" wrote me congratulations this morning and to-morrow I dine with the editor of the "Forum."

So I think I can say that if I "watch out," I'm almost a success. And "such a boy, too," they say.

I do not think, however, that I will get enough applause to turn my head. I don't see why I should. I merely did what I could, in a simple way, and recognition from such men as Howells, Garland, Flower and Shaw, has shown me that I was not altogether reprehensible.

Any particular vanity in my work is not possible to me. I merely write you these things, to let you know why I was silent for so long.

I thought if I could measure myself by the side of some of the great men I could find if I was of enough value to think of you, L. B.

They tell me I did a horrible thing, but, they say, "its great."

"And it's style," said Garland to Howells, "Egad, it has no style! Absolutely transparent! Wonderful—wonderful."

And I? I have merely thought of you and wondered if you cared that they said these things. Or wether [sic] you have forgotten?

29. TO LILY BRANDON MUNROE
c/o R. G. Vosburgh/143 E. 23ᵈ/N.Y. [Winter of 1893–1894?]

Dearest: Although I do not now know what I am to you, I can not keep from addressing you as you still are to me—dearest, the one of all. Many months—or a thousand years: I hardly know—have passed since we met and were comrades; I can readily see that, in that time, I have, perhaps, become a memory to you, a mere figure in a landscape of the past. And it is well for you if it [is] so, and for it I must be glad. Yet you, to me, are still a daily vision, a dream that is part of my life, blending itself with my occupations each day. Your face is a torturing thing, appearing to me always, with the lines and the smile that I love,—be-

---

[39] Benjamin Orange Flower, editor of *The American Sentinel* (a literary and social weekly), established *The American Spectator*, which subsequently merged into *The Arena*. Founder of *The Arena*, he was an extensive contributor to leading magazines and periodicals and was editor of *The Coming Age* (Boston), one of the editors of *New Time* (Chicago), an editor of *Twentieth Century Magazine*, and president of Menace Publishing Company.

fore me always this indelible picture of you with it's fragrance of past joys and it's persistent utterance of the present griefs which are to me tragic because they say they are engraven for life. It is beyond me to free myself from the thrall of my love for you; it comes always between me and what I would enjoy in life—always—like an ominous sentence— the words of the parrot on the death-ship: "We are all damned."

And yet, would I escape from it? Not I. It is the better part. Many men have been thus; it is not for me to object to a pain that many have carried with smiles. Besides, it is supremely true that I concieve [*sic*] those days with you well spent if they cost me years of discontent. It is better to have known you and suffered, than never to have known you. I would not exchange one little detail of memory of you; I would not give up one small remembrance of our companionship. Yet, with it, I suffer and I wished you to know it because you are a woman and though [you] may value me as a straw, you will comprehend why I felt that I must tell you of it. For, surely, it is a small thing. I ask nothing of you in return. Merely that I may tell you I adore you; that you are the shadow and the light of my life—the whole of it.

I go to Europe in about two weeks—a very short trip. If you would write me before then I could take the memory of it with me. My address is: "Care of R. G. Vosburgh, No. 143 East 23d St." [40] Do this for me, dearest, for, though it is a weakness in me, I can hardly go without it. Even though you can only consistently be cold, do me this grace.

I have not been in town long. I have had a strange life. I have recently heard that Tounley [Townley] is married. For that, I owe Dottie [Lily's sister] a necklet.[41] I am delighted to think I am in debt to her. I shall wait and get it in Paris.

The *Arena Co.* brings out a book of mine this winter.[42] I wish you to get it, for it will show you how much I have changed. The Boston critics and Mr Howells think it quite extraordinary. I could prattle on here of the men who are now my friends and of the things I now hear —I am foolish enough to desire to tell you, for I wish you to think well of the man you have made—still[.]

Write me, dearest, for I need it. I may leave sooner for Europe

---

[40] Crane roomed with Vosburgh during 1893–1894 at his studio in the Art Students' League Building; Frederick C. Gordon gives a description of it in Appendix 20.

[41] Promised on a bet that his brother Townley would not marry.

[42] The book was *Maggie;* evidently the Arena Company considered reissuing the 1893 edition. Nothing came of this, nor—as we shall see—of the trip to Europe.

than is now my plan. And in my infinitely lonely life it is better that I should have all the benefits you can say to me. Ever yours,   *S. C.*

29A. *TO CORWIN KNAPP LINSON*

Thursday, 136 W. 15th St. [New York City, 1893]

My dear C. K. Fortunately Senger [Louis Senger, Linson's cousin] wrote me simultaneously and enabled me to get your address,* that I might reply to your postal card. Mr. Barry [John D. Barry, editor of the *Forum*] is still out of town and in his absence it is impossible to get the stories you mention. Have you finished the "Ominous Baby" [43] story yet? At the present time—during these labor troubles—is the best possible time to dispose of it. I am anxious to receive it from you. Could you not send it to me shortly? I hope you are having a jolly time in the wilderness.

---

* That was a feat. My address was the nearest tree, but two village stores and the Sloatsburg postmaster knew the tree!

[43] Published in the *Arena*, May, 1894. This undated leter is from Linson's memoirs (Corwin Knapp Linson, *My Stephen Crane*, ed. Edwin H. Cady [Syracuse University Press, 1958], pp. 41–42).

2

1 8 9 4 – 1 8 9 5

Crane's literary development is traced in the letters
of this section. He tried to interest a publisher in the manuscript of
The Red Badge of Courage, after getting it typed on borrowed money,
and he finally succeeded in seeing it in print at the end of 1894, *The
Red Badge* appearing in New York and Philadelphia newspapers in
shortened form in December. In March, 1894, his poems were rejected
by Harper's, but they were given a reading at Sherry's in April; and
that month's New York *Press,* in an article by Edward Marshall on
William Dean Howells, included a note of prophetic praise of Crane
as a promising fiction writer. He was on the way up, and friends
Howells and Hamlin Garland aided him considerably. He switched
from the influence of Rudyard Kipling to that of the Howells-and-Gar-
land literary credo, as he confided to Lily Brandon Munroe—he is their
disciple and her beloved Stephen.

The letters of 1895 see him on his western trip for Irving Bacheller's syndicate, gathering material for sketches and stories. Willa
Cather reports her meeting with him in Lincoln, Nebraska, and from
New Orleans he returned the typescript of *The Red Badge of Courage*
to Ripley Hitchcock of Appleton and Company. Back in New York, he
joined the Lantern Club, formed by newspaper men with literary aspirations. His book of poems, *The Black Riders,* got a poor notice in
the New York *Tribune* in early June. With the book publication of
The Red Badge this fall, however, he made his name and, having subscribed to a Boston clipping bureau, he collected reviews of *The Red
Badge* and reports on them to Willis Brooks Hawkins: "New York,
throughout, has treated me worse than any other city. Damn New
York. Except the Evening Post. The Evening Post has just reviewed
The Black Riders beautifully" (No. 108); and six days later Crane sent

Hawkins a summary of *Red Badge* reviews from the Port Jervis *Union* as evidence that his book was well received outside of New York City (see Appendix 2).

Crane's letters to Willis Brooks Hawkins record a friendship among the most intimate and rewarding of all the many that Crane's magnetic personality won for him. They provide also the first full account of Crane's dealings with Elbert Hubbard and the dinner rendered in Crane's honor by the Society of the Philistines. What Crane felt about that affair he revealed to Nellie Crouse, but not to his friend Hawkins, to whom he wrote the same night. The incident is retold by Claude Bragdon in *Merely Players* (1929) and in *More Lives than One* (1938). "Crane made a deep impression on me, although I never saw him except that once; a youth sincere and ardent, with an inward fire greater than that of other men—so great, indeed, that it was even then burning him up."[1]

The Philistine Society dinner tendered to Crane in his honor erupted into a disorderly brawling farce; the ox led to the slaughter, Crane felt duped. The occasion underscored what was native to his temperament, disillusionment. Hubbard, aiming to make his mark in literature by editing *The Philistine*, was using Crane to obtain publicity for himself—not that he didn't sincerely admire Crane. The affair of the Philistine Society marked a turning point in Crane's outlook.

That affair is an example of the spirit of the purple cow period. In the *Bookman* of July, 1929, Claude Bragdon epitomizes the gay nineties as the purple cow period, whose spirit was caught by the so-called dinkey magazines such as *The Lark, The Chap-Book,* and *The Philistine*. (In England their counterpart was *The Yellow Book*.) They were egocentric, youthfully assertive, and critical of each other as well as of the society from which they sprang. Gelett Burgess made *The Lark* famous beyond San Francisco by "The Purple Cow." "I never saw a Purple Cow, / I never hope to see one; / But I can tell you, anyhow, / I'd rather see than be one." *The Chap-Book* (Chicago) made its mark by publishing Aubrey Beardsley's illustration for Poe's "The Masque of the Red Death," and further distinguished itself by publishing such authors as R. L. Stevenson, Stephen Crane, Henry James, George Santayana, Verlaine, and Maeterlinck.

The Philistine was the low-water mark of the purple cow period. It was

> the speaking-trumpet, so to speak, of Elbert Hubbard—"fra Elbertus"—pungent, abusive, witty, knowing, vulgar. Hubbard ap-

---

[1] *More Lives than One,* p. 242.

parently dramatized himself as a sort of composite Ralph Waldo Emerson and William Morris, but his chief claim to fame is that of being the Father of Modern Advertising. He had a perfect genius for publicity, smoking up other people's talents and throwing them away like a daily newspaper, accomplishing a considerable amount of good in the process, for to his vast clientele he sustained something of the relation of Chautauqua, disseminating about as rich a brand of "culturine" as the middle-class American stomach was able to stand.[2]

Bragdon sums it up as the age of innocence. The Gibson girl of New York City brownstones encountered literature in Hubbard's *Little Journeys,* in the *Century Magazine,* then as much a national institution of popular taste as the *Reader's Digest* today, and in "A Message to Garcia." The latter, at which Crane scoffed in one of his letters to Hubbard,[3] swept the period as a kind of Arnoldian touchstone as to what literature at its loftiest should be. "It was the Age of Innocence, and it was Golden—before the sinking of the *Titanic* and Armageddon inaugurated The Great Distrust." [4]

✻ ✻ ✻

30. HAMLIN GARLAND TO S. S. McCLURE

January 2, 1894

Dear Mr. McClure: I send here by Mr. Crane the mss. you let me read. They are good and nothing like what I looked for. If you have any work for Mr. Crane, talk things over with him and for mercy's sake! don't keep him *standing* for an hour as he did before out in your pen for *culpr*its. Yours sincerely,   *Hamlin Garland*

31. TO HOLMES BASSETT

[February 24, 1894]

. . . I have just sold another book and my friends think it is pretty good and that some publisher ought to bring it out when it has been

---

[2] Bragdon, *Merely Players* (Knopf, 1929), p. 68.

[3] "I object strongly to your paragraphs about Rowan. . . . He didn't do anything worthy at all. . . . Besides he is personally a chump and in Porto Rico where I met him he wore a yachting cap as part of his uniform which was damnable" (Letter 288).

[4] Bragdon, *Merely Players,* p. 70.

shown as a serial. It is a war-story and the syndicate people think that
several papers could use it.[5]

    ✻   ✻   ✻

John Henry Dick

Hamlin Garland lent Crane $15 to redeem from the typewriter agency
one part of the manuscript of *The Red Badge of Courage,* there in
hock as security for the cost of typing it. But Garland's account in
Roadside Meetings is not the whole story. Another account, appearing
in the *Bookman* for May, 1912, is here retold in the following letter
to "Dicon." This fellow journalist, John Henry Dick, a great friend and
fraternity brother of Crane and a writer for *Godey's Magazine,* borrowed a check for $15 from his boss and gave it to Crane. When the
canceled check with Crane endorsement came back to "Dicon's"
boss, he felt he had been tricked, because he himself had refused to
make Crane this very loan. "Dicon" [6] did not get any more commissions.

Garland lent Crane $30 in all: $15 for recovery of one-half the
manuscript of *The Red Badge,* and shortly after April 22, another $15
(see Letter 37), the second sum probably to enable Crane to repay
"Dicon." (The typist's bill was $30.)

    ✻   ✻   ✻

32. TO JOHN HENRY DICK

[Late February, 1894]

Dear Dicon: Beg, borrow or steal fifteen dollars. [McClure's] like the
Red Badge and want to make a contract for it. It is in pawn at the
typewriter's for fifteen. Thine,   *Steve*

---

[5] According to Beer (p. 288), Crane had sold *The Red Badge* to Irving
Bacheller, whose syndicate was then in the planning stage. The facts, as
subsequent letters show, contradict Beer, for the manuscript of *The Red
Badge* was out with McClure's for several months. Hamlin Garland, writing
Crane on May 8, 1894, asks whether McClure's have yet taken the war
story for serial rights. Crane in his letter to Garland on November 15, 1894,
says McClure had the manuscript for "six months," but in his letter to an
editor of *Leslie's Weekly* (No. 111) he says it was "eight months."

[6] The identification of "Dicon" derives from a letter by Rupert Hughes
to Thomas Beer dated December 24, 1921. According to Hughes, editor of
Godey's Magazine (an assistant in the eighteen-nineties), Crane never paid
back the loan to John Henry Dick.

33. WILLIAM DEAN HOWELLS TO STEPHEN CRANE
40 W 59, March 18, 1894

Dear Mr. Crane: I could not persuade Mr. Alden [7] to be of my thinking about your poems. I wish you had given them more form, for then things so striking would have found a public ready made for them; as it is they will have to make one. Yours sincerely,   *W. D. Howells*

Could you tell me where I could find a copy of *Maggie?*

34. TO LILY BRANDON MUNROE
143 East 23d St., N.Y./Care, Vosburg[h]/[March, 1894?]

Dearest: Truly, I feel that I have decieved [*sic*] you by not starting for Europe today or to-morrow but as a matter of fact, I had postponed it for two reasons. One was because my literary fathers—Howells and Garland—objected to it, and the other was because you had not answered my letter. I did not intend starting for Europe or anywheres else until I had given you sufficient opportunity to reply. It would have been a lonely business—to go so far without a word from you.

To speak, to tell you of my success, dear, is rather more difficult. My career has been more of a battle than a journey. You know, when I left you,[8] I renounced the clever school in literature. It seemed to me that there must be something more in life than to sit and cudgel one's brains for clever and witty expedients. So I developed all alone a little creed of art which I thought was a good one. Later I discovered that my creed was identical with the one of Howells and Garland and in this way I became involved in the beautiful war between those who say that art is man's substitute for nature and we are the most successful in art when we approach the nearest to nature and truth, and

---

[7] Henry Mills Alden, editor of *Harper's Magazine.* Corwin Linson in his "Stephen Crane, A Personal Record" (manuscript in Syracuse University Library), claims that the poems for *The Black Riders* were completed by February, 1894. But in a letter of May 9, 1894 (No. 39), Crane remarked to Hamlin Garland: "I have got the poetic spout so that I can turn it on or off." Later this year he was at it again, as is indicated by Howells' letter of October 2, 1894 (No. 44), and here Howells is outspoken in his dislike of Crane's "prose-poems." It was Howells' reading of Emily Dickinson's poetry that started Crane writing the strange poems that were finally printed as *The Black Riders* in 1895, published before the first edition of *The Red Badge.* That meeting with Howells occurred during the first week of April, 1893. See Letter 27 and n. 31.

[8] In August, 1892. Writing Copeland and Day in 1895 (Letter 74), Crane told his publishers that he had on hand "considerable work" not yet

those who say—well, I don't know what they say. They don't, they can't say much but they fight villianously [sic] and keep Garland and I out of the big magazines. Howells, of course, is too powerful for them.

If I had kept to my clever, Rudyard-Kipling style, the road might have been shorter but, ah, it wouldn't be the true road. The two years of fighting have been well-spent. And now I am almost at the end of it. This winter fixes me firmly. We have proved too formidable for them, confound them. They used to call me "that terrible, young radical," but now they are beginning to hem and haw and smile—those very old coons who used to adopt a condescending air toward me. There is an irony in the present situation, that I enjoy, devil take them for a parcel of old, cringing, conventionalized hens. In one magazine office once, the editor kept me waiting for a good long hour and then made a cool apology in a careless manner that I wouldn't have used upon a dog.[9] I stopped in at that office the other day to see the manager and the editor caught sight of me through the door of his office. "Ah, Crane, my dear boy," he said, "come in and have a cigar and a chat. I'm always glad to see you." And he made haste to be rid of an authoress of some kind who was haggling with him about a story. The bare-faced old grey-headed diplomatist, I wondered if he considered that I had lost my memory. "No—thanks—I'm in a hurry." He seemed really grieved.

I have two books coming out this spring.[10] I will send them to you. One, I think, will make an awful howl. I don't mind it in the least. And as my shorter work will presently begin to appear in the magazines, I will send them to you, also, if you care to have me.

If "Shore Acres" comes to Washington, I wish you would see it played. Young Franklin Garland [11] in the caste [sic] is a great friend and

---

published. "My favorites are eight little grotesque tales of the woods which I wrote when I was clever." These are his Sullivan County sketches.

[9] See Garland's letter of January 2, 1894 (No. 30), in which he took McClure to task for this incident.

[10] Neither book was printed this year. Writing Copeland and Day in August, 1894 (Letter 41), Crane expressed the wish to have his poems brought out this fall, but The Black Riders was not published until 1895. The other book Crane was counting on was probably Maggie, which Crane now thought the Arena Company would issue. It did not see hard-cover publication until 1896. Nor did The Red Badge appear this year except in a syndicated newspaper version. Neither did the European trip materialize.

[11] Hamlin Garland's brother had a part in James Herne's New England play, Shore Acres. With Herne as Uncle Nat, it opened in Chicago in May, 1892, in February, 1893, at the Boston Museum, and that autumn at the

Herne himself is a great admirer of my work, they say, so, really he must be a man of the most admirable perceptions, you know. I have accepted his invitation to see the play next Monday night. Those critics whose opinions are valuable say that Herne is the hope of the American stage, so study him.

I think I shall stay in New York until my book can be sent to the publishers and then go to Europe. I was to go this week but waited until I could overcome the objections of those fellows and until I could hear from you. I shall let you know my new plans.

So, the colonel [Lily's father] is in Washington? I lost his Brooklyn address but last week in my despair I was going over there to see if I couldn't find him. I had a vague idea of "Kent Ave." and the "Carleton House," and was going to make a search. Give him many assurances of my distinguished consideration and if he ever comes to New York—may th' divil fly away wid me but I'll open the largest bottle on Manhattan Island—no less.

Don't forget me, dear, never, never, never. For you are to me the only woman in life. I am doomed, I suppose, to a lonely existence of futile dreams. It has made me better, it has widened my comprehension of people and my sympathy with whatever they endure. And to it I owe whatever I have achieved and the hope of the future. In truth, this change in my life should prove of some value to me, for, ye gods, I have paid a price for it.

I write to our friend, the ever-loyal Miss Dottie Brandon by this same post—Heaven send her rest. Good-bye, beloved.[12]

❋   ❋   ❋

The Uncut Leaves Affair

The Uncut Leaves Society heard John Barry of the *Forum* read Crane's "poems" at Sherry's on April 14, 1894. Crane—he called them "lines,"

Fifth Avenue Theater in New York City. After running five years and still drawing large houses, it was discontinued on Herne's decision.

[12] A portion of this letter was printed in *Omnibus*, p. 648, where it is dated 1896, following the dating of Melvin Schoberlin in *The Sullivan County Sketches of Stephen Crane* (1949), where this letter was first printed (p. 19). Schoberlin dates it February 19, 1896. It seems more likely to have been written in 1894, not long after the Crane letter to Lily Brandon Munroe which is here designated for the winter of 1893–1894 (No. 29). Both letters carry the address of R. G. Vosburgh, with whom Crane lived in 1894. Other internal evidence also points to the dating of this letter for about March, 1894.

not poems—refused to read them himself. The New York *Tribune* quoted him as saying that he "would rather die than do it." He waited down the street for Louis Senger, Frederic Lawrence, and Corwin Linson, his old friends, to report on the reception his poetry made on this literary society. It is the same plight that Crane rendered in "The Making of an Orator," one of his Whilomville stories. The only time in his life that Crane did make a speech was at the banquet given in his honor on December 19, 1895, the one sponsored by Elbert Hubbard's pretentious Society of the Philistines.

Crane enclosed with his letter to Garland on April 17 a clipping of the New York *Press* for Sunday, April 15, 1894. In this same issue of the *Press* Edward Marshall, the most promising editor on Park Row, published his interview with William Dean Howells—"Greatest Living American Writer." Crane in Marshall's account comes off very well. However, Marshall erroneously identified the publisher of *Maggie* as the Arena Company, and the same error was made in the review of *Maggie* appearing in this same issue. (To this day the publisher of the 1893 edition of *Maggie* remains unknown.) Here is what the *Press* said of Crane's *Maggie:*

> *There is unquestionably truth in it, the kind of truth that no American has ever had the courage (or is it bravado?) to put between book covers before. It is a question if such brutalities are wholly acceptable in literature. Perhaps, as Mr. Howells says they will be before long. Perhaps there will always be certain phases of our life which we will not want to have woven with entire realism into our reading matter.*
>
> *This writer, however, deserves praise for one thing, surely. He has not failed to touch vice in his book where he has found it in real life; but he has not gilded it. He has painted it as it is; he has not made it clandestinely attractive. In this he rises far above such other Americans—Edgar Fawcett and Edgar Saltus, notably— as have endeavoured to gain recognition in somewhat similar fields.*

Perhaps it was at this time that Hamlin Garland presented Crane with an inscribed copy of a book of Garland's verse: "To Stephen Crane, a genius, Hamlin Garland." (Quoted from Corwin Knapp Linson, *My Stephen Crane* [1958], p. 81.)

✧   ✧   ✧

35. *TO HAMLIN GARLAND*

111 West 33d St., City/Wednesday, P.M.
[for Tuesday, April 17, 1894] [13]

Dear Mr Garland: I have not been up to see you because of various strange conditions—notably, my toes are coming through one shoe and I have not been going out into society as much as I might. I hope you have heard about the Uncut Leaves affair. I tried to get tickets up to you but I couldn't succeed. I mail you last Sunday's *Press*.[14] I've moved now—live in a flat. People can come to see me now. They come in shools [*sic*] and say that I am a great writer. Counting five that are sold, four that are unsold, and six that are mapped out, I have fifteen short stories in my head and out of it. They'll make a book. The Press people pied some of Maggie as you will note. Yours sincerely

Stephen Crane

36. *HAMLIN GARLAND TO STEPHEN CRANE*

April 17/94 [15]

You'll find me at home any morning at 12. I'd like to know how things are going with you. I am going West on the 25th. Yours sincerely

Hamlin Garland

---

[13] Wednesday was April 18; Garland replied to Crane by postal on April 17, and therefore Crane misdated his letter. In the *Bookman* for January, 1930, Garland says Crane wrote him the above in 1893, but on internal evidence he is mistaken. (Garland's reply is Letter 36.)

In Garland's *Roadside Meetings* (1930), pp. 201–2, and in the *Bookman* of January, 1930, this letter and others of Crane to Garland are inaccurately quoted, the mistakes being reprinted in *Omnibus* (1952) as the originals, for the Crane to Garland letters, were not then available. They are reproduced here for the first time from the originals in the Manuscript Division of the University of Southern California Library.

[14] The review of *Maggie* quoted above. The reviewer goes on to say: "Whether or not we can be entertained by the book, it certainly must command our respect." And he injects an advertisement note on behalf of the young and unknown writer: "It is interesting to note that in next Sunday's 'Press' Mr. Crane will describe the experience of a student of human nature among the tramps in Bowery lodging houses, under the heading of 'An Experiment in Misery'" (see Letter 37).

[15] A postal card postmarked April 18, 1894, addressed to Crane at 143 East 23d Street and forwarded to him at 111 West 33d Street. Crane had moved out of the Art Students' League Building. It was here in the studio of Frederick Gordon that Crane this fall finished writing *The Red Badge of Courage*. Crane wrote in his notebook an article describing the place and the life there: "The Art Students' League." It is reproduced for the first time in

37. HAMLIN GARLAND TO STEPHEN CRANE

April 22/94

Dear Mr Crane: I saw your study in the *Press* today.[16] It reads amazingly well. If you'll come to the stage door tomorrow night and ask for my brother he will hand to you $15, and also a pass for "Margaret Fleming."

Don't trouble yourself about the borrowing, we all have to do that sometimes. You'll soon be able to pay it back and more too. You're going to get on your feet mighty soon. *Yours sincerely*

Hamlin Garland

38. HAMLIN GARLAND TO STEPHEN CRANE [17]

474 Elm St./Chicago, Ill/May 8/94

Dear Mr. Crane: What is the state of things? Did McClures finally take that war story for serial rights? Write me all the news. I shall be here until June 1st probably.

I am nicely located near the lake and I am writing heavily each day. Keep me posted on New York affairs. Yours as ever

Hamlin Garland

39. TO HAMLIN GARLAND

111 West 33d St.,/May 9, 94

Dear Mr. Garland: I have not written you because there has been little to tell of late. I am plodding along on the Press in a quiet and effective way. We now eat with charming regularity at least two times per day. I am content and am writing another novel which is a bird.[18] That poem—"The Reformer"—which I showed you in behind Daly's [Theater] was lost somehow, so I dont think we can ever send it to the *Arena*. I can't remember a line of it.[19]

I saw "Hannele." It's [*sic*] reason for being is back somewhere in the middle ages but as an irresponsible artistic achievement it's great. I sat and glowed and shivered.

"Stephen Crane: Some New Stories," by R. W. Stallman, *Bulletin of the New York Public Library* (September, 1956), p. 60.

[16] This is "An Experiment in Misery," published in the New York *Press*, April 22, 1894, and followed by "Experiment in Luxury," April 29, 1894.

[17] Crane pasted this letter onto the flyleaf of a book signed "Crane, Brede Place" [Brede, Sussex, England].

[18] *George's Mother*, published two years later (see Letter 46).

[19] "The Reformer" was spouted off sometime after Christmas, 1893. Herne's *Shore Acres* moved from the Fifth Avenue Theater to Daly's Theater at that time and remained there until the end of the season.

When anything happens I'll keep you informed. I'm getting lots of free advertising. Everything is coming along nicely now. I have got the poetic spout so that I can turn it on or off.[20] I wrote a decoration day thing for the *Press* which aroused them to enthusiasm.[21] They said, in about a minute though, that I was firing over the heads of the soldiers. I am going to see your brother soon. Don't forget to return to New York soon for all the struggling talent miss you.[22] Yours as ever

Stephen Crane

40. *E. C. BROSS TO STEPHEN CRANE* [23]

Ridgefield, Conn.   June 21, 1894

My Dear Mr. Crane: I have a few moments to spare now while waiting for the last proofs of the paper, and so I will acknowledge the receipt of your letter and the MSS. I will mail you Garland's Poems in a day or two, after having perused them more fully. . . .

As regards the MSS. you have perused, I shall be glad to let you examine the remaining chapters as soon as completed, and I feel quite confident that you will agree that my purpose is not ill-advised, for I follow exactly what you surmise. I draw the moral that it is unfair to judge a young woman too harshly for being indiscreet through the machinations of some sneaking man devoid of principle. I have the remaining chapters all thought out and am amplifying the matter as rapidly as I can with my other work. Charlotte Carlysle marries the young college student who defies society, and he makes her an ornament of the better social world. I use Waymart, restrained as a boy, to find out the life of the so-called ruined girl, and thus the young student

---

[20] Crane wrote his first poems in the spring of 1893. He brought Garland then a dozen poems written on legal cap paper and in Garland's presence he jotted down some poems that were in his head but had not yet been drawn off. Gradually the "poetic spout" dried up, but now a year later he has it again so that he can "turn it on or off."

[21] Perhaps this is the article that appears in Daniel G. Hoffman's edition of *The Red Badge of Courage and Other Stories* (1957), entitled "The Gratitude of a Nation," which was written before Decoration Day.

[22] Garland was in Chicago; he went West on or just after April 25 and remained there all this year.

[23] Edgar Clifton Bross was editor of the *Ridgefield Press;* the manuscript was that of *God's Pay Day* (New York, G. W. Dillingham Co., 1898). A copy of this novel is owned by Karl S. Nash, present editor and publisher of the Ridgefield *Press.*

is able to bring about certain influences in her favor. Makepeace is shown up eventually as a cur and a sneak, but the end of the story does not assume that the church is responsible for the cowardice, but simply that the church would be greatly purified if it were possible to dig up the noxious weeds such as represented by Makepeace, Rev. Snell, and their ilk. Throughout there is not one line written in the spirit of enmity to absolute right living, but all the sarcastic thrusts are meant to hit hard those despicable traits of character that would blast reputation. I sincerely appreciate your criticism of the chapters you have already seen, and I trust that I will be able to let you examine in a few weeks the entire work, thoroughly revised, in type-written pages, so that you may know that I have altered much of the literary faults and toned down some of the most glaring expressions relative to the social sin. . . .[24]

I trust that you will meet with great success with your new war story, and I hope we will be able to drive about this beautiful Connecticut country some time in July or in August at the latest. . . . Very fraternally yours,   *E. C. Bross*

❈   ❈   ❈

Copeland and Day

Boston publishers of experimental poetry, Copeland and Day, were among the first of American publishers at the turn of the century to issue works of literary merit in an attractive format. Crane waited impatiently for Copeland and Day to bring out his first volume of poems, expecting it to be issued this year; but *The Black Riders* did not appear until April or May, 1895. (A second edition, prompted by the success of *The Red Badge of Courage*, was issued in 1896.) Limited to fifty copies, it was printed in green ink.

❈   ❈   ❈

---

[24] Bross had evidently found in *Maggie* the kind of novel he himself was trying to write and in its young author a sympathetic kinship with his own aims as writer and commentator on the sociological scene. It seems evident from what Bross says about his manuscript draft of the novel that he placed plot over style in importance. Crane excels in stylistic devices, not in plot; in his best works he substituted conflict for plot and dramatized his theme instead of preaching it.

41. TO COPELAND AND DAY

Interlaken Camp—Parker's Glen/Pike Co., Penn./[25]
[August, 1894]

Dear sirs:—I would like to hear from you concerning my poetry. I wish to have my out-bring all under way by early fall and I have not heard from you in some time. I am in the dark in regard to your intentions. Yours very truly   *Stephen Crane*

42. TO ODELL HATHAWAY

Hartwood, Sul Co, N.Y.[26]/Sept 7 [1894]

My dear Odell: It was a perfectly shameful thing in me not to have answered your letter sooner but it was a difficult thing to write letters at camp and since my arrival here at Hartwood tonight has been my first real opportunity. I was very glad to hear from you but I felt ashamed too because it recalled to me those days when you used to make weekly demands that I come to Middletown to visit. God always interferes when I try to stop off at Middletown. I have never succeeded in seeing any more of it than can be percieved [sic] from the railroad tracks altho the Powelson used occasionally to ask me after you quit, and one might think that God would not seriously oppose anything that a Powelson was in. I have been wondering what has become of the Sioux Indian and the other stars of the third hall at Claverack. If you have recieved [sic] any letters from them let me know. In the meantime I shall soon make a violent struggle to reach Middletown. And at any rate I remain always grateful to you for your remembrances of the old days at H. R. I.[27] Yours   *Stephen Crane*

43. TO COPELAND AND DAY

September 9, 1894

Dear Sirs: We disagree on a multitude of points. In the first place I

---

[25] At Twin Lakes, near Milford, Pennsylvania, where Crane went camping for a couple of weeks with Frederic M. Lawrence (the "Pudgy Man" of *The Sullivan County Sketches*), Louis E. Carr, Jr. (the "Little Man"), and Louis C. Senger, Jr. They had gone camping every August from 1891. (Senger lived at Port Jervis, New York, where William Howe Crane lived; Edmund Crane moved this summer to Hartwood, New York.)

In *Month at Goodspeed's* (1937) excerpts of eight Crane letters to Copeland and Day appeared, "Letters of a Shortstop," in which *The Black Riders* is mistakenly said to have been published in 1894.

[26] At Edmund's home, Edmund having moved from Lake View.

[27] Hudson River Institute.

should absolutely refuse to have my poems printed without many of those which you just as absolutely mark "No." It seems to me that you cut all the ethical sense out of the book. All the anarchy, perhaps. It is the anarchy which I particularly insist upon. From the poems which you keep you could produce what might be termed a "nice little volume of verse by Stephen Crane," but for me there would be no satisfaction. The ones which refer to God, I believe you condemn altogether. I am obliged to have them in when my book is printed. There are some which I believe unworthy of print. These I herewith enclose. As for the others, I cannot give them up—in the book.

In the second matter, you wish I would write a few score more. It is utterly impossible to me. We would be obliged to come to an agreement upon those that are written.

If my position is impossible to you, I would not be offended at the sending of all the retained lines to the enclosed address. I beg to express my indebtedness to you and remain Yours sincerely,

Stephen Crane

44. WILLIAM DEAN HOWELLS TO STEPHEN CRANE

40 W. 59, Oct. 2, 1894

Dear Mr. Crane: These things are too orphic for me. It is a pity for you to do them, for you can do things solid and real, so superbly. However, there is room for all kinds,—need if you like!

I do not think a merciful Providence meant the "prose-poem" to last. Yours sincerely,   *W. D. Howells*

45. TO COPELAND AND DAY

143 East 23d St/[October 30, 1894]

Dear sirs: I enclose copy of title poem.[28] Sincerely   *Stephen Crane*
Please note change of address.[29]

---

[28] The title poem of *The Black Riders, and Other Lines:*

Black riders came from the sea.
There was clang and clang of spear and shield,
And clash and clash of hoof and heel,
Wild shouts and the wave of hair
In the rush upon the wind:
Thus the ride of Sin.

James Joyce's poem "I Hear an Army," published in *Chamber Music* (1907), bears a striking resemblance to Crane's poem.

[29] Crane, having moved out of the Art Students' League Building in mid-April, is now back there again. This undated letter has the envelope postmarked October 30.

46. TO HAMLIN GARLAND

143 East 23d St, NYC/Thursday Nov 15th. [1894]

My dear friend: So much of my row with the world has to be silence and endurance that sometimes I wear the appearance of having forgotten my best friends, those to whom I am indebted for everything. As a matter of fact, I have just crawled out of the fifty-third ditch into which I have been cast and I now feel that I can write you a letter that wont make you ill. McClure was a Beast about the war-novel and that has been the thing that put me in one of the ditches.[30] He kept it for six months until I was near mad. Oh, yes, he was going to use it, but— Finally I took it to Bacheller's. They use it in 'January in a shortened form.[31] I have just completed a New York book[32] that leaves Maggie at the post. It is my best thing. Since you are not here, I am going to see if Mr. Howells will not read it.[33] I am still working for the *Press*.
Yours as ever   *Stephen Crane*

46A. TO CORWIN KNAPP LINSON

Continental Hotel, Philadelphia
[December, 1894]

My dear Linson: I have furnished Mr. Bacheller with your address and some time in the near future he will send for that portrait * which you so kindly consented to loan us. He wishes me to express to you our thanks for your charming generosity. Yours as ever,   S. C.

---

[30] Here, as in almost everything about Crane, we run against contradictory "facts." Beer's statement (p. 288) that Crane sold *The Red Badge* on February 24, 1894, to "Irving Bacheller's young syndicate for less than a hundred dollars," while seemingly supported by Crane's letter of that date to Holmes Bassett (No. 31), stands at odds with the fact that the war novel had been with McClure for six or eight months, presumably since February. Possibly Crane dealt with both syndicates, though this surmise seems contradicted by Crane's statement here—"Finally I took it to Bacheller's." Bacheller's syndicate was not founded until late in 1894, though most likely it was in the planning stage much earlier (see Appendix 4).

[31] *The Red Badge* was syndicated by Bacheller's agency in newspapers during early December, one month sooner than Crane here expected. It appeared, in much shortened form, first in the Philadelphia *Press*, December 3–8, and then in the New York *Press*, December 9, as well as in several other unidentified newspapers.

[32] This is *George's Mother*. Crane refers to it also in his letter of May 9 to Garland (No. 39). Corwin Knapp Linson in *My Stephen Crane* (1958), p. 82, surmises that it is Crane's *The Third Violet*.

[33] Howells, in fact, preferred *George's Mother* to *The Red Badge*.

* See frontispiece.

47. TO COPELAND AND DAY

#143 East 23d St., N.Y.C./Dec. 10, 94

Dear sirs: I would like to hear something from you in regard to the poems.

Also, I have grown somewhat frightened at the idea of old English type since some of my recent encounters with it have made me think I was working out a puzzle. Please reassure me on this point and tell me what you can of the day of publication. Yours sincerely *Stephen Crane*

48. TO COPELAND AND DAY

143 East 23d St, City/16 Dec. 94

Dear sirs:—There has been no necessity for you to wait impatiently to hear from me for I have answered each of the letters sent to me and at any rate, you have had opportunities to inform me of it since the 31st Oct. The type, the page, the classic form of the sample suits me. It is however paragraphed wrong. There should be none. As to punctuation, any uniform method will suit me. I am anxious to know the possible date of publication. Yours sincerely   *Stephen Crane*

49. TO AN UNKNOWN RECIPIENT

[Port Jervis, New York, after December 15, 1894]

. . . If you hear that I have been hanged by the neck till dead on the highest hill of Orange County you may as well know that it was for killing a man who is really a pug—No, by the legs of Jehovah! I will not insult any dog by comparing this damned woman to it. There is a feminine mule up here who has roused all the bloodthirst in me and I don't know where it will end. She has no more brain than a pig and all she does is to sit in her kitchen and grunt. But every when she grunts something dies howling. It may be a girl's reputation or a political party or the Baptist Church but it stops in its tracks and dies. Sunday I took a 13 yr. old child out driving in a buggy. Monday this mule addresses me in front of the barber's and says, "You was drivin' Frances out yesterday" and grunted. At once all present knew that Frances and I should be hanged on twin gallows for red sins. No man is strong enough to attack this mummy because she is a nice woman. She looks like a dried bean and she has no sense, but she is a nice woman. Right now she is aiming all her artillery at Cornelia's [34] new hat. I have been

---

[34] Mrs. William Howe Crane. The Port Jervis gossip reappears in *The Third Violet*, in sec. 19 of *The Monster*, and in chap. xxi of *The O'Ruddy*. As Wilson Follett points out, "Crane pilloried her over and over again, where she fitted the story and where she did not" (Introduction to *Work*, III, xvi).

deprived by heaven of any knowledge of hats but it seems to be a very kindly hat with some blue flowers on one side and a ribbon on the other. But we rustle in terror because this maggot goes to and fro grunting about it. If this woman lived in Hester Street some son or brother of a hat would go bulging up to her and say, 'Ah, wot deh hell!' and she would have no teeth any more, right there. She is just like those hunks of women who squat on porches of hotels in summer and wherever their eye lights there blood rises. Now, my friend, there is a big joke in all this. This lady in her righteousness is just the grave of a stale lust and every boy in town knows it. She accepted ruin at the hands of a farmer when we were all 10 or 11. But she is a nice woman and all her views of all things belong on the tables of Moses. No man has power to contradict her. We are all cowards anyhow. Bacheller thinks I had best start for Nevada as soon as possible, maybe before Christmas, but I should like to be with the family, of course.[35]

P.S. Somebody has written clean from California about The Red Badge.[36]

❁   ❁   ❁

Ripley Hitchcock

Crane's letters to Ripley Hitchcock, editor of Appleton and Company, are of interest as a record of an author's dealings with an American publisher, and they are of importance for the scholar wishing to set straight the record of Crane's life during the period of his writing or seeing through the press four of his early works. The letters are interesting and important because they record what the author says about his works, how he worried them into print, and what he worried about.

The publisher of almost all his major works was Heinemann, not Appleton. There must have been a good deal of correspondence between Crane and Heinemann, probably just as interesting and important as the correspondence with Hitchcock; but as the Heinemann house in London was twice gutted by fire, nothing of the Crane-Heinemann correspondence remains. For the record of Crane's deal-

---

[35] Crane did not leave for the West until the first week of February, 1895 (or after January 28).

[36] Beer (pp. 289–90) assigns this letter to "some date of late November, 1894." But The Red Badge in serialized newspaper form was not printed until the second week of December, in the New York Press. In the Philadelphia Press it ran serially on December 3–8. Crane's postscript indicates late December for the dating of this letter, before Christmas Day.

ings with his publishers, then, what remain are the letters to Ripley Hitchcock.[37] Other than these we have only his letters to James Pinker and Paul Revere Reynolds, his literary agents.

Beginning when *The Red Badge of Courage* had as yet appeared only in shortened newspaper form, the Crane-Hitchcock letters cover, first, Crane's trip to the West for the newspaper syndicate and then his political excursion to Washington for McClure. Along the way they show us Crane proofreading *The Red Badge,* taking flight from New York City to the woods at Hartwood, New York, where his brother Edmund lived, revising *Maggie,* getting *The Little Regiment* through the press, and finishing off *The Third Violet.*

Though Ripley Hitchcock may not have known it, Crane disliked him. That may be why his English publisher issued more than twice as many of Crane's books as Appleton—nine, to be exact. Appleton published four Crane works, *The Red Badge of Courage, Maggie, The Little Regiment,* and *The Third Violet;* Heinemann published not only these four but also five others, *The Black Riders, The Open Boat, Pictures of War, Active Service,* and posthumously, *Bowery Tales.*

In the letters, especially the long one of March 26, 1896 (No. 153), we can see Crane moving tentatively away from Appleton's, letting his "avarice" be appealed to, and "perhaps" violating "certain business courtesies." He lets *George's Mother* go to Edward Arnold, because the American manager of Edward Arnold is "an old school-mate" and conducts an effective "campaign." Arnold is "about to get" *The Little Regiment* when Hitchcock steps in, evidently with a better offer. Crane alludes to overtures from "nearly every representative American house," and although he disclaims any intention "of playing one house against another," at the same time he bargains for Appleton's allowing him "all the benefits I deserved. . . . If I make ill terms now there may come a period of reflection and so I expect you to deal with me precisely as if I was going to write a GREAT book ten years from now and might wreak a terrible vengeance upon you by giving it to the other fellow. And so we understand each other" (Letter 153). That must have rubbed Hitchcock like sandpaper.

Sandpaper was part of Crane's make-up—nobody was going to get the better of Stevie. In his early business dealings he used his sandpaper on Hitchcock; in his last ones he used it on Pinker—with the difference that at first it was a kind that does not scratch too much,

---

[37] Reprinted here (beginning with No. 50) from "Stephen Crane's Letters to Ripley Hitchcock," ed. R. W. Stallman, *Bulletin of the New York Public Library* (July, 1956), p. 60. The original holograph letters are in the Berg Collection of the New York Public Library.

whereas later it was a more coarse-grained variety. What Hitchcock got was the gloss of earnest innocence; what Pinker got was rough and earnest desperation. In the business of selling his stuff Crane was as shrewd a dealer as Hitchcock; from the softhearted Pinker he wrung the utmost in generous advances. He had a hardheaded bargaining drive uncommon among artists.

Putting *The Red Badge of Courage* into book form was not much of a risk for Hitchcock, for it had already passed muster with newspaper readers. *Maggie* had likewise already seen print when Hitchcock read and accepted it. Edward Arnold's publishing of *George's Mother* (June, 1896) constituted more of a gamble than Appleton's publishing of *The Little Regiment* five months later. As for Hitchcock's knowing that Crane had already written a "GREAT book," *The Red Badge*, Hitchcock had as much literary insight as his competitors in the field, if not more, but after Crane's writing *The Third Violet* (see Crane's defense of it in Letter 133), he was not sanguine about Crane's writing another. He lost out on *The Open Boat* a year later, Doubleday and McClure publishing it in the United States and Heinemann in England at the same time (April, 1898).

The Crane-Hitchcock correspondence begins with a short note about *The Red Badge of Courage*. Crane had sold an abridged version, cut down from 55,000 to 18,000 words, to the Bacheller-Johnson newspaper syndicate, and it had appeared in the Philadelphia *Press*, December 3-8, 1894, the New York *Press*, December 9, and other papers not yet identified. Crane sent the clippings to Hitchcock (Letter 50), who apparently agreed orally to publish the full book on the strength of what he then read.[38] Before going to St. Louis, Crane probably left

---

[38] According to Hitchcock, in his Introduction to *The Red Badge of Courage* (1900), Crane first came to him in December with two stories "as examples of the work which he was then doing for the newspapers. The impression made by the stories was so strong that Mr. Crane was asked if he had a story long enough for publication in book form. He replied hesitantly that he had written one rather long story, which was appearing in a Philadelphia newspaper, and 'some of the boys in the office seemed to like it.' He was asked to send the story at once, and presently there appeared a package of *newspaper cuttings* containing *The Red Badge of Courage*, which was promptly accepted for publication."

For an excellent summary of the newspaper version see W. L. Werner, "Stephen Crane and *The Red Badge of Courage*," *The New York Times Book Review*, September 30, 1945 (cf. Berryman, pp. 94 ff.). *Stephen Crane: An Omnibus*, pp. 201-17, relates the history of the variant manuscripts and the newspaper version. *Omnibus* publishes for the first time in the United States both the long- and the short-version manuscripts. (The long-version

with Hitchcock the manuscript of the complete draft. Crane was uneasy until he received an offer in writing (see Letter 61). The first six
letters all concern *The Red Badge*. They give little information about
the journalistic trip Crane was taking for the Bacheller-Johnson syndicate, beginning January 28, except the names of cities and hotels.

The second group of letters (Nos. 91, 118, 119, 133), written from
Hartwood the following winter, concern *The Third Violet*, which
Hitchcock accepted apparently with some reluctance. Most of the
remaining Crane-Hitchcock letters chart the course of the more enthusiastically received *Maggie* (see No. 138), from first rewriting to the
author's telegram (No. 192) demanding "payment . . . very important."

     ✿   ✿   ✿

50. TO RIPLEY HITCHCOCK

143 East 23d City/18 Dec 94

Dear Mr. Hitchcock: This is the war story in it's syndicate form—that
is to say, much smaller and to my mind much worse than its original
form. Sincerely   *Stephen Crane*

51. TO COPELAND AND DAY

33 East 22d St./New York [39]/Sturday [*sic*] [December 22? 1894]

Dear sirs:—It may be that I will be unable to reach Boston before I
start for the west and if it so happens,—I should like to hear how the
poems are coming on, anyway, and wether [*sic*] there is anything you
would care to have my opinion about. Sincerely yours   *Stephen Crane*

52. TO COPELAND AND DAY

143 East 23d St., N.Y.C./Jan 2, 1895

Dear sirs: I return proof sheet instantly. I do not care for a corrected
proof. I go west so soon now that the proofs will have to be hurried
along or I can get to see but few of them. I wish to know if some man-

---

manuscript received first publication in England in the Folio Society edition
of *The Red Badge of Courage*, ed. John T. Winterich, 1951). A photocopy
set of *The Red Badge* manuscripts is in the Manuscript Division of the New
York Public Library; the University of Texas Library has a set; and another
set is in R. W. Stallman's possession, the gift of Clifton Waller Barrett. The
original handwritten manuscripts belonging to the Barrett Collection are at
the University of Virginia Library.

[39] Written on stationery of the Pendennis Club, though Crane wrote
from a different address.

ner of announcement card can be printed which I can send to my friends. I think it would benefit matters greatly. Yours sincerely

Stephen Crane

53. TO COPELAND AND DAY

143 East 23d St., N.Y.C./Sunday [January 6, 1895]

Dear sirs: I enclose a copy of a recent review in the Philadelphia Press.[40] I have a good many notices but none of them are particular. Most of them call me a prominent youth. Another review that I would like to have used was published in the Arena Magazine some time in '92 I think. It was written by Garland.[41] I suppose it could readily be found at the Arena office. Some parts of it would make good extracts. Sincerely yours   *Stephen Crane*

54. TO COPELAND AND DAY

143 East 23d, NYC   [January 10, 1895]

Dear sirs: The notice by Mr Garland is in the June 93 number of the Arena on page 12 of the book notices.

I had no dedication in mind for the volume [42] but on second thoughts I would like to dedicate it to Hamlin Garland in just one line, no more: To Hamlin Garland

My friend, the artist,[43] is very busy but if you will send him here an exact rendering of the words of the cover, he may submit something shortly.

The book I wrote some time ago is difficult to procure but if I can get one I will send it to you. Sincerely yours   *Stephen Crane*

---

[40] Crane sent Copeland and Day a handwritten copy of Holland's review of *The Red Badge of Courage* appearing in the Philadelphia *Press*, December 4, 1894.

[41] Garland's review in the *Arena* appeared in June, 1893. Copeland and Day brought out an advertisement announcing publication of *The Black Riders* and quoted some of Garland's remarks about *Maggie* made in his *Arena* review: "With such a technique already in command, with life mainly before him, Stephen Crane is to be henceforth reckoned with . . . a man who impresses the reader with a sense of almost unlimited resource."

[42] *The Black Riders*, Crane's second published book, was dedicated to Garland without Garland's foreknowledge (see Letter 76).

[43] Frederic C. Gordon, the artist-friend who did the decorations for *The Black Riders*. Crane lived with him during 1893–1894 and finished writing *The Red Badge* in Gordon's studio in the old Art Students' League Building in October. Here, says Gordon, Crane also wrote *The Black Riders*. "His fortunes were then at their lowest ebb, I believe." Gordon's original cover design for *The Black Riders* is described in Letters 57, 65.

55. *TO COPELAND AND DAY*

143 East 23d St./[Monday] Jan 14, 94 [44]/[1895]

Dear sirs: I start for the west on a very long and circuitous newspaper trip on the last day of this week. I end ultimately in the City of Mexico. I will probably not return before the book is issued. If you can send me more proofs this week, I would like it. I will try to establish a means of communication with you. Any answer to a letter of mine will have to be sent very promptly or it will not reach me, as I travel quickly from city to city.

I send you a list of personal friends who would like to get that notice of the poems. I can use many more if you will send them to me in the west. Kindly preserve the list and return it to me when you have finished with it. Yours sincerely   *Stephen Crane*

Will you please send, as I requested, the size of the cover, the exact lettering upon it, and, if possible, the probable thickness of the book. The artist needs it.

56. *TO COPELAND AND DAY*

143 East 23d St./Friday [January 18, 1895]

Dear sirs: The artist wishes to know what you mean by the phrase: "Both sides the same" in relation to the book cover.

My journey to the west is delayed for ten days. Yours sincerely
Stephen Crane

Please dont destroy Ms.[45]   *Crane*

57. *FREDERIC C. GORDON TO COPELAND AND DAY*

[January ? 1895]

Gentlemen—In another package I mail you a design for cover of Mr. Crane's poems. It is drawn twice the dimensions of the book. The same design, with title and author's name omitted is intended for the back of the book.

The orchid, with its strange habits, extraordinary forms and curious properties, seemed to me the most appropriate floral motive, an idea in which Mr. Crane concurred before he left New York. I have just mailed him a tracing of the design.

---

[44] Crane's mistake; should be 1895.

[45] The handwritten manuscript of one of the poems, No. II ("Three little birds in a row"), answers perfectly Conrad's description of Crane's "regular, legible, perfectly controlled handwriting."

Will you kindly let me know whether it suits your requirements.
Very truly yours,   *F. C. Gordon*

58. *TO THE REVEREND THOMAS DIXON*

[January, 1895]

[Inscribed on a copy of *Maggie*]

It is inevitable that this book will greatly shock you, but continue, pray,
with great courage to the end, for it tries to show that environment is a
tremendous thing in the world, and often shapes lives regardlessly.
If one could prove that theory, one would make room in Heaven for
all sorts of souls (notably an occasional street girl) who are not confidently expected to be there by many excellent people.

59. *TO COPELAND AND DAY*

Cooke's European Hotel/1803 to 1811 Market Street/
St. Louis, Mo.,/Jan. 30 1894 [46] [1895]

Dear Sirs: My address for the next ten days will be "Care of Will
Owen Jones, The State Journal, Lincoln, Nebraska," and for one month
from date it will be—"Care Mr. Marrion Baker, the Times-Democrat,
New Orleans." Let me hear about the notices. Yours sincerely
                                                   Stephen Crane

When you lose track of me write in care of Bacheller and Johnson,
Tribune Building, New York.

60. *TO RIPLEY HITCHCOCK*

Cooke's European Hotel/1803 to 1811 Market Street/
St. Louis, Mo. [January 30, 1895]

Dear Mr. Hitchcock: I left New York so suddenly that I was unable to
communicate with you. My address for the next three weeks will be in
care of Mr Will Owen Jones, Editor *State Journal*, Lincoln, Neb. Afterward, I go to New Orleans and letters will reach me there if sent in
care of Mr Marrion Baker of the Times-Democrat. Any news of the
war story will be grateful to me. If you had not read the story, I would
wish you to hear the Philadelphia Press staff speak of it. When I was
there some days ago, I was amazed to hear the way in which they
talked of it.[47]

---

[46] Crane's error; should be 1895.

[47] Crane's visit with the staff of the Philadelphia *Press* is reported by
Reginald Kauffman in *Modern Culture*, October, 1895. "Who is this man
Crane, anyway?" asked one of the newsmen of the editor, Mr. Duffy. "Well,
if he keeps this up, we'll all know him in a few years." On December 4,

I will be glad to hear from you at any time. Yours sincerely
                                                    Stephen Crane

     ✿   ✿   ✿

Crane Meets Willa Cather

In Lincoln, Nebraska, Crane—waiting for some money to catch up
with him—lingered in the offices of the *State Journal* and, sitting on
the window ledge, talked with Willa Cather.

> *Quite without invitation on my part . . . [Crane] began to talk,*
> *began to curse his trade from the first throb of creative desire in a*
> *boy to the finished work of the master. . . . In all his long tirade,*
> *Crane never raised his voice; he spoke slowly and monotonously*
> *and even calmly, but I have never known so bitter a heart in any*
> *man as he revealed to me that night. It was an arraignment of the*
> *wages of life, an invocation to the ministers of hate.*[48]

Not yet twenty-four, Crane was for Willa Cather "the first man of letters I had ever met in the flesh." Shabbily dressed in a flannel shirt,
a felt hat pulled low over his eyes, with his shoes dusty and worn down
at the heels, he nevertheless wore gloves, and when he removed them,
Willa Cather noticed his artistic hands: "long, white and delicately
shaped, with thin nervous fingers." He was coughing, but Mexico
would cure that.

As for his strategies in the writing craft, "He declared that his
imagination was hidebound," to quote Willa Cather's reminiscences.
"It was there, but it pulled hard. After he got a notion for a story,
months passed before he could get any sort of personal contact with it,

---

1894, the day after the first installment of *The Red Badge* in the *Press,*
there was an editorial: "Stephen Crane is a new name, but everybody will
be talking about him if he goes on as he has begun." Also in the same issue
was an article, "The Work of Stephen Crane," signed "Holland" (see Appendix 1). An editor of Scribner's in the 1870's, Holland had seen the manuscript of *The Red Badge* some months before and had recognized at once
Crane's great powers of imagination. Berryman claims that whether anyone
ever saw the original manuscript of *The Red Badge* is not known, but Garland and Howells saw it in 1893 and Bacheller and Holland in 1894.

[48] Willa Cather, "When I Knew Stephen Crane," *Prairie Schooner,* XXIII
(1949).

or feel any potency to handle it." *He led a double life*—writing with care what pleased him, and dashing off what he could sell. While in Lincoln, he was busy writing what he could sell, journalistic pieces such as "Nebraskans' Bitter Fight for Life," which he sold to the Philadelphia *Press* and the New York *Press* this month and to the Nebraska *State Journal* (February 24, 1895). What impressed Willa Cather was his pronouncement about the writing that took painstaking care. "The detail of a thing has to filter through my blood, and then it comes out like a native product, but it takes forever." *Maggie* was not written in two nights, nor *The Red Badge* in ten days. Crane was boasting. It took him two years to finish *Maggie* and at least a year and a half for *The Red Badge.*

On February 13 Crane tried to stop a barroom fight. "But thus I offended a local custom. These men fought each other every night. Their friends expected it and I was a darned nuisance with my Eastern scruples and all that. So first everybody cursed me fully and then they took me off to a judge who told me that I was an imbecile and let me go; it was very saddening. Whenever I try to do right, it don't." Crane here echoes Huck Finn. He had been persuaded by Elbert Hubbard to read *Huckleberry Finn* before going West. Beer (p. 293) reports that Crane "changed trains once at a dreary junction town where was a hotel of a dreadful blue that fascinated him." It reappears in "The Blue Hotel," and also the barroom fight that Crane experienced.

       ❊   ❊   ❊

61. TO RIPLEY HITCHCOCK

The Lincoln/Lincoln, Neb. [February 12? 1895]

Dear Mr. Hitchcock: I've just recieved [sic] your letter. I would be glad to have Appleton and Co publish the story on those terms. I am going from here to New Orleans. The Mss could be corrected by me there in short order. I shall have to reflect upon the title.[49] I shall not be back to New York for two months. Yours sincerely *Stephen Crane*

---

[49] Hitchcock thought the title too long (see Letter 66). The manuscript Crane left with Hitchcock before going West is the long version, designated as LV (see the account of the original manuscripts of *The Red Badge* in *Omnibus,* pp. 201–24). It must have been written in 1894, before its shortened form appeared in the Philadelphia *Press.*

62. TO CLARENCE LOOMIS PEASLEE [50]

[Lincoln, Nebraska] [February 12, 1895]

. . . As far as myself and my own meagre success are concerned, I began the war with no talent, but an ardent admiration and desire. I had to build up. I always want to be unmistakable. That to my mind is good writing. There is a great deal of labor connected with literature. I think that is the hardest thing about it. There is nothing to respect in art, save one's own opinion of it.

63. TO CORWIN KNAPP LINSON [51]

New Orleans/Tuesday [February 19, 1895]

Mon ami Linson: Friedweller die schonënberger [sic] je suis dans New Orleans. Cracked ice dans Nebraska, terra del fuego dans New Orleans. Table d'hotes sur le balconies just like spring. A la mode whiskers on the citizens en masse, merci, of the vintage de 1712.

Frequented I all the time here again l'etoile de Virginitie sur St Louis Street. Sic temper tyrannis! Mardi gras tres grande but it not does until next Tuesday begin. Spiel! Senger to me one letter wrote filled with abuse. Ce matin I write un article sur le railways du South which were all made in hell.

This boarding-house est le terrible Francais. I have learned to ask for the vinegar at the table but otherwise I shall perhaps to Heaven go through starvation.[52] Yours ever   *Crane*

---

[50] A fraternity brother of Crane at Syracuse University in the spring of 1891, he published this much of Crane's letter to him in the *Monthly Illustrator* (1896). A Crane letter quoted by Hilliard in *The New York Times Supplement* for July 14, 1900, is practically a copy of this one. By "unmistakable" Crane meant "lucid." In one letter to Hilliard he says: "I endeavored to express myself in the simplest and most concise way." Again: "My chiefest desire was to write plainly."

[51] An art student at the National Academy of Design, Linson was doing drawings for illustrated magazines when Crane first met him in his studio in the winter of 1892–1893. His memoirs, written in the 1920's but not then in publishable form, were published in 1958 as *My Stephen Crane*, ed. Edwin H. Cady (Syracuse University Press). Crane's New York City days are also described by Linson in Appendix 19. Crane wrote the first draft of *The Red Badge* in Linson's room on West 30th Street. Linson published an interesting and important article on Crane in the *Saturday Evening Post*, April 11, 1903, "Little Stories of 'Steve' Crane," of which *My Stephen Crane* is an expanded version.

[52] "I tried to learn French, because my mother thought it important," Crane wrote somebody much later.

64. TO RIPLEY HITCHCOCK [53]

Hotel Royal/New Orleans, Feb. 20 1895

Dear Mr Hitchcock: If the manuscript is sent here in care of Mr Baker of the Times-Democrat I shall be able to arrange it before I depart for Mexico. I will not leave here for ten days.

I know it is a most inconvenient arrangement but as I am extremely anxious to have you bring out the book, I am hoping that the obstacles of the situation will not too much vex you. Yours sincerely

Stephen Crane

P.S. I shall only be in Mexico one week
c/o Mr Marrion Baker/Times-Democrat/New Orleans.

65. FREDERIC C. GORDON TO COPELAND AND DAY

143 East 23rd Street, New York/Feb. 25/95

Gentlemen: In regard to the cover design for The Black Riders, perhaps it would be best to have your artist adapt a portion of my drawing to your requirements, as I am unusually busy at present. If, however, you prefer to have me do it, I will undertake it at once on receipt of instructions.

As my design was not entirely satisfactory, I will submit no bill for it, but will accept such price as you judge proper under the circumstances.

A little later, if I can find the time, I shall be pleased to submit a design for your lines. Very truly yours,   *F. C. Gordon*

66. TO RIPLEY HITCHCOCK

The Tremont/Galveston, Texas/March 8, 1895

Dear Mr Hitchcock: I sent the Ms from New Orleans.[54] I made a great number of small corrections. As to the name I am unable to see what to do with it unless the word "Red" is cut out perhaps. That would shorten it. I am about to depart into Mexico for three weeks or a month. My address will be Hotel Iturbide, City of Mexico. Very truly yours   *Stephen Crane*

---

[53] A penciled note at the top—"Ms. sent by express Feb. 25"—is probably in Hitchcock's handwriting. A facsimile of this holograph letter is reproduced in "Stephen Crane's Letters to Ripley Hitchcock," ed. R. W. Stallman, *Bulletin of the New York Public Library*, LX (July, 1956), 318.

[54] Hitchcock sent the *Red Badge* manuscript by express February 25, and Crane returned it from New Orleans, revised, in early March. In addition to making "small corrections," he expunged some 2,000 words.

67. *TO EDWARD GROVER* [55]

[San Antonio, Texas, March ? 1895]

Dear Deadeye Dick: Thanks for sending back my money so fast. The hotel trun me out, as my friends of the Bowery say and I was living in the Mex diggings with a push of sheep men till my boss in New York wired me money. Now, old man, take some advice from a tough jay from back East. You say your family is all right and nobody bothers you. Well, it struck me that you are too young a kid and too handsome to be free and easy around where a lot of bad boys and girls will take your pennies. So better stay home and grow a mustache before you rush out into the red universe any more. Yours sincerely,

Stephen Crane

68. *TO DR. LUCIUS L. BUTTON*

Mahncke Hotel/San Antonio, Texas, March 12, 1895

My dear Button: I am about to venture into Mexico and sever my relations with the United States postal service so it will cost you five cents to answer this note—Hotel Iturbide, City of Mexico—

I would tell you of many strange things I have seen if I was not so bored with writing of them in various articles. This note is merely an attempt to cajole a letter out of you.

There is one thing however—I met a most intolerable duffer in New Orleans.[56] No doubt his ingenuous Akron spirit was amazed at many scenes but for my own part I felt that he should have controlled his emotion.

It is hard to feel kindly toward a man who makes you look like an unprecedented idiot and while I had only a general and humane objection to his making an ass of himself, I felt differently about myself.

He enthusiastically requested me to stop off on my way home in the spring and visit him. I modestly replied that while I appreciated his generosity and his courage, I had to die early in the spring and I

---

[55] Edward Grover, a sixteen-year-old boy, ran away from his Chicago home to become a cowboy. Crane, finding him sobbing and penniless on the Alamo Plaza, took him to a restaurant, fed him, and paid his fare on a home-bound train. An uncle met him at St. Louis and wired Crane the money to repay him.

[56] The "duffer" was from Akron; Crane is ribbing Button about his home town. It was through Button that Crane met Nellie Crouse, in a house on 34th Street, New York City, and then in the winter of 1895–1896 during a period of three months he wrote her seven letters. She too came from Akron.

feared that I would have to hurry home for the funeral but I had an
open date in 1997 and would be happy to see him in hell upon that
occasion.

Well, at any rate, I lie, for I was considerate of him, treated him
well at times, and was careful of his childish innocence. But there
should be a tariff on that kind of an export from Akron, O.

Tell Tommie Parson that this is a straight tip upon the quality of
his rivals, named Butler who let it be known that he was from Akron, O.,
although I dont see why he should. He told me that he knew your
friends there or your friends who have escaped or are about to escape
or are planning to escape, or are about to plan to escape from there.

He had fingers like lightning rods and on the street he continually
pointed at various citizens with the exclamation: "Look at that fellow!"
People in New Orleans don't like that sort of thing, you know.

I am off for Mexico tonight. Yours as ever   S. C.

P.S. Be good!

69. TO WICKHAM W. YOUNG [57]

The American Club/City of Mexico
Hotel Iturbide/City of Mexico/March 30, 1895

My dear Wick: This is to say that I am well and am going to ascend
Popocatapetl [*sic*]. Wether [*sic*] I will be well afterward is a matter of
speculation. Give my adieus in a general manner to Middletown.
Yours Sincerely   *Stephen Crane*

---

[57] A friend of Crane's vacation days at Twin Lakes, Pike County, Pennsylvania.

In one of three manuscript press dispatches headed "City of Mexico,"
Crane wrote, perhaps at this time:

A man has the right to rebel if he is not given a fair opportunity to be
virtuous. Inversely, then, if he possesses this opportunity, he cannot
rebel, he has no complaint. I am of the opinion that poverty of itself
is no cause. It is something above and beyond. For example, there is
Collis P. Huntington and William D. Rockafeller [sic]—as virtuous as
these gentlemen are, I would not say that their virtue is any ways
superior to mine for instance. Their opportunities are no greater. They
can give more in quantity but not relatively. We can each give all that
we possess and there I am at once their equal.

I do not think however that they would be capable of sacrifices
that would be possible to me. So then I envy them nothing.

70. TO COPELAND AND DAY

Port Jervis, N.Y./May 29 [1895]

Dear sirs: If it is convenient for you at this time I would greatly like a settlement in the matter of *The Black Riders*.[58] Sincerely yours

Stephen Crane

❀   ❀   ❀

The Lantern Club

The Lantern Club, formed by a group of New York newspaper men in May, 1895, was a literary club meeting in a quaint house on William Street, in the section of the city known as Monkey Hill. It began with seven members, Irving Bacheller being its perpetual president. In *Coming Up the Road* (1928) Bacheller identifies the group. He calls Willis Brooks Hawkins, who became Crane's close friend (as we see in Crane's letters to Hawkins, 1895–1897), "a most cheerful companion, a man of playful whims and quaint and delightful fancies." Post Wheeler, who later became Secretary of the American Embassy in London, also describes the Lantern Club, of which he was a charter member, in his memoirs. The charter members included Charles W. Hooke, a successful writer of mystery tales; Tom Masson, managing editor of *Life;* Edward Marshall of the New York *Press;* and Stephen Crane, whose *Maggie* and *Black Riders* stimulated the ambition of the others.

They met for luncheons and on Saturday evenings for dinner, read their short stories and poems to one another, chiefly sketches dealing with "the fading old-time color of the town," and spared no one the frankest criticism. Mark Twain came to luncheon; also Kipling, Charles Dana Gibson, Ethel Barrymore, Richard Harding Davis, Booth Tarkington, and Stanford White (the architect of Madison Square Garden, who was slain there by Harry K. Thaw over an affair with a chorus girl); and frequent visitors were William Dean Howells and Richard Watson Gilder, the old guard of the magazine world. An undated note from Bacheller, whose syndicate had published *The Red Badge* the previous December, strikes the spirit of these good-fellowship times:

---

[58] *The Black Riders*, published probably in May (Beer, p. 298, says it was published in April, 1895), was Crane's first book to be published under his name. The poems were later set to music by William Schuyler, of St. Louis.

✿   ✿   ✿

71. IRVING BACHELLER TO STEPHEN CRANE

Go now and take a drink with O'Darrow to the health of your friend
                                                           Irving Bacheller

It was Post Wheeler who urged Crane to come to New York City
"to sink or swim": Wheeler felt that that was where Crane belonged,
and it was in Wheeler's enormous loft on 23d Street that Crane wrote
The Black Riders and some of *The Red Badge*. (Precisely where Crane
wrote *The Red Badge* is a vexed issue; the honor has been claimed by
a half dozen of his rooming house friends as well as by the Crane family.) Wheeler's gambit for enticing Crane to the big city was a couple
of uncorked bottles in his studio loft.

"You appal me," Crane responded, *"by mentioning a couple of
bottles. If I were sure you meant beer no one would reply with
more fervent and fraternal joy. But I have a damnable suspicion
that you mean wine. Know then, my old companion, that I am living upon the glory of literature and not upon its emoluments.
Nevertheless we have gone too many leagues together to let the
matter of beer or wine separate us."* [59]

One oddity of the Lantern Club was the way you approached it—

*by a hanging iron stairway that climbed the side of a brick build-
ing occupied by an iron-monger. We landed on a broad roof which
was the cover of a stable-yard. From its level we ascended three
or four steps to our door. . . . Our decorations were mostly lanterns—Oriental, Colonial, ancient and medieval. We had many
varieties of these portable windows. . . . Indeed, the box of light
was our symbol. We hung an old ship's lantern on a wrought-iron
bracket outside our door. . . . Soon we named our club "The
Sign o' the Lanthorne."* [60]

---

[59] Post Wheeler, *Dome of Many-Colored Glass* (1956), p. 99.
[60] Irving Bacheller, *Coming Up the Road*, p. 280.

72. TO COPELAND AND DAY
The Hartwood Club [61]/Port Jervis, N.Y./June 8, '95

Dear Sirs: I returned from Mexico some days ago [62] but have come up here for a time because I am not in very good health. I would be glad to learn of the Black Riders. I see they are making some stir.[63] My address will be c/o Lantern Club, 126 Williams [*sic*] St.[64] NYC. Yours Sincerely   *Stephen Crane*

73. WILLIAM DEAN HOWELLS TO STEPHEN CRANE
Iroquois/Buffalo, N.Y./June 13, 1895 [65]

Dear Mr. Crane: I expect to be at home Friday night and if I'm in good repair, I shall be glad to dine with you Saturday. You won't mind

---

[61] Writing Nellie Crouse (Letter 144), Crane remarks: "In Hartwood I have a great chance to study the new-rich. The Hartwood Clubhouse is only three miles away and there are some of the new rich in it. May the Lord deliver me from having social aspirations."

[62] This letter is important as establishing Crane's return from the West much earlier than has been assumed.

[63] Reviewed in the *Bookman* for May: "All the stanzas in the little volume which has just been published were written in a sudden fit of inspiration, in less than three days, and were polished and finished and sent off within a fortnight."

The day after Crane wrote this letter a stir about *The Black Riders* was raised in the New York *Tribune*, where the new poet was scorched as "ludicrous," "a dabbler in mysteries which he is unworthy to approach." "Does Mr. Crane really believe that he is writing of things from his heart? If so, why have not his 'lines' some poetic vitality, some obvious reason for being? In their futility and affectation they strike the impartial reader as so much trash."

[64] The Lantern Club entertained Crane at dinner on April 7, 1895, according to Linson (p. 89). But Linson is in error, as Crane was then in Mexico. Crane often misspelled William Street.

[65] A week before, Howells had written a notice on *Maggie* in *Harper's Weekly*, June 8, 1895. There he gave a notice later this year (October 26) on *The Red Badge*, and on January 25, 1896, he reviewed *The Black Riders*. He had praised Crane in his interview with Edward Marshall—"A Great American Writer," Philadelphia *Press*, April 15, 1894—and in Crane's interview with him, in "Fears Realists Must Wait," in *The New York Times*, October 28, 1894, Howells had by implication praised *George's Mother* as being on the right track. Howells reviewed *Maggie* and *George's Mother* in "New York Low Life in Fiction," in the New York *World*, July 26, 1896. For the English edition of *Maggie* (1896), Howells contributed "An Appreciation."

my backing out at the last moment? Yours sincerely   *W. D. Howells*

74. TO COPELAND AND DAY
#126 Williams [*sic*] St. [Lantern Club]/New York City/
[June ? 1895]

Dear sirs/ I cant seem to light on a copy of Maggie.

I have considerable work that is not in the hands of publishers. My favorites are eight little grotesque tales of the woods which I wrote when I was clever.[66] The trouble is that they only sum 10000 words and I can make no more.

If you think you can make one of your swell little volumes of 10000, the tales would gain considerable lengthy abuse no doubt.

Mr Howells wishes the Black Riders to review in Harper's Weekly. Jordan of Current Literature wishes it for the same reason. If you could send me a few at the Lantern Club, I would like them. I am particularly anxious to see the green ones.[67]

I see they have been pounding the wide margins, the capitals and all that but I think it great. Yours sincerely   *Stephen Crane*

75. TO LILY BRANDON MUNROE
Lantern Club   126 William St/New York/[July ? 1895]

My dear L. B.: Copeland and Day of Boston which [wish] to re-print those old Sullivan County tales of mine and there is no one in the world has any copies of them but you. Can you not send them to me?[68]

Are you coming north this summer? Let me know, when you send the stories. I should like to see you again. Yours as ever   *S. C.*

76. TO HAMLIN GARLAND
Lantern Club/#126 William St.,/New York City/
[July 17? 1895][69]

Dear Mr. Garland: I have lost your address and so for certainty's sake,

---

[66] His Sullivan County sketches.

[67] Printed subsequently to the original edition, bound in gray. The edition printed in green ink and limited to fifty copies has the date 1895 on the white paper label pasted on the spine. A third edition of *The Black Riders* was issued jointly by Copeland and Day and William Heinemann in 1896.

[68] Copeland and Day did not publish them. They were not published in book form until 1949, when Melvin Schoberlin brought out *The Sullivan County Sketches.* Three of them appeared in the collected *Work of Stephen Crane,* ed. Wilson Follett (1925–1927).

[69] Dated in Garland's hand; an accompanying envelope is postmarked

send this to the Arena. I am just returned from my wanderings in
Mexico.[70] Have you seen the *Black Riders*. I dedicated them to you but
I am not sure that I should have done it without your permission? Do
you care? I am getting along better—a little better—than when I last
saw you. I work for the Bachellers.[71] Yours sincerely   *Stephen Crane*

77. TO KARL KNORTZ [72]

Parker's Glen,/Pike Co., Pennsylvania/August 3, 1895

Dear sir: I have requested the publishers to forward you at once a
copy of The Black Riders and I remain anxious to see your frank opinion of it as expressed in the Leipsic publication. Sincerely yours
                                                        Stephen Crane

78. TO COPELAND AND DAY

Parker's Glen,/Pike Co., Penn./August 3d.

Dear sirs: Please forward a "Black Riders" to the enclosed gentleman.[73] Sincerely   *Stephen Crane*

At my charge if necessary.

❋   ❋   ❋

Willis Brooks Hawkins

Willis Brooks Hawkins, editor of the Brains Publishing Company and
a charter member of the Lantern Club, was Crane's best friend. They
were all good fellows, said Irving Bacheller of the Lantern Club group,

---

New York, July 17, 1895. Garland was in Wisconsin, Crane's letter being
forwarded there from the *Arena Magazine* (Boston). Crane wrote this letter
on the reverse side of a printed folder issued by *Brains*, a periodical "devoted to the art of advertising" and managed by Crane's friend Willis
Brooks Hawkins.

[70] Crane's trip to the West lasted just four months, from the first week
of February to the first week of June.

[71] The Bacheller and Johnson syndicate.

[72] Head of the German department in the public schools of Evansville,
Indiana. He had translated Longfellow and Whittier into German (as noted
by Cady and Wells in *Stephen Crane's Love Letters*). It is not known
whether he translated *The Black Riders* into the German for publication in a
Leipsic literary periodical.

[73] The "enclosed gentleman" refers most likely to Karl Knortz (see No.
77), whose letter Crane enclosed with this one.

"but able borrowers"—and the ablest of them all was no doubt Stephen Crane. Hawkins was always helping him out of tight spots with money, an overcoat, or just good advice. His literary underwriter, Hawkins, was also one of the four executors of a will that Crane drew up in 1897, and he got the best part of Crane's literary estate—the gift of the original manuscript of *The Red Badge of Courage*, which Crane sent him early the preceding year as an expression of gratitude: "Thought maybe you'd like it." Hawkins probably felt proud to appear beside his famous friend in *The Lanthorn Book* (1898), a collection of tales and verses "Read at the Sign o' the Lanthorn."

Writing to Hawkins put Crane in the mood to discuss anything but a literary idea. He was more inclined to describe what happened while he was sailing a catboat on the lake at Hartwood, to mention some girls in the camp at Parker's Glen, or to recount experiences with a bicycle when he was a boy in military school. They did not discuss literature; they knew each other too well for that. When Crane did pour out his literary soul, it was to a woman he knew only slightly and to another woman he knew not at all.

It has been said that Crane had no intimate friends, but the correspondence with Hawkins upsets that notion. He wrote Hawkins at least thirty letters; the last one from Greece in mid-April, 1897.

✿   ✿   ✿

79. TO WILLIS BROOKS HAWKINS
Parker's Glen/Pike Co., Penn./August 9, '95

My dear Willis: I am cruising around the woods in corduroys and feeling great. I have lots of fun getting healthy. Feel great.

If anything in the way of notices comes out and you see it, send them to me here for I feel out of the world.[74]

There are six girls in camp and it is with the greatest difficulty that I think coherently on any other subject.[75]

Wish you could come up some Sunday. Only—it is with the greatest trouble that any one can reach here. Four deadly miles up the mountain from the Erie's station at Parker's Glen. If you would care to do it let me know and I will tell you how to do it.

My remembrances to Mrs. Hawkins and to Florence. Yours, as ever,   S. C.

---

[74] Reviews of his book of poems, *The Black Riders, and Other Lines*, published in May.

[75] Crane had an eye for pretty girls, as is indicated in Letter 6, written immediately after his arrival at the Delta Upsilon House at Syracuse University: "There are certainly some dam pretty girls here, praised be to God."

80. TO WILLIAM DEAN HOWELLS

August 17, 1895

[Inscribed in a copy of *The Red Badge of Courage*] [76]

To W. D. Howells this small and belated book as a token of the veneration and gratitude of Stephen Crane for many things he has learned of the common man and, above all, for a certain re-adjustment of his point of view victoriously ...cluded some time in 1892.

Stephen Crane

81. TO WILLIS BROOKS HAWKINS

Parker's Glen/Pike Co., Penn./August 18, '95

My dear Willis: The Philistine people [77] have written to me about the notice of *The Red Badge of Courage* which they wish to bring out in their September number. What shall I say in it. I dont know how to write those notices. Can you advise me concerning a little notice. (I meant to say *will* you.) I hope you are awfully well. Did you get my last letter. My remembrances to all the lanterns.[78] I am getting mighty anxious to hear the Apache Scalp Dance again. I will [go] down however in about 2 weeks more. Yours as always   S. C

82. TO RIPLEY HITCHCOCK

Parker's Glen/Pike Co. Penn/August 26 [1895]

Dear Mr. Hitchcock: The title page proof is all right. Will you write an ad. for the Philistine & send it to me here? [*Piece cut away.*] thought of using it for my "Red Badge"—. What do you think? Very truly yours

Stephen Crane

---

[76] Not presented to Howells until 1896.

[77] Harry P. Taber and Elbert Hubbard of *The Philistine: A Periodical of Protest,* published at East Aurora, New York. Crane's poems appeared in nearly every issue of the *Philistine* during 1895. A year before the magazine began actual publication (the first issue was in June), Hubbard had bought two articles from Crane, one on slum charities and the other expounding a social theory. Hubbard lost both articles on a train.

The Crane and Hawkins letters provide the first full account of Crane's dealings with Elbert Hubbard and the Philistine Society. Beer mentions Hubbard only once (p. 291) and slights the Philistine Society banquet (cf. p. 305).

[78] Members of the Lantern Club.

83. TO WILLIS BROOKS HAWKINS

Office of The Press,/Philadelphia,/Sept. 6 [1895]

Dear Willis: It is dramatic criticism and nuthin else.[79] I've taken it and am to go to work at once. I will however be in New York on Tuesday night for the dinner, and will talk at length to you. I wrote to Mr. Howells today asking him to come to the dinner.[80] Yours as ever   S. C.

84. TO WILLIS BROOKS HAWKINS

2840 Ridge Ave./Philadelphia/Tuesday¹ [September 10, 1895]

Dear old man: Things fell ker-plunk. Stranded here in Phila. Dont you care! Nice town. Got lots of friends, though, and 23,842 invitations to dinner of which I have accepted 2.

The Press wanted me bad enough but the business manager suddenly said: "Nit." Yours as ever   S. C.

85. TO WILLIS BROOKS HAWKINS

2840 Ridge Ave.,/Philadelphia/Sept. 18 [1895]

My dear Willis: I am going to stay down for a few more days. If you see anything for me in New York holler quick. I am with some friends, pretty good time but I am engaged at last on my personal troubles in Mexico.[81] Yours as ever   S. C.

86. TO WILLIS BROOKS HAWKINS [82]

165 W 23d [New York City, October, 1895]

My dear Willis: Can you bring over a poker contingent tonight. The

---

[79] As the next letter shows, Crane's attempt to hire himself out as a dramatic critic to the Philadelphia Press did not succeed. The Press had accepted in March his one piece of dramatic criticism: "Grand Opera in New Orleans." Later when he was in England, he and Conrad proposed writing a Western play, Predecessor, but the only play by Crane that was printed was Blood of the Martyr, in the Sunday New York Press in 1898.

[80] The weekly Tuesday dinner at the Lantern Club.

[81] The "personal troubles" Crane was writing had to do with his having been chased in Mexico by a "fashionable bandit" named Ramón Colorado, the episode recast in Horses—One Dash! This letter to Hawkins dates the composition of that sketch and identifies the place where it was written. It was published as One Dash—Horses! in the Philadelphia Press, January 4 and 6, 1896.

[82] Written on a Western Union telegraph blank. See also Crane's note to Hawkins to bring the boys over "for a little fiesta de poke" (Letter 157).

place is all torn to shreds—I'm moving to Hartwood but would be glad to welcome a poker party.   *S. C.*

87. *TO WILLIS BROOKS HAWKINS*

165 West 23d [New York City, October, 1895]

My dear Willis: By all means you fellows come here tonight. Looked for you this afternoon in the Downing Build'g. This will be my last game—perhaps. Expect to skip for the country. Dont let the game fall through. Yours   *S. Crane*

88. *TO WICKHAM W. YOUNG*

The Hartwood Club/Hartwood Sul Co, N.Y./Oct 21st, 1895

My dear Wick: My brother William H. is running for Surrogate of Orange County on the Democratic ticket and although I know you fellows dont care so much for politics I am immensely interested in seeing the boy make a creditable record for himself wether [*sic*] he gets elected or not. The other man is Howell from here and he isn't so nice. Surrogate isn't much of a political office any how, and you can swallow all the rest of the Republican ticket if you like. Be careful, though, about the mechanical part of it. Understand you know that this is merely a broad general hint and I know too that any kind of a man will do just as he damned pleases in the matter, but—you see how it is. Let me hear wether [*sic*] this makes you made [*sic*] or not. I am going to gun for W. W. W. and A. A., too. Yours as ever *Stephen Crane*

89. *TO WICKHAM W. YOUNG*

Hartwood, N.Y./Oct 23d, 95

My dear Wick: I am delighted at your good-nature in the election business. Will is a good fellow and very honest and clever. I would like to snare Arly and Bill Woodward but dont quite know how to go about it as I dont feel that I know them as well as I do you and any-how I hate to monkey about politics. I used to think that distinquished [*sic*] merit had some weight but it isn't worth a damn, relatively speak-ing. The man who hustles is the man who gets there and if some honest person is opposing a thief, he wants to be busy or the thief will snow him under, which is, after all, what everybody knows.

I am working pretty well here. Better than in New York. Missed my first partridge today. Crash. Yours as ever   *Stephen Crane*

90. TO WILLIS BROOKS HAWKINS

Hartwood, Sullivan County, N.Y.,/Oct. '95 [October 24]

My dear Willis: The brown October woods are simply great. There is a kitten in the stables who walks like Ada Rehan and there is a dog who trims his whiskers like the late President Carnot's whiskers. Gypsey, cousin to Greylight and blood relative of the noble Lynne bel, who lost the Transylvania so capably at Lexington this season—well, Gypsey ran away with me. What can be finer than a fine frosty morning, a runaway horse, and only the still hills to watch. Lord, I do love a crazy horse with just a little pig-skin between him and me. You can push your lifeless old bicycles around the country but a slim-limbed thoroughbred's dauntless spirit is better. Some people take much trouble to break a horse of this or that. I don't. Let him fling himself to the other side of the road because a sumach tassle waves. If your knees are not self-acting enough for that sort of thing, get off and walk. Hartwood scenery is good when viewed swiftly.

I missed my first partridge yesterday. Keh-plunk. Bad ground, 'though. Too many white birches. I haven't written a line yet. Dont intend to for some time. Clip anything you see in the papers and send it. Remember me to everybody at Greene Ave. I have heard indirectly from Brentano's that the damned "Red Badge" is having a very nice sale. Yours as always   *Stephen Crane*

91. TO RIPLEY HITCHCOCK

Hartwood, N.Y./Oct 29 [1895]

Dear Mr. Hitchcock: The story is working out fine.[83] I have made seven chapters in the rough and they have given me the proper enormous interest in the theme. I have adopted such a "quick" style for the story that I don't believe it can work out much beyond twenty-five thousand words—perhaps thirty—possibly thirty-five. Can you endure that length?—I mean, should you like the story otherwise, can you use a story that length?

Mr. Howells almost always speaks of my work in Harper's Weekly [84] and, if you cared to, a book might be sent to him.

I have lost a certain document relating to the making over of ownership of copyright. If you will send me another copy, I will sign it at once. Yours sincerely   *Stephen Crane*

---

[83] *The Third Violet.*

[84] In Howells' column in *Harper's Weekly* he reviewed *Maggie* on June 8 and *The Red Badge* on October 26, 1895.

92. TO WILLIS BROOKS HAWKINS

Hartwood, Sul. Co., N.Y./Nov. 1st, 1895

My dear Willis: My correspondence—incoming—has reached mighty proportions and if I answered them all I would make Hartwood a better class office and my brother [85] a better class postmaster for you know he is a postmaster, justice-of-the-peace, ice-man, farmer, mill-wright, blue stone man, lumberman, station agent on the P.J.M. and N.Y.R.R. and many other things which I now forget. He and his tribe can swing the majority in the township of Lumberland. By that reference to my correspondents I meant the fellows before the war. They're turning up. Heaven send them somebody to appreciate them more although it is true I write two or three perfunctory little notes each day.

There has been an enormous raft of R. B. of C. reviews and Appleton and Co. have written me quite a contented letter about the sale of the book.[86] Copeland and Day have written for my New York sketches and Appleton and Co. wish to put my new story in their Zeit-Geist series. Which I leave you alone to pronounce. Devil take me if I give you any assistance.

That's enough about books.

On the bicycle question, I refuse to listen to you. In the old days at military school I once rode a wheel—a high one—about three miles high, I think. An unsmiling young cadet brought one into the armory one morning and as I was his senior officer I took it away from him. I mounted by means of a friend and rode around and around the armory. It was very simple.

When I wished to dismount however I found I couldn't. So I rode around and around the armory. Shafer, who was champion of Pennsylvania in those old high-wheel days, watched me and said I did some things on that wheel which were impossible to him. A group of cadets gathered in a corner and yelled whenever I passed them. I abjured them at intervals to let me off that wheel but they only hollered. At last, I ran into a bench and fell neatly on my head. It broke the machine, too, praise God. Some days later I whipped the boy who had loaned it me. Not for that mind you, but for somethingelse.

I am shooting a good deal. I beat my brother the last time out. That's a good deal.

---

[85] Edmund.

[86] Crane subscribed to a clipping bureau and kept a scrapbook of reviews. On the sale of *The Red Badge* Crane wrote on December 24: "Mr. Hitchcock tells me that the book does not sell much in New York. It has gone to about 4500, though, and many of them have been sent west" (Beer, p. 302).

I have another brother [87] who is running for surrogate of Orange County and I haven't a doubt but that he will achieve a magnificent defeat. For he is a bold Democrat and they're rare birds in Orange.

Give my remembrances cordially to all your people and say that I regret the Apaches and the Pilgrims. Remember me too at the Lantern. Yours as always   *Stephen Crane*

93. *TO WILLIS BROOKS HAWKINS*

[Hartwood, N. Y., about Nov. 2, 1895]

Dear Willis: Here are two sample letters.[88]   *S. C.*

94. *GUSTAV A. ROEDELL TO STEPHEN CRANE*

Gallipolis, Ohio,/Oct. 30, 1895

My dear Sir: If it is not asking too much, dare I beg that you will do me the great honor to transcribe your poem, "He was a brave heart," [89] to insert in my copy of *The Black Riders and Other Lines?*

The favor would be valued more than I can say. I have the honor to remain/Your obliged servant,   *Gustav A. Roedell*

95. *FROM THE CORRESPONDING EDITOR OF* THE YOUTH'S COMPANION

Boston. October the 31st [1895]

My dear Sir/ In common with the rest of mankind we have been read-

---

[87] William; he lost the election. In 1894 Crane jotted down in his notebook a humorous conversation piece having to do with the defeat of Tammany Hall in the election of 1894, a sketch printed in the New York *Press* sometime in November, 1894. The notebook version, reproduced from the Crane notebook in the Barrett Crane Collection, was published in "Stephen Crane: Some New Stories," ed. R. W. Stallman, *Bulletin of the New York Public Library* (September, 1956), p. 60.

[88] See Letters 94, 95.

[89] The concluding portion of No. LXI of *The Black Riders:*

He was a brave heart.
Would you speak with him, friend?
Well, he is dead,
And there went your opportunity.
Let it be your grief
That he is dead
And your opportunity gone;
For, in that, you were a coward.

ing The Red Badge of Courage and other war stories by you.[90] And our editors feel a strong desire to have some of your tales in The Youth's Companion.

I want to invite you to submit some of your work to The Companion for consideration. While we have a number of standards inside of which all our stories have to fall I am confident that you would not find them a grave inconvenience. But to save you possible misdirection of effort, would you be so kind (if our invitation is acceptable to you) to write me and let me send you a few hints as to the kind of stories we want and dont want.

Will you also let me say that for the higher grades of work the substantial recognition which The Companion gives to authors is not surpassed in any American periodical. Very truly yours/

The Corresponding Editor

P.S. For your address I am indebted to the politeness of Messrs Copeland and Day, the former of whom is one of our editors.

96. *ELBERT HUBBARD TO STEPHEN CRANE*

Nov 5, 95

Dear Mr. Crane: The enclosed [91] sounds a bit formal but it is all straight business. I trust you will see your way clear to accept.

The newspaper men of Buffalo and even that arrant varlet on the Rochester Chronicle will co-operate with us to make the dinner a big success. Also the manager of the Associated Press. "The Red Badge" is a strong work thoroughly well sustained. I congratulate you on it. Sincerely your friend,   *Elbert Hubbard*

Send acceptance to me.

97. *FROM THE COMMITTEE FOR THE PHILISTINE SOCIETY TO STEPHEN CRANE* [92]

East Aurora, N.Y.,/Nov 5, 95

My dear Mr Crane: Recognizing your merit as a man and your genius

---

[90] There were only two other war stories then in print: "A Mystery of Heroism," the New York *Press*, August 1, 2, 1895, and "A Gray Sleeve," the Philadelphia *Press*, October 12, 14, 15, 1895.

[91] Letter 97. Crane made a handwritten copy of Hubbard's letter to send to Hawkins and wrote at the top: "Personal letter from Hubbard./ Verbatim."

[92] This letter, which Crane copied verbatim, and Hubbard's enclosing it (No. 96), Crane sent to Hawkins on November 8.

The full story of the Philistine affair is here given for the first time. Un-as a poet, and wishing that the world should know you better, the Society of the Philistines tender you a dinner to take place at the Iroquois Hotel in Buffalo in about one month.

As soon as we receive your acceptance stating the date that suits you best we will send out invitations to 200 of the best known writers, publishers and newspaper men of the United States and England.

We have already secured transportation for you and we further beg to assure you that you will be our guest as long as you remain here. We believe that aside from the charming friendly intercourse of the occasion, that the dinner will be of very great value to your books and will lead to a wider recognition of your talent.

Pray favor us with an early answer giving dates that suit you best. With high esteem, dear sir, we are/ Sincerely yours/ Elbert Hubbard/ H. P. Taber/Wm McIntosh, Man'g Ed. Buffalo *News*/ E. R. White of the *News*/S. G. Blythe Buffalo *Express*

97A. TO AN UNKNOWN RECIPIENT

[Inscribed in an 1893 edition of *Maggie*] *

With compliments.   *Stephen Crane*

Nov 5, 1895

98. TO WILLIS BROOKS HAWKINS

[Hartwood, N. Y., about November 5, 1895]

My dear Willis: I always considered Field [93] to be a fine simple spirit and I am glad his death makes you so sad.

I never thought him a western barbarian. I have always believed the western people to be much truer than the eastern people. We in the east are overcome a good deal by a detestable superficial culture which I think is the real barbarism. Culture in it's true sense, I take it, is a comprehension of the man at one's shoulder. It has nothing to do with an adoration for effete jugs and old kettles. This latter is merely

---

known to Williams and Starrett (Crane's bibliographers) were the November 5 letters of Hubbard and of the Committee for the Philistine Society. Berryman (p. 153) says that the society's invitation "had not mentioned his novel," but Hubbard in his November 5 letter praises *The Red Badge*.

* This front-cover inscription is reprinted from *Stephen Crane: A Bibliography* (1948); the inscribed copy of *Maggie* is in the Huntington Library.

[93] Eugene Field, who died on November 4.

an amusement and we live for amusement in the east. Damn the east! I fell in love with the straight out-and-out, sometimes-hideous, often-braggart westerners because I thought them to be the truer men and, by the living piper, we will see in the next fifty years what the west will do. They are serious, those fellows. When they are born they take one big gulp of wind and then they live.

Of course, the east thinks them ridiculous. When they come to congress they display a child-like honesty which makes the old east laugh. And yet—

Garland will wring every westerner by the hand and hail him as a frank honest man. I wont. No, sir. But what I contend for is the atmosphere of the west which really is frank and honest and is bound to make eleven honest men for one pessimistic thief. More glory be with them.

The novel is one-third completed.[94] I am not sure that it is any good. It is easy work. I can finish a chapter each day. I want you to see it before it goes to the Appletons.

Sometimes I go out sailing in a little boat here. The people are expecting my death shortly for the little boat leans like a shingle on a house—when she tacks—and the November winds are very strong.

My brother William went down in the Democratic wreck. Poor boy.

It is singular that the Republicans won in every place where it was to the glory of God that they should lose, and lost in every place where it was to the glory of God that they should win.

I am very contented here. For a while I felt incarcerated but not now.

Good-bye. My remembrances always to your Greene Ave castle. Your friend—ever   *Stephen Crane*

---

[94] *The Third Violet,* tentatively called *The Eternal Patience.* It was serialized a year later in the New York *Evening World,* November 4–14, and published in book form in 1897. At the end of October Crane had written "seven chapters in the rough and they have given me the proper enormous interest in the theme." Now about a week later, it is "one-third completed." In his November 15 letter to Hawkins (No. 104) he says that it is "exactly half finished," and then on November 19 it is "two-thirds done" (Letter 108). On December 27 he shipped the manuscript to Hitchcock to have it typed. He did not keep to the beginning speed of a chapter a day, but he wrote twenty-six chapters during November and December, and perhaps it was because it all came too easy for him that he was dubious about it. In name, the hero of *The Third Violet* echoes Willis Hawkins, though with the difference that the hero, William Hawker, is an impressionist painter.

99. TO WILLIS BROOKS HAWKINS

Hartwood/Nov. 8 [1895]

Dear Willis: I sent down to Port Jervis to-day to get hung up for fifty cents worth of tobacco and on the same train with the tobacco came the enclosed interesting cummunications.[95] My dress suit took to the wood long ago and my 1895 overcoat is not due until 1896. I have not owned a pair of patent leather shoes in three years. Write me at once and tell me how to get out of the thing. Of course I am dead sore but I think if you will invent for me a very decent form of refusal, I will still be happy up here with my woods. Yours as always   S. C.

100. FROM THE COMMITTEE FOR THE PHILISTINE SOCIETY TO STEPHEN CRANE [96]

East Aurora, N.Y., Nov. 10, 1895.

TO MR. STEPHEN CRANE:/ Recognizing in yourself and in your genius as a poet, a man whom we would like to know better, The Society of the Philistines desire to give a dinner in your honor early in the future. If this meets with your approval we should be glad if you will let us know upon what date you could conveniently come to us.

Elbert Hubbard./H. P. Taber, Editor of the *Philistine*./Samuel G. Blythe, of the Buffalo *Express*./Wm. McIntosh of the Buffalo *News*./ Eugene R. White of the Buffalo *News*./Philip Hale of the Boston *Journal*/Nelson Ayres of the New Orleans *Picayune*./L. H. Bickford of the Denver *Times*./Marshall Cushing of the Washington *Capital*./ Walter Blackburn Harte of *Moods*./John Northern Hilliard of the Rochester *Union and Advertiser*./   *Committee for The Society*

101. WILLIS BROOKS HAWKINS TO STEPHEN CRANE

875 Green Ave., [New York City] Nov. 11. [1895]

My dear Stephen: I intended to write to you last night, but the folks lured me into an amateur game of poker (penny ante) and I was so

---

[95] These "cummunications" were (1) a letter from the Committee for the Philistine Society, inviting Crane to attend a proposed dinner to take place at the Iroquois Hotel, Buffalo, in about one month (Letter 97) and (2) a letter from Elbert Hubbard urging him to accept the invitation and praising *The Red Badge* (Letter 96). These two letters are reproduced here for the first time.

[96] See Nos. 103, 106. This November 10 letter and Crane's reply of November 15 (No. 103) were printed later this year in Hubbard's pamphlet entitled *The Members of the Society*, published by the Roycroft Printing Shop (1895).

sleepy that I went to bed as soon as it was over. I am a bit rocky this morning—(up at the unseasonable, unreasonable hour of 7)—but I want this to get to you soon as possible so that you may answer the Buffalo fellows without delay, for you must—you just *must*—accept their invitation. There is a business side of life that must not be wholly ignored. It hasn't a leg to stand on, and there's no honest reason for its being, but here it is and—there you are. I could sit and give ten reasons why you must go to that dinner for one why you can't; and then, by gum, I can set even the one aside. You go ahead and accept. Tell me of the day you fix on, and I'll agree that you'll be togged properly for the occasion. Send me your chest measurements and your length of leg (from your crotch to your heel—you remember Lincoln's answer when he was asked how long an ideal soldier's leg should be [97]) and I'll find some way. Tell me, too, what size (anybody with an ear for rhyme would know that the next word is————), shoe best fits you. I'm not one of those proper persons who get up early in the morning to write— even letters. I'll write the letter part later. Yours, very sincerely, all the time.   *Willis B. Hawkins*

102. TO WILLIS BROOKS HAWKINS

Hartwood/Tuesday. [November 12, 1895]

My dear Willis: No, you hadnt answered my last letter. Sometimes I dont need a reply because I know you are there and everything is all right. But this time I did need a reply because my sudden escape that day I was supposed to go to your house was upon my conscience very heavily and your majestic silence was a great trouble to me. However, I am perfectly contented with your reply and the way in which you appropriate 50% of the blame. I had been carefully abusing myself for the whole affair and was quite astonished and over-joyed when you volunteered.

I am writing a story—"The Little Regiment" for McClure. It is awfully hard. I have invented the sum of my invention in regard to war and this story keeps me in internal despair. However I am coming on with it very comfortably after all.[98]

---

[97] It has been suggested that Lincoln replied that the soldier's leg ought to be at least long enough to reach to the ground.

[98] Published in *McClure's Magazine* in June, 1896, and, as the title piece to a volume of that name, by Appleton, and in 1897 by Heinemann. In contrast to the "easy work" of evolving *The Third Violet*, the difficulties Crane encountered in composing "The Little Regiment" recall the labor of pain that *The Red Badge* cost him. Crane finished the story at the end of February, 1896.

The dinner scheme mingles my emotions. In one sense, it portends an Ordeal but in the larger sense it overwhelms me in pride and arrogance to think that I have such friends.[99]

By the way, you ought to see the effect of such things upon my family. Aint they swelled up, though! Gee! I simply cant go around and see 'em near enough. It's great. I am no longer a black sheep but a star. Yours, always   S. C.

103. TO THE COMMITTEE FOR THE PHILISTINE SOCIETY BANQUET

Hartwood, N.Y./Nov. 15, 1895

To Mr. Elbert Hubbard, Mr. Harry P. Taber, Mr. Eugene R. White, Mr. Wm. McIntosh, Mr. Walter Blackburn Harte, Mr. S. G. Blythe, Mr. John Northern Hilliard, Mr. Philip Hale, Mr. Nelson Ayres, Mr. L. H. Bickford, Mr. Marshall Cushing of the Society of the Philistines./ Gentlemen: The only obstacle in the way of my accepting an invitation at once so cordial and so kind is the fact that an acceptance, it seems to me, is a tacit admission of my worthiness in the circumstances. Believe me, this sense of embarrassment that I should be at all considered as a fit person for such distinction is my solitary discomfort. But I have industriously blunted this sense and can say that it will deal me great pleasure to dine with the Society of the Philistines on Thursday evening, Dec. 19th.

I beg to thank you, gentlemen, and pray believe me that I am ever Very Sincerely Yours,   *Stephen Crane*

104. TO WILLIS BROOKS HAWKINS

Hartwood, N.Y. [About November 15, 1895]

My dear Willis: Upon my soul when I first read your letter I was ashamed that I had written you about it at all. Then when I reflect I find I wrote you because the letter delighted and charmed me and I had to whoop it up to somebody. But heavens, to think you would

---

[99] The author of these illusions suggests his counterpart Henry Fleming in *The Red Badge*, for the actual dinner at Buffalo was a vulgar orgy of chaos and stupid bickering among the thirty hosts collected in a private room of the Genesee House—not at all the glorious tribute of friends that Crane here anticipates with "pride and arrogance." After the event Crane saw himself as the deluded hero, the dupe of his own vainglorious notions, and it is because of this change of vision that this Philistine affair has importance in any account of Crane's life. It marked a turning point in Crane's outlook.

allow me to make a victim of you! For, blast it all, on the strength of your letter I have accepted the invitation. At first, as I said, I was dismayed at your letter but, confound it, you might understand that I blush for myself more still when I think I was low enough to grab at your generosity.

I told the Philistines that any date in late November or early December would suit me. When they write, you shall hear from me at once. I shall go and I shall have a dandy time. I know and am satisfied that it will do me an immense amount of good. My chest, bad luck to it, measures 35 inches—scant—and my leg is a 33—worse luck. And foot —rot it—is a seven. There! It is over. I feel as if I have told you that I am a damned thief.

Heaven send you rest, Willis, and in your old age may you remember how you befriended the greatest literary blockhead in America from himself.

The novel is exactly half finished. It seems clever sometimes and sometimes it seems nonsensical.[100] I hope to show it you in less than two months. The Evening Post has come out very grandly in support of the Black Riders. And the Boston papers have said some fine things about the Red Badge.

What do you suppose made the Philistines do this dinner thing? Was it because I wrote for their magazine? You could have knocked me down with a gas-pipe when I got their bid. Until today I was very miserable about it for I of course was resolved to refuse the offer. But, bad luck to me again. I was delighted with your letter and accepted it "within-side" of thirty minutes.[101]

The woods up here are all dun and dusk and purple save where they are pines or white birches. The little lake is like blue crystal./ I am as always Willis/Your good friend   *Stephen Crane*

105. ELBERT HUBBARD TO STEPHEN CRANE [102]

Nov 16, '95

My Dear Mr Crane: I am delighted with your letters of acceptance,

---

[100] *The Third Violet* was serialized in November, 1896, in *Inter Ocean* and published in book form by Appleton and Heinemann in 1897.

[101] Elbert Hubbard, without asking permission, printed Crane's letter of acceptance in the Buffalo newspapers, and Crane in commenting on this public appearance of his private letter, wrote Nellie Crouse that he would have been more hypocritical in phrasing it had he known it was to appear in print (Letter 122).

[102] This holograph letter, reproduced here for the first time, was enclosed in Crane's letter to Willis Hawkins (No. 106).

and write now merely to acknowledge your letters and thank you. We want this dinner to be perfect and complete in all its appointments and therefore we will submit proof of invitations and list of invited guests to you for suggestion and revisal.

I feared you might think we were merely contemplating a pleasant meeting and dinner with you. But it is more than this—you represent a "cause" and we wish in a dignified, public (and at the same time) elegant manner to recognize that cause.

I fear it will be fully Dec 15th before arrangements can be fully perfected.

Will write you soon again and inform you of exactly what arrangements are being made. Yours Truly   *Elbert Hubbard*

106. TO WILLIS BROOKS HAWKINS

Hartwood, N.Y./Nov. 15th [for November 17, 1895] [103]

Dear Willis: Herein enclosed letter of Hubbard. Write to me quick and tell me that you don't think I am a villian [sic]. Would you come out to Buffalo for the dinner?

I am getting frightened already. Imagine me representing a "cause." Yours always   *Stephen*

107. TO ELBERT HUBBARD

Hartwood, N.Y./Nov. 18 [1895]

My dear Mr. Hubbard: Your photograph came today and I thank you heartily for it. I have none of mine own but I have been looking sideways at photograph galleries for some time and I am quite sure that I will be able to compass the thing before I come to Buffalo.

I am quite an old reader of your Little Journeys and I think them the best things that have been said. Yours very sincerely

Stephen Crane

108. TO WILLIS BROOKS HAWKINS

Hartwood/Nov. 19 [1895]

My dear Willis: I have no late news from Buffalo, although Hubbard sent me his picture some days ago. He is a clever-looking duck. I hope

---

[103] Crane misdated this letter. The Hubbard letter he enclosed in his letter to Hawkins is dated November 16, and therefore Crane must have written this one on the sixteenth or seventeenth. Willis Hawkins answered him the same day he received it (the eighteenth). Crane constantly misdates events.

by all means you can come to the Buffalo dinner. For heaven's sake, begin to think about it now and then by the time the day comes around it will seem easy.

There is a clipping bureau in Boston which is said to only send in it's bills once in three months, so when they wrote me the other day I took them up. I got forty-one new reviews of the Red Badge. And, oh, say, most of 'em were not only favorable but passionately enthusiastic. They didn't skirmish around and say maybe—perhaps—if—after a time —it is possible—under certain circumstances—but.

No; they were cock-sure. The above is a fair sample of New York literary criticism. The fellows in Boston, ten of them,—had a real nice fit. In the west, the Chicago Post and the Minneapolis Tribune were the best but there were a lot of other good ones. About six in the patch are roasts. One is a copy of the Tribune's grind. New York, throughout, has treated me worse than any other city. Damn New York.[104] Except the Evening Post. The Evening Post has just reviewed The Black Riders beautifully.

There—I'm through talking about them but then you know there is nobody here whom one can talk to about them at all. It sounds sort of priggish, somehow. And it is I have no doubt excepting that it is right to be elated when almost all the writers and reviewers seem to have really read the thing.

The new novel is two-thirds done.[105] I gave the first eighteen chapters to my brother Teddie [106] to read. He finished them up without a halt. He is an awful stuff in literature. I am a little dubious about his performance. Seems to me it throws rather a grimly humorous light on the situation. Understand, he thinks my style wouldn't be used by the devil to patch his trousers with. I think he—Teddie—discovered the fellow and the girl in the story and read on to find out if they married. He hung around for a time asking for more chapters but I sent him away.

Dont you forget to keep deciding every day that you are coming to the Buffalo thing.

I lost my temper to-day—fully—absolutely—for the first time in a good many years. I sailed the cat-boat up the lake today in the stiffest breeze we've had in moons. When I got near to the head of the lake, the boat was scudding before the wind in a manner to make your heart

---

[104] Crane sent Hawkins on November 25 a clipping of "Stephen Crane's Talent" in the Port Jervis *Union,* quoting reviews outside New York City; this article is reproduced in Appendix 2.

[105] *The Third Violet.*

[106] Teddie is Edmund Crane.

leap. Then we got striking snags—hidden stumps, floating logs, sunken brush, more stumps,—you might have thought ex-Senator Holman of Indiana was there. Anything that could obstruct, promptly and gracefully obstructed. Up to the 5th stump I had not lost my philosophy but at the 22d I was swearing like cracked ice. And at the appearance of the 164th, I perched on the rail, a wild and gibbering maniac. It is all true. I cant remember when I was so furiously and ferociously angry. Never before, I think.

Teddie has a Belton setter named Judge. When the girls run Judge out of the kitchen, his soul becomes so filled with hate of the world, that outside, he pounces on the first dog he meets. This is all right if it happens to be one of the hounds. They are only pups. He whales them and they roar. But sometimes the first dog he meets is the collie and the collie, after recovering from his surprise, simply wipes up the place with him. But this causes no change in Judge's way. Little dog, or big dog, hound or collie, put him out of the kitchen and he pounces on the first one. This is the way I felt up the pond. But there was nobody there.

Dont you miss the Buffalo dinner. Yours always   S. C.

109. TO WILLIS BROOKS HAWKINS

Dec. 20 [for November 20, 1895]

Dear Willis: Date for dinner Wednesday, Dec. 18.[107] Don't say at Lantern Club that you are coming. Other invitations there supposed to be complimentary. Do you follow me? Yours as ever   S. C.

110. TO WILLIS BROOKS HAWKINS

Hartwood/Nov. 25 [1895]

My dear Willis: I have been frantically hustling of late to make some money but I haven't achieved a cent mainly because I want it so badly. Frank Leslie's Weekly wrote me that my story was very stunning but that the tale "When Greek meets Greek" was going to run until February and they didnt feel justified in buying a serial at this moment. Irving Bacheller had tried hard to accept a story of mine, he said, but he said that he couldn't. Stone and Kimball wrote me that they wanted something for the Chap-book and I immediately fired something at them. I hope for the Lord's sake it goes, but it would be my luck if it

---

[107] Crane misdated the letter. The Philistine Society banquet took place on Thursday, December 19, in Buffalo; it was held at the Genesee House, not at the Iroquois Hotel as originally planned.

didnt.[108] I send you a clipping which may convey a general impression of Red Badge notices—outside of New York.[109]

I have send [sent] a little story to Irving [110] but it is so tiny—the Lantern Club will grab every cent. I tell you these things to convey a sense of how loyally and stoutly I have tried to pull you out of the hole you slid yourself into. When you dont write I begin to think you are disgusted with me. Adios. Yours as ever   *Stephen Crane*

111. TO AN EDITOR OF LESLIE'S WEEKLY

[About November, 1895]

. . . I can't do any sort of work that I don't like or don't feel like doing and I've given up trying to do it. When I was at school few of my studies interested me, and as a result I was a bad scholar. They used to say at Syracuse University, where, by the way, I didn't finish the course, that I was cut out to be a professional base-ball player. And the truth of the matter is that I went there more to play base-ball than to study. I was always very fond of literature, though. I remember when I was eight years old I became very much interested in a child character called, I think, Little Goodie Brighteyes, and I wrote a story then which I called after this fascinating little person. When I was about sixteen I began to write for the New York newspapers, doing correspondence from Asbury Park and other places. Then I began to write special articles and short stories for the Sunday papers and one of the literary syndicates, reading a great deal in the meantime and gradually acquiring a style. I decided that the nearer a writer gets to life the greater he becomes as an artist, and most of my prose writings have been toward the goal partially described by that misunderstood and abused word, realism. Tolstoi is the writer I admire most of all. I've been a free lance during most of the time I have been doing literary work, writing stories and articles about anything under heaven that seemed to possess interest, and selling them wherever I could. It was hopeless work. Of all human lots for a person of sensibility that of an obscure free lance in literature or journalism is, I think, the most discouraging. It was during this period that I wrote "The Red Badge of Courage." It was an effort born of pain—despair, almost; and I believe that this made it a better piece of literature than it otherwise

---

[108] The *Bibliography* lists only one Crane piece in *Chap-Book* (Chicago), an article on Harold Frederic, March 15, 1898.

[109] A clipping of a summary of the reviews of *The Red Badge*, appearing in the Port Jervis *Union* earlier this month, reproduced here for the first time. (See Appendix 2.)

[110] Irving Bacheller.

would have been.[111] It seems a pity that art should be a child of pain, and yet I think it is. Of course we have fine writers who are prosperous and contented, but in my opinion their work would be greater if this were not so. It lacks the sting it would have if written under the spur of a great need.

But, personally, I was unhappy only at times during the period of my struggles. I was always looking forward to success. My first great disappointment was in the reception of "Maggie, a Girl of the Streets." I remember how I looked forward to its publication, and pictured the sensation I thought it would make. It fell flat. Nobody seemed to notice it or care for it. I am going to introduce Maggie again to the world some time, but not for a good while.[112] Poor Maggie! she was one of my first loves.

I suppose I ought to be thankful to "The Red Badge," but I am much fonder of my little book of poems, "The Black Riders." The reason, perhaps, is that it was a more ambitious effort. My aim was to comprehend in it the thoughts I have had about life in general, while "The Red Badge" is a mere episode in life, an amplification. A rather interesting fact about the story is that it lay for eight months in a New York magazine office waiting to receive attention. I called on the editor [113] time and again and couldn't find out whether he intended to publish it or not, so at last I took it away. Now that it is published and the people seem to like it I suppose I ought to be satisfied, but somehow I am not as happy as I was in the uncertain, happy-go-lucky newspaper writing days. I used to dream continually of success then. Now that I have achieved it in some measure it seems like mere flimsy paper.

112. WILLIAM DEAN HOWELLS TO HARRY P. TABER

40 West Fifty-ninth Street/Dec. 8, 1895

My dear Sir: I am sorry to be so busy and so far away that I cannot hope to come to your dinner for Mr. Crane. It is good to find people generally appreciating a talent known in its rarity to two or three of us

---

[111] Crane's viewpoint that literature is the product of "a great deal of labor" is echoed in Letters 125, 137.

[112] J. Herbert Welch published this letter on May 28, 1896, in *Leslie's Weekly:* "The Personality and Work of Stephen Crane." Welch reported that Crane had said this much "the other day," but Crane must have written this letter much earlier because *Maggie* was in the press during May, 1896— it was published in June. *Maggie* was in process of revision in February. Crane's letter was again published in *Omnibus*, pp. 627–29.

[113] McClure.

earlier; and I am glad that Mr. Crane's laurels are growing in his youth, when he can have pleasure in them. With sincere thanks for your invitation, Yours truly   *W. D. Howells*

113. *JOHN NORTHERN HILLIARD* [114] *TO STEPHEN CRANE*

Rochester, N.Y./December 14th 1895

Dear Sir/ I am running in the Union a series of Illustrated articles on— American and Foreign Authors. Sketches of such writers as Eugene Field, Donald G. Mitchell, Hamlin Garland, Sara[h] Orne Jewett, James Whitcomb Riley W. D. Howells and others equally as noted have appeared. I should like to run a series of articles concerning your-self if you will send us a photograph as our portraits are printed in half tone and on excellent paper.

Please write your name across the photograph, that it may be re-produced with it. Also jot down some notes of your life and work, which will be written up in a sketch, which will include a review of your work. If you have a scrap of manuscript to send we will repro-duce that, too.

This series is attracting considerable notice and comment in this part of the world. Trusting to hear from you as soon as convenient I remain/Very sincerely yours   *John N. Hilliard/Editor*

114. *TO WILLIS BROOKS HAWKINS*

[Hartwood, N.Y., about December 15, 1895]

My dear Willis: You harrow me a little bit. My transportation is to be by the Erie. I was hoping all along that you were going to go by the Erie. You were to be the moral reinforcement which I sought. I cant come to N.Y., because it requires "dough." I have mapped out my two or three shekels so that I will return home smiling but broke and in the smoking-car. I bought to-day one full dress shirt and what goes with it. I have a damn fine hat. I have no overcoat save that little gauze one which you may remember. Nor no dress-suit. My brother has (had) a pair of patent leathers and I am sleeping with them under my pillow. I've got 'em.

There is a peach of a row on in Buffalo. The Saturn Club, the

---

[114] Hilliard moved from the Rochester *Union and Advertiser* to the Rochester *Post-Express* some time during 1896–1897. This form letter elic-ited Crane's January 2, 1896, response (see No. 125). Older than Crane, Hilliard said he was a friend of his as early as April, 1893, when Crane bor-rowed Hilliard's suit to appear for tea with Howells (so Beer's legend has it). The night before Crane died he expressed an intention to write Hilliard.

Browning Clubs, etc., have heard somehow of me and—Hubbard says
—are planning to dine me. All the *Philistines* are hot. Wrote swearing
letters to and from to each other. Hubbard enclosed letters to me without comment. I of course wrote him that it would naturally be hard
for me to offend people who only intended to be kind but that for my
very short stay I would consider that I had engaged myself to the
Philistines. I didnt see what else to do when I could percieve [*sic*] by
their letters that the *Philistines* were likely to be very much injured.
They called the others a "god damned lot of old tabies." [*sic*]

I enclose you copy of a London letter.

In the matter of the Saturn Club—I don't deride a dinner from the
Saturn Club. No. But then I have to proceed by the atmosphere when
I get there.

And now, Willis, old man, when I get in all this flumy-doodle business and see you behind there moving the scenes and knowing all the
time what a damned fool I am and what a ridiculous hole I'm in, I get
fair feeble-minded with dwelling upon it. I leave it all to you. For my
part I wish the whole thing was in Ballywhoo because while I look
forward to it as probably the greatest pleasure of my life, I feel as if I
were astride of your shoulders. And if I could stop the thing now I
would. Yours alway   S. C.

I go to Port Jervis on Sunday. My address—Port Jervis, N.Y. c/—W. H.
Crane

115. WILLIS BROOKS HAWKINS TO STEPHEN CRANE

Tuesday Dec 17 [1895]

My dear Stephen: I addressed a note to you at Hartwood last night.
You may not get it in time, so I repeat its contents: I go by the Central
—*must*. I leave here Wed. night, reach Buffalo probably by noon Thursday. I shall go straight [to] the Genesee, where the dinner is to be, and
shall ask for you. If you have not yet arrived I will wait for you at the
Genesee. If I go out I will leave a note for you with the clerk. If you
reach the Genesee before do you either wait for me or leave a note for
me. I shall express an overcoat to you this afternoon. In Buffalo we will
fix up the dress suit question. You bring along your shirt, hat & shoes.
I will attend to coat, vest and trousers.

I like this sort a thing. Don't you let it bother you a bit. It isn't as
if I were rich. It's one poor devil faking up a way for another poor
devil to get his fingers into pie. I haven't had any fun at all lately, and
this is a real enjoyment. We'll have a bully time. I wish I could go by
the Erie, but I can't. Let me get you as soon as you reach Buffalo—

before you fall into the hands of the Philistines if possible. It will be
better so. Your friend   *Willis B. Hawkins*

116. TO WILLIS BROOKS HAWKINS

Buffalo [December 19, 1895]

Dear Willis: Back at four, old man   *S. C.*

❋   ❋   ❋

The Banquet in Honor of Stephen Crane

"In Honor of Mr. Stephen Crane" the Society of the Philistines printed
a banquet menu folder presenting three dozen tributes and regrets of
authors and journalists unable to attend, including messages from
William Dean Howells, Hamlin Garland, Louise Imogen Guiney, Bliss
Carman, and Ambrose Bierce, who wrote: "Were it not for the miles
which separate us, I would be with you." There were notes from
Richard Harding Davis, Ripley Hitchcock, and S. S. McClure, and a
pert one from the editor of the *Albany Express:* "I have a profound
admiration for a man who, casting to the winds rhyme, reason and
metre, can still write poetry." From Amy Leslie, of the *Chicago News,*
there was a more personal note: "My most gentle thoughts are tinged
with envy of you who are so lucky as to meet Stephen Crane." There
was also a verse parody of Crane by Hayden Carruth ("I saw a Man
reading an Invitation"), and quotations from Crane's poems appeared
on the back cover.[115] Crane wrote the note below to Willis Hawkins
two days after the banquet. He stayed on in East Aurora with Elbert
Hubbard and Taber for four days.

❋   ❋   ❋

117. TO WILLIS BROOKS HAWKINS

East Aurora, [New York]/Saturday [December 21], 1895

Dear Willis: I am coming to New York on Tuesday morning.

Stephen Crane

[P.S.] *I wish I could too!/Elbert Hubbard*

---

[115] The Buffalo *Evening News,* December 20, reported the banquet:
"The Philistines at Dinner," "Mr. Crane is unquestionably a Philistine, according to the definition of the society, for he writes what pleases him, in
his own way, and takes all the chances of its pleasing any one else. The purpose of the Philistines is to encourage just such independence and individu-

118. TO RIPLEY HITCHCOCK

Hartwood, N.Y./Dec 27, 95

Dear Mr Hitchcock: I forward you today my new story: "The Third
Violet," in the original manuscript for the typewriting was so bad I am
obliged to consider the original better.[116] Moreover as I am considering a start very shortly to some quarter of the world where mail is uncertain, I am in haste for your opinion. I was not in the least offended
at the "puppet" thing. Thought it was all right. Yours sincerely

Stephen Crane

119. TO RIPLEY HITCHCOCK

Hartwood/Friday [December 27, 1895]

Please acknowledge reciept [*sic*].

Dear Mr. Hitchcock: Enclosed is "The Third Violet" in ms. There is
only one. Typewriting is too new an art for the woods. If you think it
well, have the thing type-writen—charged to my c/o—and send me
the type written one to save the story.   *S. C.*

120. TO JOHN PHILLIPS OF THE
PHILLIPS-AND-McCLURE SYNDICATE

Hartwood, N. Y./Dec. 30 [1895]

Dear Mr. Phillips: Your project [117] it seemed to me would require a
great deal of study and a great deal of time. I would be required to

---

ality in literature and other matters, and Mr. Crane was thus in the house
of friends though personally known beforehand to none of the Philistines
here."

[116] Crane had completed one-third of *The Third Violet* by November 8.
Hitchcock begged Crane to think over the novel before it was printed, being
dubious about it. Crane admitted that many scenes were too compressed,
"but the story had appeared as a serial and it was 'dishonest' to change the
thing now that it had been offered to readers" (Beer, p. 377).

This letter was sent separately from the manuscript (see No. 119).

[117] Civil War stories. This project became *The Little Regiment*, published late the next year by Appleton's. Instead of writing sketches of particular battles, Crane finally wrote imaginary war stories: "The Little Regiment," "Three Miraculous Soldiers," "A Mystery of Heroism," "An Indiana
Campaign," "A Gray Sleeve," and "The Veteran." The best of the lot is "A
Mystery of Heroism," which deals with an incident that might have occurred
in any war. The incident, but not the theme, is echoed in Conrad's "Heart
of Darkness" (1898).

give up many of my plans for this winter and this I am reluctant to do. I dont know how you would advise going about it but one of the first things I would want to do, would be to visit the battle-field—which I was to describe—at the time of year when it was fought. The preliminary reading and the subsequent reading, the investigations of all kinds, would take much time. Moreover, if I did not place the only original crown of pure gold on the heads of at least twelve generals they would arise and say: "This damned young fool was not there. I was however. And this is how it happened." I evaded them in the Red Badge because it was essential that I should make my battle a type and name no names but in your case, it would be very different. In the spring when a good deal of my work will be done and the anniversaries of the fights begin to occur, I think I would like to do the work and if you send me the name of the battle you first wish me to tackle I will try to do some reading on it. I am not very leisurely just now for I have a good many orders and requests, and I am busy at them. Yours sincerely   *Stephen Crane*

121. TO WILLIS BROOKS HAWKINS

Hartwood, N.Y./Dec 31st [1895]

Dear Willis: Back and retired once more to corduroys. I send overcoat tonight. Pray heaven I have not got you into trouble by keeping it too long. Write me your impressions of the dinner as soon as you get time. Hubbard and Taber think you are just the smoothest guy in the world. The reason I wrote you that I would be in NY was because they told me my passes would be over the Central but as it turned out, they were to Port Jervis over the Erie. I am very anxious to hear wether [*sic*] you are satisfied with the dinner. I did not drink much but the excitement soon turned everything into a grey haze for me and I am not sure that I came off decently.[118]

---

[118] To commemorate the Philistine Society banquet Hubbard printed three pamphlets of souvenir material—the letters of invitation and acceptance in *The Members of the Society;* the menu and additional responses and an unsigned new Crane poem ("I have heard the sunset song of the birches," printed there for the first time) in *The Time Has Come;* and in the May issue of Hubbard's *Roycroft Quarterly,* as "A Souvenir and a Medley," tributes to Crane and seven poems by him. Hubbard exploited the whole thing to the utmost.

On New Year's Eve Crane wrote Nellie Crouse a long letter (No. 122) and satirized the Philistine affair in describing what happened at the dinner, but he expressed himself quite differently here in writing to Willis that same night.

I sent my new novel down to Appleton's yesterday.[119] Will let you know it's reception. If you see Colonel Floyd give him my kindest regards. I think you and him [sic] made the big hit at Buffalo. The agony of the Indians over the fact that you left the boat in the middle of the Fox River may have led you to think differently but it is true. Write me soon. Yours as ever   *Stephen Crane*

✿   ✿   ✿

Nellie Crouse

Crane evidently fell in love with Nellie Crouse on first sight. They met at a tea in January, 1895, in New York City, when Lucius L. Button introduced Crane to some of his Akron, Ohio, friends. Not until he had struck fame with *The Red Badge* did he write her, first in December and finally from Washington, D.C., in March, 1896—seven letters in all.

Crane's letters to Nellie Crouse are outspoken, bitter, and satirical. The satire (as one reader of them puts it) "is indicative of his devastatingly ironical attitude towards everything which he believed to be insincere." They reflect Crane's depression and change of heart following his self-deluded experience of the Philistine Society fiasco.

✿   ✿   ✿

122. TO NELLIE CROUSE
                                       Hartwood, N.Y./Dec. 31st [1895]

Dear Miss Crouse: I embrace with pleasure the opportunities of the walrus. I knew little of the Philistines until they sent me this letter [the letter of November 10 from the Committee for The Society, which Crane here transcribed]. . . . I was very properly enraged at the word 'poet' which continually reminds me of long-hair and seems to me to be a most detestable form of insult but nevertheless I replied [Crane here quotes his November 15 letter (No. 103)]. . . . I am convinced that I would have written a worse letter if I had had the slightest idea that they were going to print it. I went to Buffalo and this is not at all what happened: [120] [Here Crane attached to his letter a clipping of "The

---

[119] *The Third Violet*, which Crane sent to Hitchcock on December 30, or on December 27, according to his letter to Hitchcock (No. 119).

[120] What happened is detailed in Frank Noxon's letter of 1926 (see Appendix 24). To Claude Bragdon, whose version of the affair differs from Noxon's account, Hubbard's now historic Philistine dinner seemed in retrospect "still a distressing memory—like the sight of a young ox led to the slaughter. At first the dinner was dominated by a lot of drunken pseudo-reporters, who had come there with the evident intention of turning the

Philistines at Dinner," from the Buffalo *Evening News* of December 20]. . . .

However it is one man's idea of what happened and not altogether wrong in proper names. I had a good time and caused them considerable trouble in inventing nice things to say to me.

I do not suppose you will be overwhelmed with distinction when I tell you that your name is surrounded with much sentiment for me. I was in southern Mexico last winter for a sufficient time to have my face turn the color of a brick side-walk. There was nothing American about me save a large Smith and Wesson revolver and I saw only Indians whom I suspected of loading their tomales with dog. In this state of mind and this physical condition, I arrived one day in the city of Puebla and there I saw an American girl. There was a party of tourists in town and she was of their contingent. I only saw her four times— one in the hotel corridor and three in the street. I had been so long in the mountains and was such an outcast, that the sight of this American girl in a new spring gown nearly caused me to drop dead. She of course never looked in my direction. I never met her. Nevertheless I gained one of those peculiar thrills which a man only acknowledges upon occasion. I ran to the railroad office. I cried: "What is the shortest route to New York." I left Mexico.

I suppose you fail to see how this concerns you in anyway! And no wonder! But this girl who startled me out of my mountaineer senses, resembled you. I have never achieved the enjoyment of seeing you in a new spring gown but this girl became to me not an individual but a sort of a symbol and I have always thought of you with gratitude for the peculiar thrill you gave me in the town of Puebla, Mexico.

The lives of some people are one long apology. Mine was, once, but not now. I go through the world unexplained, I suppose. Perhaps this letter may look like an incomparable insolence. Who knows. Script is an infernally bad vehicle for thoughts. I know that, at least. But if you are not angry at me, I should like you to tell me where Button is at. I lost him almost a year ago and I have never been able to discover him. I suppose it is his size. He could be so easily overlooked in a crowd. Yours sincerely　　　　　　　　　　　　　*Stephen Crane*

---

whole affair to ridicule by their ribald and irrelevant interruptions, much to the distress, naturally, of Hubbard and us others. When these men were finally cowed into some semblance of order Crane was forced to his feet to respond to Harry P. Taber's tribute to 'the strong voice now heard in America—the voice of Stephen Crane.' " It was Bragdon who cowed the rowdies into order. Bragdon's accounts of the affair are given in the *Bookman* for July, 1929, in his *Merely Players* (1929), and in his *More Lives than One* (1938).

123. TO CURTIS BROWN [121]

Hartwood, N.Y./Dec. 31st, 1896 [for 1895]

My Dear Curtis, Thank you for your kind words and for *Sketch* clipping.[122] I hear the damned book ("The Red Badge of Courage") is doing very well in England. In the meantime I am plodding along. I have finished my new novel—"The Third Violet"—and sent it to Appleton and Co., as per request, but I've an idea it won't be accepted.[123] It's pretty rotten work. I used myself up in the accursed "Red Badge." Yours as ever,   *Stephen Crane*

---

[121] Literary agent; at this time Sunday editor of the New York *Press*.
[122] This item has not been traced.
[123] Appleton's published *The Third Violet* in 1897.

3

1 8 9 6 – 1 8 9 7

THE MOST IMPORTANT EVENT of 1896 for Stephen Crane was his meeting with Cora Howorth, who called herself Cora Taylor. Cora's first marriage to Thomas Vinton Murphy had ended in divorce. She soon afterward married Captain Donald William Stewart—later K.C.M.G.—from whom she was now separated, though not divorced. How she came by the name "Taylor" is not known, but it was probably a name she took for business reasons—comparable to Crane's own use of "Johnston Smith," the pseudonym under which he wrote *Maggie*. Crane met her in November in Jacksonville, Florida, where she was the hostess and proprietress of the Hotel de Dream. Crane and other newspaper men, waiting to go to Cuba, were often at her place—among them E. W. McCready, whose reminiscences of Cora and Stephen are given in Appendix 25.

The year begins with Crane continuing his love letters to Nellie Crouse, writing her (No. 131): "I perceived that the fight was not going to be with the world but with myself." The issue of discussion in Letter 144 is the man of fashion; to the society men Crane prefers the aristocrat—"He is like a thorough-bred horse." Crane's passion for horses echoes from letter to letter. In January he visited the battlefields of Virginia, in preparation for writing some war stories, and wrote Ripley Hitchcock, editor of Appleton & Company: "People may just as well discover now that the high dramatic key of the Red Badge cannot be sustained (Letter 133). He began to revise *Maggie* and thought of making a trip to London. In March he visited Washington, D.C., to do a book for S. S. McClure on political society, a project he abandoned, and he returned to New York and had a poker game with Willis Brooks Hawkins and other friends. At the year's end he was in trouble over money allegedly borrowed from Amy Leslie, former actress and drama critic of the Chicago *Daily News*.

On New Year's Day, 1897, he was shipwrecked en route to Cuba, and out of this *Commodore* disaster he re-created his experiences in "The Open Boat." Then unable to get to Cuba, he went to Greece as war correspondent for the New York *Journal*. Cora Taylor rejoined him in London and went with him to Greece as war correspondent for the *Journal*, the first woman war correspondent, writing under the pseudonym of "Imogene Carter." [1] They went to London when the war ended, and in July they rented a house at Oxted, Surrey.

They began their life together in debt, and they ended it still in debt. As we see in his letters to Paul Revere Reynolds, beginning with No. 200, Crane had overdrawn his accounts with S. S. McClure and his other publishers, and hard luck in money matters plagues him constantly. In September Crane and Cora visited Ireland with Harold Frederic, the novelist, and Kate Lyon, for whom Harold had left the wife who would not give him a divorce to marry Kate. In October Crane met Joseph Conrad, and after that first meeting they remained close friends, as many Conrad letters testify. One of the most interesting is a Conrad letter recently discovered in The Library of Congress, written long after Crane's death (see Appendix 16).

These 1897 letters tell the story of Crane's writings after Paul

---

[1] A rival claimant to being "the first woman war correspondent at the front" turned up on the field in the person of one Harriet A. Boyd, a Smith College graduate in Greece when the war broke out, who volunteered as a nurse. A feature story by Miss Boyd appeared in the New York *Journal*, Sunday edition of April 25, describing her experiences in nurses' training and announcing other articles to follow. But Miss Boyd failed to qualify for the hospital unit and promptly signed up with the *Journal* as a war correspondent. Her next article, datelined from Volo, was featured with the headline: "Only Woman War Correspondent at the Front." But "Imogene Carter's" dispatch of April 29 had already appeared in the *Journal*: "Woman War Correspondent at the Front. Goes for the Journal. . . . Only Woman on the Scene." The ensuing mix-up is to be explained by the probability that Harriet Boyd, after washing out with the hospital unit, cabled the *Journal* office in New York and got the assignment as woman representative at the front, whereas "Imogene Carter's" job must have been arranged by Stephen in Athens through John Bass, the *Journal* man in charge there. The *Journal* records were lost in a fire that gutted the old building on Nassau Street; but there can be no doubt about the *Journal*'s desire to have a woman correspondent at the front.

"Imogene Carter" also published in some other paper an earlier dispatch, April 26, "War Seen Through a Woman's Eyes" (unpaged clipping in the Butler Library Crane Collection); and again in the New York *Journal*, Athens, May 9, "Imogene Carter's Pen Picture of the Fighting at Velestino," bringing the number of her published dispatches on record to three.

Revere Reynolds became his agent. "The Bride Comes to Yellow Sky,"
"The Monster," "A Man and Some Others," and "Death and the Child,"
were written in this period.

❄   ❄   ❄

124. TO WILLIAM DEAN HOWELLS [2]

Hartwood, N.Y./January 1st [1896]

Dear Mr. Howells: Every little time I hear from some friend a kind
thing you have said of me, an interest which you have shown in my
work. I have been so long conscious of this, that I am grown uncomfortable in not being able to express to you my gratitude and so I seize
the New Year's Day as an opportunity to thank you and tell you how
often I think of your kind benevolent life. Sincerely yours,

Stephen Crane

125. TO JOHN NORTHERN HILLIARD

Hartwood, N.Y./January 2ᵈ [1896]

Dear Mr. Hilliard: If you will pardon this kind of paper,[3] I think I will

---

[2] For Howells' reply see Letter 130.

[3] Written on blue-lined paper (8 by 12½ inches) with red-lined margin,
almost like the legal cap used for writing *The Red Badge*. Crane is replying
to Hilliard's letter (No. 113).

The full text of this letter is reproduced here for the first time. Portions
of it (quoted or paraphrased) were printed in a recently discovered article
by John Northern Hilliard appearing on February 8, 1896, in the Rochester
Union and Advertiser: "The Hideousness of War/Stephen Crane and *The
Red Badge*." Hilliard was then an editor of that newspaper. In publishing
Crane's letter Hilliard cut and interpolated as he pleased. In reprinting it on
April 18, 1900, in the Rochester *Post-Express*, of which Hilliard became an
editor in 1896, he said that it had been written a few weeks before.
In *Omnibus* (pp. 689–91) it is dated therefore as "about February, 1900."
We see now that it was written on January 2, 1896, but we have to account
for certain variants occurring in the so-called February, 1900, letter ascribed
in *Omnibus* to Joseph O'Connor, who was editor of "Literary Notes"–the
column in which this variant letter appeared–in the Rochester *Post-Express*.
This variant letter reads: "On the first day of last November I was precisely
29 years old, and had finished my fifth novel, 'Active Service.'" Crane, however, was in fact but twenty-eight then. It seems likely that when Hilliard
published the original (the January 2, 1896, letter) in the *Post-Express* in
1900, he tampered with it to bring it up to date so that it would appear to
be a recently written letter. It does not seem likely that Crane wrote Hilliard
in 1900 a letter which is an almost exact copy of the one he had written
him in 1896. The 1896 letter reads: "On the 1st day of November, 1895,
I was precisely 24 years old."

be able to [tell?] you more easily what you wish to know. However even then I am not sure that I will succeed as I am not much versed in talking about myself. As to the picture I am sorry I cannot give you one but I haven't had a picture taken since early boyhood.[4]

Occasionally, interested acquintances [sic] have asked me if "Stephen Crane" was a nom de guerre; but it is my own name. In childhood, I was bitterly ashamed of it and now, when I sometimes see it in print, it strikes me as being the homliest [sic] name in created things. The first Stephen Crane to appear in America, arrived in Massachusetts from England in 1635. His son Stephen Crane settled in Connecticut and the Stephen Crane of the third American generation settled in New Jersey on lands that now hold the cities of Newark and Elizabeth. When the troubles with England came, he was president of both Colonial Assemblies that met in New York. Then he was sent by New Jersey to the Continental Congress and he served in that body until just about a week before the Declaration was signed, when the Tories made such trouble in New Jersey that he was obliged to return and serve as speaker in the colony's assembly. He died in the old homestead at Elizabeth when the British troops were marching past to what pappened [sic] to be the defeat at Trenton. His eldest son commanded the 6th New Jersey infantry during the Revolution and ultimately died the ranking Major-general in the regular army from an old wound recieved [sic] in the expedition to Quebec. The second son became the ranking commodore in the navy at a time when the title of admiral was unknown. The youngest son, while proceeding to his father's bedside, was captured by some Hessians and upon his refusing to tell the road by which they intended to surprise a certain American out-post, they beat him with their muskets and then having stabbed him with their bayonets, they left him dead in the road. In those old times the family did it's duty.

Upon my mother's side, everybody as soon as he could walk, became a Methodist clergyman—of the old ambling-nag, saddle-bag, exhorting kind. My uncle, Jesse T. Peck, D.D., L.L.D., was a bishop in the Methodist Church. My father was also a clergyman of that church, author of numerous works of theology, an editor of various periodicals of the church. He graduated at Princeton. He was a great, fine, simple mind.

As for myself, I went to Lafayette College but did not graduate. I found mining-engineering not at all to my taste. I preferred base-ball.

---

[4] That is the photograph of Crane in military uniform taken in 1888 at the Hudson River Institute (reproduced in *Stephen Crane: A Bibliography*, p. 85).

Later I attended Syracuse University where I attempted to study literature but found base ball again much more to my taste. At Lafayette I joined the Delta Upsilon fraternity.

My first work in fiction was for the *New York Tribune* when I was about eighteen years old. During this time, one story of the series went into the *Cosmopolitan*.[5] Previous to this I had written many articles of many kinds for many newspapers. I began when I was sixteen. At age of twenty I wrote my first novel—*Maggie*.[6] It never really got on the market but it made for me the friendships of W. D. Howells and Hamlin Garland and since that time I have never been conscious for an instant that those friendships have at all diminished. After completing *Maggie* I wrote mainly for the *New York Press* and for the *Arena* magazine. The latter part of my twenty-first year I began *The Red Badge of Courage* and completed it early in my twenty-second year. In my twenty-third year, I wrote *The Black Riders*.[7] On the 1st day of November, 1895, I was precisely 24 years old. Last week I finished my new novel: "The Third Violet." It is a story of life among the younger and poorer artists in New York.

I have only one pride and that is that the English edition of *The Red Badge of Courage* has been recieved [*sic*] with great praise by the English reviewers. I am proud of this simply because the remoter people would seem more just and harder to win.

I live in Hartwood, Sullivan Co., N.Y., on an estate of 3500 acres

---

[5] "A Tent in Agony," in the series of Sullivan County sketches, was published in *Cosmopolitan*, December, 1892. Crane was then twenty-one (not eighteen, as he has it).

[6] In the spring of 1891 he began writing *Maggie*. He was then nineteen.

[7] Elsewhere Crane claimed "I wrote the things in February of 1893" (see Beer, p. 297), but he did not write them until after hearing Emily Dickinson's poetry read to him by Howells, and this inspirational meeting did not occur until the first week of April, 1893. He was then not yet twenty-two. He made two visits to Garland's Harlem apartment, first with the manuscript of *The Red Badge* (as yet untitled) and then with the manuscript of a dozen short poems written on legal cap. Garland was much impressed by the poet's "air of detachment. It was precisely as if some alien spirit were delivering these lines through his hand as a medium." " 'There is a ghost at your shoulder,' I said in mock seriousness, 'but not the ghost who gave you *The Red Badge of Courage*. This is the ghost of militant agnosticism—a satirical ghost.' " What this also tells us is that Garland saw first the manuscript of *The Red Badge* and then the manuscript of the poems (in Berryman's account this sequence of visits to Garland is reversed). From Garland's "Stephen Crane as I Knew Him," *Yale Review*, April, 1914. See *Omnibus*, Part VI: Poems, pp. 565 ff.

belonging to my brother and am distinguished for corduroy trousers and briar-wood pipes. My idea of happiness is the saddle of a good-riding horse. . . .

I am not so sure that the above is what you want but I am sure that it is the most complete I have ever written. I hope you will like [it] and if you find that you need enlightenment on certain points, let me know. Please remember me to Mr. Bragdon.[8] With assurances of my regard I am Very sincerely   *Stephen Crane*

My father died when I was seven y'rs old. My mother when I was nineteen.

126. TO CORWIN KNAPP LINSON

Hartwood, N.Y., January 4th, 1896

Dear CK: The lot of truck which I left in your studio would be very acceptable to me just now if you will bundle them up and express them to me C.O.D. I don't doubt but what you will be glad to see them out. There is some "lines" [poems] among them which I will be very glad to get; and also my contract with Copeland and Day, and with Appleton & Co. Please ship the whole business to me here at Hartwood. I am sorry to trouble you but I am too poor to come down to New York. Remember me to Jaccaci.[9] Yours as ever,   *S. C.*

127. TO NELLIE CROUSE

Hartwood, N.Y./January 6th. [1896]

Dear Miss Crouse: Of course it was my original belief that you would not be offended at my letter. I had formed a much higher opinion. If you had rushed out and defended your dignity when it was not assailed, I would have been grievously disappointed. I felt that I was doing something unusual but then I believed I saw in your eye once that the usual was rather tiresome to you. I am galloping all around the point of the argument but then—you know what I must mean—and it is awfully complimentary.

I am sorry that you did not find the "two poems"—mind you, I never call them poems myself—in the *Philistine*. No more did I. But as a matter of truth, the *Philistine* will have something of mine in every number in 1896 so if you ever see that little book again this year, you will on search discover the lost one. I never encourage friends to read my work—they sometimes advise one—but somehow I will be glad to

---

[8] Claude Bragdon, who had met Crane at the Philistine Society banquet.
[9] August F. Jaccaci, art editor of the new *McClure's Magazine*.

send you things of mine. Not because I think you will refrain from advising one either. But simply because I would enjoy it—sending them, I mean. I think your advice would have a charm to it that I do not find in some others.

I observe that you think it wretched to go through life unexplained. Not at all. You have no idea how it simplifies matters. But in your case I make humble concession and I am prepared to explain anything at all which I can find power to do. I have been told 84676 times that I am not of the cream of mankind but you make a sort of an inference that I might myself think I was of it, so I hasten to say that although I never line the walls or clutter the floors of ballrooms, my supreme detestation is dowdy women although they may be as intellectual as Mahomet. If you had seen me dashing through the back streets of Buffalo to escape the Browning Club, you would believe me. I am not sure that they were very anxious either, but then I was anxious, and I would not have been caught for a great deal.

When you said that Hitchcock mentioned me, I was alarmed for I thought you meant Ripley Hitchcock [10] of New York and I knew just how he would mention anybody save himself and God. I resolved to overthrow him on the first opportunity. But then I perceived that you meant Hitchcock of Buffalo. His name, you understand, is Hitchy. If you had said that Hitchy mentioned me, I would have known at once.

I am sending you by this mail a newspaper clipping of "A Grey [sic] Sleeve." [11] It is not in any sense a good story and the intolerable pictures make it worse. In England, it comes out in a magazine and if I had a copy I would send you one, in order to make you think it was a better story but unfortunately I have not yet seen the English periodical.

I must here candidly say that I am not insanely desirous of knowing Button's location. Originally, it was a pretext. But still I am glad to know that you know where he is and I would be glad to have you find out for me, for he is as good an Indian as ever lived.[12]

I am not very much on newspaper work now but in the spring I am wanting very much to go to Arizona to study the Apaches more. There is a man in Boston who has been unwise enough to ask me to write a play for his theatre and I wish to have some Apaches in it.

---

[10] Though Crane seems to have disliked Hitchcock, he nevertheless made him one of the executors of his will.

[11] In the Philadelphia *Press*, October 12, 14, 15, 1895, and in the *English Illustrated Magazine*, January, 1896.

[12] Lucius L. Button, of Akron, introduced Crane to Nellie Crouse at a tea in New York (see Letter 68).

For instance the music of their scalp dance is enough to set fire to a stone church. And in this connection I intend going west on the Erie. This route leads through Akron, as I distinctly remember. Furthermore,—if I don't go to Arizona—and I shall at any rate go to Buffalo and if you will please tell me that Akron is not far from Buffalo, I will make an afternoon—or possibly evening—call on you. Sure.

I am deeply interested concerning that lot of things which you say you wish to know. I pledge myself to "'fess" if it ruins my egotism for a fortnight. Anyhow, it is a very comfortable and manful occupation to trample upon one's own egotism. When I reached twenty-one years and first really scanned my personal egotism I was fairly dazzled by the size of it. The Matterhorn could be no more than a ten-pin to it. Perhaps I have succeeded in lowering it a trifle. So you will please keep in mind that there is a young [*missing word*] corduroy-trousered, briar-wood smoking young man—in Hartwood, N.Y. who is eagerly awaiting a letter from you. Sincerely yours,   *Stephen Crane*

128. TO JOHN PHILLIPS OF THE PHILLIPS-McCLURE SYNDICATE

Hartwood/January 9th. [1896]

Dear Mr. Phillips: The only battle one could well do during this time of year is Fredericksburg. It was fought in December and no doubt the color of things there now would be the very same color of things of the days the battle was fought. I however could not arrange to go down there before the middle of February.[13]

Fredericksburg is to me the most dramatic battle of the war. The terrific assault of the Union army on the impregnable had something in it of the fury of despair. It had been goaded and hooted by the sit-stills until it was near insane and just as a maddened man may dash his fists against an iron wall, so did the Union army hurl itself against the hills back of Fredericksburg.

If you intend to have me do the thing, let me know soon. I want to understand Fredericsburg [*sic*] completely as far as the books will teach it and then after that, the other things. Yours sincerely

Stephen Crane

129. TO NELLIE CROUSE

Hartwood, N.Y./January 12th. [1896]

Dear Miss Crouse: How dreadfully weary of everything you are.

---

[13] Crane went to Virginia in late January, 1896, to study battlefields. Other than Frederic M. Lawrence's recollection as given in his letter to Thomas Beer (see Appendix 21), there is no proof that Crane visited Fredericksburg and the battlefields in Virginia in 1893 (contra Berryman, p. 71).

There were deeps of gloom in your letter which might have made me wonder but they did not, for by the same token, I knew of them long ago. As a matter of truth, I learn nothing new of you from your letters. They merely substantiate previous opinions.

For my own part, I am minded to die in my thirty-fifth year. I think that is all I care to stand. I don't like to make wise remarks on the aspect of life but I will say that it doesn't strike me as particularly worth the trouble. The final wall of the wise man's thought however is Human Kindness of course. If the road of disappointment, grief, pessimism, is followed far enough, it will arrive there. Pessimism itself is only a little, little way, and moreover it is ridiculously cheap. The cynical mind is an uneducated thing. Therefore do I strive to be as kind and as just as may be to those about me and in my meagre success at it, I find the solitary pleasure of life.

It is good of you to like "A Grey [sic] Sleeve." Of course, they are a pair of idiots. But yet there is something charming in their childish faith in each other. That is all I intended to say.

When I implored you to advise me, I knew very well you would not. But still I was crushed to an infinite degree when you suggested that I should take knowledge from the reviewers. Oh, heavens! Apparently you have not studied the wiles of the learned reviewer very much or you never would have allowed yourself to write that sentence. There is only one person in the world who knows less than the average reader. He is the average reviewer. I would already have been a literary corpse, had I ever paid the slightest attention to the reviewers. It may seem to you that I take this ground because there have been so many unfavorable reviews in America. Take this then from England:

> The "Red Badge of Courage" has fascinated England. The critics are wild over it, and the English edition has been purchased with avidity. Mr. Crane has letters from the most prominent of English publishers asking for the English rights to all of his future productions.

Now I have never taken the trouble to look up a single one of these English reviews although I hear from all sides how enthusiastic they are.[14] As for the English publishers I wrote them that I remembered

---

[14] The chief impetus for Crane's American success was provided by British praise, and the tumultuous reception accorded *The Red Badge* by the British journals was first noted by Harold Frederic's London dispatch in *The New York Times* on January 26, 1896: "Stephen Crane's Triumph— London Curious About the Identity of America's New Writer." (Crane wrote

thinking The Red Badge a pretty good thing when I did it, but that it had no attractions for me now and as for any other books I had not then the slightest knowledge of being able to write them. So, you see if I despise reviewers it is not because I have not received favorable notice in some quarters.

I am dejected just now because I have to start for New York tonight and leave the blessed quiet hills of Hartwood. McClure is having one of his fits of desire to have me write for him and I am obliged to go see him. Moreover, I have a new novel coming out in the spring and I am also obliged to confer with the Appleton's about that.[15] But I am hanged if I stay in New York more than one day. Then I shall hie me back to Hartwood.

Why, in heaven's name, do you think that beer is any more to me than a mere incident? You don't, as a matter of fact. You were merely warning me. Teas bore me, of course, because all the girls gibber. But then you didn't mean that I might run into a regular tea.

Of course, I knew of the young man who wrote the back-hand. Not that he wrote a back-hand; but then I knew that he had come and gone. Writers—some of them—are dreadfully impertinent about knowing things. Once upon a time there was a young woman but her sister married a baronet and so she thought she must marry a baronet, too. I find it more and more easy to believe her stupid. This is rather lame consolation but I have known it to work.

Your admission that many people find you charming, leads me to be honest. So prepare. I called once in 34th St., when you were there, didn't I? Well, I was rather bored. I thought you very attractive but then I was bored, because I had always believed that when I made calls I was bored. However to some sentence of mine you said: "Yes, I know," before I had quite finished. I don't remember what I had said

---

Ripley Hitchcock of Appleton's that he was "very much delighted" with Frederic's article.) Once the United States got wind of it, his book "swept the country," leading the best-seller lists by March and April in sixteen cities and going through fourteen American printings that year (*Omnibus*, p. xxii).

[15] *The Little Regiment, and Other Episodes of the American Civil War* (a collection of short stories), which Crane finished the next month. In his letter to the editor of *The Critic* he calls it a "novelette for S. S. McClure— *The Little Regiment* which represents my work at its best I think and is positively my last thing dealing with battle." Appleton's published *The Little Regiment* in July and reissued *Maggie* in June. In England Heinemann published *The Red Badge of Courage* and *Maggie*, and Edward Arnold brought out both here and in England *George's Mother*. *The Black Riders* was also printed in England this year, and so 1896 proved to be Crane's most fruitful year.

but I always remembered your saying: "Yes, I know." I knew then that you had lived a long time. And so in some semi-conscious manner, you stood forth very distinctly in my memory. In New Orleans I met a fellow—awful chump—who said he was from Akron, O.[16] After a decent interval, I mentioned my meeting you. I was delighted to find that he knew you. I said you were very charming and ultimately he said "rather queer girl, though." Of course he said you were charming, too, but then the slightly dazed manner in which he said "rather queer girl" impressed me. He apparently did not understand you and he being such a chump, I thought it a very good sign. You know the Mexican incident.[17] It was very strange. When I arrived in New York I called at once at 34th St. Nobody was there. Long afterward, I sent the menu of that dinner at Buffalo.

There is the whole episode. You have been for me a curiously potential attraction. I tell it you frankly, assured that no harm could come from any course so honest. I don't know what it is or why it is. I have never analyzed it. Couldn't. I am bound to let my egotism have swing here and tell you that I am an intensely practical and experienced person, in fear you might confuse the word "poet" with various kinds of crazy sentiment.

I have said sometimes to myself that you are a person of remarkably strong personality and that I detected it in New York in that vague unformulating way in which I sometimes come to know things; but then I don't even know this. In short, I want to be frank but I don't know precisely how. One thing however, is certain. I would like to know you. And when Akron becomes possible to me, I shall invade Akron.

You will feel embarrassed. I'll bet on it. Here is a young man who proclaims an admiration of you from afar. He comes to Akron. You don't care either way but then you feel a sort of moral responsibility. Great Scott! What a situation!

The Bookman next month is I believe going to use a photograph of me which is worse than one in the Chicago *Echo*. It is worse because it looks more like me. I shall expect an answer soon. You have not yet told me where is Button. I enjoyed your last letter immensely and

---

[16] The "awful chump" was the "intolerable duffer" Crane met in New Orleans, referred to in his letter to Dr. Lucius L. Button (see No. 68).

[17] Crane refers here to an adventure experienced in Mexico the previous summer and faithfully recorded in "One Dash—Horses," written in 1895 and published January 4 and 6, 1896, in the Philadelphia *Press*. He sent a clipping of the story to Nellie Crouse with this letter, as we see from Letter 131.

understood your point-of-view exactly. I am going to take this letter to Port Jervis with me tonight so that your answer may come quicker. Very sincerely yours   *Stephen Crane*

130. WILLIAM DEAN HOWELLS TO STEPHEN CRANE

40 West Fifty-ninth Street./Jan'y 26, 1896

Dear Mr. Crane: Your New Year's greeting was very pleasant to me, and I have been enjoying for your sake your English triumphs.[18] I am glad you are getting your glory young. For once, the English who habitually know nothing of art, seem to know something.—For me, I remain true to my first love, "Maggie." That is better than all the Black Riders [19] and Red Badges.

You have a lot of good work in you, and the whole of a long life to get it out.

I wish you could come sometime to see me. Yours sincerely,

W. D. Howells

131. TO NELLIE CROUSE

Hartwood, N.Y./Sunday [January 26, 1896]

Dear Miss Crouse: I am just this moment back to the hills. I was obliged to go down to Virginia [20] from New York and so the time of my little journey was unduly prolonged. I was impatient to get your letter and so had it forwarded to New York where I got it two days ago but was so badgered with silly engagements that I did not really own a minute in which I could reply. Sometimes people revenge themselves for delayed letters by calmly delaying the reply but I know you will not treat me to any such injustice.

I told you indeed that I was a practical and experienced person but your interpretation in this last letter was perhaps a little too wide. I did not say so to "warn" you. I mentioned it in a sort of a wonder that anyone so prodigiously practical and experienced should be so

---

[18] "Stephen Crane's Triumph," Harold Frederic's London article in the Sunday *Times Supplement,* to which Crane refers in his letter to Howells (No. 132) and again in letters to Hawkins, McClure, and Hitchcock. Frederic's novel, *The Damnation of Theron Ware,* appeared in March, 1896. When Crane settled in England, he and Frederic became great friends; he wrote an article on Frederic for the Chicago *Chap-Book,* in 1898.

[19] Reviewed, not exactly favorably, by Howells in *Harper's Weekly,* January 25, 1896.

[20] To study Fredericksburg and other battlefields for the Civil War stories he was then writing.

attracted by a vague, faint shadow—in fact a young woman who crossed his vision just once and that a considerable time ago. This is the thing that makes me wonder. Your letters, however, have reinforced me. I know much more of you now than I did before you amiably replied to my first letter and I know now that my instinctive liking for you was not a mistake.

I am afraid you laugh at me sometimes in your letters. For instance when you speak of a likelihood of being aghast at being left alone with such a clever person. Now that is really too bad of you. I am often marvelously a blockhead and incomparably an idiot. I reach depths of stupidity of which most people cannot dream. This is usually in the case of a social crisis. A social crisis simply leaves me witless and gibbering. A social crisis to me is despair. When I am really myself however, I am all right, being a good fellow, I think, and quite honest and simple. On most occasions I contrive to keep myself that way but sometimes the social crisis catches me unawares. The "Great Scott" in my letter was intended to show me stupid, witless, gibbering, despairing when I meet you in Akron. I only wish it could be in riding weather. I could bring some togs and I dare say I could rent some kind of a steed in Akron. My pilgrimage to the west via the Erie will please me immensely if it achieves a ride, a tea and *An Evening Call*, in Akron. Considering February weather, I can forego the ride. The story "One Dash—Horses," which I sent you celebrates in a measure my affection for a little horse I owned in Mexico. I just thought to tell you. I was about to say however that you must submit to my being quite serious over the stop-off at Akron. As sure as February appears you can expect to be bored by *An Evening Call*.

I have some friends departing for London on the 29th of February and as some people in London have requested me to come over and be looked at and as S. S. McClure, Limited, has requested me to go to London for him, I am mildly tempted, but expect to decline. Travelling is a great deal of trouble. If however you have in mind any new excursions to the land where all bad newspaper articles come from, you ought to let me know for then I would feel capable of overcoming my inertia.

You don't mean to soberly say that you thought I was anything but very ordinary when I called in 34th St.? I was sure that on that occasion I was stupid. In truth I sometimes secretly wail over the fact that women never see the best traits of a man—not, at least, in our conventional intercourse. Many a duffer shines like a sun and many a brave man appears a duffer. To offset this, women have a sort of an instinct of discovery. Still I am sure that no women—not even the women who have cared for me—ever truly knew the best and worst of me. There are three men in this world who know me about as I am but no woman does.

I see that I am in danger of wandering. I meant to say that in all social situations I am ordinarily conscious of being minute. At a dinner the other night in New York—the Lantern Club—they drank a very kind toast to me and to see all those old veterans arise and looked [*sic*] solemnly at me, quite knocked the wind from me and when it came my turn to get up I could only call them damned fools and sit down again. They were all old friends. At Buffalo however where everyone was strange, I was as cold as iced cucumbers when I arose and I said what I had to say very deliberately. The social crisis catches me sometimes and sometimes it doesn't. At Buffalo however I didn't talk as well as I could talk and to a woman I never talk as well as I can talk. Now that is exactly what I mean. And I never made a call, fought a tea, or sat on the sands by the mournful sea, that I didn't come away much discontented. So, you see, when my mind recalled the evening on 34th St., I was always disgusted for I distinctly remembered that I was more than usually stupid on that occasion. And this is why I was bored then. It wasn't because I didn't know I was meeting a very charming girl, because I did know it. It was simply because it was my experience and, later, my habit to be bored when calling. Button, good a soul as he is, only dragged me forth on that call because he was exhibiting his literary friend. You know what I mean. It seems that to some men there is a mild glamor about their literary friends and they like to gently exhibit them. I was used to it and usually submitted as decently as possible. It is awfully nice to be exhibited like a stuffed parrot. They say that Davis [21] enjoys it. I should think he would. He has, I believe, the intelligence of the average saw-log and he can no doubt enjoy anything. And now with this illumination of the subject you will better understand why I say I was bored.

This is manuscript paper and I think it is perfectly plain. Otherwise, several editors would by this time have tomahawked me. Your paragraph relating to the tangle of my letters was a remarkable case of supreme and undaunted assurance. I have been patiently and humbly working at your pages, fitting them this way and that way, trying them one way and then another, performing puzzle solutions on them and exhausting half the devices of the Chinese in efforts to form the proper sequence, when, glory to you, along you come with an ingenuous request to be more plain.

---

[21] Richard Harding Davis, later a fellow war correspondent with Crane in the Greco-Turkish and Spanish-American wars.

No, I know you are not cynical. But then you are very tired. I am, too, very tired. So you think I am successful? Well I don't know. Most people consider me successful. At least, they seem to so think. But upon my soul I have lost all appetite for victory, as victory is defined by the mob. I will be glad if I can feel on my death-bed that my life has been just and kind according to my ability and that every particle of my little ridiculous stock of eloquence and wisdom has been applied for the benefit of my kind. From this moment to that deathbed may be a short time or a long one but at any rate it means a life of labor and sorrow. I do not confront it blithely. I confront it with desperate resolution. There is not even much hope in my attitude. I do not even expect to do good. But I expect to make a sincere, desperate, lonely battle to remain true to my conception of my life and the way it should be lived, and if this plan can accomplish anything, it shall be accomplished. It is not a fine prospect. I only speak of it to people in whose opinions I have faith. No woman has heard it until now.

When I speak of a battle I do not mean want, and those similar spectres. I mean myself and the inherent indolence and cowardice which is the lot of all men. I mean, also, applause. Last summer I was getting very ably laughed at for a certain book called The Black Riders. When I was at my publishers yesterday I read long extracts from English newspapers. I got an armful of letters from people who declared that The Black Riders was—etc, etc,—and then for the first time in my life I began to be afraid, afraid that I would grow content with myself, afraid that willy-nilly I would be satisfied with the little, little things I have done. For the first time I saw the majestic forces which are arrayed against man's true success—not the world—the world is silly, changeable, any of it's decisions can be reversed—but man's own colossal impulses more strong than chains, and I perceived that the fight was not going to be with the world but with myself.[22] I had fought the world and had not bended nor moved an inch but this other battle—it is to last on up through the years to my grave and only on that day am I to know if the word Victory will look well upon lips of mine.

It is a pretty solemn thing to talk thus and if you were not you, I would re-write that paragraph and write it much better but I know you will understand. To become frank still further, it seems to me that I like you wonderfully more, after confessing so unreservedly.

Dont trouble to locate Button. As I said, it was originally merely an expedient.

---

[22] Henry Fleming in The Red Badge came to the same conclusion.

I am a very hurried writer but I hope my innumerable editings will not make you impatient.

I don't like to appear common-place but I remember that Button had your photograph and it seems to me that one who pays you such such [*sic*] reserved and unreserved, conditional and unconditional devotion as do I, might be one of the chosen. If you refuse, I shall go and slay Button for his impertinence.

I remain in the hope that you will do it. And remember that you are supposed to reply at once to this letter. Yours sincerely

Stephen Crane

132. TO WILLIAM DEAN HOWELLS

Hartwood, N.Y./Jan 27. [1896]

Dear Mr. Howells: I had just become well habituated to abuse when this bit of a flurry about the red badge [*sic*] came upon me. I am slightly rattled and think it best to cling to Hartwood where if I choose to shout triumphant shouts none can hear me. However I have not yet elected to shout any shouts. I am, mostly, afraid. Afraid that some small degree of talk will turn me ever so slightly from what I believe to be the pursuit of truth, and that my block-head will lose something of the resolution which carried me very comfortably through the ridicule. If they would only continue the abuse.[23] I feel ably [*sic*] to cope with that, but beyond I am in great doubt. Yours sincerely   *Stephen Crane*

133. TO RIPLEY HITCHCOCK

Hartwood, N.Y./January 27 [1896]

Dear Mr. Hitchcock: I fear that when I meet you again I shall feel abashed. As a matter of truth, New York has so completely muddled me on this last visit that I shant venture again very soon. I had grown used to being called a damned ass but this sudden new admiration of my friends has made a gibbering idiot of me. I shall stick to my hills.

I think it is as well to go ahead with The Third Violet. People may just as well discover now that the high dramatic key of The Red Badge cannot be sustained. You know what I mean. I dont think The Red Badge to be any great shakes but then the very theme of it gives it an intensity that a writer cant reach every day.[24] The Third Violet is a

---

[23] The abuse, mainly of *The Black Riders,* by reviewers.

[24] Echoed in his letter to S. S. McClure: "I feel I could do something then to dwarf the Red Badge, which I do not think is very great shakes" (No. 135). Again in his letter to Hilliard in 1897 he disparages *The Red Badge* ("a mere episode"); and, although he objected to "preaching" in literature, he preferred *The Black Riders* on the ground that his verse represented "the more ambitious effort."

quiet little story but then it is serious work and I should say let it go.[25]
If my health and my balance remains to me, I think I will be capable
of doing work that will dwarf both books. Yours sincerely,

Stephen Crane

134. TO WILLIS BROOKS HAWKINS

Hartwood, N.Y./January 27th [1896]

My dear Willis: There are none of my friends whom I could treat so
shamefully and none who can make me feel so utterly dejected over it
afterward. But oh you dont know how that damned city tore my heart
out by the roots and flung it under the heels of it's [sic] noise. Indeed
it did. I couldn't breathe in that accursed tumult. On Friday it had me
keyed to a point where I was no more than a wild beast and I had to
make a dash willy-nilly. It was a disgraceful retreat but I think you
will understand me. I feel myself perfectly capable of any sacrifice for
you now with the sting of that retreat still upon me. But as to that past
thing I will have to throw myself upon your mercy. I am coming down
again in about two weeks. Yours invariably   S. C.

P.S.: I am expressing you the original ms of The Red Badge. Thought
maybe you'd like it.[26]   S. C.

[P.P.S.] DID you see Sunday's Times.

135. TO S. S. McCLURE

Hartwood, N.Y./January 27th. [1896]

Dear Mr. McClure: I think my retreat to Hartwood was quite a mas-
terly move on my part for I feel so much more quiet and undisturbed
and the noise of the trees cannot muddle me as does the city. I am getting the Fredericksburg row into shape. I dont know how much you
were going to pay me for the little "Three Miraculous Soldiers" [27] but
if you can send me twenty-five more dollars to last until my February

---

[25] Hitchcock was dubious about *The Third Violet*, and as Crane confessed to Hawkins, "I am not sure that it is any good" (Letter 98).

[26] What Crane sent was the final handwritten manuscript containing a
portion of an earlier draft written on the back sides of the loose sheets.
Hawkins had them bound into a notebook in order to preserve the manuscripts.

[27] Published in the St. Paul *Pioneer Press* and in *Inter Ocean,* March
15, and in the *English Illustrated Magazine,* May, 1896.

ship comes in, it would assist the Cranes of Sullivan County very greatly.

I think the agreement with you is a good thing. I am perfectly satisfied with my end of it but your end somewhat worries me for I am often inexpressibly dull and uncreative and these periods often last for days.

I see by Sunday's Times, that the Englishmen are mildly curious about me. Many of my friends—quite a number, I mean—are going to Europe on the 29th February.[28] If you could think out some campaign for me I might go but I feel reluctant.

Whenever you have some article or other in mind, let me know at once. Beware only how you catch me up here without car-fare to N.Y. That is the spectre that perches on the back of the Crane "child of promise."

I think it will be of a great advantage to me to have you to invent subjects for me. By the way I would like to go to the scene of the next great street-car strike. I feel I could do something then to dwarf the Red Badge, which I do not think is very great shakes. Yours sincerely   *Stephen Crane*

136. *TO S. S. McCLURE*

Hartwood, N.Y./January 28 [1896]

Dear Mr. McClure: I feel for you when I think of some of the things of mine which you will have to read or have read. If you dont like the enclosed please return it to me here. Sincerely   *Stephen Crane*

137. *TO JOHN NORTHERN HILLIARD* [29]

[January, 1896?]

. . . As far as myself and my own meagre success are concerned, I began the battle of life with no talent, no equipment, but with an ardent admiration and desire. I did little work at school, but confined my abilities, such as they were, to the diamond. Not that I disliked

---

[28] He refers to these friends in Letter 139 to Nellie Crouse, and in Letter 144 he jokes with her about taking the same ship, as she apparently plans also to go to Europe.

[29] Hilliard evidently asked Crane for more information, and this represents presumably Crane's reply. Hilliard submitted extracts from Crane's letters to the Literary Supplement of *The New York Times*, where they appeared (July 14, 1900) after Crane's death. There are three letters to Hilliard—the January 2, 1896, letter (No. 125), this one now dated for January, 1896, and the letter Crane wrote Hilliard from England in 1897 (No. 216).

books, but the cut-and-dried curriculum of the college did not appeal
to me. Humanity was a much more interesting study. When I ought to
have been at recitations I was studying faces on the streets, and when
I ought to have been studying my next day's lessons I was watching
the trains roll in and out of the Central Station. So, you see, I had, first
of all, to recover from college. I had to build up, so to speak. And my
chiefest desire was to write plainly and unmistakably,[30] so that all men
(and some women) might read and understand. That to my mind is
good writing. There is a great deal of labor connected with literature.
I think that is the hardest thing about it. There is nothing to respect in
art save one's own opinion of it. . . .

The one thing that deeply pleases me in my literary life—brief and
inglorious as it is—is the fact that men of sense believe me to be sincere. "Maggie," published in paper covers, made me the friendship of
Hamlin Garland and W. D. Howells, and the one thing that makes my
life worth living in the midst of all this abuse and ridicule is the con-
sciousness that never for an instant have those friendships at all diminished.[31] Personally I am aware that my work does not amount to a
string of dried beans—I always calmly admit it. But I also know that
I do the best that is in me, without regard to cheers or damnation.
When I was the mark for every humorist in the country I went ahead,

---

[30] By "unmistakably" Crane meant lucid, for elsewhere he says: "I endeavored to express myself in the simplest and most concise way." Again:
"My chiefest desire was to write plainly." See his letter to Peaslee: "I always
want to be unmistakable. That to my mind is good writing." The first sentence and the concluding sentences in this section of Crane's letter duplicate
almost word for word what Crane wrote Peaslee (Letter 62).

[31] This second section of extracts from Crane's letter to Hilliard—here
dated for January, 1896—was published in Vincent Starrett's *Men, Women
and Boats* (1921) and again in *Bibliography* (1948), but the source is not
there given. It was published on April 18, 1900, in the Rochester *Post-
Express*, of which Hilliard had been an editor since 1896. In *Omnibus* this
portion of Crane's letter is incorrectly ascribed to Joseph O'Connor, also an
editor of the *Post-Express*. (The correction is based on the evidence of the
new Crane to Hilliard Letter 125.) This extract and others were printed also
in the *Literary Digest*, June 23, 1900, and later in the London *Academy*,
August 11, 1900. This portion is identified in the *Academy* as having been
written "shortly after the publication of 'The Red Badge of Courage' and
'The Black Riders,' when ridicule and personalities were volleyed across the
net of criticism." Both extracts, says the *Literary Digest*, were written to the
same man. In the second sentence Crane repeats what he wrote Hilliard in
Letter 125. Extracts from Crane's letters to Hilliard also were printed in the
Literary Supplement of *The New York Times*, July 14, 1900.

and now, when I am the mark for only 50 per cent of the humorists of the country, I go ahead, for I understand that a man is born into the world with his own pair of eyes, and he is not at all responsible for his vision—he is merely responsible for his quality of personal honesty. To keep close to this personal honesty is my supreme ambition.[32] There is a sublime egotism in talking of honesty. I, however, do not say that I am honest. I merely say that I am as nearly honest as a weak mental machinery will allow. This aim in life struck me as being the only thing worth while. A man is sure to fail at it, but there is something in the failure.

138. TO RIPLEY HITCHCOCK

Hartwood, N.Y./February 2ᵈ [1896]

Dear Mr Hitchcock: I am very glad to hear you speak as you do concerning *Maggie*. I will set to work this month rewriting it. I have no more pictures until they come from New York where I sat the last time I was down.[33] They should reach me soon. I was very much delighted with Frederick's [*sic*] letter in the Times.[34] I see also that they are beginning to charge me with having played base ball. I am rather more proud of my base ball ability than of some other things. I am coming down to New York this month and will come to see you first thing. Yours sincerely   *Stephen Crane*

139. TO NELLIE CROUSE

Hartwood, N.Y./February 5 [1896]

Dear Miss Crouse: Your photograph came today. Of course you know how very grateful I am to you. I had expected to hear from you on Mon-

---

[32] Another variant on this Crane statement appears in Beer, p. 381: "For I understand that a man is born into the world with his own pair of eyes, and he is not at all responsible for his vision—he is merely responsible for his quality of personal honesty. To keep close to this personal honesty is my supreme ambition." The very same dictum forms part of Conrad's aesthetic credo.

[33] The photograph was taken at the Lantern Club, as is shown by Crane's reply to the editor of *The Critic*, who also asked for a photograph (Letter 146). When Hubbard requested a picture, Crane promised that he would take one to Buffalo; and when Hilliard asked him for one the following December, Crane replied that he had no recent one at hand. In Letters 141, 142 he begs off on requests for photographs. In his letter to Nellie Crouse (No. 129) he said that the *Bookman* and *Echo* were publishing his photograph.

[34] The London *Times Supplement* for January 26: "Stephen Crane's Triumphs."

day but that day as well as Tuesday were times of disaster. At noon to-day, however the coming of the portrait relieved me. I am sure now, still more, that you are precisely the kind of young woman I have judged you. However, you have awed me. Yes, indeed, I am awed. There is something in your face which tells that there are many things which you perfectly understand which perhaps I don't understand at all. This sounds very vague but it is nevertheless very vague in my mind. I think it means that I am a savage. Of course I am admittedly a savage. I have been known as docile from time to time but only under great social pressure. I am by inclination a wild shaggy barbarian. I know that I am hopelessly befogging my meaning but then at best my mean-ing is a dim thing. I intend to say at any rate that the light of social experience in your eyes somewhat terrifies this poor outer pagan.

Well, it is better that I should gibber in the above lines. Otherwise I would have bored you with long descriptions of how charming I think the portrait.

I am engaged in rowing with people who wish me to write more war-stories.[35] Hang all war-stories. Nevertheless I submitted in one case and now I have a daily battle with a tangle of facts and emotions. I am however doing the thing in a way that is not without a mild satis-faction for me.

I believe I told you in my last chronicle—my letters arise almost to the dignity of chronicles; they are so long—that I might go over to England on the 29th.[36] Well, I've almost given up the plan. The pub-lishers and things in London seem anxious for me to come, and people on this side furnish me with unlimited introductions. So the journey seems so easy and simple that I am quite out of the humor of it. I dont think I shall go on until next fall. Do you come east in the summer? I hope so. I never work in the summer. It is one long lazy time to fool away. Just now we in Hartwood are being drearily snowed upon. Sometimes I am much agitated at the thought that perhaps the little train won't be able to struggle up the mountain and deliver my mail. As yet however nothing has happened to it. Did not you once ask me if Hartwood is out of the world? It is—very much. New York is only 104 miles but it is a terrible 104 miles, and the mail service is wretched.

I have about four new books coming out.[37] Sometimes I feel like

---

[35] Phillips and McClure.

[36] He broached this notion to McClure in Letter 135.

[37] These were *George's Mother* (published in May in New York by the English house of Edward Arnold, and the following month in London by the same house); *The Third Violet,* in periodical publication during Novem-ber, 1896, and in book form in 1897; *The Little Regiment,* published in

sitting still and watching them appear. However, they are not good enough to delight me at all.

I wonder if you have a copy of *The Black Riders*. If you have not, let me know. I might as well let you know the worst of me at once. Although *Maggie* perhaps is the worst—or the most unconventional— of me.

I hope you will keep me no longer in anxiety by not writing. Of course I know that if you sent the picture you wouldn't write, and if you wrote, you wouldn't send the picture. So, possessing the picture I can forego the letter this week. Early next week, however, I shall not be so submissive. To add to the situation, no mail route, I imagine, can be so laboriously intricate as the way between Akron and Hartwood. Yours sincerely   *Stephen Crane*

140. TO RIPLEY HITCHCOCK

[Hartwood, N.Y., February 4–6? 1896]

Dear Mr. Hitchcock: I am working at *Maggie*. She will be down to you in a few days. I have dispensed with a goodly number of damns. I have no more copies of the book or I would have sent you one.

I want to approach Appleton & Co on a delicate matter. I dont care much about money up here save when I have special need of it and just at this time there is a beautiful riding-mare for sale for a hundred dollars. The price will go up each week, almost, until spring and I am crazy to get her now. I dont want to strain your traditions but if I am worth $100. in your office, I would rather have it now.[38] [*Incomplete*]

McClure's Magazine in June and then by Appleton's in book form in November; and *A Souvenir and a Medley,* a miscellany containing among other things eight poems by Crane. (This identification corrects the surmised list in *Love Letters,* p. 45.) Though *Maggie* was also published this year, *Maggie* was not one of the "four new books coming out," as it was printed first in 1893.

Also in 1896 *The Black Riders* was published in England, and *The Red Badge of Courage* by Heinemann.

[38] During December, 1895, when Crane visited Elbert Hubbard, he fell in love with a little brown horse, Peanuts, and, according to letters of the Crane family, he purchased him with money earned from the sale of a short story. On the other hand, here he is writing Hitchcock in February and asking for an advance of $100 for the purchase of a horse. Peanuts was clever, playful, and tricky; one never knew what he was going to do next. And that was perhaps why Crane had special affection for him—he was as unpredictable as his master. Crane was an excellent horseman.

Beer (p. 305) has Crane riding Peanuts in January, but Crane did not

141. TO AN ADMIRER OF HIS WORK [39]

Hartford [*sic*], N.Y./February 6th [1896]

Dear sir: I don't thing [*sic*] it possible to get my photograph. They have been mostly amateur things. Very truly yours,   *Stephen Crane*

142. TO RIPLEY HITCHCOCK

Hartwood, N.Y./February 7th. [1896]

Dear Mr Hitchcock: I enclose you a letter from Syracuse written in the usual nervy vein of college editors. I am not trembling with anxiety to have them print my picture and I am sure it makes me apprehensive at a prospect of their reviewing The R.B. I have written them that I have requested you to send them a cut and a book but I dont request it.[40] [*Incomplete*]

143. TO RIPLEY HITCHCOCK

Hartwood/Monday [February 10, 1896]

Dear Mr Hitchcock: I am delighted with your prompt sympathy in regard to the saddle horse. It is a luxury to feel that some of my pleasures are due to my little pen. I will send you *Maggie* by detail. I have carefully plugged at the words which hurt. Seems to me the book wears quite a new aspect from very slight omissions.[41] Did you know

---

leave Hartwood all that month, and his letter to Hubbard (No. 147) inquiring about the noble horse indicates that he had not yet obtained Peanuts—not until mid-February. In any case, the mare he asks Hitchcock money for is not Peanuts.

[39] Reprinted from *Meditations of an Autograph Collector* (1902), p. 14. It was perhaps this sort of thing that Beer had in mind when he called Crane's correspondence uninteresting (see also Letter 142).

[40] The book was not reviewed, and no photograph of Crane appeared during 1896 in *The University Herald*. A fraternity brother of Crane, John W. Sadler, published in its January, 1895, issue a notice about the forthcoming book: " 'The Red Badge of Courage' is the title of a new novel by Stephen Crane, ex-'94. The story has attracted considerable attention, and Mr. Crane is looked upon as one of the most promising young writers before the public by such an able critic as William D. Howells."

[41] The omissions include the portrait of a character who appears only in the 1893 edition of *Maggie* and who provides thus an addition to the nine persons Maggie encounters on her predestined journey to the river. The omitted character is "a huge fat man in torn and greasy garments." See R. W. Stallman, "Stephen Crane's Revisions of *Maggie: A Girl of the Streets*," *American Literature*, XXVI (January, 1955). On the genesis and designed intention of *Maggie* see *Omnibus*, pp. 3–20. For an analysis of the novel see R. W. Stallman, "Stephen Crane's Primrose Path," *New Republic*, September 19, 1955, p. 133.

that the book is very short? Only about 20000 words? Yours sincerely
Stephen Crane

144. TO NELLIE CROUSE

Hartwood/Feb. 11th [1896]

[*No salutation*] Wherever that letter went is more than I can imagine.
It certainly never reached Hartwood. I am grieved at the prospect of
never seeing it but I console myself a little with the remembrance that
you wrote it. There is some consolation in that, you know.

Your recent confession that in your heart you like the man of
fashion more than you do some other kinds of men came nearer to my
own view than perhaps you expected. I have indeed a considerable
liking for the man of fashion if he does it well. The trouble to my own
mind lies in the fact that the heavy social life demands one's entire
devotion. Time after time, I have seen the social lion turn to a lamb
and fail—fail at precisely the moment when men should not fail. The
world sees this also and it has come to pass that the fashionable man
is considerably jeered at. Men who are forever sitting with immovable
legs on account of a tea-cup are popularly supposed to be worth little
besides. This is true in the main but it is not without brave exceptions,
thank heaven. For my part, I like the man who dresses correctly and
does the right thing invariably but, oh, he must be more than that, a
great deal more. But so seldom is he anymore than correctly-dressed
and correctly-speeched, that when I see a man of that kind I usually
put him down as a kind of an idiot. Still, as I have said, there are exceptions. There are men of very social habits who nevertheless know
how to stand steady when they see cocked revolvers and death comes
down and sits on the back of a chair and waits. There are men of very
social habits who know good music from bad, good poetry from bad—
(a few of 'em)—good drama from bad—(a very few of 'em)—good painting from bad. There are very many of them who know good claret and
good poker-playing. There are a few who can treat a woman tenderly
not only when they feel amiable but when she most needs tender-treat-
ment. There [are] many who can ride, swim, shoot and sail a boat, a
great many. There are an infinitismal [*sic*] number who can keep from
yapping in a personal way about women. There are a large number
who refuse to haggle over a question of money. There are one or two
who invariably mind their own business. There are some who know
how to be frank without butchering the feelings of their friends. There
is an enormous majority who, upon being insured of safety from de-
tection—become at once the most unconventional of peoples.

In short they are precisely like the remainder of the race, only they
devote their minds to riding smoothly. A slight jolt gives them the impression that a mountain has fallen upon them.

I swear by the real aristocrat. The man whose forefathers were men of courage, sympathy and wisdom, is usually one who will stand the strain whatever it may be. He is like a thorough-bred horse.[42] His nerves may be high and he will do a lot of jumping often but in the crises he settles down and becomes the most reliable and enduring of created things.

For the hordes who hang upon the out-skirts of good society and chant 143 masses per day to the social gods and think because they have money they are well-bred—for such people I have a scorn which is very deep and very intense. These people think that polite life is something which is to be studied, a very peculiar science of which knowledge is only gained by long practice whereas what is called "form" is merely a collection of the most rational and just of laws which any properly-born person understands from his cradle. In Hartwood I have a great chance to study the new-rich. The Hartwood Clubhouse is only three miles away and there are some of the new rich in it. May the Lord deliver me from having social aspirations.

I can stand the society man, if he don't interfere with me; I always think the society girl charming but the type that I cant endure is the society matron. Of course there are many exceptions but some I have seen struck me afar off with the peculiar iron-like quality of their thick-headedness and the wild exuberance of their vanity.

On two or three occasions I had some things read at Sherry's [43] and later by chance met people who had been there. I distinctly remember some compliments paid me very graciously and confidently by a woman. Nothing so completely and serenely stupid have I ever witnessed. And the absolutely false tongue of her prattled away for ten minutes in more lies than are usually heard at one time. Of course it was nothing to me if she liked my stuff and it was nothing to her. She was merely being [sic] because she indifferently thought it to be correct at that moment, but how those old cats can stand up and lie until there is no breath left in them. Now, they think that is form, mind you, but, good heavens, it isnt. They think that a mere show of complacent idiocy is all that is necessary to a queen of society. Form really is truth, simplicity; when people surround it with falsity, interpret it as mean-

---

[42] "A good saddle horse is the one blessing of life," Crane wrote his college friend Peaslee, and repeated the same words in writing the editor of *The Critic* (Letter 146).

[43] John Barry's reading of Crane's poems at Sherry's was reported in the New York *Tribune*, April 26, 1894. Barry reviewed *The Red Badge* in the *Literary World*, January 11, 1896, and published "A Note on Stephen Crane" in the *Bookman*, April, 1901.

ing: "lies," they become not society leaders but barbarians, savages, beating little silly tom-toms and flourishing little carved wooden goblins. They really defy every creed of this social god, the very diety [*sic*] which they worship.

I am rather apprehensive. I detest dogma [44] and it strikes me that I have expressed too many opinions in this letter. When I express an opinion in writing I am in the habit of considering a long time and then formulating it with a great deal of care. This letter however has been so hasty that I have not always said precisely what I intended to say. But at any rate I hope it will be plain that I strongly admire the social God even if I do despise many of his worshippers.

As for the man with the high aims and things—which you say you like in your soul—but not in your heart—I dont know that he is to my mind any particular improvement on the society man. I shouldn't care to live in the same house with him if he was at all in the habit of talking about them. I get about two letters a day from people who have high literary aims and everywhere I go I seem to meet five or six. They strike me as about the worst and most penetrating kind of bore I know. Of course I, with my meagre successes, would feel like an awful duffer if I was anything but very, very considerate of them but it is getting to be a task. Of course that is not the kind you meant. Still they are certainly people of high aims and there is a ridiculous quality to me in all high ambitions, of men who mean to try to make themselves great because they think it would [be] so nice to be great, to be admired, to be stared at by the mob. "Well," you say, "I didnt mean that kind of high aim either." Tolstoy's aim is, I suppose—I believe— to make himself good.[45] It is an incomparably quixotic task for any man to undertake. He will not succeed; but he will even succeed more than he can ever himself know, and so at his nearest point to success he will be proportionally blind. This is the pay of this kind of greatness.

This letter is certainly not a conscience-smiter but I hope you will reply to it at the same length that you claim for the lost letter.

I may go to Chicago in late February or early March—over the Erie's lines.[46] I wish you would tell me more about your European trip. By the way, if you forbid me going over on the same boat, it must be because you think I am not clever. Yours sincerely   *Stephen Crane*

---

[44] He had, as Beer says, no patience with doctrines; the Episcopal Church he thought an inanity because the teachings of Christ had been perverted into formulas.

[45] On Tolstoy, Crane's ideal, see Letter 216.

[46] Nothing came of this.

145. TO RIPLEY HITCHCOCK

Hartwood/Feb 15. [1896]

Dear Mr Hitchcock: I send you under two covers six edited chapters of Maggie to see if they suit. The remainder will shortly follow. Sincerely   *S. C.*

146. TO THE EDITOR OF THE CRITIC

Hartwood, N.Y./Feb. 15, 96.

Dear Sir: There is a very excellent photograph of me in the possession of Mr. King, the artist, c/ The Lantern Club, 126 William St., New York. It is a picture that has never been used for publication and is I think a very good portrait. I have forwarded him your letter with a request to send you a picture.

I began writing for newspapers when I was 16. At 18 I did my first fiction—for the N.Y. Sunday Tribune—sketches. At 20 I began *Maggie* & finished it when I was somewhat beyond 21. Later in the same year I began *The R. B. of Courage* and finished it some months after my 22nd birthday.[47] *The Black Riders* were written in that year. When I was 23, I devoted most of my time to travelling for the Bachellor [*sic*] and Johnson syndicate and in writing short stories for English magazines. This winter I wrote a novel: "The Third Violet," which is to be published by the Appletons. Beforehand, however, they are to bring out in connection with William Heineman [*sic*] a new edition of *Maggie*.[48] I am now finishing a novelette for S. S. McClure called The Little Regiment which represents my work at its best I think and is positively my last thing dealing with battle.

When I look back on this array it appears that I have worked but as a matter of truth I am very very lazy, hating work, and only taking up a pen when circumstances drive me.

I live at Hartwood very quietly and alone, mostly, and think a good saddle-horse is the one blessing of life.[49] Sincerely yours,

Stephen Crane

P.S. If in doubt concerning certain facts apply to S. S. McClure.

---

[47] See also Letter 125.

[48] *Maggie* was published in June; in the United States by Appleton and in England by Heinemann.

[49] The final two paragraphs of this letter are almost identical with what Crane wrote Clarence Loomis Peaslee in 1896: "When I look back on this array, it appears that I have worked, but as a matter of truth I am very lazy, hating work and only taking up a pen when circumstances drive me. I live

147. TO ELBERT HUBBARD [50]

165 West 23d St.,/New York City [mid-February, 1896]

My dear Hub: I've been a rampant wild ass of the desert with my feet never twice in the same place but at last I am settled down finally & feel that my first occupation should be the writing of a profound apology to you for my curious silence. I expect to be in East Aurora in about 2 weeks—at least if I am still at liberty to purchase that noble horse? At that time we will chew the rag at great length and finally decide all these contested points. Yours always,   S. C.

148. TO WILLIS BROOKS HAWKINS

Cosmos Club/Washington [51]/Mch 15. [1896]

Dear Willis: It was a woman! Dont you see? Nothing could so interfere but a woman. How sorry I am that I treated you so badly and yet how full how absolute is the explanation—a woman. I shall want to know at once how angry you are. I am sure, of course that you have been very much offended but it is a woman, I tell you, and I want you to forgive me. Yours as ever   *Stephen Crane*

149. TO RIPLEY HITCHCOCK

The Cosmos Club/Washington, D.C. [March 15? 1896]

Dear Mr Hitchcock: Of course eccentric people are admirably picturesque at a distance but I suppose after your recent close-range ex-

---

at Hartford [*sic*], N.Y., very quietly and alone mostly." "I think a good saddle-horse is the one blessing of life." Peaslee published portions of Crane's letters to him in the *Monthly Illustrator*, August, 1896.

Crane repeats himself from letter to letter, with only slight variations in phrasing, and the duplication is most marked when he is summing up his career and ancestry in response to requests for such information. His book inscriptions likewise tend to run to formula.

This letter, reprinted from *Omnibus* (pp. 646–47), was first printed in the *Colophon*, July, 1930, where, six months later, Vincent Starrett appraised it as "the most important Crane discovery of recent years."

[50] The original of this letter is tipped into the flyleaf of the copy of *A Souvenir and a Medley* belonging to the Dartmouth College Library. It was published by Herbert Faulkner West in *A Stephen Crane Collection* (1948).

[51] McClure sent Crane to Washington to do a book on political society. Crane once remarked that he "was a socialist for two weeks but when a couple of socialists assured me I had no right to think differently from any other socialist and then quarrelled with each other about what socialism meant, I ran away" (Beer, 359 f.).

periences with me, you have the usual sense of annoyance. After all, I cannot help vanishing and disappearing and dissolving.[52] It is my foremost trait. But I hope you will forgive me and treat me as if you still could think me a pretty decent sort of chap.

I am almost settled in Washington but for some time yet I hope to see the city in the manner of a stranger. My address will be the Cosmos Club. You must send me the edited Maggie.[53] I am going to settle down to New York work in lazy Washington. I have had enough tea. Yours sincerely   *Stephen Crane*

150. TO VIOLA ALLEN

The Cosmos Club/Washington, D.C./March 15th, 1896

My dear Miss Allen: I am very glad to be able to forward you by this mail a copy of The Red Badge. My years at Claverack are very vivid to me. They were I believe the happiest period of my life although I was not then aware of it. Of course, you were joking when you inferred that I might not remember you And Anna Roberts! And Eva Lacy! And Jennie Pierce! Alas, Jennie Pierce. You must remember that I was in love with her, madly, in the headlong way of seventeen. Jennie was clever. With only half an effort she made my life so very miserable.

Men usually refuse to recognize their school-boy dreams. They blush. I dont. The emotion itself was probably higher, finer, than anything of my after-life, and so, often I like to think of it. I was such an ass, such a pure complete ass—it does me good to recollect it. Yours sincerely,   *Stephen Crane*

151. TO NELLIE CROUSE

33 East 22d, NYC/March 1st and 18 [1896]

[*No salutation*] Do you know, I have succeeded in making a new kind of an idiot of myself. They had a winter party at Hartwood and after I had sat before twelve fire-places and drank 842 cups of tea, I said:

---

[52] Crane apparently broke engagements not only with Hawkins (Letter 148) but also with Hitchcock. He had had a fling with some woman in New York City, perhaps with Amy Leslie (see pp. 118–122).

[53] Published in June by Appleton's, it appeared the same month in England but with the title altered. The hardened Maggie became, in the Heinemann edition, "A Child of the Streets." The subtitle "A Story of New York" was abandoned in the 1896 editions; it appears only in the 1893 edition (*contra* Berryman, p. 32). The Heinemann edition carried "An Appreciation" by William Dean Howells.

"I shall escape." And so I have come to New York. But New York is worse. I am in despair. The storm-beaten little robin who has no place to lay his head, does not feel so badly as do I. It is not that people want to meet me. When that happens I can endure it. But it is that mine own friends feel bitterly insulted if I do not see them twelve times a day—in short they are all prepared to find me grown vain.

You know what I mean. That disgraceful Red Badge is doing so very well that my importance has widened and everybody sits down and calmly waits to see *me be a chump.*

Dear me, how much am I getting to admire graveyards—the calm unfretting unhopeing [*sic*] end of things—serene absence of passion—oblivious to sin—ignorant of the accursed golden hopes that flame at night and make a man run his legs off and then in the daylight of experience turn out to be ingenious traps for the imagination. If there is a joy of living I cant find it. The future? The future is blue with obligations—new trials—conflicts. It was a rare old wine the gods brewed *for mortals.* Flagons of despair—[54]

The Cosmos Club/Washington   Washington, D.C./March 18 [1896] [55]

Really, by this time I should have recovered enough to be able to write you a sane letter but I cannot—my pen is dead. I am simply a man struggling with a life that is no more than a mouthful of dust to him. Yours sincerely   *Stephen Crane*

152. TO RIPLEY HITCHCOCK
                    The Cosmos Club/Washington, D.C./Mch 23d [1896]

Dear Mr Hitchcock: I will begin to drive Maggie forward. Is The Red

---

[54] Crane's gloomy mood is, however, contradicted in the lightheartedness of his letter to Viola Allen (No. 150), written March 15. Not that he wasn't affected by Nellie Crouse's dismissal of him:

> *Oh, a rare old wine ye brewed for me*
> *Flagons of despair*
> *A deep deep drink of this wine of life*
> *Flagons of despair.*
>   *Dreams of riot and blood and screams*
>   *The rolling white eyes of dying men*
>   *The terrible heedless courage of babes*

The manuscript of this fragment is in the Butler Library Crane Collection and was published in Daniel G. Hoffman's, *The Poetry of Stephen Crane* (1957).

[55] Crane finished writing his March 1 letter to Nellie Crouse on the eighteenth; this postscript concludes his correspondence with her.

Badge going yet? Greeley by the way told me yesterday that it had been filed in the "archives" of the war department.

Your man Marcus Benjamin has been awfully good to me here, putting himself out generously.

I am all very well and am gradually learning things. I have been already in a number of the senatorial interiors. But I want to know all the congressmen in the shop. I want to know Quay of Pennsylvania. I want to know those long-whiskered devils from the west. So whenever you see a chance to send me headlong at one of them, do so.

Do you think The Atlantic Monthly would like The Third Violet? I enclose a note from them. Yours sincerely   *Stephen Crane*

153. TO RIPLEY HITCHCOCK

The Cosmos Club/Washington, D.C./ March 26. [1896]

Dear Mr Hitchcock: I have not told you that I am beset—quite—with publishers of various degrees who wish—or seem to wish—to get my books and who make me various offers. Some of them are little firms but I think nearly every representative American house has made overtures of some kind to me as well as five or six London firms. I have not thought it worth while to talk much about it and in fact this letter contains the first mention of it, I believe. I have not considered at all the plan of playing one house against another but have held that the house of Appleton would allow me all the benefits I deserved. Without vanity I may say that I dont care a snap for money until I put my hand in my pocket and find none there. If I make ill terms now there may come a period of reflection and so I expect you to deal with me precisely as if I was going to write a GREAT book ten years from now and might wreak a terrible vengeance upon you by giving it to the other fellow. And so we understand each other.

As for Edward Arnold, his American manager is an old schoolmate and ten-year's friend of mine and he conducted such a campaign against me as is seldom seen. He appealed to my avarice and failing appealed to my humanity. Once I thought he was about to get "The Little Regiment," when you stepped in and saved it. Finally I thought of a satirical sketch of mine—an old thing, strong in satire but rather easy writing—called Dan Emmonds and I gave it to him.[56]

---

[56] Harry Thompson was the "old school-mate." What he succeeded in obtaining from Crane was not "Dan Emmonds" but *George's Mother*, which Arnold published in the United States in May and in England in June. Appleton's brought out *The Little Regiment* in October, after the title piece (a short story) had appeared in *McClure's Magazine* for June. Berryman (p. 134) takes "Dan Emmonds" for a variant title to *George's Mother*. But

You know of course that my mind is just and most open but perhaps in this case I violated certain business courtesies. But, before God, when these people get their fingers in my hair, it is a wonder that I escape with all my clothes. My only chance is to keep away from them.

I sent you three pictures yesterday.

It would oblige me very much if you would have a check for my initiation fee sent to the secretary of the Author's Club. Yours sincerely   *Stephen Crane*

154. TO RIPLEY HITCHCOCK

The Cosmos Club/Washington D.C./March 30 [1896]

Dear Mr Hitchcock: You may see me back in New York for good by the end of this week. These men [congressmen] pose so hard that it would take a double-barreled shotgun to disclose their inward feelings and I despair of knowing them. Yours sincerely   *Stephen Crane*

155. TO WILLIS BROOKS HAWKINS

Cosmos Club/Washington, D.C./March 31 [1896]

My dear Willis: You are the only friend I ever had who possessed the decency to forgive me for being an ass and your value has doubled in my eyes. I intend to come back to New York this week. Washington pains me. By the way, the three who I would like to see at the dinner are my brother, for one, William H. Crane, Port Jervis, N.Y., Col. Floyd, and Underwood Johnson of the Century.

Will probably see you at lunch on Saturday. Very much yours
S. C.

156. TO RIPLEY HITCHCOCK

165 W 23d/Thursday [April 2, 1896]

Dear Mr Hitchcock: I am engaged on the preface.[57] Dont let anyone put chapter headings on the book. The proofs make me ill. Let somebody go over them—if you think best—and watch for bad grammatical form & bad spelling. I am too jaded with Maggie to be able to see it. Yours   *Crane*

"Dan Emmonds" is a manuscript that was never printed; it was still "Dan Emmonds" in 1900 when James B. Pinker, and later G. H. Perris, were unsuccessfully peddling it. The manuscript of "Dan Emmonds" is in the Butler Library Crane Collection.

[57] The preface to *Maggie* never materialized, at least not in print.

157. TO WILLIS BROOKS HAWKINS

[165 West 23d Street, New York City, early April, 1896]

Dear Willis: I am returned. Can—will—you bring the boys over for a little fiesta de poke tonight.[58] Charley, Fairman & you will do if you cannot raise more. Yours   S. C.

158. TO WALLIS McHARG [59]

Hartwood, New York [Early April, 1896]

. . . When people see a banker taking a glass of beer in a cafe, they

---

[58] Another occasion for poker playing took place in June, this time with Stephen as host to Fairman, Hawkins, and D. "Dysenpith" (?). Fairman is here named Bill, but it seems likely that he is the same Leroy Fairman we hear about in the Amy Leslie affair. The names of the poker contingent are written on the card table cover used on this occasion, and Stephen, while keeping the score, doodled and, like Stephen Dedalus in Joyce's *Portrait of the Artist as a Young Man*, scribbled his name on the table cover over and over again: "Stephen Crane, Chauncey Depew, Stephen Crane, Chauncey Depew, Stephen Crane." This paper table cover, preserved by Hawkins, is in the Barrett Collection at the University of Virginia.

Card games figure in several of Crane's short stories, as in "The Blue Hotel." "Midnight Sketches," in *Work*, Vol. XI (1926), contains "Poker Game."

Crane's hobbies, as his letters show, were horseback riding and card games. He loved horses, he loved dogs, and he had a quick eye for women. Also, he had a quick eye for cards. In the Barrett Collection (not before now reproduced) are two Crane inscriptions related very likely to Crane's appeal to Hawkins to summon "a little fiesta de poke tonight." The first note precedes that get-together; the second, written subsequently, announces in gloating terms Crane's triumph at the card table.

1

Shanley's

My dear Willis: Howard was not at home. Answer by this boy if you corraled [*sic*] him later. Yours   S. C.
His address is #10 West 19.

2

[Written on the back of an illustrated playing card printed with the legend: WHICH IS THE FATAL CARD? Crane sent this card to Hawkins, inscribed thus:] Didn't I rather hock their game?

[59] A schoolboy chum whose life Stephen had saved by pulling him out of the surf. That Beer (p. 307) dates this letter March, 1896, indicates that Beer did not have access to the Crane-Hawkins letters, for Crane was still in Washington in March. He did not get back to Hartwood until early April.

say, There is Smith. When they behold a writer taking a glass of beer, they say, Send for the police! No great law of nature can be proved from this but it pretty often hits me that people are ingenious blockheads. I have been to Washington about a book on political society for Mr. McClure but I came straight back.

159. TO THE EDITOR OF THE NEWARK SUNDAY CALL [60]

[165 West 23d Street, New York City] April 29, 1896

Dear Sir: I was born in Newark on the 1st of November, 1871. The house was No. 14 Mulberry place. I understand the neighborhood is rather tough now, so that I am not too stringent on that point, although it makes no particular difference. My father was the Rev. J. T. Crane, D.D., presiding elder of the Newark district. The family moved from there to Bound Brook. My great-great-great-grandfather was one of the seven men who solemnly founded Newark. He was Jasper Crane. His farm came into the southwest corner of Market and Broad streets. His son Stephen Crane, M.C., moved to Elizabeth, where my grandfather and my father were born. During the Revolution the Cranes were pretty hot people. The old man Stephen served in the Continental Congress (for New Jersey) while all four sons were in the army. William Crane was Colonel of the Sixth Regiment of New Jersey Infantry. The Essex Militia also contained one of the sons.

I am not much on this sort of thing or I could write more, but at any rate the family is founded deep in Jersey soil (since the birth of Newark), and I am about as much of a Jerseyman as you can find. Sincerely yours,   *Stephen Crane*

160. TO RIPLEY HITCHCOCK

Port Jervis, N.Y./May 29 [1896]

Dear Mr Hitchcock: I have again taken to the woods and I shall try to

---

[60] Written in answer to a request for a record of himself and his people, this letter was published in the Newark *Sunday Call*, May 3, 1896, where Crane was hailed as "A new star in the literary firmament, . . . a fair-haired youth, who, having passed through a storm of adverse criticism, is now hailed far and wide as a genius. Things as extravagant in praise, as the former notices of him were extravagant in condemnation, are now being said. . . . It is even said of this new star that if he never produces another thing [other than *The Red Badge*], he has done enough to save the fag end of the century from literary disgrace, which is no small matter."

Crane's letter was reprinted in the New York *Sun*, June 10, 1900, with a long article tracing Crane's ancestry ("Stephen Crane, Jerseyman"), and again in the Newark *Sunday Call*, June 17, 1923.

remain here for I am certainly unable to withstand the fury of New York. Are you bringing out *Maggie* soon? I am planting some financial seed up here and I would. [*Incomplete*]

161. TO RIPLEY HITCHCOCK

Hartwood/Saturday [June 6 or 13 (?) 1896]

Dear Mr Hitchcock: Through the fault of the U.S.P.O. Dept.—no less —proofs [61] did not reach me until today. I return them herewith. I have asked Arnold's to come up here and I will reiterate to you.

[*Stephen Crane*] [62]

[*Letter Cut*]

The copy was not complete. Used June McClure's.

162. TO E. J. EDWARDS[?] [63]

New York City/June 14. [1896]

[Inscribed in a copy of *George's Mother*]

To my friend Eddie in memory of our days of suffering and trouble in 217th St.   *Stephen Crane*

163. TO DeWITT MILLER [64]

Mr. DeWitt Miller/ July 3d, 96

[Inscribed in a copy of *Maggie*] [65]

It is indeed a brave new binding and I wish the inside were braver.

Stephen Crane

---

[61] Proofs of *The Little Regiment,* which included the story "The Little Regiment," published in the June issue of *McClure's Magazine.* The title story of the collection was finished in February; Crane had thought then to do a Civil War play with Clyde Fitch.

[62] Crane's signature is excised from the holograph letter, and above the scissored portion is written in another hand (Hitchcock's?) Crane's name. Someone wanted Crane's signature, and Hitchcock, to oblige, cut out that portion.

[63] Edwards gave Crane a place to sleep in his room on West 217th Street during the early part of 1892.

[64] Identity not known.

[65] The 1896 edition of *Maggie: A Girl of the Streets,* published by D. Appleton and Company, was announced in the *Publishers' Weekly,* June 13.

164. TO H. P. TABER: EDITOR OF THE PHILISTINE

[Undated]

[Inscribed in a copy of *Maggie*] [66]

My dear Tabor: I wrote this book when I was very young so if you dont like it, shut up. But my best wishes go with it.   *Stephen Crane*

165. TO HAMLIN GARLAND

[165 West 23d Street, New York City/July 1896]

Dear Mr. Garland: Just heard you were in town. I want you to dine tonight with me at the Lantern Club. Sure!! Roosevelt [67] expects to be there. He wants to meet you. Don't fail. I will call here at six— again.[68] Yours   *Crane*

166. TO HAMLIN GARLAND

New York City/July, 1896

[Inscribed in a copy of *George's Mother*]

To Hamlin Garland of the great honest West,[69] from Stephen Crane of the false East

---

[66] Crane sent Taber this inscribed copy of the 1893 edition some time subsequent to the honorary dinner tendered him by the Society of the Philistines in December, 1895. Until then Crane had not met Taber, and his first appearance in the *Philistine* was in June, 1895, with the poem "I stood upon a high place," reprinted from *The Black Riders* (1895). The *Philistine* published in February, 1896, "What says the little sea-shell," and in March the sketch "Great Mistake," and in October "The Ominous Baby," reprinted from the *Arena* (1894). That Crane sent Taber this 1893 *Maggie* sometime during the first half of 1896 or at the end of 1895 is evidenced also by the contents of his inscription. That he knew him only slightly is shown by his misspelling Taber's name. This copy of *Maggie*, in original wrappers, is in the Houghton Library.

[67] Theodore Roosevelt, President of the New York City Board of Police Commissioners. Crane dined at his house in July. On July 20 Roosevelt wrote Crane that it would be all right for him to call on him at eleven o'clock: "I have much to discuss with you about 'Madge.'" On August 18 Roosevelt wrote Crane to thank him for an autographed copy of *George's Mother* (see Letter 171).

[68] This handwritten postal card Crane left at Garland's hotel and with it an inscribed copy of *George's Mother* (see Letter 166). Garland pasted this card in the inscribed copy, and years later, probably when in his seventies, he penciled on the half-title page of this book the note given in No. 167.

[69] Garland, in *Afternoon Neighbors* (1934), shifts his point of view—he now dislikes the Middle West.

167. *HAMLIN GARLAND'S NOTE IN* GEORGE'S MOTHER

As I read this book now it appears an unimportant youthful venture. It is a heightened, artificially colored transcript of life. It is Crane, the boy, telling of things he has seen but putting his own psychology into his observations. His English is admirable, concise, vivid and unfaltering. It will live only as a literary phase of a brilliant young literary man, whose later phases were not much more important. Crane never quite grew up in any sense. Disease came in to weaken his work and death cut it short. His marvelous command of simple English words is his chief claim to distinction to me now as it was in the days when I first knew him.

168. *WILLIAM DEAN HOWELLS TO STEPHEN CRANE*

Far Rockaway, [Long Island]/July 30, 1896

My dear Mr. Crane: I send you my notice of your last books,[70] which has been vexatiously delayed. It ought to have been out a month ago.

We are hoping for a little glimpse of you here before the season is over. Yours cordially   *W. D. Howells*

169. *TO WILLIAM DEAN HOWELLS*

McClure's Magazine/[Sunday] August 15– [1896]

Dear Mr. Howells: I was away in the country when your essay appeared in the World—so deep in the woods in fact that word of it was much belated. It is of course the best word that has been said of me and I am grateful in a way that is hard for me to say. In truth you have always been so generous with me that grace departs at once from my pen when I attempt to tell you of my appreciation. When I speak of it to others however I am mightily fluent and use the best terms every time. I always thank God that I can have the strongest admiration for the work of a man who has been so much to me personally for I can imagine the terrors of being indelibly indebted to the Chump in Art or even to the Semi-Chump in Art.

I would like to know Mr. Cahan.[71] I am reading his book and I

---

[70] Howells reviewed *George's Mother* and *Maggie* in "New York Low Life in Fiction," in the New York *World*, July 26, 1896, and wrote "An Appreciation" in the Heinemann edition of *Maggie*, published in June. (Reissued in *Bowery Tales*, 1900.) Howells wrote Hamlin Garland on July 22, 1896: "What a boom Crane has had! Have you read George's Mother? Mrs. Howells thinks it the best of all.—He's a good boy, with lots of sense."

[71] Abraham Cahan, editor of the *Jewish Daily Forward*, published this year *Yekl, A Tale of the New York Ghetto*. In Howells' "New York Low Life

am wondering how in the name of Heaven he learned how to do it. I am going tomorrow on a business journey and shall be gone until Wednesday. Upon my return I shall call at Far Rockaway and I hope then you will tell me where to find him. I have a delicious feeling of being some months ahead of him in the recognition, critically, and I would like to take some trouble in looking him up at his home. Sincerely yours   *Stephen Crane*

170. WILLIAM DEAN HOWELLS TO STEPHEN CRANE

Far Rockaway,/August 15, 1896

Dear Mr. Crane: Come a week from the time you mention—that is, come Wednesday the 25th, and spend the night and the next day with us, so as to get in two sea baths. Take the 3:20 p.m. train from the L.I.R.R. station at the East 34th st. ferry, and you will arrive here at 4:10; we will meet you and go at once to the beach with you.

Cahan lives at 213 East 6th St. He will be glad to see you, and is a fine fellow—school teacher, and editor of the Yiddish socialist paper. We all join in regards to you. Yours cordially   *W. D. Howells*

171. THEODORE ROOSEVELT TO STEPHEN CRANE [72]

New York, Aug. 18, 1896

My dear Mr. Crane:—I am much obliged to you for "George's Mother" with your own autograph in the front. I shall keep it with your other books. Some day I shall get you to write your autograph in my "Red Badge of Courage," for much though I like your other books, I think I like that book the best. Some day I want you to write another story of the frontiersman and the Mexican Greaser in which the frontiersman shall come out on top; it is more normal that way! [73] I wish I could have seen Hamlin Garland, but I am leaving in a few days for a three weeks trip in the West.

---

in Fiction" Cahan is headlined "as a New Star of Realism" and Crane is linked with him for having drawn "the Truest Pictures of East Side Life." Howells had sent Crane a clipping of this essay with his letter of July 30, but Crane first sees it now, just back from Hartwood two weeks later. Howells then replies the same day (Letter 170).

[72] At the time Roosevelt wrote this letter he was President of the New York City Board of Police Commissioners. On Crane and the police, see Dr. Frederic M. Lawrence's letter (Appendix 21).

[73] "A Man and Some Others," published in the *Century*, February, 1897, relates the story of a frontiersman, formerly a bouncer at a Bowery saloon, who dies in a gun fight with José and a band of Mexican "greasers."

This evening I shall be around at the Madison Square Garden to see exactly what the Police do.[74] They have a very difficult task with a crowd like that, because they have to be exceedingly good humored with the crowd, and they also have to please the Managers of the meeting who know nothing about crowds, and yet they have to control twenty thousand people. I will say one thing for them at the Bryan meeting; we have not had a single complaint of clubbing or brutality from any man claiming to have suffered; the Managers of the meeting and the Manager of the Garden have both written us in the warmest terms. I hope soon to see you again. Sincerely yours,

Theodore Roosevelt

172. TO WILLIAM DEAN HOWELLS

Hartwood, N.Y./Saturday [August 21, 1896]

Dear Mr. Howells: Just received your note and I shall be very glad to come out on Wednesday [the 25th] afternoon. I think however that I shall be obliged to return to New York Wednesday night. Sincerely yours   *Stephen Crane*

173. TO AN UNKNOWN RECIPIENT

New York/Aug. 29, 1896

[Inscribed in a copy of *Maggie*, 1893 edition]

And the wealth of the few shall be built upon the patience of the poor/ Prophecy not made B. C. 1090   *Stephen Crane*

174. TO MISS BELLE WALKER

141 East 25th St./New York City/Sept. 8th. [1896]

Dear Miss Walker: I think the motif of the story is properly strong. "You will never hold the cross toward me." That, I think is very effective. One thing I must say at once: Take the diamond out of that man's shirt immediately. Dont let him live another day with a diamond in his front. You declare him to be very swell and yet you allow him to wear a diamond as if he were a saloon proprietor or owned a prosperous livery stable. It is of the utmost importance that you remove the dia-

---

[74] Crane and the police did not get along, and Roosevelt's defense of them replied to Crane's criticism. *Book News*, September, 1896, said about Crane: "He will publish a new series of stories, or a long story, he has not definitely decided which, in which will be presented the life of the metropolitan policeman."

mond at once for our fin de siecle [editors] [75] have keen eyes for that sort of a mistake.

Frankly I do not consider your sketch to be very good but even if you do me the honor to value my opinion, this need not discourage you for I can remember when I wrote just as badly as you do now. Furthermore there are many men, far our superiors who once wrote just as badly as I do today and no doubt as badly as you. Yours sincerely   *Stephen Crane*

175. TO PAUL REVERE REYNOLDS

Sept. 9th/96

Dear Mr. Reynolds,—/ I leave you a story of something over 5000 words, which I would like you to sell if you can. It is one of the best stories [76] that I have done and the lowest price that I could take for it would be $350. I think it is worth more however, if it once strikes the right place, but don't sell it please to some publication that will print it in 1897 and pay in 1898. There are so many of that kind of offices and I would rather take the bottom price if it was represented by cash. Please let

---

[75] In turning to a new page, Crane forgot the word "editors" then inserted it above the phrase "another day with a diamond in his front." It obviously belongs here.

[76] This is "A Man and Some Others," which Reynolds submitted to Richard Watson Gilder of the *Century Magazine*. Crane's mix-up with the police and gossip attaching to his name brought Gilder to ask indignantly of Reynolds what Crane meant by getting into such a mess when he had sold a story to the *Century Magazine*. Gilder postponed publication of "A Man and Some Others" until February, 1897, when the gossip had died down.

Gilder objected also to certain phrases in the manuscript. He wrote Reynolds on October 24, 1896:

My dear Mr. Reynolds: I am truly obliged to Mr. Crane for getting out that hackneyed "crown of thorns."

You may think me over anxious, but I am particularly sorry he did not change that "B'Gawd." It is difficult to know what to do with swearing in fiction. When it appears in print it has an offensiveness beyond that of the actual word; and it is never true or "realistic" because, if the actual oaths were printed just as the swearer swears it would be as unendurable among men as among gods.

I am a sincere well-wisher of the author, and I am anxious that this story should not attract unfavorable criticism in any details; so I particularly ask him through yourself to omit that expression, for his sake as well as yours. Sincerely,   *R. W. Gilder*

me know within a couple of days whether you also arrange for the English rights. My English Market has always been pretty good and I would not care to have both English & American rights sold for 350. but I would expect for the English rights about 25 pounds. I wish you therefore every luck with the story and please let me hear from you when convenient. Don't go to Bacheller or McClure. Yours truly,/ Dictated by S. C.   (*signed*) *Stephen Crane*

   ❀   ❀   ❀

Cora Taylor

In November, 1896, Crane first met Cora Taylor in Jacksonville, Florida, where she was operating the Hotel de Dream, a boardinghouse and night club.[77] Her father John Howorth was a painter, her great-grandfather George Howorth had an art gallery in Boston at 26 Kneeland Street, the house where Cora was born. Her father died when she was six years old and her mother remarried within a year. Nothing is known of Cora Howorth's life in the years between, until, while still very young, the marriage in New York to Thomas Vinton Murphy, which lasted but a few months. Two and a half years later in London she married Captain Stewart, the younger son of an English baronet. This marriage too was unsuccessful, and when they separated, her husband refused her a divorce. Crane, trying to get to Cuba to report the rebellion there for Bacheller, waited all November and December in Jacksonville, and was a frequent visitor during this time at the Hotel de Dream and other night spots. At the time of his first meeting with "Miss Cora," as she was known to guests of the hotel, Crane inscribed a note to "C. E. S." (Cora E. Stewart) and gave her an inscribed copy of *George's Mother.*

   ❀   ❀   ❀

---

[77] A night club in the Victorian era—in the United States, we perhaps should say in the heyday of Carry Nation—was classified among the haunts of sin. Technically, at any rate, the Hotel de Dream was not a house of prostitution and there were no girls boarded on the premises. Cora bought the business and leased the place from one Ethel Dreme, in March, 1895. The spelling of the name Hotel de Dream is confused and controversial, later detractors of Cora Taylor seeing in it an opportunity for vulgar caricature. We have adhered to the spelling in the McCready MSS as most likely the one used by Cora herself, a reflection of her somewhat unpredictable sense of humor colored by romanticism.

176. TO C. E. S.[78]

Jacksonville, Fla./Nov 4th, 1896
[for November 14?]

Brevity is an element that enters importantly into all pleasures, of life, and this is what makes pleasure sad; and so there is no pleasure but only sadness.   *Stephen Crane*

If Crane's note and inscribed copy of *George's Mother* (No. 177) are correctly dated November 4, Crane must have traveled a good deal these first weeks of November; for he was in Cambridge on the seventh to report "How Princeton Met Harvard at Cambridge" (published in the New York *Journal*, November 8, 1896), and the previous Saturday he had covered another football game, reporting it in the New York *Journal* for November 1: "Harvard University Against the Carlisle Indians." This puts him in Cambridge on the weekend of October 31, in Jacksonville by the following Wednesday (November 4), and back in Cambridge that weekend—by Saturday, November 7. And then back in Jacksonville by the twelfth (Beer dates Crane's letter from Jacksonville to Miss Catherine Harris as November 12). It seems more likely that Crane misdated his inscribed copy of *George's Mother* and his note to Cora—November 4 for November 14. This theory has apparent support in what the Syracuse University *Herald* reported about Crane's departure for Cuba: "Mr. Stephen Crane, ex-'94, left New York for Cuba on Friday, November 13, to report the Cuban war news for the New York *Journal*. He postponed his journey a week in order to defy superstition by starting on a so-called unlucky day." If he postponed his departure from New York City a week, he was not in Jacksonville on November 4. But if he left for Jacksonville not until the thirteenth, he could not have written Miss Harris from Jacksonville on the twelfth. The *Herald's* sophomoric superstition about the thirteenth would not have influenced Crane. It seems reasonable to assume that he left for Jacksonville the weekend of November 7 and reached Jacksonville some days before writing Miss Harris on November 12. If so, he misdated his inscriptions to Cora. The curious thing about Crane is that so many facts pertaining to him resist certitude.

177. TO CORA TAYLOR

Nov. 4,/96 [for November 14?]

[Inscribed in a copy of *George's Mother*]

To an unnamed sweetheart   *Stephen Crane*

---

[78] This note was first printed in Melvin H. Schoberlin's study of the *Sullivan County Sketches* (p. 11).

178. *TO MISS CATHERINE HARRIS*

[Jacksonville, Florida/November 12 ? 1896]

[*No salutation*] Thank you very much for your letter on Maggie. I will try to answer your questions properly and politely. Mrs. Howells was right in telling you that I have spent a great deal of time on the East Side and that I have no opinion of missions. That—to you—may not be a valid answer since perhaps you have been informed that I am not very friendly to Christianity as seen around town.[79] I do not think that much can be done with the Bowery as long as the [*word blurred*] are in their present state of conceit. A person who thinks himself superior to the rest of us because he has no job and no pride and no clean clothes is as badly conceited as Lillian Russell. In a story of mine called "An Experiment in Misery" I tried to make plain that the root of Bowery life is a sort of cowardice. Perhaps I mean a lack of ambition or to willingly be knocked flat and accept the licking. The missions for children are another thing and if you will have Mr. Rockefeller give me a hundred street cars and some money I will load all the babes off to some pink world where cows can lick their noses and they will never see their families any more. My good friend Edward Townsend—have you read his "Daughter of the Tenements"?—has another opinion of the Bowery and it is certain to be better than mine. I had no other purpose in writing "Maggie" than to show people to people as they seem to me. If that be evil, make the most of it.

❋   ❋   ❋

Amy Leslie

Amy Leslie, former actress and since 1889 dramatic critic on the Chicago *Daily News,* lent Crane some money on November 1, 1896, and sued him for recovery of it in early January, 1898. She declared that he had repaid her only $250 of the original $800 loan. The letter below

---

[79] Nor was he friendly to temperance leaders, although his own father—author of *The Arts of Intoxication*—subscribed to the cause and his mother, Helen Peck Crane, was an active participant in the work of the organization headed by Miss Willard, the Woman's Christian Temperance Union. "Frances Willard," he told Miss Harris, "is one of those wonderful people who can tell right from wrong for everybody from the polar cap to the equator. Perhaps it never struck her that people differ from her. I have loved myself passionately now and then but Miss Willard's affair with Miss Willard should be stopped by the police" (Beer, p. 359).

has importance; it suggests that Amy Leslie was infatuated with Crane and that he had the burden of appeasing a brokenhearted and mentally sick woman.

❀   ❀   ❀

179. TO WILLIS BROOKS HAWKINS

Jacksonville, Fla.,/Nov. 29, 1896

My dear Willis: I am here in Jacksonville and feeling very good. I am very much obliged to you for allowing me to plant certain responsibilities upon your noble shoulders and I know that you will carry it out with every consideration for your old friend. By the way, I have planted another responsibility upon your noble shoulders. I have just written to my brother Will that in case my journey was protracted by casuses [sic] which you can readily imagine, I wish you to serve with Mr. Howells, Mr. Garland and Mr. Hitchcock as my literary executors.

In case you see Amy from time to time encourage her in every possible way. Of course feminine nature is mighty peculiar and she might have that singular ability to get rid of mournful emotions which is possessed by a great many of her sex, but I was positively frightened for the girl at the moment of parting and I am afraid and worried now. I feel that no one hardly could need a friendly word more than this poor child,[80] and I know you are just the man to do it in a right way if the chance presents itself. Hooke fastens his intellect so securely to some damned molecule that he loses sight of a broad question and I do not think he is very efficient as a bracer. It broke my heart to leave the girl but I could feel comparatively easy now if I could feel that she had good friends. There is not one man in three thousand who can be a real counsellor and guide for a girl so pretty as Amy, and this will present itself to your mind no doubt as a reason for supposing that Charley would not be very capable in the position. Her sister [81] is a good hearted sort of a creature, but she is liable to devote most of her attention to herself and besides that Amy is mentally superior to her in every way. The sister is weak, very weak, and so I am sure that she would be of no help to Amy in what is now really a great trouble. I do not want to bore you with any of my affairs but I am obliged to feel that you are about the only man who could possibly help me and do it

---

[80] Amy Leslie was almost twenty years older than Crane, who was twenty-five on November 1.

[81] Mrs. O'Brien, with whom Amy Leslie lived on West 25th Street. Charley, referred to in letter 157, was a poker-table friend of Crane.

in the way that would count for some good, so just remember this and when you think some times of your friend remember that he has left behind him one to whom he would count favors done as favors done to himself. By my remarkable use of bad English in parts of this letter you can see that I am dictating [82] and you know very well that I am not used to dictation because my brain is too slow, but I have no doubt you will be able to make out what I mean. Yours always

Stephen Crane

My best to old Bill Fairman.[83]

180. TO WILLIAM HOWE CRANE

[Jacksonville, Florida] November 29, 1896

[Dear Will:] I was off to Cuba before I had a chance to even inform you of it from New York. I fooled around town for over a month expecting to go at any time . . . suddenly received orders to skip and I left New York that very night. . . . [The collecting of my stories] will make considerable work, but there are some of them which I would hate to see lost. Some of my best work is contained in short things which I have written for various publications, principally the New York *Press* in 1893 [1894] or thereabouts. There are some 15 or 20 short sketches of New York street life and so on which I intended to have published in book form under the title of "Midnight Sketches." That should be your first care.[84] . . . my saddle horse [Peanuts] I

---

[82] Crane's typewritten letters, of which this is one, are rare.

[83] A crony of Crane's poker-table days.

[84] Crane's will, made out before leaving Florida, has been lost, except for these fragments of his letter to William and his mention of it to Hawkins on November 29: "I wish you to serve with Mr. Howells, Mr. Garland and Mr. Hitchcock as my literary executors," (Letter 179). According to Beer (p. 313), "William Crane was to be his sole executor and to receive a third of the estate, Edmund Crane was to have another third, and the remainder was divided between his two other brothers" (Townley and Wilbur; there was yet another brother George, the eldest, with whom Stephen seems to have had little contact). On November 29, 1896, Crane wrote further details regarding his will in this letter to William Howe Crane. But in April before he died (on June 5, 1900) Crane made a new will leaving to Cora all his personal effects, and until she should remarry, all the income from his estate. Should she marry again, one-half of his estate was then to be divided between Edmund and William, the other half going to his namesake Stephen (Edmund's baby son, born in 1900). William was made executor of the American branch of his estate, and his London solicitor Alfred T. Plant, English executor, with power over the income from America which was to be sent to Plant after payment of debts. This 1900 will, which was made in

would not like to have sold. I would prefer that he be kept in easy service at Hartwood and have him cared for as much as possible by Ed himself or by somebody whom it is absolutely certain would not maltreat him . . . and all I can add now is my love to you and Cornelia and all the babies.

181. TO WILLIS BROOKS HAWKINS

[Telegram. Jacksonville, Florida, to New York] Dec. 24, 1896

Leave soon. Telegraph frankly Amy's mental condition. Also send fifty if possible. Will arrange payments from Appleton. Troubled over Amy.

✿   ✿   ✿

Disaster at Sea

The steamer *Commodore*, with an expedition for the Cuban insurgents, sank with her cargo of arms and ammunition about fifteen miles off Mosquito Inlet during the night of January 1. The Florida *Times-Union and Citizen* on Sunday, January 3, announced that all twenty-eight men on the vessel had reached shore safely, twelve of them arriving in Jacksonville the night before by railway from Daytona Beach. The other sixteen, it reported, were expected there "this morning" (January 3). But the newspaper account was in error. On Monday, January 4, the New York *Press* reported that seventeen men had been accounted for "last night" (January 3), "with a slight chance of seven more yet alive." Among those saved was Stephen Crane. ("Young New York Writer Astonishes the Sea Dogs by His Courage in the Face of Death.")

✿   ✿   ✿

182. MORTON TO CORA TAYLOR [85]

[St. James Hotel, Jacksonville, Florida] 9 pm
[January 2, 1897]

My dear Miss Cora/I am very sorry that I have no encouraging word

England was filed there, and in Goshen, Orange County, New York. (No mention of it is made in Beer or in Berryman.)

The original source for Letter 180 remains unidentified. The first and final portions have been extracted from Berryman (pp. 148, 171) and the middle portion from Beer (pp. 313–14). Unfortunately, neither Berryman nor Beer documents source materials.

[85] Morton was the night clerk at the St. James and one of the "gang" who frequented the Hotel de Dream. This handwritten letter probably was delivered to Cora by messenger.

to send you. The eleven men who were saved have arrived in town. One of them saw Mr Crane get out of his berth and dress himself with that same non-plussed [nonchalant] manner, characteristic of him. He entered the boat containing the 16, which is reported to have swamped. There is conflicting rumors as to the empty boat being washed ashore. Some say it has been washed ashore at Port Orange—others say not. The Operator at New Smyrna tells me that he has it pretty straight that it came in, bottom up. God save Crane if he is still alive. You are welcome   *Morton* [86]

183. CORA TAYLOR TO STEPHEN CRANE

[Telegram. Jacksonville to Daytona, Florida] Jan 3 1896
[for 1897]

Telegram received Thank God your safe have been almost crazy   *C. T.*

184. MORTON TO STEPHEN CRANE

[Telegram. Jacksonville to Daytona, Florida] [January 3] 189[7]

The wake held at the St James last night turned into a Jubilee today. Just carried the news down home. All well there, congratulations from the gang   *Morton*

185. CORA TAYLOR TO STEPHEN CRANE

[Telegram. Jacksonville to Daytona, Florida] Jan 3, 1896
[for 1897]

Come by special today never mind overcharges answer and come surely   *C. T.*

---

[86] Another note in another hand reads: "Have just conversed with Phonse Fritot. [Alphonse W. Fritot, an employe of the Florida East Coast Railway and manager of the Jacksonville Terminal.] He fears the worst. Carter is here telling us the story from what he gathered from the rescued." W. R. Carter was editor and publisher of the *Jacksonville Evening Metropolis*.

Crane's "death" was reported in Hubbard's *Philistine:* "I have gibed Stephen Crane, and jeered his work, but beneath all the banter there was only respect, good-will—aye! and affection. He is dead now—Steve is dead. How he faced death the records do not say. . . . *He died trying to save others.* So here's to you, Steve Crane, wherever you may be!" Hubbard in this same issue corrects himself: "LATER: Thanks to Providence and a hencoop Steve Crane was not drowned after all—he swam ashore."

186. MORTON TO STEPHEN CRANE

[Telegram. Jacksonville to Daytona, Florida] 189[7]

I am right here within call anything I can do command me   *Morton*

187. MANAGER OF THE ST. JAMES [87] TO STEPHEN CRANE

[Telegram. Jacksonville to Daytona, Florida] 189[7]

Cora will be there on noon train   *M[anager] St James*

188. MORTON TO STEPHEN CRANE

[Telegram. Jacksonville to Daytona, Florida] 189[7]

Marshall [88] Wires "Congratulations on plucky and successful fight for
life. Dont wire. But write fully from Jax. will wire money today" 4
telegrams here for you nothing important except above.   *Morton*

189. TO WILLIS BROOKS HAWKINS

[Telegram. Jacksonville, Florida, to New York] 1/7 1897

Thanks awfully old man [89] greeting to club [90] send mail here   *Crane*

190. TO CORA TAYLOR [91]

[Jacksonville, Florida, January, 1897]

To C. E. S./Love comes like the tall swift shadow of a ship at night.
There is for a moment, the music of the water's turmoil, a bell, perhaps, a man's shout, a row of gleaming yellow lights. Then the slow
sinking of this mystic shape. Then silence and a bitter silence—the
silence of the sea at night.   *Stephen Crane*

---

[87] This wire was actually sent by the assistant manager, James Harrison.

[88] Sunday editor of the New York *Journal;* he had been with the New
York *Press* in 1893 and with the New York *World* in 1894.

Omnibus (pp. 448–76) reproduces newspaper accounts of the *Commodore* shipwreck, with "Stephen Crane's Own Story," from the New York
Press (cf. Berryman, pp. 159–60).

[89] Hawkins had wired Crane some money when the news reached him
that Crane had been saved.

[90] The Lantern Club.

[91] Pasted on the reverse side of this sheet is an envelope postmarked
January 26 and addressed "Stephen Crane, Esqr.," at Hartwood, New York.
The postmarked letter, we presume, was forwarded to Crane from Hart-
wood to Jacksonville.

191. TO LYDA [92]

Jacksonville, Fla./February 18,/1897

[Inscribed on the flyleaf of an 1896 edition of *Maggie*]

To Lyda/From her friend/ Stephen Crane

192. TO RIPLEY HITCHCOCK

[Telegram. Jacksonville, Florida, to New York] Feby 24 1897

Wire here Heinemans payment little regiment or maggies very important   ***Stephen Crane***

193. TO EDMUND CRANE

[Jacksonville, Florida] March 11, 1897

I have been for over a month among the swamps further South [of Jacksonville], wading miserably to and fro in an attempt to avoid our derned U.S. Navy. It can't be done. I am through trying. I have changed all my plans and am going to Crete.[93]

✿   ✿   ✿

Crane En Route to the Greco-Turkish War

Unable to get to Cuba, Crane set off for Greece as war correspondent for the New York *Journal*. About the middle of March he was in New York City, en route to London and Paris. In New York he met a young Hearst newspaperman, Robert H. Davis, who records reminiscences of this occasion in his introduction to *The Work of Stephen Crane*, Vol. 11 (1925). He wanted to meet Crane mainly to tell him what Ambrose Bierce, the literary lion of San Francisco, had said of *The Red Badge of Courage:* "This young man has the power to feel. He knows nothing of war, yet he is drenched in blood. Most beginners who deal with this subject spatter themselves merely with ink." [94] One of Crane's artist friends of the old days, Corwin Knapp Linson, had a farewell dinner

---

[92] Lyda de Camp, a well-known madam, proprietress of a sporting house in Ward Street which was known as "the line."

[93] "I am going to Greece for the *Journal* and if the Red Badge is not all right I shall sell out my claim on literature and take up orange growing." So Crane wrote someone at this time. This note is reprinted from Beer (p. 318), and the above portion of Crane's letter is reprinted from Thomas L. Raymond, *Stephen Crane* (1923), p. 11.

[94] Bierce's melodramatic acclaim of Crane has a hollow ring to it, and so too do most of Bierce's short stories. An exception is "An Occurrence at

with Crane, at which Stephen confided to Linson his intentions regarding Cora—of marriage.

In London, on March 26, Crane was at the Savage Club with his new friend, Harold Frederic, whose London report on *The Red Badge* had promoted Crane's reputation at home the year before, and on March 29 he was given a luncheon at the Savoy by Richard Harding Davis and presented to James M. Barrie. Frederic saw Crane off at Dover for Paris on April 1; the following day Arnold Henry Sanford Bennett, a Canadian who spoke French, guided Crane around Paris. Bennett had married a French woman in 1896; she died in 1899, and Crane remarked in a letter about Bennett: "Destiny sets an alarm clock so as to be up early and strew banana peels in front of him. If he trusts a friend, he is betrayed. If he starts a journey, he breaks an ankle. If he loves, death comes to her without a smile." Beer reports that Bennett "was so shy that he dropped the name Arnold after the popularity of Arnold Bennett began."

Cora, meanwhile, accompanied by an older friend, Mrs. Ruedy, had rejoined Stephen in London and was with him on the Channel crossing, together with Bennett and Richard Harding Davis, also en route to the Greek war. Davis, who probably had met Cora earlier at the Hotel de Dream, gossiped in letters home to his family about "a bi-roxide blonde" who had left her husband to run after Stephen Crane. Davis soured on Crane thereafter.[95] Cora and Mrs. Ruedy traveled with

---

Owl Creek Bridge," which Crane advised Richard Harding Davis to read. "Nothing better exists," said Crane. "That story contains everything."

Although Bierce praised *The Red Badge* to Davis, he expressed pleasure when it received an unfavorable review in the New York *Journal* of May 22, 1896. He wrote the reviewer, Percival Pollard, on May 25 from Washington, D.C.: "I valued it, I really believe, more for its just censure of the Crane freak than for its too kindly praise of me. I have been hoping some one still in the business of reading (I have not myself looked into a book for months) would take the trouble to say something of that kind about that Crane person's work" (the original of this letter is in the Berg Collection at the New York Public Library). Bierce knew very little about current literature. In the San Francisco *Examiner* of July 26, 1896, Bierce remarked that "Mr. Percival Pollard . . . has dragged to upper day two worse writers than Stephen Crane, . . . the names (H. W. Phillips and Rupert Hughes . . .) are unfamiliar to me; and I had thought that there could be only two worse writers than Stephen Crane, namely two Stephen Cranes" (Paul Fatout, *Ambrose Bierce: The Devil's Lexicographer* [1951], p. 220).

[95] See Scott C. Osborn, "Stephen Crane and Cora Taylor: Some Corrections," *American Literature* (November, 1954); and "The 'Rivalry-Chivalry' of Richard Harding Davis and Stephen Crane," *ibid.* (March, 1956).

Crane on a wild journey through the Balkans, ending at Athens, after a brief stopover in Constantinople.

Crane wrote somebody from Basel: "I now know that I am an imbecile of rank. If nobody shoots me and I get back alive through those Indians in London I will stay home until there is a nice war in Mexico where it does not matter what you talk so long as you can curse immoderately. Willie Hearst has made a bad bargain." The Greco-Turkish War, lasting but one month, began April 18.

✿   ✿   ✿

The Amy Leslie Affair

In an item captioned "Stephen Crane Sued," the New York *Daily Tribune*, for January 4, 1898, reported a suit in Supreme Court that Amy Leslie brought against Crane to recover $550, the plaintiff alleging that she gave the defendant $800 on November 1, 1896, to deposit in the bank. "Instead of depositing it in her name, she says, he placed it to his own credit." The fact is that Crane had deposited $500 on November 25 with Willis Hawkins with instructions to pay it out to Miss Leslie in certain prescribed sums periodically; when that sum was paid out, Hawkins' connection with the matter was ended. Crane sent him another sum, but Hawkins washed his hands of the whole affair, and meanwhile Miss Leslie took the issue to court. (Amy Leslie's letters to Hawkins and his accounting of sums received and paid out are at Dartmouth College Library.)

✿   ✿   ✿

194. TO WILLIS BROOKS HAWKINS [96]

Grand Hotel D'Angleterre/Athens/(Greece) [April 18, 1897]

Willie:/ Have mailed at [to] 25th St—one hundred for Amy / Yours / S

A draft on Cooks.

195. TO WILLIS BROOKS HAWKINS

Grand Hotel D'Angleterre/Athens/(Greece) [April 18, 1897]

Dear Willie   Have mailed you cooks draft for one hundred for Amy / C

---

[96] This note and No. 195 are postmarked April 18, 1897. No. 194 was addressed to Hawkins, c/o Lantern Club, while No. 195 was sent to Hawkins, c/o Bacheller Syndicate, New York City.

196. TO WILLIS BROOKS HAWKINS

Grand Hotel D'Angleterre/Athens/(Greece) April 27 [1897]

Dear old man: I enclose a pony [97] for Amy. Give her my love. Tell her there is lots more coming. Just off again to see fight. I love Amy. Yours   **S.**

Tell Fairman [98] go to hell./[Enclosure] $100 ck

      ❀ ❀ ❀

"Imogene Carter"

With the war over by May 20, Crane returned to London—and with him went Cora Taylor, who had served with Crane in Greece as war correspondent for the *Journal* under the pseudonym "Imogene Carter." Two of her dispatches appeared in the *Journal* under her by-line, one other in a source untraced. These three are all that are thus far known to have been published. But she wrote other articles in collaboration with Crane, in the form of a series of unsigned newsletters issued from London and syndicated to various newspapers in the United States. These pieces (some of which are wholly by Cora, some by Stephen, and others reworked from notes dictated by him to her) contain chit-chat of the doings of the English aristocracy, their country houses, visiting royalty, fashion notes, travel notes, sports items, and so forth. (The holograph manuscripts are in the Stephen Crane Collection at Butler Library.) These articles—erroneously connected with a letter written by Crane to Paul Revere Reynolds in October, 1897—have given rise to the belief (otherwise without foundation) that "Imogene Carter" did not write her own dispatches from Greece (see Berryman, pp. 181–82). "You might go to Curtis Brown, Sunday Editor of the *Press*," Crane wrote Reynolds from England, "and say how-how from me. Then tell him this *in the strictest confidence,* that a lady named Imogene Carter whose work he has been using from time to time is also named Stephen Crane and that I did 'em in about twenty minutes on each Sunday, just dictating to a friend" (Letter 200). Though something of an exaggeration, this last statement clearly refers to the London newsletters that had appeared in the New York *Press*, not to the Greek war dispatches that Curtis Brown had never seen.

---

[97] Slang for £25.

[98] Miss Leslie's agent. Possibly the same "Bill" Fairman who was Crane's friend and crony at poker-games with Crane and Hawkins.

✿   ✿   ✿

197. IMOGENE CARTER TO STEPHEN CRANE

Athens/May 22/97

[Inscribed on a photograph of Cora in war correspondent's field dress]

To me old pal Stevie with best wishes—   *Imogene Carter*

198. TO MR. HARRIS [99]

London/June, 1897

[Inscribed in a copy of *The Third Violet*]

Dear Mr. Harris: This book is even worse than any of the others.

Stephen Crane

✿   ✿   ✿

The Cranes Go to England

Crane and Cora, whose husband had refused her a divorce, remained unmarried this summer and fall. In September, when they were in Ireland with Harold Frederic and Kate Lyon (who for similar reasons could not marry), Henry Sanford Bennett received a letter—dated September 2 from Paris—announcing Crane's marriage to Cora. Our conjecture is that some friend had posted it there for him, as a ruse to comfort the conventionally-minded Bennett, who had been with Crane and Cora on the Channel crossing.

✿   ✿   ✿

199. TO HENRY SANFORD BENNETT

(Paris, France; September 2, 1897)

. . . Frederic and Mr. Heinemann have been urging me to stay in England for a time. So my wife—after practicing nine days I can write that without a jump—and I will be hunting a house or an attic in London pretty soon.[100]

---

[99] A friend of Harold Frederic [Frank Harris?]. *The Third Violet* was published in May by Heinemann in England and by Appleton in New York.

[100] In early July they took a house called Ravensbrook at Oxted, Surrey. It was not far from Harold Frederic's place, Homefield, at Kenley; and within a few miles at Limpsfield, the Cearne, lived the Garnetts. Here also the Conrads visited the Cranes. In August, 1897, the London *Bookman* announced: "Mr. Stephen Crane has settled down in this country for an indefinite period."

200. TO PAUL REVERE REYNOLDS [101]

[Ravensbrook, Oxted, Surrey, October, 1897]

Dear Mr. Reynolds: Good: Now we can do something. I will allow you ten percent on the sales and refer everything to you, giving you the clear field which is your right. You will have the whole management as in the theatrical business.

Now one of the reasons of this thing is to get me out of the ardent grasp of the S. S. McClure Co. I owe them about $500, I think, and they seem to calculate on controlling my entire out-put. They have in their possession "The Monster" (21,000 words) and "The Bride Comes to Yellow Sky" (4500) both for the American rights alone.[102] The American rights alone of "The Monster" ought to pay them easily, minus your commission. No; perhaps it wouldn't pay them fully but it would pay them a decent amount of it. Then the American rights of "The Bride"—I judge to be worth $175.

As for my existing contracts there are only two. I. To write an article on an engine ride from London to Glasgow for the McClures. II. To give them my next book. Of course these would go on as if I had not called in your assistance.

Robert McClure here in London told me he thought you had "The Monster" in New York but I judge, if that were so, that you would have mentioned it in your letter this morning. I will write to Phillips [103] and ask him to let you have it under the agreement that the money

There is no evidence (other than this doubtful letter) that Crane ever actually married Cora. That Eben Alexander, American Minister at Athens, mentioned "Mrs. Stewart" in writing Crane on July 14 indicates that Stephen had not married Cora in Greece. Two letters to Cora from her brother-in-law Sir Norman Robert Stewart, both written after Crane's death (March 9, 1901, and November 17, 1901), contain inferential evidence that she had not been successful during his lifetime in persuading her husband, Captain Stewart, to grant her a divorce to marry Crane. (These letters are in the Butler Library Crane Collection, and are reproduced in Lillian Gilkes' biography of Cora Crane.) H. G. Wells provides another parallel situation to that of Harold Frederic: factors, both, which may have influenced Crane to settle in England.

[101] Crane met Reynolds early in 1896, when *The Red Badge of Courage* suddenly swept the United States. He met him at a luncheon given by Irving Bacheller, and arranged then for Reynolds to be his literary agent.

[102] On September 9 Crane wrote his brother Edmund from Ireland: "Finished a novelette of 20,000 words—'The Monster.'" "The Bride Comes to Yellow Sky" was written at Ravensbrook during September or October, and by February, 1898, Crane had finished "The Blue Hotel."

[103] A partner in S. S. McClure Co.

minus your commission shall be paid to them. Then *if* the money for
"The Monster" goes far toward paying my debt, you can ask them
about "The Bride."

"The Bride Comes to Yellow Sky" is a daisy and don't let them
talk funny about it.

Now as for the newspaper business we can do large things. The
Herald pays me $100 per article of between 3000 and 4000 words. The
World has never paid me over $50 and expenses but could be brought
to $75 or $100, I think.[104] Now that of course is a big graft to play as
long as I am here in Europe. As for the *Journal* I have quite a big misunderstanding with them and can't get it pulled out straight. They say
I am over-drawn. I say I am not. I have sent them an installment of
my Irish Notes that I am doing here for the Westminster *Gazette* and
would send them more if it were possible to hear from them. I would
send you the Irish Notes and also my London Impressions from the
Saturday Review—for the *Journal*, if we could get some definite statement from them.[105] My idea was that they would go in with that stuff
on the editorial page. Twenty-five dollars per installment would be
enough. If the *Journal* will explain why they say I am over-drawn I
am the last man in the world to kick and will pay the a/c in work.

Then on the other hand instead of fooling with the big newspapers, here is another scheme. You might go to Curtis Brown, Sunday
Editor of the *Press* and say how-how from me. Then tell him this *in the
strictest confidence*, that a lady named Imogene Carter [106] whose work
he has been using from time to time is also named Stephen Crane and
that I did 'em in about twenty minutes on each Sunday, just dictating
to a friend. Of course they are rotten bad. But by your explanation he
will understand something of the manner of the articles I mean to
write only of course they will be done better. Ask him if he wants
them, signed and much better in style, and how much he will give.
Then if he says all right you might turn up a little syndicate for every
Sunday. You can figure out that I should get about £10 per week out
of it. Then—you do the business—I do the writing—I take 65 per cent
and you take 35. The typewriting expenses in New York we share alike.

---

104 Crane "got high prices for his work, at least £10 a thousand words,"
according to Cora in a letter written in late 1900, and occasionally as much
as £30.

105 Two of his "Irish Notes" were printed in the United States but not
until 1899 and then only in *The Philistine*. "London Impressions" appeared
in the London *Saturday Review* during July and August, 1897.

106 "Imogene Carter," "the first woman war correspondent" (Cora
Taylor).

You do a lot of correspondence, that's all—and keep your eyes peeled for new combinations.

Write me at once. Good luck to you. Yours very truly

Stephen Crane

201. TO WILLIAM CRANE

c/o William Heineman[n]/21 Bedford St., W.C./London
Sat., Oct. 29. [1897]

My dear William: I got your letter this morning. I have been wanting to write you for some time about the library but have been quite too busy. For my part I would gladly give to you power to choose my part of the library. Take an encyclopaedia and as many histories as possible and then let the others have a chance. It cant matter so much to me and I feel that I have not treated the others very fairly in the matter. If you go to Asbury Park, look up my two swords—I wore them at Claverack—and keep them for me.

I have been in England, Ireland, Scotland, Wales, France, Turkey and Greece. I have seen Italy but never trod it. Since I have been in England I have been in dreadfully hard luck. I have been here four months and one month I was laid up by the carriage accident. In the working three months I have earned close to 2000 dollars but the sum actually paid in to me has been only £20. 17s. 3d—about 120 dollars. In consequence I have had to borrow and feel very miserable indeed. I am not sure that I am not in trouble over it.

McClures, with security of over 1000 dollars against my liability of four hundred, refuse to advance me any money. And yet they think they are going to be my American publishers.

I am working now on a big novel.[107] It will be much much longer than The Red Badge. My next short thing after the novelette (The Monster) was The Bride Comes to Yellow Sky. All my friends come here say it is my very best thing. I am so delighted when I am told by competent people that I have made an advance. You know they said over here in England that The Open Boat (Scribner's) was my best thing. There seem so many of them in America who want to kill, bury and forget me purely out of unkindness and envy and—my unworthiness, if you choose. All the hard things they say of me affect me principally because I think of mine own people—you and Teddie [Ed-

---

[107] *Active Service,* begun at the suggestion of Harold Frederic but put aside; finished the next year in Havana, except for the last chapters, which had to be rewritten. It was published in 1899. In his letter to Reynolds in December, 1897, Crane says that his new Greek novel is not yet begun (*contra* Beer, p. 328).

mund] and the families. It is nothing, bless you. Now Dick Davis [108] for instance has come to like the abuse. He accepts it as a tribute to his excellence. But he is a fool. Now I want you to promise to never pay any attention to it, even in your thought. It is too immaterial and foolish. Your little brother is neither braggart or a silent egotist but he knows that he is going on steadily to make his simple little place and he cant be stopped, he cant even be retarded. He is coming.

Sometimes I think you and old Ted worry about me and you may well worry! I have managed my success like a fool and a child but then it is difficult to succeed gracefully at 23. However I am learning every day. I am slowly becoming a man. My idea is to come finally to live at Port Jervis or Hartwood. I am a wanderer now and I must see enough but—afterwards—I think of P. J. & Hartwood.

Ted wrote to me that he wanted to go to Klondike. At least he hinted at a desire. In less than a week, I happened to get a letter from the Bachellers asking me to go there. I do not believe there is exactly too much money in it for me but there will be enough to clear all heavy expenses and so I have accepted the offer in the hope that I may be able to do some small service to Ted—if he really means it.

I go to the Soudan in about a month. The English forces are surely going to Khartoom [sic]. Perhaps I may be able to write you from there.[109] That would be nice. I wanted badly to go to India to see the frontier row there but English papers discouraged me. They said it would be all over before I could get there. That was eight weeks ago and the war is still in full blast. The Afridis have thrashed the life out of the Englishmen on one or two occasions but we dont hear about it.[110] That is the Englishman's strong point. However I hope there will be some good fighting in the Soudan before long.

I am sorry about the arm. Perhaps, after a time, it will regain its

---

[108] Richard Harding Davis.

[109] Crane went neither to the Klondike nor to Khartoum. In July he had written his brother Edmund: "Expect to hear from me in the Soudan. The S. A. fight is off." The closest Crane ever got to Africa was in writing about it in his first short story or sketch, published while he was at Syracuse University, in the *University Herald*, May, 1891. The setting of this sketch, "The King's Favor," is British South Africa.

[110] Crane refers to the Tirah campaign under General Sir William Lockhart begun on October 18, 1897, against the Afridis, in the North-West Province of India. On October 20 the British forces in storming the Dargai heights lost 199 killed and wounded. Crane wrote up the campaign, or some portion of it, and sent Paul Reynolds, his literary agent in New York City, a thousand words for him to place with the *Press* or the *Journal* (see Letter 219).

strength. So Helen has a sweetheart? [111] I got her letter but she didn't mention it. That reminds me—my stamp collection! If Tounley [Townley, Crane's brother] hasn't hocked it, it is now valuable. He had a good claim on it in a way. He gave me the start and, afterward, contributed largely. Try to get it at Asbury Park. Give Helen charge of it and then she and I can be partners. She had better then get a good catalogue that gives valuations.

The Irish Notes [112] and so on, which appear in the Journal are written really for The Westminster Gazette and The Saturday Review.

I suppose it would be the proper thing for me to write long descriptions home of what I see over here but I write myself so completely out in articles that an attempt of the sort would be absurd.

I am just thinking how easy it would be in my present financial extremity to cable you for a hundred dollars but then by the time this reaches you I will probably be all right again. I believe the sum I usually borrowed was fifteen dollars, wasn't it? Fifteen dollars—fifteen dollars—fifteen dollars. I can remember an interminable row of fifteen dollar requests.

Tell Cornelia [113] I still refer to her as the most delicately perfect cook—upon a given material—of the world and I have dined in all the best places of Paris and England. Give her my steadfast love.

I should like to see this famous pony. It appears to me that Edna might write and describe it. Your loving brother   S.

* * *

Joseph Conrad

Crane did not meet Conrad until October, although he had asked about him immediately on arrival in London from New York in March. At that time he first met Harold Frederic; Conrad was the other person he hoped to meet in England. In October S. S. Pawling of the publishing firm of William Heinemann took Crane and Conrad to luncheon. The two tramped the streets all afternoon from Green Park to Kensington Gardens and, after stopping for tea, resumed their stroll

---

[111] Helen, William's daughter, was about sixteen. She later visited Crane at Brede Place. She died in the spring of 1921.

[112] Only two of the four "Irish Notes" have been traced as having appeared anywhere but in The Philistine in 1899.

[113] William Crane's wife. Cora Taylor was also a wonderful cook. Among Crane's British guests (including Henry James) she was famous for her biscuits.

through uncharted mazes of streets to Tottenham Court and finally to Monico's for late night supper and chitchat about Balzac and his *Comédie Humaine*. Conrad records that they parted "with just a hand-shake and a goodnight—no more—without making any arrangements for meeting again, as though we had lived in the same town from child-hood and were sure to run across each other next day. It struck me directly I left him that we had not even exchanged addresses; but I was not uneasy. Sure enough, before the month was out there arrived a postcard [from Ravensbrook] asking whether he might come to see us." [114] On November 9 Conrad sent him an inscribed copy of his first novel, *Almayer's Folly*, and Crane—before he had received it—wrote Conrad on the eleventh.

❋   ❋   ❋

202. A CONRAD INSCRIPTION

9th Nov. 1897

[In a copy of *Almayer's Folly*] [115]

To Stephen Crane with the greatest regard and most sincere admiration from
                                                          Jph Conrad

203. TO JOSEPH CONRAD

Ravensbrook,/Nov 11 [1897]

My dear Conrad,/ My first feat has been to lose your note and so I am obliged to send this through Heineman [*sic*]. I have read the proof sheets which you so kindly sent me and the book is simply great. [116]

---

[114] See Conrad's introduction to Beer's *Stephen Crane* (1923) and in Beer's *Hanna, Crane, and the Mauve Decade* (1941), or the shorter version of this memoir in *Notes on Life and Letters* (1921), first published in 1919: "Stephen Crane: A Note Without Dates." On Conrad's friendship with Crane see also Jessie Conrad, *Joseph Conrad and His Circle* (1935), and "Recollections of Stephen Crane," *Bookman*, April, 1926.

[115] Cora Crane wrote on the flyleaf: "This book belongs to Mrs. Stephen Crane, 6 Milborne Grove, Boltons, South Kensington, 1898." She lived in this rented house with her friend Mrs. Brotherton after Crane's death, from September, 1900, until near the end of April, 1901, when she returned to the United States to stay.

[116] *The Nigger of the "Narcissus,"* begun in the autumn of 1896 and finished February 19, 1897, appeared in Henley's *New Review* that year and in book form in December. It was on the ground of the *Nigger* that Crane wanted to meet Conrad, and Conrad—already familiar with *The Red Badge*—considered Crane "as eminently fit to pronounce a judgment on my first consciously planned attempt to render the truth of a phase of life in

The simple treatment of the death of Waite [sic] is too good, too terrible. I wanted to forget it at once. It caught me very hard. I felt ill over that red thread lining from the corner of the man's mouth to his chin. It was frightful with the weight of a real and present death. By such small means does the real writer suddenly flash out in the sky above those who are always doing rather well. In the meantime I have written to Bacheller and told him to be valiant in the matter of "The Nigger"—I have also written some other little notes to America.

I am afraid you must write to me soon so that I can finally nail your address and put it away in my little book. I was very stupid. Are you quite sure you could not come down for a Sunday luncheon with Mrs Conrad? Say your own date, barring this next one. We could then keep you as long as you would stay.

Did not we have a good pow-wow in London? Faithfully yours
Stephen Crane

204. TO HENRI D. DAVRAY [117]

Ravensbrook,/Nov 11. [1897]

Dear Sir: I am today taking the liberty of sending you a copy of a little book of mine—The Black Riders—in hopes that some happy accident will persuade you to read it. My importunity is not without it's darker side. My dearest wish is to see these simples translanted [sic] into French.[118] Some of my other books have recieved [sic] German and Russian translations but, let alone translations, the British public nor even my own American public will not look at The Black Riders.

---

the terms of my own temperament with all the sincerity of which I was capable." Crane, having read the *Nigger* serially in the *New Review*, wrote Hamlin Garland about it (see Letter 207).

On a visit in late November Harold Frederic quarreled with Crane about Conrad's *Nigger*. Beer (p. 330) reports that Crane crashed his revolver down upon a dessert plate and yelled: "You and I and Kipling couldn't have written the Nigger!" (See Letter 208, n. 123.)

[117] Henri D. Davray, reviewer for the *Mercure de France* (Paris), gave favorable notice of Conrad's *The Nigger of the "Narcissus"* in the London *Daily Telegraph*, December 8, 1897. With Francis Vielé Griffin, Davray translated *The Red Badge* under the title *La Conquête du Courage* (Paris: Mercure de France, 1911).

[118] There is no record of a French translation. Alain Bosquet in *Anthologie de la Poèsie Americaine des Origènes à Nos Jours* (1956) introduced three Crane poems in translation with the note: This "poète concis et rageur, est de ceux qui ont fait le plus pour dénoncer l'absurdité d'un monde matérialiste; il n'est pas sans rappeler Corbière et LaForgue" (Daniel G. Hoffman, *The Poetry of Stephen Crane* [1957], p. 31).

Thus my letter to you is in the nature of an appeal. I wish the distinction of appearing just for a moment to the minds of a few of your great and wise artistic public. I do not know if this will appear absurd to you. At any rate, I send you the book. You will tell me? Perchance, there would be a publisher who would print it. What I wish is the distinction. My American publishers, who own the copyrights, would readily agree. I hope I do not bore you too much? If you reply to this letter I shall be delighted. Faithfully yours   *Stephen Crane*

205. *JOSEPH CONRAD TO STEPHEN CRANE*
Stanford-le-Hope/Essex 16th Nov. 1897

My Dear Crane,/ I must write to you before I write a single word for a living to-day. I was anxious to know what you would think of the end. If I've hit you with the death of Jimmy [119] I don't care if I don't hit another man. I think however that artistically the end of the book is somewhat lame. I mean after the death. All that rigmarole about the burial and the ship's coming home seems to run away into a rat's tail—thin at the end. Well! It's too late now to bite my thumbs and tear my hair. When I feel depressed about it I say to myself "Crane likes the damned thing"—and am greatly consoled. What your appreciation is to me I renounce to explain. The world looks different to me now, since our long powwow. It was good. The memory of it is good. And now and then (human nature *is* a vile thing) I ask myself whether you meant half of what you said! You must forgive me. The mistrust is not of you—it is of myself: the drop of poison in the cup of life. I am no more vile than my neighbours but this disbelief in oneself is like a taint that spreads on everything one comes in contact with: on men—on things—on the very air one breathes. That's why one sometimes wishes to be a stone breaker. There's no doubt about breaking a stone. But there's doubt, fear—a black horror, in every page one writes. You at any rate will understand and therefore I write to you as though we had been born together before the beginning of things. For what you have done and intend to do I won't even attempt to thank you. I certainly don't know what to say, tho' I am perfectly certain as to what I feel.

I know it is perfectly right and proper from a ceremonial point of view that I should come to you first. But, my dear fellow, it's impossible. My wife is not presentable just now. And, joking apart, I wouldn't dare let her undertake a journey—even of the shortest. As to myself I would come speedily and I shall come as soon as I can get away with a free mind. Meantime show your condescension by coming to me first.

---

[119] James Wait in *The Nigger of the "Narcissus."*

After this week I haven't any engagements. Just drop a postcard say-ing *I'm coming* and I shall meet the train from Fenchurch Street. You have trains at *11.20 am 1.45 pm 3.28 pm 5.5 pm 5.53 pm 8.13 pm*. Last train to town at night is at *8* arrives in London at *9.30*. But we can put you up in a bachelor's quarters. I should love to have you under my roof. And come soon for when the circus begins here and the house is full of doctors and nurses there will be no place for the poor literary man. Finish to catch the post. Ever yours   *Jph. Conrad*

206. TO EDWARD GARNETT [120]

Ravensbrook,/Nov 16 [1897]

Dear Mr. Garnett:/ I am sorry that I could not get over to you on Tuesday [121] and sorry too that I have let so much time pass without saying so. Will you come over to luncheon at two on Sunday? Faith-fully yours   *Stephen Crane*

207. HAMLIN GARLAND TO STEPHEN CRANE

23 Grammercy [*sic*] Park [New York City]/Nov. 29/97.

Dear Mr. Crane: I was very glad to hear from you and from Mr Con-rad. I wish you had written another page to tell me how you were getting on and what you intended to do. I heard you were to make your home in England but this I take to be somebody's lie. I shall not believe it till you write and tell me so.

Mr Conrad's work is not known to me, I am sorry to say, but I shall be all the more delighted to have a copy of the book you speak of. Beeman now has some five of my books. What do you hear of them there? Is he considered a good publisher?

Dont let yourself lie fallow. I do not see much of you lately—This is good if you are working on some large thing. With best word. Yours sincerely   *Hamlin Garland*

208. CORA CRANE TO HENRY SANFORD BENNETT

[Ravensbrook, November 29, 1897]

As Stephen is asleep I have taken the liberty of opening your telegram. Will you do a distracted wife a favour? I know that Stephen wants to see you as soon as possible. But we have been overwhelmed with call-

---

[120] English critic and friend of Conrad. His essay "Stephen Crane: An Appreciation" in the *Academy*, December 17, 1898, together with H. G. Wells's appraisal of 1900 are among the best critical studies of Crane during the two decades, 1895–1915.

[121] Tuesday is today; next Sunday is the twenty-first.

ers all week. He is desperately trying to finish a story.[122] Just this morning a literary boy who lives in the neighbourhood imposed himself on us from 9 to 4![123] So I am not going to tell Stephen that Mrs. Bennett and you have arrived in London. Please telegraph or write again, day after tomorrow. I know this is rude. . . .

209. AN AMERICAN LAWYER [124]

[November 30, 1897]

Mr. [John] Stokes [125] gave me a note of introduction to Mr. Crane and he was very pleasant in a quiet, boyish way when I got to his house. It surprised me how little he uses slang when his books are full of it and how young he is. Mrs. Crane asked me to stay for lunch. She is a southerner [126] and very nice. I should imagine her to be six or seven years older than Mr. Crane with big blue eyes and reddish hair. Mr. Frederic, the New York *Times* correspondent came in the middle of the lunch with five other men and it was very embarrassing for Mrs. Crane as they were not expected. Mr. Frederic is not at all agreeable. He is funny in a sarcastic way about politics and people but he kept interrupting everybody else and was downright rude to Mr. Crane several times. They made Mr. Crane shoot with his revolver after

---

[122] "Death and the Child," a story drawn from his Greco-Turkish War experiences. Crane slept late this morning, having returned from Stanford-le-Hope, where on Sunday, November 28, he visited Conrad (see Letter 213).

[123] As Letter 209 shows, Harold Frederic brought five men next day—November 30—uninvited at lunchtime. A few days later—Beer says "early in December"—Frederic quarreled with Crane over Conrad's *The Nigger of the "Narcissus,"* then appearing in the *New Review,* and Crane's own story "The Monster." At this quarrel Sanford Bennett was present, according to Beer's account (p. 330); and in Berryman's version of this episode (p. 205) it also appears that Bennett and his wife were guests one or two days at Ravensbrook. Among other visitors on November 30 was an American lawyer who describes the occasion in Letter 209. Then Crane fled to London on December 1 and locked himself in a hotel room in order to finish "Death and the Child" (see Letter 211). The visit of the Bennetts and the quarrel with Frederic probably took place soon after his return to Ravensbrook.

Frederic wrote an unsigned review of *The Nigger of the "Narcissus"* in the *Saturday Review,* LXXXV (1898).

[124] The American lawyer, writing his wife an account of his visit, is unidentified by Beer (pp. 330 ff.).

[125] Cousin of the Duke of Norfolk.

[126] She was born in Boston, and was five or six years older than Crane. Born 1865 (not 1868, as given on her tombstone in Evergreen Cemetery in Jacksonville, Florida), she died in 1910.

lunch and he is a fine shot.[127] Some children came over from the next house to watch and Mrs. Crane made biscuit for tea. She is a wonderful cook.

210. JOSEPH CONRAD TO STEPHEN CRANE

[Stanford-le-Hope] 1st Dec. 1897.

My Dear Crane:/ Glad to hear you haven't had your head taken off. We had here on Monday a high tide that smashed the sea-wall, flooded the marshes and washed away the Rwy line. Great excitement.

But *my* great excitement was reading your stories. Garnett's right. *A Man and Some Others* [128] is immense. I can't spin a long yarn about it but I admire it without reserve. It is an amazing bit of biography. I am envious of you—horribly. Confound you—you fill the blamed landscape—you—by all the devils—fill the sea-scape. The boat thing [129] is immensely interesting. I don't use the word in its common sense. It is fundamentally interesting to me. Your temperament makes old things new and new things amazing. I want to swear at you, to bless you—perhaps to shoot you—but I prefer to be your friend.

You are an everlasting surprise to one. You shock—and the next moment you give the perfect artistic satisfaction. Your method is fascinating. You are a complete impressionist.[130] The illusions of life come out of your hand without a flaw. It is not life—which nobody wants—it is art—art for which everyone—the abject and the great—hanker—mostly without knowing it. Ever yours,   *Jph. Conrad*

---

[127] Ford Madox Ford (the novelist and friend of Conrad, Henry James, and Edward Garnett) was a nearby neighbor at Limpsfield and called on Crane this fall. "I can see him sitting in the singularly ugly drawing room of the singularly hideous villa he lived in for a time at Oxted. Then he wore —I dare say to shock me—cowboy breeches and no coat, and all the time he was talking he wagged in his hand an immense thing that he called a gun and that we should call a revolver. From time to time he would attempt to slay with the bead-sight of this Colt such flies as settled on the table, and a good deal of his conversation would be taken up with fantastic boasts about what can be done with these lethal instruments. . . . And Crane in those days, and for my benefit, was in the habit of posing as an almost fabulous Billy the Kid, just as later, to épater Henry James, he insisted on posing as, and exaggerating the characteristics of, a Bowery boy of the most hideous type" (New York *Herald Tribune Books,* January 2, 1927, p. 1).

[128] In the *Century,* February, 1897 (see Letter 175, n. 76).

[129] "The Open Boat," in *Scribner's Magazine,* June, 1897.

[130] Conrad repeats this insight in Letter 213.

211. TO AN UNKNOWN RECIPIENT [131]

[London, December 3, 1897]

I have been staying at this hotel two days so as to finish some work. Cora just now wires me that she has got rid of some people who have been boarding with us for three days, so I can go home.

212. TO ACTON DAVIES

[Ravensbrook,/Sunday, Dec. 5? 1897]

. . . Will you see if X and Y could let me have what they borrowed last May? I took X's note for $300 and Y owes me about $250. I hate to press nice fellows but it costs me more to live over here than I was led to believe and some of these Comanche braves seem to think I am running a free lunch counter. Seven men have been staying over Sunday.[132]

213. JOSEPH CONRAD TO EDWARD GARNETT

[Stanford-le-Hope] 5th Dec. 1897

My dear Garnett,/ The *Nigger* came out to-day I believe but is not advertised in the *Sat. Review*. As soon as I get my copies I shall forward a specimen to the Cearne.

I had Crane here last Sunday. We talked and smoked half the night. He is strangely hopeless about himself. I like him. The two stories are excellent. Of course, "A Man and Some Others" is the best of the two but the boat thing ["The Open Boat"] interested me more. His eye is very individual and his expression satisfies me artistically. He certainly is *the* impressionist and his temperament is curiously unique. His thought is concise, connected, never very deep—yet often startling. He is *the only* impressionist and *only* an impressionist.[133]

---

[131] Sanford Bennett?

[132] Acton Davies in New York collected nothing from Crane's friends. Crane's business affairs were by now muddled, and he had been driven into debt by his overgenerosity in affording hosts of hangers-on the hospitality of Ravensbrook and in loaning them money. "Money Crane desperately needed, affluent as he might seem to these harpies; for the rest, letters, written in his clear round backhand script, reveal his optimism in the full tide of creative work. He was writing, writing, writing, and though the debt collector was always just around the corner, he saw prosperity as surely ahead" (Frederick Lewis Allen, *Paul Revere Reynolds* [1944]).

[133] Edward Garnett defined Crane as an impressionist in the *Academy* (1898), and Conrad in "A Note Without Dates" wrote of Crane in 1919: "His impressionism of phrase went really deeper than the surface. In his

Why is he not immensely popular? With his strength, with his rapidity of action, with that amazing faculty of vision—why is he not? He has outline, he has colour, he has movement, with that he ought to go very far. But—will he? I sometimes think he won't. It is not an opinion—it is a feeling. I could not explain why he disappoints me—why my enthusiasm withers as soon as I close the book. While one reads, of course he is not to be questioned. He is the master of his reader to the very last line—then—apparently for no reason at all—he seems to let go his hold. It is as if he had gripped you with greased fingers. His grip is strong but while you feel the pressure on your flesh you slip out from his hand—much to your own surprise. This is my stupid impression and I give it to you in confidence. It just occurs to me that it is perhaps my own self that is slippery. I don't know. You would know. No matter.

My soul is like a stone within me. I am going through the awful experience of losing a friend. Hope [134] comes every evening to console me but he has a hopeless task. Death is nothing—and I am used to its rapacity. But when life robs one of a man to whom one has pinned one's faith for twenty years the wrong seems too monstrous to be lived down. Yet it must. And I don't know why, how, wherefore. Besides there are circumstances which make the event a manifold torment. Some day I will tell you the tale. I can't write it now. But there is a psychological point in it. However this also does not matter.

The *Nigger* is ended and the *New Review* stops. I suppose you've heard already. Henley printed the Preface at the end as an Author's Note. It does not shine very much, but I am glad to see it in type. This is all the news. No criticisms have appeared as yet. I am trying to write the *Rescuer* [135] and all my ambition is to make it good enough for a magazine—readable, in a word. I doubt whether I can. I struggle without pleasure like a man certain of defeat. Drop me a line.

214. TO PAUL REVERE REYNOLDS

[Ravensbrook, December, 1897]

Dear Reynolds: I send you the child story of the Greek business.[136]

---

writing he was very sure of his effects. I don't think he was ever in doubt about what he could do. Yet it often seemed to me that he was but half aware of the exceptional quality of his achievement" (*Notes on Life and Letters* [1921]).

[134] His friend, Captain G. F. W. Hope.

[135] Not published until 1920 and then entitled *The Rescue—A Romance of the Shallows*.

[136] "Death and the Child," published in *Harper's Weekly*, March 19, 1898.

McClure has a call on it. He should give $300 for it—at least. The English rights are sold.

I have made a proposition to McClure that he advance £200 on the 1st of January for the book rights of my new Greek novel—not yet begun.[137] If he takes that offer he may want to hold back on payment for this story. I wouldn't have done it if I was not broke. For heaven's sake raise me all the money you can and *cable* it, *cable* it sure between Xmas and New Year's. Sell "The Monster"! [138] Don't forget that—cable me some money this month.   S. C.

215. JOSEPH CONRAD TO STEPHEN CRANE

Stanford-le-Hope/24th Dec. 1897

My Dear Crane,/ Just a word to wish—from us both—to you and Mrs. Crane all imaginable prosperity and all the happiness that may be found in this merry world.

How are you getting on? I struggle along feeling pretty sick of it all. The New Year does not announce itself very brightly for me—and that's a fact. Well! A bad beginning may make a good ending tho' I don't believe it much.

Criticisms (!) are coming in. Some praise, some blame, both very stupid. Yours ever   *Jph. Conrad*

P.S. Have you seen the *Daily Tele.* article by that ass Courtney? [139] He does not understand you—and he does not understand me either. It is the most *mean-minded* criticism I've read in my life. That's a feather in our caps, anyhow. Do you think I tried to imitate you? No Sir! I may be a little fool but I know better than to try to imitate the inimita-

---

[137] *Active Service.*

[138] This was rejected by the *Century*, Richard Watson Gilder protesting to Paul Reynolds: "We couldn't publish that thing with half the expectant mothers in America on our subscription list!" (Beer, p. 329.)

[139] *The Daily Telegraph*, December 8, reviewed *The Nigger*, which had appeared in *The New Review*, XVII (1897), from August through December, and Courtney's claim of Crane's influence on Conrad's novel was repeated the next year when the serialized narrative was printed in book form. *The Speaker* (1898) compared *The Nigger of the "Narcissus"* to *The Red Badge of Courage* as "a worthy pendant" and joined Conrad and Crane to "a whole school of descriptive writers of a new class, who aspire to make visible . . . the inside of great scenes" (John D. Gordan, *Joseph Conrad* [1941], p. 287). Crane's influence is seen not only in *The Nigger* but also in *Lord Jim.*

ble. But here it is. Courtney says it. You are a lost sinner and you have led me astray. If it was true I would be well content to follow you but it isn't true. Three cheers for the Press! Your   *J. C.*

216. TO JOHN NORTHERN HILLIARD

[Ravensbrook, 1897?]

. . . I have only one pride—and may it be forgiven me. This single pride is that the English edition of "The Red Badge" has been received with praise by the English reviewers. Mr. George Wyndham, Under Secretary for War in the British Government, says, in an essay, that the book challenges comparison with the most vivid scenes of Tolstoi's "War and Peace" or of Zola's "Downfall"; and the big reviews here praise it for just what I intended it to be, a psychological portrayal of fear.[140] They all insist that I am a veteran of the civil war, whereas the fact is, as you know, I never smelled even the powder of a sham battle. I know what the psychologists say, that a fellow can't comprehend a condition that he has never experienced, and I argued that many times with the Professor. Of course, I have never been in a battle, but I believe that I got my sense of the rage of conflict on the football field, or else fighting is a hereditary instinct, and I wrote intuitively; for the Cranes were a family of fighters in the old days, and in the Revolution every member did his duty. But be that as it may, I endeavored to express myself in the simplest and most concise way. If I failed, the fault is not mine. I have been very careful not to let any theories or pet ideas of my own creep into my work. Preaching is fatal to art in literature. I try to give to readers a slice out of life; and if there is any moral or lesson in it, I do not try to point it out. I let the

---

[140] In *The New Review*, January, 1896, Wyndham called Crane a great artist and *The Red Badge* "a remarkable book." "Mr. Crane's picture of war is more complete than Tolstoi's, more true than Zola's." Crane dipped into Zola's *Débâcle* sometime before writing his own war novel, but he never finished reading it. He disliked Zola's statistical realism and Tolstoi's panoramic method. He found *Peace and War* (as he called it) tiresome: "He could have done the whole business in one third the time and made it just as wonderful. It goes on and on like Texas." *Anna Karenina* was "too long," and Tolstoi stopped to preach. Nevertheless, Tolstoi was the writer he most admired. "I think Tolstoy greater than any other novelist because he is a greater artist. His morality is simply that of Christ" (*Omnibus*, p. 181).

Beer (p. 380) reports Crane telling Mark Barr: "You can never do anything good aesthetically—and you can never do anything with anything that's any good except aesthetically—unless it has at one time meant something important to you."

reader find it for himself. The result is more satisfactory to both the reader and myself. As Emerson said, "There should be a long logic beneath the story, but it should be kept carefully out of sight." Before "The Red Badge of Courage" was published, I found it difficult to make both ends meet. The book was written during this period. It was an effort born of pain, and I believe that it was beneficial to it as a piece of literature. It seems a pity that this should be so—that art should be a child of suffering; and yet such seems to be the case.[141] Of course there are fine writers who have good incomes and live comfortably and contentedly; but if the conditions of their lives were harder, I believe that their work would be better. Bret Harte is an example. He has not done any work in recent years to compare with those early California sketches. Personally, I like my little book of poems, "The Black Riders," better than I do "The Red Badge of Courage." The reason is, I suppose, that the former is the more ambitious effort. In it I aim to give my ideas of life as a whole, so far as I know it, and the latter is a mere episode, or rather an amplification. Now that I have reached the goal, I suppose that I ought to be contented; but I am not. I was happier in the old days when I was always dreaming of the thing I have now attained. I am disappointed with success, and I am tired of abuse. Over here, happily, they don't treat you as if you were a dog, but give every one an honest measure of praise or blame. There are no disgusting personalities.

217. TO JAMES GIBBONS HUNEKER [142]

[Ravensbrook, December ? 1897]

. . . They [Englishmen] will believe anything wild or impossible you

---

[141] Writing Clarence Loomis Peaslee (Letter 62), Crane expressed the same dictum: "There is a great deal of labor connected with literature. I think that is the hardest thing about it." Here too he echoes himself in saying that "I endeavored to express myself in the simplest and most concise way," for in his letter to Peaslee of 1895 he wrote: "I always want to be unmistakable. That to my mind is good writing." This in turn repeats what Crane wrote to Hilliard in an early letter, and again his view of the creative process as involving "an effort born of pain" is differently phrased in Letter 111 to an editor of *Leslie's Weekly*.

[142] American music critic and writer. A friend of Crane, Huneker never dealt in his criticism with Crane's works nor mentioned him in his correspondence with other friends. In the *Musical Courier* for June 13, 1900, Huneker wrote: "I knew Stephen Crane who died last week. He was a good fellow and a promising writer." Huneker added that Crane lacked "the sustaining power or formal gifts of Frank Norris," a viewpoint with a measure of truth; but Crane in what works he achieved far surpasses Norris. That

tell them and then if you say your brother has a bathtub in his house they—ever so politely—call you a perjured falsifier of facts. I told a seemingly sane man at Mrs. Garnett's that I got my artistic education on the Bowery and he said, "Oh, really? So they have a school of fine arts there?" I had, you see, just told Mrs. Garnett [143] while this mummy listened all about the Bowery—in so far as I could tell a woman about the Bowery—but that made no difference to this John Bull. Now I am going to wave the starry flag of freedom a little even if you contemn the practice in one who knows not Balzac and Dostoywhat'shisname. You Indians have been wasting wind in telling me how "Unintrusive" and "DELICATE" I would find English manners. I don't. It has not yet been the habit of people I meet at Mr. Howells or Mr. Phillips or Mrs. Sonntag's to let fall my hand and begin to quickly ask me how much money I make and from which French realist I shall steal my next book. For it has been proven to me fully and carefully by authority that all my books are stolen from the French. They stand me against walls with a teacup in my hand and tell me how I have stolen all my things from De Maupassant, Zola, Loti and the bloke who wrote —I forget the book.[144]

Huneker was ignorant of Crane's artistry and achievement and did not take him seriously except as a café companion is indicated by his lukewarm appraisal: Crane would have written a strong book someday!

[143] Constance Garnett, wife of the literary critic Edward Garnett, was the translator who pioneered in bringing the great Russian writers to the English reading public. Her translations included works of Tolstoi, Turgenev, Dostoevski, Gogol, and Chekhov.

[144] Garnett insisted that Crane must have read French authors, and Crane replied, "I never read a word of French in my life." But he admitted, when Garnett asked him about Maupassant, that he had read Henry James's critical essays on the French authors. Beer quotes a letter Crane wrote to a woman, discussing Zola's *Nana*: "This girl in Zola is a real streetwalker. I mean, she does not fool around making excuses for her career. You must pardon me if I cannot agree that every painted woman on the streets of New York was brought there by some evil man. Nana, in the story, is honest. . . . Zola is a sincere writer but—is he much good? He hangs one thing to another and his story goes along but I find him pretty tiresome" (Beer, p. 318.)

Crane, writing somebody and in much the same literary vein as here to Huneker, reported on the literary figures of London: Oscar Wilde is "a mildewed chump. He has a disease and they all gas about him as though there was a hell and he came up out of it. . . . Mr. Yeats is the only man I have met who talks of Wilde with any sense. The others talk like a lot of little girls at a Sunday School party when a kid says a wicked word in a corner" (Beer, p. 327).

"I should say that Mr. Wells will write better and better when he sticks to characters altogether and does not so much concern himself with narrative. I may be wrong but it seems to me that he has a genius for writing of underclass people more honestly than Charles Dickens. . . . I will bet all my marbles and my best top that Walter Besant is forgotten in twenty years. . . . Every one tells me that Mr. [Robert Louis] Stevenson was a fine fellow but nothing on earth could move me to change my belief that most of his work was insincere" (Beer, pp. 379–80). On October 12, 1897, Crane wrote somebody: "I believe in ghosts. Mr. Stevenson has not passed away far enough. He is all around town" (Beer, p. 326).

4

THE LETTERS in this section continue the Conrad friendship begun in 1897 and the relationship with Crane's literary agent in New York City, Paul Revere Reynolds. They see into print "The Monster," "The Blue Hotel," "The Price of the Harness," and many other works. In April Crane left England for Cuba to report on the Spanish-American War, and Cora during his absence was faced with financial problems as Crane sent her nothing.

Harold Frederic, the American novelist, had a house on the coast of Ireland, loaned him by a wealthy admirer, and Cora visited Harold and Kate Lyon there. Then in June she visited Brede Place,[1] a fourteenth-century manor house owned by Clara (Mrs. Moreton) Frewen, one of the three celebrated Jerome sisters and aunt of Sir Winston Churchill; Cora began arrangements for renovation and rental of the house from the Frewens at a nominal sum. But Stephen lingered on in Havana all summer and fall; he did not reach England until the second week of January, 1899.

Conrad was enthusiastic about "The Price of the Harness," which appeared in December in *Blackwood's Edinburgh Magazine,* and Edward Garnett, literary critic and friend of Conrad and of Moreton Frewen, published an important study of Crane's artistry in the *Academy* this December: "Stephen Crane: An Appreciation."

At Brede Place Crane spent the last full year of his short life. Financial troubles and ill-health continued to plague him. He was

---

[1] Clara Frewen, according to her daughter Clare Sheridan, had fallen in love with Brede Place and bought it from her husband's elder brother, Sir Richard Frewen (Clare Sheridan, *To the Four Winds* [André Deutsch, London, 1957], p. 23).

threatened with bankruptcy and tried desperately to write himself out of debt, but he never succeeded. He began writing three types of stories: Whilomville stories of childhood, war tales, and tales of Western American life similar to "Twelve O'Clock." "You grumble at the English market," James B. Pinker (Crane's London literary agent) wrote him, "but it has not yet had a fair chance. It won't be sluggish when you give it what it wants and a reasonable time" (Letter 286). By the end of April, 1899, Crane finished twenty-two chapters of *Active Service*, which he had written mainly in a first draft while in Cuba. By the end of August he completed the war tales, comprising *Wounds in the Rain* and had written most of *Great Battles of the World*.

War Is Kind, his second book of poems, was published in 1899. He undertook contracts for a novel on the American Revolution, a work he abandoned for a satirical romance of old Ireland, *The O'Ruddy*. He visited the Continent and Ireland. In October he was desperate again for money, although he produced for Pinker an incredible number of short stories for the sixpenny magazines, an output in fact so large that Pinker warned him not to dump too many on the market for fear of spoiling it. On November 4 Crane sent Pinker a masterpiece, "The Upturned Face."

The year ended with a house party at Christmastime. Henry James, George Gissing, Joseph Conrad, and H. G. Wells contributed to the writing of a play, "The Ghost," and autographed a program commemorating this event. James, Gissing, Conrad, and Robert Barr were not among the guests; but Wells, H. B. Marriott-Watson, A. E. W. Mason, and Edwin Pugh were at the party, which Wells remembered as "an extraordinary lark." Crane paid all the expenses of "The Ghost" production, which had a tryout at the Brede Hill Schoolhouse. This house party was the last occasion for any merriment at Brede Place; before the guests departed, Stephen had a hemorrhage of the lungs. Cora concealed the truth from all but Wells. It was the beginning of the end.

❊   ❊   ❊

218. JOSEPH CONRAD TO STEPHEN CRANE

[Stanford-le-Hope, Essex] Wednesday [January 12? 1898]

My dear Crane/ I hope you haven't been angry with me. Fact is my dear fellow I've been having a hell of a time—what with one thing and another.[2] Had I come that day I would have been no good at all. I am hardly yet in a decent frame of mind.

I am very curious to know your idea; [3] but I 'feel somehow that collaborating with you would be either cheating or deceiving you. In any case disappointing you. I have no dramatic gift. You have the terseness, the clear eye, the easy imagination. You have all—and I have only the accursed faculty of dreaming. My ideas fade—yours come out sharp cut as cameos—they come all living out of your brain and bring images—and bring light. Mine bring only mist in which they are born, and die. I would be only a hindrance to you—I am afraid. And it seems presumptuous of me to think of helping you. You want no help. I have a perfect confidence in your power—and why should you share with me what there may be of profit and fame in the accomplished task?

But I want to know! Your idea is good—I am certain. Perhaps you, yourself, don't know how good it is. I ask you as a friend's favour to let me have a sketch of it when you have the time and in a moment of inclination. I shall—if you allow me—write you *all* I think of it, about it, around it. Then you shall see how worthless I would be to you. But if by any chance such was not your deliberate opinion—if you should really, honestly, artistically think I could be of some use—then my dear Crane I would be only too glad to work by your side and with your lead. And quién sabe? Something perhaps would get itself shaped to be mangled by the scorn or the praise of the Philistines.

Take your time and answer me. My wife sends kind regards. We

---

[2] With writing *Lord Jim*, for one thing; Conrad had to keep up install-ments in *Blackwood's Magazine*.

[3] The idea of the proposed play consisted (Conrad relates in his intro-duction to Beer's *Stephen Crane*) "in a man personating his 'predecessor' (who had died) in the hope of winning a girl's heart. The scenes were to in-clude a ranch at the foot of the Rocky Mountains, I remember, and the action I fear would have been frankly melodramatic. Crane insisted that one of the situations should present the man and the girl on a boundless plain standing by their dead ponies after a furious ride (a truly Crane touch). I made some objections. A boundless plain in the light of a sunset could be got into a back-cloth, I admitted; but I doubted whether we could induce the management of any London theater to deposit two stuffed horses on its stage."

are standing by for a regular bust-up. It may come any day.[4] I can't write. The D'ly Mail has given a bad notice to the *Nigger*. There is no other news here. Yours ever   *Jph. Conrad*

This letter has been held back and now since I can't come I send it. My sister in law [5] must go away tomorrow, and I can't leave my wife all alone here.

Do write your idea. I am anxious. Yours   *J. C.*

219. TO PAUL REVERE REYNOLDS

[Ravensbrook] Jan. 14 [1898]

Dear Reynolds:/ I enclose you a thousand words on the Alfridi [Afridi] [6] business. It might go to the *Press* and be syndicated, or else to the *Journal*.

I received your letter yesterday and promptly cabled you that McClure was not concerned in the matter. When I sent him "The Monster" I owed him a lot of money but when I paid him up, I went to see Robert McClure here and he agreed that "The Monster" was released. He said he would inform the N.Y. office to that effect or even write the same to you, if I liked. I said I did like but it seems the affair was bungled. McClure's claim on the story was one which I gave him through courtesy and honor—no other. Your final manipulation of the novelette I consider very brilliant and I am sorry to see it handicapped by that Scotch ass.

In all the months I have been in England I have never received a cent from America which has not been borrowed. Just read that over twice! The consequences of this have lately been that I have been obliged to make arrangements here with English agents of American houses but in all cases your commission will be protected. This is the best I could do. My English expenses have chased me to the wall. Even now I am waiting for you to cable me my share of the Monster money and if there is a fluke I am lost.

Don't kick so conspicuously about the over-charge on the damned manuscripts. If I was a business man, I would not need a business man to conduct my affairs for me. I will try to do better but if I shouldn't, don't harangue me. The point is of minor importance.

---

[4] The birth of their first child, born January 15 (see Letter 220).

[5] Dolly, Mrs. Conrad's sister, whom Conrad described as "a young person with her hair down her back, and of extreme docility." She later stayed with the Conrads six months to help Mrs. Conrad.

[6] On the Afridi business see Letter 201. Publication of this article remains unidentified.

I have withheld the "Death and the Child" story from an English sale because I think you can hit one of the three big fellows with it. "The Five White Mice" is sold in England.[7] Faithfully yours,

Stephen Crane

220. JOSEPH CONRAD TO STEPHEN CRANE

[Stanford-le-Hope, Essex] 16th Jan 98

My Dear Crane/ Don't you bother about writing unless you feel like it. I quite understand how you feel about it—and am not likely to forget you because you don't write. Still mind that when you do write you give me a very great pleasure.

A male infant arrived yesterday [8] and made a devil of a row. He yelled like an Apache and ever since this morning has been on the warpath again. It's a ghastly nuisance.

Look here—when you are coming to town next time just fling a sixpence away on a wire (the day before) to me and I shall try to run up too. If detained shall wire care Heinemann. Ever yours   *Jph. Conrad*

Say—what about *The Monster*.[9] The damned story has been haunting me ever since. I think it must be fine. It's a subject for you.

221. JOSEPH CONRAD TO CORA CRANE

[Stanford-le-Hope, Essex] 25 Jan 98

Dear Mrs. Crane:/ My wife shall write as soon as she is allowed to sit up. Meantime let me send you our warmest thanks for the beautiful flowers and for your very kind invitation.

---

[7] *Harper's Weekly* published "Death and the Child" in March, 1898. "The Five White Mice" was printed in the New York *World*, April 10, 1898, and, with "Death and the Child," appeared in *The Open Boat and Other Stories*, published in England by Heinemann and in the United States by Doubleday & McClure (1898). Reynolds sold "The Monster" to *Harper's Magazine*, where it appeared in August, 1898.

[8] Conrad's first son, Borys, was so named because Conrad wanted to give him a purely Slavonic name "and yet easy for foreigners to pronounce and write." So he wrote Mme. Zagórska, his cousin in Poland, but Conrad, writing to her, misdates the birth of his son, "The child was born on the 17th of this month" (*Joseph Conrad: Life and Letters*, ed. G. Jean-Aubry [1927], I, 224–25).

[9] Crane must have outlined the story to Conrad. To Harold Frederic "The Monster" was offensive; he told Crane to throw it away (Beer, pp. 329–30).

I would hesitate to inflict myself upon you with the tribe—but since you call your fate upon your own head the temptation to please ourselves is too irresistible. So, all being well, we shall descend upon your peaceful homestead on the 19th.[10] I have grounds for hope that by that date my wife shall be able to travel. We shall meantime devote all our energies to the taming of the Baby lest he should break out and devastate your countryside, which, I feel, would put you and Crane in a false position vis-à-vis your neighbours. Perhaps a strong iron cage would be the most effective expedient; however we shall judge at the time the exact degree of his ferocity and act accordingly. . . .

The child is, I am sorry to say, absolutely callous to the honor awaiting him of his very first visit being to your house. I talked myself hoarse trying to explain to him the greatness of the occurrence—all in vain. I want Crane to give it his artistic benediction and call upon its head the spirit—the magnificent spirit that is his familiar—the genius of his work. And then when our writing days are over he who is a child today may write good prose—may toss a few pearls before the Philistines. I am dear Mrs. Crane your most obedient and faithful servant.   *Jph. Conrad*

222. JOSEPH CONRAD INSCRIPTION TO STEPHEN CRANE [11]

[Inscribed in a copy of *The Nigger of the "Narcissus"*(?)]

2 Feb. 1898

To/Stephen and M [*hole torn here*] with the author's/affectionate regard

223. JOSEPH CONRAD TO STEPHEN CRANE

[Stanford-le-Hope] 5th Febr. 98

Dear Stephen—/ We got home last night. Ever since I've left you I

---

[10] See Letter 226 on the Conrads' visit to the Cranes on Saturday, February 19. They visited the Garnetts on February 3–4 (see Letter 223). Cf. Jessie Conrad, "Recollections of Stephen Crane," *Bookman* (April, 1926), pp. 134 ff.

[11] Not signed, but in Conrad's handwriting. On the back of this flyleaf torn from an unidentified book Cora wrote an account of Conrad after the Cranes moved to Brede Place in Sussex:

"Joseph Conrad. Both these names are Christian names. . . . He is a Pole of noble family. His father died in Siberia and he was there when an infant with his mother. Their estates were confiscated. He was educated in France and speaks and acts like a Frenchman. Went to sea when seventeen and has had the most wonderful adventures, particularly in the South Sea Islands. He is a master in Merchant Service. In 1898 he lived at Ivy Wall's

am wondering how you have passed through your crisis. I would like to hear all is well; it hurts me to think you are worried.[12] It is bad for you and it is bad for your art. All the time I was at the Garnett's we have been talking of you. We conclude you must be kept quiet; but who is going to work that miracle?

We trust in Mrs. Crane and in the sagacity of publishers. That last is not much to trust to—I admit. Still! . . .

I've had letters of thanks from Pearson and Blackwood for inducing you to call on them. The Pearson man writes he hopes they shall be able very soon to do something quite satisfactory to Mr. Crane "if he gives us an opportunity." The Blackwood man sends an invite to lunch for the week after next to you and me if you will condescend to accept that invitation through me. It appears old Blackwood is coming to London himself to make your and my acquaintance. He is a good old Scotchman and if you like the idea drop me a line to name the day. It is left to you.

Your whiskey old man has effected a cure and I feel quite fit for work. How long that disposition will last only the devil in charge of my affairs knows. I miss you horribly. In fact Ravensbrook and its inhabitants have left an indelible memory. Some day—perhaps next year —we must take a house together—say in Brittany for three months or so. It would work smoothly—I am sure. . . .

Give us some news—good, if you can. Ever yours   *Jph. Conrad*

224. TO PAUL REVERE REYNOLDS

[Ravensbrook] Feb. 7 [1898]

Dear Reynolds:/ I am sending you by the Majestic (Wednesday) a new novelette, "The Blue Hotel." To my mind, it is a daisy. I have left every solitary right free—English book, English serial, American book, American serial—so that you can sell the story to Harper's Magazine for the volume.[13] You might gently intimate to them that $500 is about the price I am led to expect for a story of ten thousand words. As for "Death and The Child" it is to go to the McClure book. So is "The Five White Mice." [14]

[sic] Farm, Stanford-Hope, Essex. His son Borys was born there on January 15, 1898. 1899 he moved to Pent Farm near Hythe, Kent." (Actually, the Conrads moved to Pent Farm in October, 1898.)

[12] Worried over his debts, as is shown by Letter 224.

[13] The volume in which "The Blue Hotel" appeared was *The Monster and Other Stories,* published in 1899 by Harper & Brothers. "The Blue Hotel" first appeared in November and December, 1898, in *Collier's Weekly.*

[14] The McClure book is *The Open Boat and Other Stories,* published in 1898 by Doubleday & McClure.

Besides it would be absurd to conjoin "Death and The Child" with "The Monster." They don't fit. It would be rotten. Now, "The Blue Hotel" goes in neatly with "The Monster" and together they make 32,000. Very little more is needed for a respectably sized $1.00 book, and that can be readily submitted within the next six weeks.

If the Harpers take this story, try to get them to produce that 50 £ which is to be paid for the book rights. I shall need every sou for the next two months. And if it hadn't been for your handsome management of the Harpers I would have been stumped absolutely. As you see, I am buckling down and turning out stuff like a man. If you hold your fine gait it will only be a short time before we are throwing out our chests.

There are a few odds and ends of affairs, such as the Journal business and so on that I wish you would get settled up. A ten pound note even fills me with awe.

You must understand as my confidential agent that my settlement in England cost me in the neighborhood of $2000 worth of debts. Your payments from the Harpers knocked a comfortable hole in them but I must have about $1200 more. This would have been simple if it were not for that black-mail at Appleton's.[15]

However, now that I am in it, I must beat it and I feel that with your help the affair will not be too serious. I will bombard you with stuff. Then, if you sell Harper's "The Blue Hotel," cable the money instantly.[16] I have got big matters to attend to this month. Get me through this and I am prepared to smile.

In a cable-gram, never mind the word "dollars." I will understand that you always speak in U. S. money. My replies should also be understood in U. S. terms. Yours faithfully   S. C.

------

[15] What this indicates is that Crane's royalties on *The Red Badge of Courage* were legally tied up through the lawsuit Amy Leslie brought against Crane for recovery of money she had allegedly loaned him.

[16] Reynolds did not sell "The Blue Hotel" to Harper's. Crane wrote frantically: "Try to sell it as soon as possible. I must have some money by the first of April." Reynolds next tried Scribner's, but they declined it and so did the *Atlantic Monthly*. A letter of Walter H. Page rejecting "The Blue Hotel" is printed in Frederick Lewis Allen, *Paul Revere Reynolds* (1944). (All Crane to Reynolds letters are reproduced from this source.) In April Reynolds sold it for $300 to *Collier's Weekly*, where it appeared at the end of this year (November 26, December 3).

Crane had begun work in 1897 on a series of historical pieces, undertaken as potboilers, which eventually became *Great Battles of the World* (1901). But research on this project bored him, and he laid it aside to write "The Monster" and "The Blue Hotel."

❀ ❀ ❀

Harold Frederic

By February, Crane's nerves had snapped. But Harold Frederic, whose enemies have hit him with every hard name in the book, showed himself the most forgiving of men. (Crane had already quarreled with Frederic over "The Monster" and Conrad's *Nigger of the "Narcissus."*) A house in Ireland, "a mansion on the sea," had been lent to the Frederics by a wealthy woman admirer of Harold. And Frederic wrote Crane: "We think of it solely with reference to your sharing it with us. The expenses will be very light. I am going to finish my book there! We can work as well as loaf."

In a letter written perhaps a year or two earlier, Frederic exhibited his volatile temperament: "Mr. Edward Garnett would be an El Dorado to an American publisher of the superior class. He seems to be able to scent a new talent in fiction from a thousand miles and as a critic he possesses both sincerity and distinction of manner. He should be made known to Americans. . . . Henry James is an effeminate old donkey who lives with a herd of other donkeys around him and insists on being treated as if he were the Pope. He has licked dust from the floor of every third rate hostess in England. . . . Mr. James recommended Mr. Crane's novel before me in the house of our one mutual acquaintance [Ford Madox Hueffer?] and I was deterred from reading it for some days for that reason. With his usual lack of sense or generosity he described the book as an imitation of Zola's 'The Downfall' which it resembles as much as I do Ellen Terry." Beer (p. 321) quotes this as being the only Frederic letter known to him.

The case for James was made by Crane in an 1898 letter (shortly after February 5); it serves as a reply to Frederic's unkind criticism of the master of them all. Crane wrote somebody: "I agree with you that Mr. James has ridiculous traits and lately I have seen him make a holy show of himself in a situation that—on my honour—would have been simple to an ordinary man. But it seems impossible to dislike him. He is so kind to everybody" (Beer, p. 334).

❀ ❀ ❀

225. HAROLD FREDERIC TO CORA CRANE

Homefield,/Kenley,/Surrey./February 8th, 1898

My dear Cora:/ Forgive the informality of my taking the matter away from Kate, and myself answering your characteristically kind and straightforward letter of Sunday.[17]

I left Ravensbrook on Saturday dismayed at the proportions of the mistake I had made in opening up the Irish business at all. My error arose from my taking as my guide the very delightful memories we both have and cherish of the Irish trip last autumn. I had not at all realized—up to the time of our discussions last week—that so much had changed since then. You see you and Stephen then were still in the chrysalis stage, so to speak, of housekeeping, and you were both relatively fresh from the haphazard, bohemian life of the campaign in Thessaly. It was comparatively easy for you both, therefore, to fall in with the general views of the organizer of the picnic. How charmingly you both did so we shall never forget. And you were both ill, too, and that contributed its very sweetening effect, in our minds, to what we look back upon as one of the happiest times of our life. It has been borne in upon me, however, by practically every word that has been exchanged about the new project, that the conditions are all altered—and I am greatly distressed and angry at my own simplicity in not having seen this in time to avert the unhappy blunder of making the proposition. I am more vexed about my stupidity than you can think—but it never occurred to me that since last Autumn Ravensbrook has defined for itself a system and routine of its own—quite distinct, as is natural, from the system of Homefield—and that an effort to put these two side by side under one roof would necessarily come to grief. There would be the common bond of great and deep personal attachment between the two households, of course—but when it came to a test of strength between that and the divergent impetus of two wholly different sets of habits, I have seen too much of the world to doubt that the bond would be injured much more easily than the habits would be harmonized. And God forbid that that should happen.

I don't want to go any further into the matter. It is all very heart breaking to me—to us—and I wish with sharp emphasis that Mrs. Rice had never offered me the house at all. As I have said, I take all the blame upon myself. . . . I think . . . if we were all off on a holiday, with no necessity of work for either Stephen or me, we could probably take a sufficient number of these differences by the scruff of the neck,

---

[17] This letter has not come to light.

and thrust them back where they belong. But with the necessity of work weighing upon us both, I am frankly afraid of the experiment.

Yet I have built so fondly on the project of having some long, good fishing days alone with Stephen—and there are such a multitude of like attractions for us all . . . I want earnestly to set before you a kind of alternative. Do you and Stephen and Mrs. Ruedy [18] carve out of your spring a three weeks of entire leisure (and I will make that period free for myself, or nearly free) and come over and visit us at Ahakista. Everything then will be perfectly simple, and I surely need not waste words in saying how warmly you would be welcome. Bring Adoni [19] with you.

Kate is going to write you tomorrow. Meanwhile I beg you both to read into my letter all the regret and affection which your hearts will tell you I wanted it to contain. Yours always,   *Harold*

226. JOSEPH CONRAD TO STEPHEN CRANE

[Stanford-le-Hope] Tuesday [February 15, 1898] [20]

My dear Crane./ I've been rather seedy lately—all worry I think. But I am going to put my worries aside and have a real good time with you. I shall wire you on Sat. [21] by what train we are coming; some time in the afternoon but not late. I shall bring a lot of paper and you shall

---

[18] Cora's friend and companion, Mrs. Charlotte Ruedy, from Akron, Ohio, a city associated in Stephen's memory with Nellie Crouse and with "an intolerable duffer" who bored him. Mrs. Ruedy had also a middle name, Matilda, by which she is called in Cora's sketchy but colorful account of the wild journey with Stephen, Mrs. Ruedy, and two other persons through the Balkans in wintertime en route to the Greco-Turkish War. Mrs. Ruedy was with Cora at the Hotel de Dream in Jacksonville and accompanied her in March, 1897, when she left to rejoin Crane in London. She was with the Cranes throughout their stay at Ravensbrook, but returned to the United States after they moved to Brede Place. An unattractive caricature of Mrs. Ruedy is given in Crane's *Active Service*.

[19] Adoni Ptolemy, one of the pair of Greek refugees whom the Cranes brought back from Greece. Adoni became their butler at Ravensbrook—"a butler in shirt sleeves," Crane called him.

[20] On this day, February 15, the battleship *Maine* blew up. Later Crane wrote somebody: "This war will be fought in English. I can at least swear in Spanish and it will be more comfortable all around. But I have not decided on going yet" (Beer, p. 339).

[21] The Conrads, accompanied by Dolly (Mrs. Conrad's sixteen-year-old sister), visited "Ravensbrook" on Saturday, February 19, and stayed four days.

find a pen. I am anxious to know what you have done with your idea for a play. A play to write is no play.[22] I believe you can do anything. Ever Yours   *J. Conrad*

Our kindest regards to Mrs Crane. Baby sends a friendly howl.[23]

227. JOSEPH CONRAD TO CORA CRANE

Tuesday [March 15? 1898]

Dear Mrs. Crane/ I am sorry to say I am not well enough to keep Stephen's engagement for Saturday evening. It is nervous trouble and the doctor advises me to keep very quiet. I think I ought to follow his advice. A dinner in town means sleeping in town and I simply don't feel equal to it. I hope Stephen won't be angry; but really I do not feel at all well. I am writing today to Meldrum[24] saying that Stephen would like to meet Mr. Blackwood if it can be managed on Saturday next. If the thing is arranged I shall try to come up on that day for the lunch, but must get home in the afternoon.

I am so glad Stephen is writing; it consoles me for my own inability to work. I haven't written three pages since I left you. I simply *can't.* I am like a man under a fiendish spell cast over the power of thinking.

My wife and Dolly send their love to you all. Believe me dear Mrs. Crane   Your faithful and affectionate servant   *Joseph Conrad*

228. TO JOSEPH CONRAD

'Ravensbrook,'/March 17th [1898]

My dear Conrad,/ I am enclosing you a bit of original ms. under the

---

[22] Crane in January had suggested the idea of a play to be done in collaboration with Conrad, and on February 3 Conrad wrote E. L. Sanderson: "Stephen Crane is worrying me to write a play with him. He won't believe me when I swear by all the gods and all the muses that I have no dramatic gift. Probably something will be attempted but I would bet nothing shall be done" (*Life and Letters*, I, 228).

Crane about this time was writing somebody: "Oscar Hammerstein couldn't get people to make bigger fools of themselves. Except Willie Hearst nobody understands the popular mind as well as Oscar. I see no difference between the *Journal* and Hammerstein's roofgarden. You could get the blonde with the tincan in her gullet and the comic speaker and the song about mother's wayward boy in both shows. I must affiliate with Hammerstein. Mr. Conrad and I are writing a new kind of play" (Beer, p. 338).

[23] Conrad called his infant son "The Ominous Baby"—a reference to the title of an early Crane New York City sketch.

[24] London literary consultant to William Blackwood and Sons, Conrad's publishers.

supposition that you might like to keep it in remembrance of my warm and endless friendship for you.[25] I am still hoping that you will consent to Stokes' invitation to come to the Savage on Saturday night.

Cannot you endure it?

Give my affectionate remembrances to Mrs. Conrad and my love to the boy. Yours always,   *Stephen Crane*

You *must* accept, says Cora and I, our invitation tò come home with me on Sat. night.

229. JOSEPH CONRAD TO CORA CRANE

17. 3. 98

My dear Mrs. Crane/ You are both awfully good to me. The only reason why I would hesitate to accept your kind proposal [26] is that I am afraid the company of a wretched creature like me *wont* do any good to Stephen, who is an artist and therefore responsive to outside moods. Now my mood is unhealthy; and I would rather forbear seeing Stephen all my life—(notwithstanding my affection for the man and admiration for the artist)—than bring a deteriorating element into his existence. You, knowing him better than any one, may tell best whether my fear is justified.

However for this time I am inclined to be selfish and say yes. I haven't yet heard from the Blackwood man.[27] I instructed him to write

---

[25] Crane's gift to Conrad of a manuscript recalls his gift to Hawkins of the manuscript of *The Red Badge* in January, 1896. This letter was first printed in Conrad's introduction to Beer's *Stephen Crane* (1923), but Conrad misdated it 1899. This is one of *Two Letters from Stephen Crane to Joseph Conrad* (First Editions Club, 1926); the other is Letter 203.

[26] To come to Ravensbrook on Saturday night, the nineteenth.

[27] Meldrum did not reply in time to keep the engagement that week; the luncheon took place on the following Friday, March 25. Conrad did attend the dinner on Saturday, March 19: "We had a very amusing time with the Savages. Afterwards Crane refused to debauch because it was on that evening that Crane told me of a subject for a story—a very exceptional thing for him to do. He called it 'The Predecessor'. . . . He wanted me to share in a certain success—'a dead-sure thing,' he said. His was an unrestrainedly generous temperament" (Conrad in his introduction to Beer's *Stephen Crane* [1923], p. 231). Nothing came of the intended collaboration between Crane and Conrad, neither on the play nor on the story, "The Predecessor." Crane first proposed the collaboration idea, if not the plot of the play, in January (cf. *Joseph Conrad: Life and Letters* [1927], I, 228; also see Letter 218).

Beer (p. 336) quotes a portion of a Crane letter relating to this occasion

direct to Stephen about the Saturday lunch business. We shall no doubt
both get a letter tomorrow (Friday). If *yes* we shall meet where he
appoints. If *not* then perhaps Stephen would wire to me on Saturday—
as early as possible.

Wife and Dolly send their love to all, and I am dear Mrs. Crane
always most faithfully your   *Jph. Conrad*

230. JOSEPH CONRAD TO CORA CRANE

24th March 98

Dear Mrs. Crane/ Thanks for your letter. I am glad to hear Stephen is
at work. I am not.

I shall be at Heinemann's a little before one. I think it's the best
place for us to meet on Friday before going to feed at old Blackwood's
expense. The time of feeding is 1.30 and the locality the Garrick Club.

Jessie and Dolly send their best love to you and Mrs. Rudie.[28]
The baby has set up a carriage and is so puffed up with pride that
there is no bearing him. He behaved like an accomplished ruffian
when Stephen was here and has hurt my feelings so much that we
haven't been on speaking terms since.

I am, dear Mrs. Crane,/ Most sincerely yours   *Jph. Conrad*

✿ ✿ ✿

Crane Leaves England for Cuba

Crane, once he decided to go to Cuba to report on the Spanish-American War, left England so swiftly that guests coming to Ravensbrook
were surprised to find him gone. "Only after he sailed the *World*
cabled to secure his services, and he did not present himself at the
office in New York until a naval recruiting bureau had declined his
body. Then he was off to Key West" (Beer, p. 338).

Conrad took Crane to the office of *Blackwood's Magazine* and
obtained an advance of £50 to get him to Cuba, for which Conrad

---

of the dinner at the Savage: "American troops always run at the first shot
and there is no such thing as the U.S. Navy. These matters were clearly
proven to me last night at the Savage by a Mr. Wyndham who once met
General Grant. I have vainly tried to tell some good men and true that
Cuba is not on friendly terms with California but they will have it that one
gets on a tug at San Francisco to go to Havana."

[28] Conrad had difficulty with this name, which appears under a variety
of spellings in his letters. She is Cora's friend and companion, Mrs. Charlotte Ruedy.

pledged his own work as security should unforeseen circumstances prevent Crane from fulfilling his bond. Sanford Bennett supplied an additional £10.

※　※　※

231. TO SANFORD BENNETT

[London, April, 1898]

Sorry not to have seen you. I have raised the wind and sail tomorrow. Nothing I can do for Harold.[29] Barr will look after him.[30] Write me at Hartwood, N.Y., care of Edmund Crane. Shall get myself taken in the Navy if possible.

232. JOSEPH CONRAD TO CORA CRANE

19th April 1898

My dear Mrs. Crane/ We imagine how lonely you must have felt after Stephen's departure. The dear fellow wired me from Queenstown,[31] just before going aboard I suppose. Jess is very concerned about you and wishes me to ask you to drop her a line on your arrival in Ireland.[32] I think your going there would be a good thing as solitude after separation is sometimes very hard to bear.

We thought of asking you to come here at once but on receiving Stephen's wire I imagined you were all in Ireland already. However you will be more entertained and more comfortable at the Frederic's for a time, and on your return to England I hope will have the will and the courage to undertake the risky experiment of coming to us with Mrs. Ruedy. Moreover I fancy Stephen's absence won't be very prolonged and we may have the felicity of seeing you all here together. I trust you will let me know how he fares whenever you hear from him. He is not very likely to write to anyone else—if I know the man. . . . I am as usual ineffective and lazy.

Believe me dear Mrs. Crane your very faithful friend and servant

Jph. Conrad

---

[29] Harold Frederic, who was ill; he had a stroke in August and died on October 19.

[30] Robert Barr, who completed Crane's unfinished novel, *The O'Ruddy*, after Crane died. Barr at Woldingham and Frederic at Kenley were both near neighbors of the Cranes at Oxted.

[31] Queenstown (now Cobh), county Cork, Eire.

[32] Conrad kept in touch with Cora throughout the nine months of Stephen's absence. Immediately after his departure Cora went to Ireland to visit the Frederics, taking with her Mrs. Ruedy and Adoni Ptolemy.

233. TO ROBERT BARR

[Key West, Florida,³³ May, 1898]

You should see the jay who runs the table here. He is straight out of a dime novel, moustache and all, with bunches of diamonds like cheap chandeliers on each hand. Now I owe Harold [Frederic] an apology for laughing when he said they would tear me in pieces the minute my back was turned. Hi, Harold! I apologize! Did you know me for a morphine eater? A man who had known me for ten years tells me that all my books are written while I am drenched with morphine. The joke is on me.

234. TO DOROTHY BRANDON ³⁴

Off Havana ³⁵/May 19 [1898]

My dear Dot: I do not know if you will forgive me but at least let me explain that I was the victim of a strange set of circumstances. When I was in Washington I suddenly recieved [*sic*] notice that there was to be a big fight off Havana and I was to go there instantly. I flew; I did not telegraph because I could not explain well enough by wire and returning now from Porto Rico I find my first real opportunity to write you a note. Will you forgive me? I have not changed in the least and you may be sure that the S. Crane you knew so well long ago would not seem thoughtless if he could help it.

I am going to England as soon as the war is over and I wish you would send me the address of your sister ³⁶ there. My address will be Key West Hotel, Key West. Adios.   S. C.

235. TO AN UNKNOWN RECIPIENT

[June 2, 1898]

[Aboard *The Three Friends*]

The sailormen of Sampson's ³⁷ big canoe ought to make us all ashamed

---

³³ Crane sent the *World* twenty dispatches between April 27 and July 9; then, back in New York City, he was refused an advance by Pulitzer's paper. He signed up with the *Journal* and sent it twenty dispatches between August 5 and November 9 (they are listed by Ames W. Williams in *New Colophon*, April, 1948).

³⁴ Sister of Lily Brandon Munroe. Mrs. Munroe was then living in Washington, D.C., having divorced her husband sometime before 1898. Crane had made a hurried trip to Washington especially to see Lily. As this letter indicates, he intended to return to Cora.

³⁵ Crane wrote this letter in pencil from the Titchfield Hotel, Port Antonio, Jamaica; the envelope is postmarked New York, June 19, 1898.

³⁶ The sister was Stella Brandon, who married a German named Schmidt and lived in Baden-Baden for years.

³⁷ Admiral William T. Sampson, of whom Crane wrote a tribute in

of our trade. The papers come aboard the flagship and who, I ask, want to see this goulash of legendary lies and solemn rumours? We do, we the cynics of Fleet Street and Park Row, the Rudyards, the lords of the popular mind. The Jackies just look at all this manure and say, Well—and go on polishing brass. Davis [38] and I tried to make them excited by donations of headlines and they said, Well—and peeled more onions. It is now the fashion of all hotel porches at Tampa and Key West to run Davis down because he has declined a captaincy in the army in order to keep his contract with his paper. The teaparty has to have a topic.

236. CORA CRANE TO MORETON FREWEN [39]

Ravensbrook/June 10th '98

Dear Mr. Frewen:/ . . . I received a cable on Wednesday from Mr. Crane from Jamica [sic] saying letters were delayed but I expect to hear from him any day now that he is satisfied with my arrangements for Brede.[40] I can, however, safely say that we will take it on the terms named in my letter and as soon as I hear from Mr. Crane I will write you a formal letter to that effect. I am glad that you do not think lawyers necessary, as I have had such an awful dose of them the past few days. I am very much disgusted with the English justice shown Americans. It seems the job masters [41] here can take mild Americans out in their traps which they can, without fear of punishment, turn upside down and dump the passengers out on the road, ruin their clothes and scar them for life. So I never want to see another lawyer if I can avoid it.

By next week I hope to forward you the formal letter and will then have the architect start repairs. And try to be already in camp at your wonderful old house when Mr. Crane returns.

I will be very much obliged to Mrs. Frewen if she will send me the literature which bears on the early history of the house. Would you

---

"War Memories": "Admiral Sampson is to me the most interesting personality of the war" (*Work of Stephen Crane* [1925–1927], IX, 225–26).

[38] Richard Harding Davis.

[39] Owner of Brede Place.

[40] The Cranes obtained the house through Edward Garnett, the literary critic and friend of Moreton Frewen.

[41] These fulminations against lawyers and "English justice" refer to a carriage accident of the previous summer, in which Cora and Crane both suffered injuries. A suit for damages brought by the Cranes against the jobmaster evidently had got nowhere.

object to its being used in an article? [42] And may I ask you for the photos you told me that you had of Brede?

Please give to Mrs. Frewen my thanks and regards Very truly yours,   *Cora Crane*

P.S. I will try to arrange to keep your caretaker who's [*sic*] looks I liked very much. I will go to Brede one day next week and see her and will then write you on the subject.   *C. C.*

236A. CORA CRANE TO AN UNKNOWN RECIPIENT [43]

[Ravensbrook, June 16, 1898]

Dear Sir: Mr. Crane cables me that he has recieved [*sic*] no letters from me. Will you kindly let me know if you forward them as received? As it is of great importants [*sic*] my letters reach him. Yours truly/ Mrs. Stephen Crane   *Cora Crane*

237. JOSEPH CONRAD TO CORA CRANE

Stanford-le-Hope/27 June 1898

Dear Mrs. Crane:/ I am, we are, horribly ashamed of ourselves for leaving your good and welcome letter so long without a reply. But we reckon upon your generous forgiveness.

I was delighted to hear good news of dear Stephen. The life on board that tug [44] of his will set him up in strength and appetite for years. Have you heard from him since you wrote? [See Letter 236A.] I suppose he landed with the army and is in the thick of everything that's going. I've only heard lately he is going to write for Blackwood. They think a lot of him and expect—as well they may—first rate work. Meldrum was here (I suppose you've heard of him? Blackwood's man in London) the other day and spoke of Stephen with real enthusiasm. They are anxious but not impatient. . . .

It looks as though the war would drag after all. I think you had

---

[42] The architect was W. Harrison Cowlishaw, brother-in-law of Constance Garnett. Crane wrote no article about Brede Place, but he described it in "The Squire's Madness," published in October, 1900, in *Crampton's Magazine*. This story was completed by Cora. In her own story, "Cowardice," Cora pictures in colorful detail the exterior and interior of the house, with notes on its history, and special attention to the ghost. "Cowardice" was sold in 1901 to the Northern Newspaper Syndicate, an English chain serving the northern counties, and was published on October 4, 1902.

[43] This letter, in the Clifton Waller Barrett Collection at the University of Virginia, may have been sent to someone at the Key West Hotel or at the New York *World*.

[44] The *Three Friends*.

better *not* wait for Stephen's return and come to us with Mrs. Ruedy (to whom my respectful duty) *at least* for the promised day and for longer if you can stand it. I am afraid you would get bored. We lead a wretched, shut-up existence in the most primitive surroundings.

Jessie will write to suggest the time but in reality you must consult your own convenience. The poor girl is doing all the housework, nursing and cooking, herself. She is very cheerful about it but it makes me miserable to see her toiling like this from morning to night. Oh! for a success, a beastly popular success! I long for it on that account. My work goes on desperately slow. I think with difficulty and write without enthusiasm but still the book crawls on towards its lame and impotent end. But the end is not yet. Enough lamentations! . . .

My wife and Dolly send their very best love to you and Mrs. Ruedy, and I am, dear Mrs. Crane, Your most obedient and faithful friend and servant   *Jph. Conrad*

PS   I was so pleased to hear my tales are a success amongst the socialists of Tennessee. I feel quite proud of it.

238. *TO MRS. BOLTON CHAFFEE* [45]

[Cuba, July, 1898]

. . . You must be careful about feeding runaway dogs. Mr. Bemis [46]

---

[45] Mrs. Chaffee had been a guest of the Cranes at "Ravensbrook" three months before Crane wrote this letter. Now in Cuba, it was rumored, as reported by Beer, that Crane had eloped with the wife of General Adna Chaffee, the hero of El Caney, and had fled with her to San Francisco. Beer states incorrectly that General Chaffee was unmarried. What started the gossip was Crane's being seen with Mrs. Bolton Chaffee on the verandah of Chamberlain's Hotel at Old Point Comfort, Virginia. This incident occurred July 13. The hotels of this resort were jammed with fashionable ladies from New York and the wives of naval and military officers, and Crane, fatigued and ill, lolled on the verandah: "The verandah was crowded with women in light, charming summer dresses," Crane wrote, "and with spruce officers from the fortress. It was like a bank of flowers. It filled me with awe. . . . Across the narrow street on the verandah of another hotel was a similar bank of flowers. Two companies of volunteers dug a lane through the great crowd of the street and kept a way, and then through this lane there passed a curious procession. I had never known they looked like that. Such a gang of dirty, ragged, emaciated, half starved and bandaged cripples I had never seen. . . . Then there were many stretchers, slow moving. When the crowd began to pass the hotel the banks of flowers made a noise which could make one tremble . . . something beyond either a moan or a sob. Anyhow the sound of women weeping was in it—the sound of women weeping" (Beer, p. 352).

[46] Floyd Bemis, a Southerner. In March, 1893, Crane was pointed out

informs me that you and I are sinners and that we have flown to San
Francisco. They have promoted you to the rank of Mrs. Brigadier General Chaffee. Perhaps it is not known to you—and it has not long been
known to me—that my name in New York is synonymous with mud.
Give my regards to your husband and tell him the cigars made many
correspondents happier. My friends will pile a mountain of lies on me
but they will smoke my cigars as freely as I smoke theirs. That is
cynicism.

239. DR. EDWARD LIVINGSTON TRUDEAU [47]
TO CORA CRANE

Paul Smith's/In the Adirondacks/Paul Smith's, N.Y.
September 16 [1898]

Dear Madam/ Your husband had a slight evidence of activity in the
trouble in his lungs when he came back here this summer but it was
not serious and he has improved steadily I understand since he came.
I have only examined him once but he looked very well and told me
he was much better last time I saw him. Very truly yours

E. L. Trudeau

240. EDITOR OF COLLIER'S WEEKLY
TO PAUL REVERE REYNOLDS

Collier's Weekly/521–547 West Thirteenth Street
New York, September 20, 1898

Dear Mr. Reynolds:–/ I enclose the Gissing story and Sarah Grand's
story, neither of which we can use.

　　With regard to the "Blue Hotel," I had intended publishing it

---

to him as "an eccentric who spent all his time in dives of the Bowery and
was the outcast son of an Episcopal bishop."

[47] World-famous lung specialist and founder of the Cottage Sanitarium
at Lake Saranac, N.Y. This letter replies to an inquiry by Cora. Her letter is
not preserved, and the records of the sanitarium do not show that he was
ever a patient there. Dr. F. B. Trudeau, son of Dr. E. L. Trudeau writes:
"However, this can very often be explained by the fact that he was undoubtedly a private patient of my Father's here in town and hence would
not come under the jurisdiction of the Sanitorium" (Dr. F. B. Trudeau to
Lillian Gilkes, September 28, 1954).

　　Richard Harding Davis told Thomas Beer that Crane, on returning to
New York City from Cuba, was coughing badly and spitting blood.

　　The war ended in mid-August. Crane had gone from Key West to the
fighting front, to Jamaica, to Old Point Comfort, to Puerto Rico, and finally
to Havana.

before Christmas, or the week immediately after, but I cannot lay my hands on it at present. Do you remember the date on which you left the shortened version here?[48] It was in manuscript, not typewriting; was it not? Kindly let me hear from you with regard to this. Very truly yours,   *Robert J. Collier/Editor*

❈   ❈   ❈

Stephen Crane Disappears

The Crane family learned of Stephen's "marriage" to Cora when Cora cabled William Howe Crane to ascertain the whereabouts of Stephen. William wrote Thomas Beer years later that after Stephen went to Puerto Rico, "the boy got a room in a boarding house in Havana. He used to give his letters to one of the servants to mail. Five or six of the letters that he wrote to his wife were never received. He was very busy trying to finish a novel [*Active Service*] and some short stories. His wife cabled me asking for his address. She also cabled to Reynolds and some others. For about ten days we were in the dark. There is a news story that Steve was hidden in Havana forty days." Somebody sent Cora a Florida newspaper announcement[49] that Crane was missing,

---

[48] The shortened version presumably ended at "This registers the amount of your purchase" (*Omnibus*, p. 529).

Robert Collier wrote to Reynolds, April 26, his acceptance of "The Blue Hotel": "I write to confirm the agreement made with regard to LeGallienne's war poem, for Seventy-five Dollars, and Stephen Crane's story, shortened to seven thousand five hundred (7,500) or eight thousand (8,000) words, for Three Hundred Dollars."

Walter Hines Page, then editor of the *Atlantic Monthly*, said that "The Blue Hotel" was "a pretty good story" but declined it for his magazine, preferring "to use in the Atlantic only those stories that may be afterwards published in book form by Messrs. Houghton, Mifflin & Co., or stories from authors whose books come to us."

[49] This was the *Florida Times-Union and Citizen* (published in Jacksonville) of September 10, as Letter 241 shows. But William Crane is in error in supposing that the *Times-Union* story was inspired by Cora. A letter to her from Robert Barr in September indicates that she had no knowledge of the story's authorship: "If what Hurst [Hearst] cables is true, then I should hate to put down in black and white what I think of S. Crane. If he has not disappeared, and if he has been drawing money for himself, while leaving you without cash, then that article about his disappearance in the Florida paper is a put up job. . . ."

Crane in Havana, meanwhile, was calling no less urgently for money, as we see in subsequent letters to Reynolds this fall. Cora, in desperation, cabled the Secretary of War (see No. 242).

that he had disappeared from the Hotel Pasaje—he had moved to a boardinghouse in order to save expenses. William Crane goes on to add: "Some of his wife's cables and letters were not judicious. She cabled a very talkative newspaper man she had known in Jacksonville and he put a yarn around that Steve had abandoned her. There was a great deal of nasty talk about it" (William Howe Crane to Thomas Beer, in "Mrs. Stephen Crane," *American Mercury*, March, 1934).

     ✿   ✿   ✿

241. CORA CRANE TO PAUL REVERE REYNOLDS [50]

Ravensbrook/Sep 25th '98

Dear Sir: In answer to your letter of the 16th Sep. I would say that it was my intention to write you today for news of Mr. Crane. The last news I had direct from him, was dated Key West Aug 16th. On the 22nd of Sep. I got a Florida paper stating that Stephen Crane was missing and that fears were entertained for his safety. This was the "Times Union" of Jacksonville Sep. 10th. It said that Mr. Crane had entered Havana as a tobacco buyer. And that he dissapeared [*sic*] about Sep. 6th from Hotel Pasaje Havana. I am in great distress of mind as I can get no news through the Journal office here. Mr. Crane's affairs here need his attention. I am in *great* need of money. And I fear that we will lose our home here if I cannot get money to pay some pressing debts. The Journal is behaving very shabily [*sic*]. I have been served with two summonds [*sic*] so you can see how bad matters really are. If you can collect any money due to Mr. Crane please cable it to me without delay. This being so helpless in a foreign country together with my fears for Mr. Crane are almost driving me mad. Will you use your influence with Mr. Hearst. He has no right to allow a man like Stephen Crane to be missing for over three weeks without using means to find him. And if he allows Stephen Cranes [*sic*] wife to be turned out of her home, while Stephen is risking his life in his service, I have told Mr. Creelman I would let every correspondent in London know about it. Both Harold Frederic and Robert Barr would let the world

[50] A portion of this letter was quoted in Frederick Lewis Allen, *Paul Revere Reynolds* (1944), pp. 59–60, and reproduced in *Omnibus*, p. 684 n. The complete text is here given for the first time.

Cora's citation of dates, in writing to Reynolds, indicates that the Florida newspaper article that reached her on September 22 was the first word she received of Crane's supposed disappearance.

know over their own signatures. I beg you to let me hear any news by cable. Very Truly Yours   *Cora Crane*

The British Consul at Havana is in charge of the Journal affairs./   C.C.

242. CORA CRANE TO THE SECRETARY OF WAR [51]

Ravensbrook/25th Sep. 98

Dear Sir: If there is any way in which you can communicate the fact of Stephen Cranes [sic] disappearance to the U.S. authorities at Havana will you do so! He entered Havana about Sep. 1st as a tobacco buyer. Stopped quietly at Hotel Pasaje and was watched by the police and was missing about Sep. 6th to 8th. If you receive any information about him I beg you will send it to me as I am very much alarmed as to his safety. Yours Resply [Respectfully]   *Cora Crane* (Mrs. Stephen Crane) [52]

243. TO PAUL REVERE REYNOLDS

Havana, Sept. 27. [1898]

My dear Reynolds:/ Now this is IT.[53] If you don't touch big money for it I wonder!

---

[51] Reprinted from *Colophon* of April, 1940. The original holograph letter is on file in the National Archives, Washington. Cora's cablegram to the Secretary of War, a shortened version of the letter, was relayed to the Adjutant General's Office, where it seems to have remained stuck until October 9, when it was transmitted to General J. F. Wade in Havana, U.S. officer in charge of evacuation of Americans from Cuba. General Wade then inquired of some newspaper men who told him Crane had not been out of the city, and reported back to Washington October 27: "After these inquiries Mr. Crane called and expressed regret at having caused so much trouble. I do not know his business or why he has not communicated with his family."

[52] A search of records in Jacksonville, New York City, London, and Edinburgh turns up no evidence of a civil marriage ceremony ever performed for Stephen Crane and Cora Howorth Stewart, or of a divorce ever obtained by Cora from Captain Stewart (see Letter 199, n. 100). To Conrad, Crane offered the explanation on his return from Cuba that they had waited to be certain that Cora's English husband was really deceased before they broke the news of marriage; and now it was "a relief to have it over" (from an unpublished letter of Thomas Beer). In Athens, Cora had gone by her married name, Stewart. Eben Alexander, American Minister to Greece, is commonly thought to have married Stephen and Cora in Athens, but Alexander in his correspondence refers to Cora as "Mrs. Stewart." Not until December, 1899, does he address her as Mrs. Crane.

[53] "The Price of the Harness," which Reynolds sold to *Cosmopolitan*.

Cable me when you make sale and how much. English copy goes to Blackwood.

244. CORA CRANE TO PAUL REVERE REYNOLDS [?]

Ravensbrook/Sep. 29th

Dear Sir: Thanks for your card. Will you let me know if Mr. Crane gets my letters and where he is at the time this reaches you. The report that he was "missing from Havana" caused me great distress. Will you tell him when you write, that "Illustrated Bits" have written asking to see him twice. I refered [sic] them to Hienemann [sic]—who has the matter in hand. They plagiarized "The Bride Comes to Yellow Sky." I transfered [sic] the copyright to Hienemann who is sueing [sic.] My letters seems [sic] to go astray so I will be glad if you can tell Mr. Crane this. Yours very truly/   Cora Crane [54]

Pardon paper.

245. TO PAUL REVERE REYNOLDS

[Havana, Cuba, early October, 1898]

My dear Reynolds:/ *Did* you get my story: "The Price of the Harness"? [55] I am worried for fear it is lost. Cable.

I am now sending you a *peach*. I love it devotedly. Sell to anybody if the price is grand enough. Otherwise remember that *Blackwood's* have a call on me. Send all letters here.   Crane

I *love* this story.[56]

---

[54] Here, and in other letters to Reynolds of this period, Cora's nervousness and emotional strain are apparent in her frequent misspellings and occasional syntactical slips.

[55] Published in *Cosmopolitan* and in *Blackwood's Edinburgh Magazine*, both in December, 1898.

[56] Crane, in Havana, was writing "story after story, article after article, and sending them on [to Reynolds] with brief penciled scrawls on cheap ruled pad paper; sometimes his vehement notes were written in a shaky hand on old telegraph blanks. Always they glowed with enthusiasm over his work and appealed for instant payment.

"Crane was enamored of Havana, and as Reynolds sold his stories one by one, he began to think of spending the winter in the lazy old city. At the same time Mrs. Crane was writing to the agent to persuade him that he must come speedily back to England" (*Paul Revere Reynolds*, p. 62; see also Letter 252).

246. CORA CRANE TO PAUL REVERE REYNOLDS

Ravensbrook/Oct. 18th 1898

Dear Sir: Thank you for your letter of 10th. This post also brought me
a letter from the British Consul at Havana, who says Mr. Crane is
no longer with the "Journal," that I have no cause to worry because of
Mr. Cranes [*sic*] health or for fear of police, but he does give the
impression that something is wrong, that Mr. Crane is in some sort of
difficulty. He says that Mr. Crane has left the Hotel Pasaje, that he
does not know his address, but has advertised in a local paper saying
that he had cables & letters for him.

I fear Mr. Crane is having money trouble and beg that you will
write him as soon as possible and tell him of the important work there
is to be done here. Ever so many people have written for stories ect.
[*sic*]

I am very much worried and will be glad if you will use every
effort to induce Mr. Crane to leave Cuba & return to his work. Very
Sincerely yours   *Cora Crane*

247. TO PAUL REVERE REYNOLDS

Havana/Oct. 20 [1898]

My dear Reynolds:/ I enclose a "personal anecdote" thing for Mc-
Clure. Hit him hard. Hit him beastly hard. I have got to have at least
fifteen hundred dollars this month, sooner the better. For Christ's sake
get me some money quick here by cable.

The "Intrigue" lot goes to Heinemann.[57] Yours,   *Crane*

   ❋   ❋   ❋

Cora Appeals for Aid for
Harold Frederic's Orphaned Children

When Harold Frederic died on October 19, Cora immediately took in
Kate and her three children at Ravensbrook. The friends of the lawful
Mrs. Frederic, also then living in England with her four children,

---

[57] A series of sentimental love poems. Heinemann did not publish
Crane's poems. *War Is Kind* was published only in the United States, by
Frederick A. Stokes Company, spring, 1899. For the set of poems compris-
ing "Intrigue" see *The Collected Poems of Stephen Crane,* ed. Wilson Fol-
lett (Knopf, 1930), pp. 111–25, and Daniel G. Hoffman, *The Poetry of
Stephen Crane* (1957).

formed a committee to raise funds for their support. The committee publicized an appeal in the London *Daily Chronicle* and further championed the cause of the widow Frederic by having Kate and the Christian Science practitioner who had visited Frederic brought under arrest, charged with manslaughter.

Cora meanwhile organized a committee to raise funds to support Kate's three children, and she wrote to all subscribers of the rival group urging them to stretch their charity to include all seven of Frederic's orphans. John Scott-Stokes gave her much help as co-chairman, handling committee funds.

Bernard Shaw, at his most Shavian, replied to Cora's appeal: "We have three very expensive orphans on hand already—parents alive in every case. My impulse is to repudiate all extra orphans with loud execrations. . . . I should simply take them out into the garden and bury them." [58] Nevertheless, he enclosed £5.

Henry James, who had signed the other appeal, sent her £5 "for the purpose you wrote me of"—though hard-pressed himself just then. "Deeper than I can say is my commiseration for those beautiful little children."

Karl Harriman in *New Hope* (October, 1934) speaks of Cora's appeal on behalf of Kate's children, and attributes to Hall Caine—to whom Stephen had given the sobriquet of "Christ on the Mount of Man"—a curt refusal. But Harriman's memory thirty-five years later plays him false. Harriman adds a cipher and some tears, Cora's, to Henry James's contribution—making it £50 instead of £5—and he was mistaken also in this other instance. Hall Caine wrote Cora (letter in the Butler Library Crane Collection):

"I sympathize very heartily with the object you have in view, and will take a sad kind of pleasure in helping it some little." He had been asked to contribute to the other fund, "and it would be my desire to contribute in some degree to both. I have been away in America, and know little or nothing of the facts of the case, but of course it does not require much knowledge to make one feel the justice of your plea. What I had to say on Frederic's walk of life I said to the man while he was alive. It would seem to me that the time is gone by for further discussion of that subject. A man's children are his children, and that is all that remains to be said on the subject."

*   *   *

---

[58] Quoted from *Columbia Library Columns* (February, 1953).

248. JOSEPH CONRAD TO CORA CRANE

Pent Farm.[59] Postling./Stanford Near Hythe,/28th Oct 98

My dear Mrs. Crane/ Just a word in haste to tell you I shall try to do what I can. Don't build any hopes on it. It is a *most* remote chance— but it's the only thing I can think of. What kind of trouble is Stephen in? [60] You make me very uneasy. Are you *sure* you can bring him back. I do not doubt your influence mind! but not knowing the circumstances I do not know how far it would be feasible. In Stephen's coming back to England is *salvation* there is no doubt about that.

Will he come? *Can* he come? I am utterly in the dark as to the state of affairs.

We recognize your good heart in your acts.[61] God forbid that we should throw the first—or even the last stone. What the world calls *scandal* does not affect me in the least. My sincere approval and high recognition of the course you've taken is not based on Christian grounds. I do not pretend to that name—not from irreverence but from my exalted idea of that faith's morality. I can't pretend to such moral- ity but I hold that those that *do* pretend and boast of it should *carry it out* at the *cost of personal sacrifice,* and in *every respect.* My admira- tion of your courageous conduct exists side by side with an utter dis- approval of those whom you (in *your* own extremity) befriend. They invoke the name of a Faith and they've dragged its substance pretty well through the mud. It may be only folly—of course—unutterable *folly.* But it looks worse. The only Christian in sight in this whole affair is you, my dear Mrs. Crane—exercising that rarest of the Creed's vir- tues: that of Charity.

I would not have said all this but your good friendly letter, I con- sider, has in a sense authorized me to speak.

I would of course have done what you wish without a moment's delay but the exact truth is I've only £8 in the bank and am in debt to publishers so heavily that I can't go to them for more. Or else I would do it, believe me. I've tried however to do something but *don't reckon on it* and do not relax your efforts in other directions. I am a poor busi-

---

[59] The Conrads had recently moved from Stanford-le-Hope in Essex to Pent Farm in Kent. An amusing account of Pent Farm is given in David Garnett, *The Golden Echo* (Chatto & Windus, 1953), p. 63.

[60] Conrad here refers to Cora's letter to Reynolds of October 18, in which she dwells on the apprehension, touched off by the British consul's communication from Havana, that "Mr Crane is in some sort of difficulty" (Letter 246).

[61] Her concern for Kate Frederic's children.

ness man and can't give you any hints as to raising money on life insurance. Couldn't Stokes advise you?

Jess shall write tomorrow. I will let you know shortly (I hope) whether my plan has been of any good. Affectionately and faithfully Yours   *Jph. Conrad*

249. *JOSEPH CONRAD TO CORA CRANE*

1st Nov 98

Dear Mrs. Crane/ Yours to hand. That's what I'm doing; trying to get at B'wood [Blackwood]. I took Mr. Meldrum into our confidence. He is an admirer of Stephen. What you say about your husband is golden truth.

To B'wood I suggested a loan of £50 on three securities. *One* (for which they would care most) *Stephen's work, second* your property, *third* my own undertaking to furnish them copy to the amount advanced should unforeseen circumstances prevent you and Stephen from paying him back as soon as he may expect.

We must approach B'wood through Meldrum who is *most* friendly. B'wood himself is a good kind man but must be handled cautiously. It is better done through me and Meldrum. How it will turn out it is impossible to say. It will also require time. I am writing to M. again this post.

Before you give *bill of sale* on furniture *make sure* the furniture dealer or dealers (from whom you bought) are paid *in full* as in the contrary case you would make yourself liable to prosecution.[62] My letter to Stephen is sent through *Reynolds.*

I am sure you are doing and planning for the best. That is the way to rescue poor Stephen. I only wish I had something to pawn or sell; you would not have to wait long for means. As it is I've only my work and that I've offered to B'wood for what it is worth. Most faithfully yours   *Conrad*

Jessie sends lots of love. She is very much concerned and anxious about your health.

---

[62] While Crane continued drawing money from the New York *Journal*—his last dispatch was dated November 9 from Havana—and from Paul Revere Reynolds, who probably was advancing him sums against stories and articles received, he was sending Cora nothing. To support the loan that Conrad was now seeking through Meldrum from Blackwood and Sons, Cora was now to give a bill of sale against her furniture. See *Joseph Conrad: Letters to William Blackwood and David S. Meldrum,* ed. William Blackburn (Duke University Press, 1958), pp. 31 ff.

250. TO PAUL REVERE REYNOLDS

Havana/Nov. 3rd. [1898]

My dear Reynolds:/ Just received letter concerning "The Price of the Harness." If Blackwood can't take it for Dec. ask them to give it to Pinker.[63] Somebody must have it. With Pinker it is worth £36.[64] We can't lose it.

Damn Walker. The name of the story is "The Price of the Harness" because it *is* the price of the harness, the price the men paid for wearing the military harness, Uncle Sam's military harness; and they paid blood, hunger and fever.[65] Let him if he likes conjure some inflammatory secondary title. He is a fool.   *Crane*

251. JOSEPH CONRAD TO CORA CRANE

Thursday [November 3, 1898]

Dear Mrs. Crane/ I forward you Meldrum's letter. He is a man of good counsel and you can see for yourself that he is anxious to do something. Please read his letter with care. His suggestion is worth consideration. The same ideas occurred to me. If I had the means there would have been no need to mention them, but as you see if we are to do something we must have recourse to strangers. . . .

Would Stephen come back by himself if written to? Would he tell us *how much* is wanted to enable him to leave Havana? Would he recognize the engagements we would enter into here for means to bring him back? His future is here—I firmly believe—but will he see

---

[63] James Pinker, London literary agent for Crane.

[64] Beer says Crane's contracts with Pinker were for £40 per thousand words. Ford Madox Ford in *Portraits From Life* speaks of Crane getting £20 per thousand words. Crane was among the highest paid writers in England, but Cora is closer to the mark in saying that he averaged "seldom less than ten pounds."

[65] On its first appearance "The Price of the Harness" was called "The Woof of the Thin Red Threads," Crane taking that title from a phrase in Part V of the story. The final title of his war novel, *The Red Badge of Courage,* was similarly derived from a phrase struck off in the writing of the story (in chap. ix).

While in Havana, before starting north later this month, Crane finished writing *Active Service,* probably in first draft only, as he worked on it again later in England. Beer (p. 355) has it that Crane started north in October; but this November 3 letter to Reynolds, as well as the other Crane-Reynolds letters and those of Cora, were not available to Beer.

it?[66] Whatever happens the matter must be kept quiet, and his reputation shielded. I know of personal knowledge that B'wood is a little angry. A short letter from Stephen saying that he could not send anything would have made all the difference. It is too late now. What do you think of writing him a strong letter urging his return and saying that we keep £50 ready for that purpose if he gives his word.[67] Please write. Always yours   *Conrad*

252. CORA CRANE TO PAUL REVERE REYNOLDS

Ravensbrook/Nov. 9th '98

Dear Mr. Reynolds: Thank you for your letter of Oct. 31st. I understand that Mr. Crane is wanted to do some work here, and that the Saturday Review has cabled to him and offered him money to return to England (£50). I *know*, that a friend [68] has written him, and that the letter should reach him not later than the 11th of this month, offering to cable him enough money to get home if he needs it. It is the opinion of all the men who know, that Stephen's future is in England. No matter what he writes, there is [sic] *always* favorable notices in every English paper. He has a great vogue here and now he must return if he is ever going to do more great work. A man must have pure wholesome air if he wishes to succeed in art. I beg you will advise Mr. Crane to return to England. He has a great future and a wonderful home awaiting him. I will write to the people who have written about stories and tell them you have stories of Mr. Cranes [sic]. Very truly yours   *Cora Crane*

P.S. I will be glad of any news of Mr. Crane.

---

[66] Crane finally saw it (as Conrad saw it) and returned to Cora and England.

[67] Conrad's second appeal to Blackwood was unsuccessful. But £50 was obtained from Heinemann against future works of Crane. This money was cabled to General Wade for transmittal to Crane in Havana by kindhearted Jack Stokes. On November 14 Stokes wrote Cora: "Cable despatched this morning to 75 Aguacale, Havana. Same text as Friday with addition as follows 'Money shortly through General Wade.' Just one word shortly to tell you, once and for all, that neither you nor Stephie owe me any money. What I have done is off my own bat. . . ." Later Stokes wrote again: "I dont think the cables I sent for you came to more than £15 if so much. . . . Anyhow I had not the slightest idea of ever asking you or Stephie for it and the receipts went into the wastebasket." As these funds did not suffice, Crane obtained $50 from Willis Brooks Hawkins (see Letter 259).

[68] Joseph Conrad. This must have been one of the letters William Crane

253. *WILLIAM HOWE CRANE*
     TO PAUL REVERE REYNOLDS

Port Jervis, N.Y./Nov. 10/98

Dear Sir:–/ Stephen Crane, my brother, telegraphs me from Havana
to loan him some money and asks me to notify you.

Can you tell me what the urgency is or whatever you may have to
do with it? I shall be greatly obliged. I have written him at Havana,
but my letters were returned as uncalled for. Do you know his city
address there. Yours truly,   *Wm. H. Crane*

254. *ROBERT BARR TO CORA CRANE*

[Late November?] 1898

Dear Mrs. Crane:/ This summons does not need to worry you. There
are eight days before anything can be done. If there is any mistake in
the account, there will be still further delay if you say you will defend
action. However it is not likely that there is any mistake so you can
count on eight days. I will keep this summons to show to Creelman [69]
unless you object. I would send you a cheque only my bank account is
at present overdrawn, but if there is no cash before the eight days I
will go to this grocer, & make myself personally responsible for the
debt, & he will accept my surety. The trouble is that the butcher may
do likewise & his bill is more serious. I will stay in town on Friday
night & come right through to Oxted on Saturday, bringing this summons with me, when I will see the grocer. Of course the grocer is perfectly within his right in doing this.[70] It has been noised about the
place that you are going to leave & he knows he wont have your custom much longer anyhow, so doubtless, having been bilked before, he
fears he is going to be cheated again. The only person at fault is
Stephen Crane, & as he is not within cursing distance there is no use
in swearing. I am sure, however, that the cash will be in from the
Journal before many days, & then everything will run smoothly again.
Most sincerely yours   *R. B.*

---

recalled, to Thomas Beer, as "not judicious" (see also Letter 246).

[69] James Creelman, London representative of the New York *Journal*.

[70] Barr got advice from a lawyer about the summons. "All you have to
do is to give notice that you are a married woman, that it is your husband's
debt and that he is in America and will pay when he returns. It would be
better to have a lawyer do this" (Barr to Cora, dated "Friday 5:15 P.M.,
1898").

✿   ✿   ✿

Stephen Crane Leaves Havana

Crane left Havana in mid-November and spent a month in New York
City, where he hunted for a house, had luncheons with William Dean
Howells and visited bars with James Huneker. On November 23 in
Delmonico's Crane was slandered by a drunk (Thomas McCumber),
and Richard Harding Davis threw the gossipmonger out. "Three or
four times," said Huneker, "when he had been spending the whole
evening with Ryder [Albert Pinkham Ryder, the painter] and myself
I would be told in the morning how drunk and disorderly he had been
the night before by men who had not seen him. For a mild and melancholy kid he certainly had fallen completely into the garbage can of
gossip" (Beer, pp. 357, 361). Leaving a theater with Mrs. Sonntag, a
white-haired woman of forty-three and a cripple, Crane in the first
week of December was accosted by a policeman and would have been
booked on a trumped-up charge had not a priest (Mrs. Sonntag's
cousin) intervened.

Crane was absent from England for nine months. On December
20 he cabled Cora. He sailed for Gravesend from Havana on the
Manitou the first week of January, 1899. John T. Winterich, in his introduction to the Folio Society edition of *The Red Badge of Courage*
(1951), errs in saying that "at the end of 1899 he was back in England"
—even if his date is a misprint for 1898. Crane did not get home until
January 10 or 11, 1899.

Though a niece of Crane is positive that he did not visit his relatives after his return from Cuba, some of his late December letters
(according to Beer) are dated from Hartwood—letters to Mrs. Sonntag,
Appleton, and Edward Garnett. These letters are no longer among
Beer's papers. Perhaps the Hartwood address is explained by the as-
sumption that he continued to use Hartwood for his mailing address.

✿   ✿   ✿

255. TO MRS. WILLIAM SONNTAG [71]

[New York City] November 28, 1898

Mrs. William Sonntag,/ How do you persuade anybody to anything
by cables and letters? I am very anxious to have Mrs. Crane come to

---

[71] This letter was first published in Thomas Beer's article "Mrs. Stephen
Crane," *American Mercury* (March, 1934), and reprinted in *Omnibus* (pp.
684–85).

this country. Mrs. Crane is very anxious to have me come back to England. We are carrying on a duel at long range, with ink.[72]

256. JOSEPH CONRAD TO CORA CRANE

Pent Farm/Stanford, Near Hythe/4th Dec 1898

My dear Mrs. Crane/ You made us quite happy with your letter. I had a couple of pretty bad days just before; having heard from Meldrum about that wretched McQueen [73] you may imagine how sick I felt. I did not write to you at once because I did act to think of some other expedient. I would have gone to London to seek [it] had it not been for my reumatism [rheumatism] which kept me on my back in bed 2 days and even when I got up I could not do more than hobble across the room. I was at my wit's end. Luckily it's over. I dreaded opening your letter, having nothing to propose or suggest. It was an immense relief to hear that you had been lucky in some other quarter. Do you think Stephen will be in England before Christmas? This story in B.[74] is magnificent. It is the very best thing he has done since the Red Badge—and it has even something that the Red Badge has not—or not so much of.[75] He is maturing. He is expanding. There is more breadth and somehow more substance in this war-picture. We (I had two men visiting me last week) are delighted with this bit of work. It is Stephen all himself—and a little more. It is the very truth of art. There is an added ampleness in his method which makes me augur a magnificent future for his coming work. Let him only come—and work!

Excuse me if I end here. I am in arrears with my correspondence—besides other worries. Ah! but I do feel relieved.

---

[72] In one of his letters of this time Crane expressed his decision to leave the United States: "I am going to stay in England for some time. It seems that in New York, outside the immediate circle of men who know me well, I am some kind of Simon Legree who goes around knocking women into the gutter and then walking on them. If I was a grocery boy or a hired man or a bank clerk no one would give a cuss what I did. But I am a writer so all bets are doubled" (*Omnibus* [p. 685], where this letter was published for the first time).

[73] John Macqueen, London publisher, whom Meldrum tried unsuccessfully to interest in lending Cora money to bring Stephen home.

[74] "The Price of the Harness."

[75] "The Price of the Harness" is by no means the best thing Crane had done since *The Red Badge;* then he had created, for one thing, "The Open Boat." Conrad, as he himself declared, was no critic.

Jess sends congratulations and best love. Believe me always most
faithfully yours   *Jph Conrad*

257. EDWARD GARNETT TO CORA CRANE

Private House/British Museum/W C./20 Dec. 98

Dear Mrs Crane,/ I send you a few words I wrote on Stephen the
other day.[76] I was asked for it in a hurry, & had not time to do Stephen
justice. There are things you will like in it, & things, perhaps, you
wont. But I meant to add in it that I looked forward to seeing Stephen
do the novel of the American journalistic world, some day. A thing
great, & on a larger scope than he has yet done.

At any rate, excuse the article's deficiencies, & believe me   Yours
very truly   *Edward Garnett*

Conrad writes a fortnight back that Stephen is coming home. I'm
afraid he has had a very sick time out there.

258. JOSEPH CONRAD TO CORA CRANE

Pent Farm/Stanford, Near Hythe/23/12/98

My dear Mrs. Crane:/ . . . I wish you could have given us some news
from Stephen.[77] Well, please God you will have your mind and your
heart at rest soon. I need not tell you it is the fervent wish of those
who live here and however ineffectually, but none the less sincerely
take part in your anxieties and hopes. May the Xmas be a season of
joy indeed and the new year a year of peace to you. Amen.

Our heartiest and friendliest wishes to the good Auntie Ruedy.
We trust to see you all *three* here before the young year has the time
to grow old or even middle aged. Let us share in all that befalls you
as you have done me the honor to allow me heretofore. I am dear Mrs.
Crane your faithful friend and servant   *Jph Conrad*

259. WILLIS BROOKS HAWKINS TO STEPHEN CRANE [78]

[Telegram. New York to Jacksonville, Florida]
Dec 28 1898

Received of Willis B. Hawkins Fifty Dollars. To be paid to Stephen
Crane, Jacksonville, Fla.

---

[76] His essay "Stephen Crane: An Appreciation," *Academy*, December
17, 1898.

[77] Cora at this point knew only that Stephen, having given up the
notions of finding a house in New York City or of buying a ranch in Texas,
was returning to England.

[78] This telegram, not before noticed, aids in substantiating the fact that

260. CORA CRANE TO MRS. ALICE CREELMAN [79]

Dec. 30th [1898]

Dear Madam:—/ I thank you for your reply to my letter asking for *private* subscription for the support of the three youngest children of the late Harold Frederic. In justice to their mother, let me say, that she refused, absolutely, to join in a public appeal for help, thinking, as I do, such an appeal in shocking taste. Nor did she have any knowledge, until yesterday when I wrote informing her, of *this* fund for the children.

The people whom you have heard "discuss this unfortunate scandal" are, naturally, not the people one would look to for help in this matter. The nasty taste that such discussion would leave in their mouths—would strike through to the organ which they use solely to pump blood—blood soured by lack of true charity—to the brain. One wonders if they think themselves christians? [*sic*] And how they dare to set themselves up as models of virteous [*sic*] morality, when they have the example of Christ's loving kindness to sinners, before them.

How can we judge another, we that are so full of sin and weakness? And how can any creature knowing itself mortal lose an opportunity to be charitable in the true sense? Judging not!

To me, the supreme egotism of women who never having been tempted, and so knowing nothing of the temptation of another's soul, set themselves upon their pedestals of self-conceit and conscious virtue, judging their unfortunate sisters guilty alike, is the hardest thing in life. If we women who are beloved and sheltered, would help those less fortunate of our sex to help themselves (and this is not done by using a club or turning our-selves into shrews under the cover of outraged innocence) the world would be a sweeter, purer place to live in and we ourselves would be more worthy of happiness. . . .

. . . I have sheltered these children for five months in my own home and with my own name—and if all the world line themselves up to fight these babies, I will still shelter *them* & God will help me, [until such time as their mother can take them *canceled*]   Yours Very Truly

Cora Crane

Crane was out of pocket, as usual, and drew when in a pinch on his old friend Hawkins, rather than his brothers William and Edmund. Presumably he was en route to Havana, from where he sailed home to England (see Letter 261).

[79] Wife of James Creelman of the New York *Journal*, in London. She opened Cora's letter in his absence and answered Cora's appeal on behalf of Kate and Frederic's three children. Mrs. Creelman wrote in the best style of outraged womanhood, and Cora replied by counterattack.

I would say it is my wish to board *the children* with some very good
Catholics in the country.

❀ ❀ ❀

Brede Place

"I hope that the perfect quiet of Brede Place and the freedom from a
lot of dear good people, who take his mind from his work, will let him
show the world a book that will live" (Letter 261). Cora did her best at
Brede Place to fend off the "Indians"—Crane's word for unwanted
visitors—but they continued to slip past her defenses, while among the
circle of their chosen friends the Cranes did nothing to curb their
entertaining. Though he did not always play the part, Crane bled himself financially in order to support it—namely, the part of "Baron
Brede," as Sanford Bennett called him. A paradox established itself, as
Beer (p. 378) aptly puts it: "To some of his English friends Brede
seemed a Bohemian stronghold while roaming Americans thought
Stephen Crane in severe evening dress surrounded by formal gowns
and black coats a most unhallowed spectacle, the Bohemian turned
snob." He liked it both ways.

He would shock them by combining the role of the Western cowboy with the role of Baron Brede: "He wore riding breeches and
puttees, like a stable boy, a flannel shirt, belt, and no coat—the sort of
costume that so shocked Henry James. When Stephen learned *that* he
always affected the rig when he called on James." When Brede Place
was visited by Crane's brother, his indifferent brother Wilbur, and
Helen (William's daughter), Cora tactfully said: "We'll not dress tonight. Wilbur didn't bring his evening things." The Cranes at Brede
Place customarily dined in evening dress—Stephen in dinner jacket
rather than in tails. (One surmises that Wilbur was duly impressed;
because he had married a housemaid, he was the downgraded member
of the Crane clan.) In July a certain journalist made himself the guest
of the Cranes for four days before Cora managed to dismiss him, and
Crane wrote James Pinker, his literary agent: "If you don't tell some
of these lice that Cora and I aren't running a hotel I'll have to advertise
the fact in the *Times!*" "How," he asked Sanford Bennett, "does it
come to pass that anybody in England thinks he can come and stay
with me before I've asked him and patronize my wife's housekeeping?"
He wrote to Elbert Hubbard: "I must have Egyptian blood in me.
Mummies rise from the tomb and come to pay calls that last for days"
(Beer, p. 372). Henry James, bicycling from nearby Rye, and Conrad
and other friends had license to come and go as they pleased. "He was

always glad to see Mrs. Richie and her daughters, Robert Barr, Mark Barr, H. G. Wells, and A. E. W. Mason. He wrote: 'John Stokes and George Lynch have the kindness to let Cora know when they are coming but would to God that some of the other Indians would write and ask.' " (Beer, p. 378.)

Of Brede Place, Crane wrote to Sanford Bennett: "It is a pretty fine affair and Cora believes that Sir Walter Scott designed it for her. They began one wing in 1378 and somebody kidded it with heavy artillery in Cromwell's time. We shall move in as soon as we can. I enclose 10 pounds. Do I owe you more than that?" (Beer, p. 363.) Bennett's loan, added to Conrad's loan, had aided Crane in getting to Cuba the previous year. In August Crane wrote a Cromwellian story, "Siege," dealing with the Sussex Valley near Brede Place.

Brede Place is "one of the greatest treasures of Sussex, an ancient house" purchased by the Frewens in 1708. It is said to be as perfect an example of a medieval home as is to be found in England. It is associated mainly with the Oxenbridges, a historical family, "whom the church and the Manor House commemorate in stone. . . . In the Oxenbridge Chantry of St. George's, Brede, are their tombs, and Sir Goddard, who attended Henry VIII to the Field of the Cloth of Gold, lies there in recumbent stone, but his rusty helm rests in the alcove on the side of the family chapel at Brede Place. On the very stone door posts of Brede the beautifully cut lettering of JOHN OXENBRIDGE is extant." He died in 1572, and Sir Goddard in 1531.[80] The Brede Chantry possesses not only the sculptured tomb of Sir Goddard, but also the cradle of Jonathan Swift. The estate belonged in the time of Richard II to John atte Ford and was known then not as Brede Place but as Forde, passing to the Oxenbridges in the fifteenth century. Before the Conquest the land belonged to the monastery of Fécamp, and was known then as "a property called Bretda," King Canute referring to it in a charter of 1017. It was then an outpost of Normandy. Queen Emma, wife of two English kings and mother of two others, converted Brede into a Norman foothold. The successful landing of William the Conqueror owes to her more than to anyone else.

Without Brede, William might not have landed, might perhaps never have ventured. But he could count on these few square miles, a convenient bridgehead, and situate almost exactly opposite. That Brede served its purpose may well be surmised by

---

[80] This information is drawn from a series of articles on Brede Place in the *Sussex County Magazine*, III (October, 1929), V (July, 1931), V (August, 1931); for copies of these magazines we are indebted to Roger M. Frewen.

*the fact, registered in Doomsday Book, that when William tri-
umphantly swept along the coast, laying "waste" as he went, the
land of Brede remained untouched!* [81]

Ford Madox Ford (then Ford Madox Hueffer) dramatizes with
lacrimae rerum his impressions of Brede Place.

> *Amongst a perfect wilderness of cats and monkeys there would be
> at least one just soul who was really devoted to Steevie* [sic]*—Con-
> rad, or occasionally the old man himself* [Henry James], *or Mr. Gar-
> nett. . . . But I could not stand the sunlight there. It filtered down
> into those dark green places and was ghastly. . . . All the mass of
> the building of gray stone with mullioned, leaded windows, offer-
> ing a proud and sinister front to sunlight coming through lowering
> clouds. On the bank which supported it played all the things in
> the world that nobody wanted—unwanted children, dogs, men, old
> maids—like beachcombers washed up on green sands. And behind
> the facade, a rabbit warren of passages with beer barrels set up at
> odd corners, and barons of beef for real tramps at the kitchen
> door, and troops of dogs and maids and butlers and sham tramps
> of the New York newspaper world and women who couldn't sell
> their manuscripts. . . .*
>
> *And poor, frail Steevie, with all the organs of his body mar-
> tyred to the waters of Cuba. . . . Poor, frail Steevie, in the little
> room over the porch in the E* [the ground plan of the house, which
> had been added to by Sir Goddard Oxenbridge, was in the form
> of an E in honor of Queen Elizabeth, as was customary in the
> building of the Elizabethan period], *writing incessantly—like a
> spider that gave its entrails to nourish a wilderness of parasites.
> For, with his pen that moved so slowly in microscopic black trails
> over the immense sheets of paper that he affected, he had to sup-
> port all that wilderness. That was the thought I could not bear.*[82]

David Garnett reports that Hueffer had once shed tears over his
own singing of a sentimental ballad, and Garnett who had known
Hueffer from boyhood chuckles, "arch liar," softening the judgment
thus: "He improvised a suitable part to play—in fact, he dramatized a
fleeting but sincere emotion. I have never known anyone else behave
in such a way—but I can imagine Dickens doing so." [83] But another

---

[81] Quoted from Clare Sheridan, *My Crowded Sanctuary* (Methuen,
1945), pp. 3–4. For a gift of this book we are indebted to Roger M. Frewen.

[82] F. M. Ford, in the *American Mercury*, January, 1936; and in *Mightier
Than the Sword* and *Portraits From Life* (1937).

[83] *The Golden Echo*, p. 129.

visitor, Edith Richie (Mrs. I. Howland Jones), dismisses Hueffer's lachrymose picture of "the ill-fated mansion . . . in a damp hollow . . . full of evil influences" in one word: "Rubbish! It stood high, looking down over the valley where flocks of sheep cropped the good grass." [84]

A. E. W. Mason, writing Vincent Starrett in 1945 (see Appendix 27), recalls the occasion of his visit to "Brede Place" for the 1899 Christmas party, to which Crane had invited the leading figures of the countryside:

"The house, which frankly was not in a state to be occupied, was sketchily furnished and I think there was arranged a dormitory in which six or seven men slept. I know that I was given a room to myself but warned not to open, except very cautiously, two great doors which enclosed one side of it. There was no electric light and naturally enough I opened very carefully the two doors. I found that if I had taken one step forward, I should have stepped down about thirty feet into the chapel, this being the private pew or box of the owners of the house. We had, I remember, rushes on the floor instead of carpets, and there were other disadvantages which meant nothing to us, for we were all of us young."

＊　＊　＊

261. CORA CRANE TO EDWARD GARNETT

Ravensbrook [First week of January, 1899]

Dear Mr. Garnet[t]: Thank you so much for sending me the clipping.[85] I like it very much indeed—one must value a true opinion: but I disagree with you when you say that he may fail when the "picturesque phases of the environment that nurtured him give out." The beautiful thoughts in Stephen's mind are simply endless! His great difficulty is the lack of that machine-like application which makes a man work steadily. I hope that the perfect quiet of Brede Place and the freedom from a lot of dear good people, who take his mind from his work, will let him show the world a book that will live.

He has been hard at work upon a war story [86] but what it is like I do not know.

---

[84] Edith R. Jones, "Stephen Crane at Brede," *Atlantic Monthly*, July, 1954.

[85] The *Academy* essay of December 17 (see Letter 257).

[86] *Active Service*, which Crane worked on in Havana but did not finish.

From the Cooks tourist people, I learn that Stephen starts from Havana for home this week.[87] We will let you know when he arrives and I hope you will be one of the first to welcome him. It will be such larks taking him to Brede Place. Perhaps you could manage to give us a day and go too?

. . . Our best wishes for this New Year. Very Sincerely Yours

Cora Crane

262. EDWARD GARNETT TO CORA CRANE

The Cearne/Kent Hatch/Edenbridge/8. Jan. 98 [1899]

Dear Mrs Crane,/ I am very pleased to get your letter & know that you took my criticism in the spirit in which it was written.[88] It is difficult to even give one's impression truly—one goes a little to the left hand or the right hand—& one may give views which the one who knows, as you know, sees is a partial misunderstanding.

I should enjoy very much making one of the party to take Stephen to Brede. Let me know when he is back. Yours very truly

Edward Garnett

263. CORA CRANE TO EDWARD GARNETT

Ravensbrook/Tuesday [January 10, 1899]

Dear Mr. Garnett: I am, at every moment, expecting a wire saying that the ship which carries my dear one, is sighted. The "Manitou," she is due today or tomorrow morning and I shall, if I have time, go to Gravesend to meet Stephen.

We will go to Brede, perhaps on Thursday or Friday.[89] I will wire you. But stop in if your [sic] passing and see Stephen.

---

[87] Beer (p. 363) quotes only two sentences from this letter and carelessly assigns it the date of January 10, 1899. Obviously, Crane could not start for home from Havana the week of January 10 and arrive there January 11. But Cora is here concealing from Garnett the fact that Stephen was a month or longer in New York, before making up his mind to return to England. Conrad's letter of December 4 (No. 256) points to the fact that she had received word of his previous departure from Cuba, headed for New York, and that she at once communicated the glad news to Conrad, expecting Crane would sail immediately for England.

Crane landed at Gravesend on January 10 or 11 (see Letter 263), and he and Cora visited Brede Place on January 17 (see Letter 265).

[88] Garnett's *Academy* essay on Crane (see Letter 257).

[89] Stephen and Cora visited Brede the next Tuesday, January 17 (see Letter 265).

I am so hoping bad weather has not detained the ship. Very Sincerely yours
                                                                    Cora Crane

264. *JOSEPH CONRAD TO STEPHEN CRANE*

Pent Farm,/Stanford, near Hythe/13 Jan 99

My dear Stephen—/ I am more glad than I can say to hear of you being here at last. You haven't lost time in looking up the old Academy.[90] I only heard of it today. Thanks very much for your second wire. All this would be damnable bosh but for the 50 gs. which just save me from battering my head against the walls.

I long to hear your news. And let me tell you at once that the *Harness*[91] is the best bit of work you've done (for its size) since the *Red Badge*. There is a mellowness in the vigour of that story that simply delighted me. Several fellows wrote to me about it as soon as it came out. Lucas [E. V. Lucas], Hueffer [Ford Madox Ford], Graham [R. B. Cunninghame Graham] and others you don't know. More power to your pen. I feel a new man since this morning's wire. It was good of you to think of me at once. I intended to wire myself today inquiring. Well that's all over now. I mean where to locate you when I think of you—which is often—very. I've been nearly dead and several times quite mad since you left. This is no joke, it is the sober truth. I haven't been able to write and felt like cutting my throat. Not a ghost of a notion in my head, not a sentence under the pen. Well. Never mind. It's a little better now. What have you got in *your head*? You must be full of stuff. I suppose the "Dead Man"[92] story will have to wait till you unload your new experience. I know whatever it is it will be *good*. It will be great! You think I might have given a whole sheet of paper for your welcome, but may I be shot if I can find another piece. I am coming to see you directly I finish a rotten thing I am writing for B'wood [*Blackwood's Magazine*]. It *is* rotten—and I can't help it. All I write is rotten now. I am pretty well decayed myself. I ought to be taken out and flung into a dusthole—along with the dead cats—by heavens! Well. Enough. I don't want to bore you into a faint in your first week in Merry England. Ever yours
                                                                    Conrad

---

[90] Edward Garnett's "An Appreciation of Stephen Crane," published in the *Academy* (see Letters 257, 261, 262). In *Friday Nights* (1922) Garnett reissued this appraisal in expanded version. Americans learned of Garnett's praise of Crane in the *Literary Digest*, January 21, 1899: "An English Appreciation of Stephen Crane."

[91] "The Price of the Harness."

[92] "The Upturned Face," a story Crane had not yet written. It is among Crane's richest works.

265. CORA CRANE TO EDWARD GARNETT

Ravensbrook/Jan. 19th '99

Dear Mr. Garnett: I thank you so much for your cheque for the three little children of the late Harold Frederic. My fund is now £49.9.0— less four weeks living they have had out of it £8. It is very kind of you to help me and I'm sure you will be blessed for your charity.

On Tuesday afternoon [January 17],[93] Stephen suddenly made up his mind to go to Brede, so off we went to Hastings. We drove out and of course it was very dark—Stephen was mad over the place. We tramped, later, after a supper of ham & eggs beside the kitchen fire— to a cottage in the village and put up for the night there. Then spent the day at Brede. We are going to move Heaven and Earth to get there. Stephen said that a solemn feeling of work came to him there so I am delighted. Come to see us soon. Very Sincerely yours

Cora Crane

266. TO JAMES B. PINKER [94]

Ravensbrook,/Feb 1, 99

Dear Mr. Pinker:— I enclose you a short story (3500 words) which is in the same series with "Lynx Hunting," "The Monster," and "His New Mittens." [95] We like it a little—Harper's, in one sense has the bookrights to this series but this right is mainly based upon an artistic reason—the fact that I do not think it correct to separate the stories. (Harper's have the rights to the Monster.)

You will be glad to know that I am now writing a story with which you can have good game: "God Rest Ye, Merry Gentlemen." [96] We are sure that you will like it.

Of course, you will understand that although I say nothing to you of money matters, our affairs at this time are in a woeful condition.

The MS of "The Angel Child" [97] has been sent to Reynolds. Yours faithfully   *Stephen Crane*

---

[93] Contra Beer (p. 363): "So, on January 16th, they drove from Hastings through twilight and Crane saw his next home by the pleasant glow of lamps."

[94] Crane's literary agent in London.

[95] *Harper's Magazine* published "Lynx Hunting" in September, 1899. In 1898 *Harper's* had published "The Monster" in August and "His New Mittens" in November.

[96] Published in *Cornhill Magazine*, May, 1899.

[97] The original of "The Angel Child" was Cora Howorth. *Harper's Magazine* printed this story in August, 1899.

❀ ❀ ❀

Stephen Crane in Debt

Crane had no sooner landed in England than creditors leaped at him, issuing judgments right and left. The rent for one year at Ravensbrook (£91) had not been paid, and other sums were due the Oxted dairy and the butcher and the grocer. A three-cornered correspondence began now between the Cranes, James Pinker (literary agent) and Alfred T. Plant (solicitor) on behalf of Crane. Crane was threatened with bankruptcy.

❀ ❀ ❀

267. TO JAMES B. PINKER

Ravensbrook/Feb 4th. '99

Dear Pinker:—/ A long day with Dominick [98] made me so tired by the time I reached home that I was quite incapable of keeping my promise to you. As regards the Solicitors,[99] Dominick also bravely offered to go and stand in the breach. I then thought it best to hold you in reserve. Dont you think so? Dominick says that he will have no hesitation in giving the Solicitors to understand that Stokes and Co., will come to my assistance to some extent at least. As the Solicitors had asked me that morning wether [*sic*] or no the Stokes people would not give a guarantee of the debt, Dominick's remarks will doubtless please them. I will let you know of course how things turn out and I will be glad if you will let me know any thing you hear through Dominick.

I have told Pawling that if "disposing of the lines (poems) is giving him any trouble" I would like to have them handed over to you. Have you done anything about Tauchnitz? [100] I suppose Heinemann controls the European rights to all my books?

[98] London representative for Frederick A. Stokes & Co., publishers.

[99] The solicitors—Morrisons & Nightingale—for Whiteley's Department Store, to whom the sum of £98 9s was owing, part of which was for the unpaid balance on the purchase of a piano in 1897. They wrote Pinker, and he in turn wrote Crane that the matter "appears more serious than you thought, and I confess that I do not see a way out of the difficulty at the moment. Of course, we can straighten things gradually as the work comes along" (letter in the Butler Library Crane Collection, dated February 13, 1899).

[100] Sidney Pawling of Heinemann's, who had introduced Crane to Conrad in 1897. The poems are *War Is Kind*, published in 1899 only in the United States by Frederick A. Stokes & Co. Tauchnitz is a German publisher.

Let me know when you hear from Meldrum as the idea of writing stories for the purpose of getting them buried forever in Scotland makes me very unhappy.

Please tell Meldrum [101] that I am unwell so that he won't be indignant because I have not come to see him.

Dominick wishes me to write a letter (which is to remain in your hands) setting forth an acknowledgement of a little temporary mortgage upon the royalties of my four Appleton books viz: The Red Badge of Courage, The Little Regiment, Maggie, and The Third Violet, the royalties being at fifteen per cent and free of all claims. It is Dominick's idea that this letter should be addressed to you and remain in your hands.

Will you draw up a letter of this kind and send it to me for my signature?

"God Rest Ye, Merry gentlemen" is coming on finely. If you conclude that "The Angel Child" is not a good opening gun, bury it in the heather i.e. send it to Blackwood. The next story will be a better one. Yours faithfully   *Stephen Crane*

268. TO THE REVEREND CHARLES J. LITTLE [102]

Brede Place, Brede,[103] Northiam, Sussex./England./Feb. 6th. '99

Dear Doctor Little:—/ I am quite sure that you will not remember me at all since I was merely a student of yours at Syracuse University and one of many hundreds. I distinctly confess that I had not the ability to impress myself upon you through my mental endowments but I remember your telling me once that I impressed myself upon you through a resemblance to "John" whom you knew when you were at Dickinson College. After a certain examination in the French Revolution you called me to the desk and told me to beware—that I was going

---

[101] Besides McClure ("that Scotch ass"), the names of Blackwood and Meldrum are added to the lengthening list of editors and publishers who had earlier come to Crane's rescue and against whom he now turned.

[102] Professor of History and Logic at Syracuse University, 1885–1891, he later became president of the Garrett Biblical Institute, Evanston, Illinois.

History, which Little taught at Syracuse University, was Crane's favorite subject. But Crane was an indifferent student, and no semester grades were posted after his name at the end of his single semester's survival at Syracuse, in the spring of 1891. The dean suggested that it would not be wise for him to return that fall unless he underwent a change of intention. Letter 276 is Little's reply.

[103] The Cranes did not move to Brede Place until February 12 (see Letter 271).

very wrong indeed. It has stuck in my mind for years that some of the information you had recieved [sic] of me was quite false. Candidly, I was worse than I should have been but I always had a singular faculty of having it said that I was engaged in crimes which are not of my accomplishments. Indeed, this singular faculty has followed me out of college into real life.

As to my little career, I'm sure I have nothing to say unless it be to the man who expressed such a generous interest in my welfare so long ago. True, it was mainly because I resembled "John" but I have never forgotten what you said to me. I am not one of the foolish ones who would say to you that your talk to me directed or changed my life but I would say to you that I remember with so much gratitude the words you spoke, they have been to me so much of a strength in life that my first fear is that amid your interest in the hundreds of students who year by year pass under your eye, you have totally forgotten your one-time interest in me.

It is a little thing to talk about but I have written several little books which have editions in New York, London, Paris, Leipsic, Vienna and in the English colonies.

It is indeed such a little thing to talk about that I would not bring it to your attention if I was not in the hopes of recalling to your mind the man who resembled "John" and to tell you that some silly talent of mine has been brought to light. In closing, I can only hope that you will remember the lad who resembled "John" and remember, also, that he often tells about his fireside the tale of the man who exhorted him—somewhat without accurate knowledge in regard to crime—but with such kindliness and interest—indeed almost affection—that the lad has almost made it a part of his creed of conduct.

I hope that you will be disposed to answer this note even if it is only three lines but anyhow remember there is one who will always be grateful to you. Yours faithfully   *Stephen Crane*

269. TO MRS. MORETON FREWEN

February 7 1899

[Inscribed in a copy of *The Open Boat and Other Stories*]

Dear Mrs. Morton Frewen/ You, with the rest of the world, have herein a further proof of my basic incapacity. However there are some stories of Americans and some stories of America in the book which may remind you of somebody better [104] but, in any case, allow me to present my esteem   *Stephen Crane*

---

[104] Probably Bret Harte or Ambrose Bierce, both of whom had lived for a time in London and whose work exerted a lasting influence on Crane.

270. TO JAMES B. PINKER

Ravensbrook,/Feb. 9th. 1899

Dear Pinker:—/ Morrisons and Nightingale have been seen and they express themselves willing to stand off the rent [105] *if* you will give them a guarantee that the rent will be paid, time not specified.

They said: "If Mr. Crane's money for *ms.* comes through Mr. Pinker's hands of course Mr. Pinker will be willing to guarantee the amount of rent." Of course I dont want to let you in for any strange game but this seems to me to be my *only* way clear. Really your position would be simply that of a buffer-state. I hesitate to ask you to do it but there is absolutely no other way. If you think you can stand it do so and God be with you.

This will enable me to move almost at once to Brede and get a fair chance at myself.

Morrison[s] and Nightingale are an old fashioned English firm of solicitors and they require of me that you write to them first. This is an added indignity but I hope you will see your way clear to do it and to make your letter to them very strong. Answer me, if you can, by the first post. Morrisons and Nightingale's address is Reigate, Surrey. Yours faithfully   *Stephen Crane*

271. CORA CRANE TO MRS. EDWARD PEASE [106]

Brede Place/Monday [February 13, 1899]

My dear Mrs. Pease:/ This is just a line to say we are here. We came yesterday with the dogs and are camping out until our things arrive. It is very jolly and we are happy. The children [107] were so very glad to see us. They look better already.

Mr. Crane was so much pleased with the book. He has heard a great deal about Fiona MacCleod [108] but has never seen this book of hers. It was such a graceful thought to send it, but you are always doing nice things for us.[109] "The Peases" are our one regret of Oxted

---

[105] Rent the Cranes owed on Ravensbrook.

[106] Edward Pease was secretary of the Fabian Society.

[107] The children mentioned here are Héloïse and Barry Frederic, aged five and four, who remained with the Cranes at Brede Place in the care of a governess, Mrs. Burke, until Crane's death.

[108] Fiona Macleod was the pseudonym of William Sharp (1855–1905), Scottish poet and man of letters.

[109] In anticipation of their move to the drafty old house, Mrs. Pease sent the Cranes a warming pan. Cora, on February 7, reciprocated with the gift of two of Stephen's manuscripts, "The Angel Child" and "The Lover and the Telltale."

but we shant lose you altogether, you will write to us and you will come often to visit us.

This house is more wonderful to us than ever, and it seems as if we must wake up to find there is no "truly Bweed" after all—as Barry says.

The children, Mrs. Burke, Mrs. Ruedy and the Cranes send their best love to you all. Ever fondly yours   *Cora Crane*

272. TO JAMES B. PINKER

Brede Place/[February 16? 1899]

Dear Pinker: I send you a rattling good war story—I think 5330 words. Please send me a checque for £40 so that I will get it on Sunday morning. If you have to dispose of the U.S. rights of any of the stories you had better consult me. I know my U.S. market. Yours faithfully   S. C.

P.S:. I should think this would go to the Strand.[110] How am I going? Strong?

273. TO MR. COLLIS [111]

Brede Place/Feb. 18th—'99

Dear Sir:—/ Thank you very much for your kind note of the 15th—. Was the "Blue Hotel" sold at all in England? If it was not I suppose you still have that typed copy? and I would be very glad if you would send it to me. Since it has already been published in America I suppose there is very little use of keeping it going here. However you

---

Eleven-year-old Michael Pease had formed an unrequited attachment to seven-year-old Helen Frederic while the Frederic orphans and their mother were staying with Cora at Ravensbrook. Around this infant heart affair Crane sketched the story of Jimmie Trescott's love letter in "The Lover and the Telltale."

The friendship between the Cranes and the Pease family did not lapse when the Cranes moved from Oxted to Brede Place. On January 4, 1900, Stephen, then recovering from his first attack of hemorrhages, sent Mrs. Pease an inscribed copy of *The Monster*, which had just been published in New York by Harper's (see Letter 322A).

[110] The *Strand Magazine* published "Revenge of the Adolphus" in September, 1899.

[111] Collis had an agency known as The Author's Syndicate. By what method of rationalization did Crane convince himself of the propriety of his dealing with Collis at the very time he was sending urgent appeals to Pinker to save him from bankruptcy? One recalls his earlier dealings with Appleton's editor, Ripley Hitchcock; his admitted violations of "certain business courtesies" (see Letter 153).

might let me know to what papers and magazines you have sent it to
[*sic*] Yours faithfully   *Stephen Crane*

274. *TO JAMES B. PINKER*

Brede Place/Sunday [Feb. 19, 1899]

Dear Pinker: I am mailing you at this time a whacking good Whilomville Story—4000 words—and I am agitatedly wiring you at the same
time. You are possibly able to forgive me by this time for the way I
put upon you. I must have altogether within the next ten days £150—
no less, as the Irish say. But, by the same token, I am going to earn it—
mainly, in Whilomville Stories for they are sure and quick money. £40
of my £150 have I done yesterday and today but for all your gods,
help me or I perish. Yours faithfully   *C.*

275. *TO JAMES B. PINKER*

Brede Place/Feb 21st '99

My dear Pinker:/ Morrison[s] and Nightingale have written to me
that you guaranteed nothing but the £40—which I made over to you
from Reynolds. I am in hopes that either your language was of dubious
meaning or else that they are mistaken. Please [let] me know at once
by wire here at Brede Place   Yours Faithfully   *Stephen Crane*

276. *THE REVEREND CHARLES J. LITTLE*
TO STEPHEN CRANE

Evanston, Illinois/Feb. 23, 1899

Dear Mr. Crane:/ "John" [112] of whom you write was a clever lad,
quite capable of writing "silly books"; if he had not hurried quite so
fast, in his eagerness "to tread the floors of hell." As I remember "John"
he was a young Apollo, lithe, vigorous, handsome; if you reminded me
of him, I must have discerned in you potencies of various kinds and
feared that they might end in blight as "John" did. The ruin of "John"
that you recall to me is still a poignant recollection; I should be glad
to be quit of all responsibility for it. We teachers, I fear, handle life
rather carelessly and "John's" blood has not yet ceased crying from
the ground. Well! I am glad you have kept to the highway. There are
so many cross-cuts to hell, that I wonder always when a full-blooded
adventurous lad gets safely established on the main road.

But you must be in error at one point. I surely did not talk to you
of "crime." For I know of no reason for my doing so. Crime is rather

---

[112] As Crane refers to him in Letter 268.

an ugly word. Indeed my pen balks at it now. And besides that, my impressions, I fancy, came rather from what I saw than from what I had heard. The resemblance to "John" quite probably aroused forebodings and led to interpretations of expression and bearing that the future has not wholly discredited. For I dealt rather with what might than with what must be. And the "silly books" of which you speak so disparingly [sic] and, yet with proper pride, have not concealed the "might be" altogether. At least so it seems to me who know them slightly. It amuses me, grey-headed fellow that I am, to hear an artist talk of crime. He, of all men, never knows it. He is taken up much with its picturesque aspects. He knows how to use the criminal, actual or potential; but in order to use him, he denaturalizes, derealizes him. The words are vile enough; but they alone will say just about what I mean. And this he does in the *very instant of perception*. In his eagerness to portray, he changes form and color, while he looks, and never sees men and women as they are. It is, I fancy, different with men whose knowledge of crime begins with the sorrow that it causes. Mine began, in this wise, very early. My earliest recollections are of crime and its consequences. For me it has no picturesque aspects; although it may, like a cancer, have picturesque associations. True, my knowledge of it is limited by the sources from which I have drawn it—an unpleasantly large and various assortment of family skeletons, and early and dangerous acquaintance with the slums of Bedford St. and St. Mary St. in Philada., the revelation of the criminal court, the Reformatory and the Insane Asylum; but above all from the perpetual study of the criminal that escapes the jail and seems to escape, in this world, the judgement of God. Add to this a fairly large acquaintance with the memoirs of men and women who have sinned in many languages and through many centuries. Of course, this kind of knowledge is a form of ignorance. To know poison, one must have it in one's blood. And even then, the experimenter encounters a peculiar difficulty; the poison destroys his power to perceive its effects. And I am glad to learn that your knowledge of crime is not of this sort. You see, too, that I would not over-value it, if it were; I should still insist upon "correcting the compass" before trusting wholly to its indications. It pleases me to sit at your fireside, invisibly, and to be talked about, as I appear to your kindly imagination. I have no share in anything that you have done or won. Many, indeed, are the influences that make and save a soul. It is barely possible that the moan of my early experiences and later sorrows vibrated through my clumsy speech and awkward thinkings and gave them a touch of enduring pathos. This, I fancy, rather than any words of mine has survived in your memory, and it pleases me to have it so. The best of our books are "silly" and our

knowledge vanishes away. But love never faileth. And, therefore, if a
face should haunt me tomorrow as yours did aforetime, I shall speak
as I did then, wisely or foolishly, as the thoughts may bubble up within
my brain. You younger men are what you will be,—sometimes, at least;
we older men, alas, must be, what we are. We have exhausted our
chances; and there are no more tickets for the transformation baths on
sale. Yours very truly,   *Charles J. Little*

277. TO JAMES B. PINKER

Brede Place/Sunday [February 26? 1899]

My dear Pinker: I am sending you another of the Whilomville stories
for Harper and Bros. It is 4095 words and for it they will pay you (at
$50 per thousand) something over forty pounds. Please send me £30
by next post. I need it badly.

   If you can stick to your end, all will go finely and I will bombard
you so hard with ms that you will think you are living in Paris during
the siege. Yours faithfully   *SCrane*

278. TO JAMES B. PINKER

Brede Place/Tuesday [February 28? 1899]

My dear Pinker: I am sending you 2 copies of a short story of a little
over 4500 words. I hope you sent the £10 to Plant [113] and hope you
will send me a further checque of £25 by next post.

   My short stories are developing in three series. I. The Whilomville
stories. (always to Harpers.)/II. The war tales./III. Tales of western
American life similar to "Twelve O'Clock."

   It might be well to remember this. For instance if you could pro-
visionally establish the war tales with one magazine and the western
tales with another as the Whilomville yarns are fixed with Harper's, it
would be very nice.

   Today I will dictate for you some information as to my U.S.
market. Faithfully yours   C

279. TO MR. COLLIS

March 2nd— '99

Dear Mr. Collis:—/ I am quite sure that the best thing to do with the
"Blue Hotel" [114] is to take it to the Westminster Gazette and sell it

---

[113] Crane's solicitor, Alfred T. Plant.
[114] Published in *Collier's Weekly*, November 26 and December 3, 1898.
The *Bibliography* (1948) does not list the *Westminster Gazette*. Although
it probably was also published there, it has not been traced.

for about fifteen pounds. I have always been a bit of a fad with them and when ever I have to sacrifice myself upon the alter [sic] of copyright, I have found them good priests. The Editor has changed since my day but I think you will find them willing. This is the only thing which I can think of.

I am very much obliged to you for the attention you have given the story. If you ever get down into this dark corner of the world I am always free and at home on Thursdays. Yours faithfully

Stephen Crane

280. EDMUND B. CRANE [115] TO STEPHEN CRANE

Hartwood N.Y. Mch. 2, '99

Dear Stephen,/ Congratulations on your marriage. Give our love to your wife.

We are in the midst of a howling blizzard today. The snow is falling fast, and, driving across the pond piles in a drift below the house. We are having severe weather this winter.

Did I write you that I was in the ice business? I built a house 40 × 60 with twenty foot posts last year and this year have built one 12 feet longer. Hartwood Lake ice is making a way for itself in Port Jervis, and I look forward to the time when we will furnish half the ice used there. We have beautiful ice 20 to 27 inches thick and clear as glass.

Your pony [116] with a mate pulled an ice wagon last summer, and was very useful. It did not hurt his health or spirits, he is as gay as ever, and a good deal tougher. I ride him often in preference to driving over the rough roads, and find him a hand-full sometimes. We are all very fond of him. Mame would pull my hair if I did not treat him

---

[115] Edmund Crane, Stephen's brother, was postmaster of Hartwood, proprietor of the general store, ice dealer, and justice of the peace. This letter must have been a reply to Stephen's follow-up announcement from England of the "marriage."

[116] Stephen's little brown horse Peanuts figured prominently in Cora's disagreements later with Stephen's brothers over the estate. The will Crane had made in Florida before sailing in the *Commodore* was lost. A few weeks before he died he summoned Plant, the solicitor, to Brede Place and made a new will, naming Plant and William Crane coexecutors respectively for the English and American branches of his estate. On August 21, 1900, Will wrote Cora: "Ed says that his bill against the horse was $129, at a rate of board fixed by Stephen himself, before Ed commenced to use it, and that he is willing to keep the horse for the bill; but that if he gives up the horse, he will make that claim against the estate. I should favor letting him keep the horse." Peanuts was sold; Cora protested.

right. She drives him anywhere and he jogs along very demurely. When I have the reins he is apt to cut up, shying, and jumping, and making believe kick. He has the best disposition of any horse I have had here. He drives very nicely to a buggy, and never breaks a trot to run. Under saddle he never trots. Being so knowing we use him in all sorts of ways: in snaking small timbers, or drawing the ice marker, plowing in team in light soil, hauling fire wood from shop, feed from the depot, and find him very useful. I can drive him the 15 miles to Port Jervis (with a mate), and you know the roads, in from 1.30 to 2 hours. One and a half hours if I am in a hurry, and two hours easily.

He is as sound as a dollar, and only shows that he has been worked by the collar mark on his neck, and his tail being shorter.

If you should ever want him, come and get him, but if you do not, he can stay with us as long as I keep a horse. . . .

Wish I could see the house at Brede Place. Our house could be stored in your big hall. When I become a wealthy ice dealer I will come over to see you. I have hunted more this season than ever before. . . . Your loving brother   *E. B. Crane*

I have considerable mail for you. Shall I send it on? Have also clippings from A. C. Bureau   *Ed.*

281. CORA CRANE TO JAMES B. PINKER

Brede Place/March 6th 1899

Dear Mr. Pinker:—/ Mr. Crane yesterday received a cable from Mr. Reynolds saying "God Rest Ye, sold 300." We do not know if this means that he has sold the international serial rights and wishes it withdrawn from the English market, or if the telegraph people have made one of their usual errors and that the cable means that Mr. Reynolds has simply *sold* the American serial rights. At any rate Mr. Crane wishes you to hold it until he is sure.

I cannot understand what can be the reason for the English publishers refusing such stuff as those children [sic] stories and "God Rest Ye." They seem to fancy themselves as judges of literature but to me they appear to be a good set of idiots to refuse really clever and artistic stuff and to print the rot they do. Mr. Reynolds has pleased us very much by his prompt placing of these stories.[117] We hope that you will be equally successful in placing the serial rights of "Active Service" and in also, perhaps by pointing out to London publishers that Harpers have not only thought "Lynx Hunting" and "The Angel Child" good

---

[117] Cora's lecture tone in regard to Reynolds' success with the Whilomville stories is similar to Crane's in Letter 284.

enough but have asked for *all* the "Whilomville" stories that Mr. Crane may write, that they have a lot to learn and that the firm of Pinker are the people to teach them. It is a good opportunity for you to let them know that there are others, as we say in America.

We hope now to soon put at rest any doubts Mssrs. [*sic*] Morrisons and Nightingale may have. Half of the novel [118] should reach you by Thursday.

We hope that you will soon be able to give us a few days at Brede Place. Yours truly   *Cora Crane*

282. JAMES B. PINKER TO CORA CRANE

James B. Pinker/Artistic and Literary Agent
Effingham House,/Arundel Street,/Strand,/London. W. C.
March 9, 1899

Dear Mrs. Crane,/ I have withdrawn "God Rest Ye, Merry Gentlemen" until we know the meaning of Mr. Reynold's cable; but I wish we could make some arrangement to prevent the possibility of Mr. Reynold's and my operations overlapping. Editors are not pleased if I go and talk a great deal about a story and ask them to pay special attention to it, and then withdraw it.[119]

In condemning English editors for their want of appreciation, one must remember that Mr. Crane's reputation is not established on this side as it is in the States, so that his name does not carry so much weight with the readers of sixpenny magazines, which are, after all, what one has most to depend on.

I am glad to hear that I may expect the MS. of the novel soon. I suppose you have arranged so that in the event of my finding a serial opening Heinemann will hold the novel over. Of course, if it is published serially, Methuen's novel [120] will have to come out first.

With kind regards/Yours sincerely,   *James B. Pinker*

---

[118] Crane is generally thought to have finished *Active Service* in Cuba.

[119] Reynolds makes the same complaint to her later on in regard to *The O'Ruddy:* "I wish I could also know where it has been offered by Mr. Pinker so that I might not offer it twice to the same people. You spoke of its having been offered to McClure, the Journal and Tillotson. Has it been offered elsewhere? I spoke of it to Pearson's Magazine and found it had been offered there, so apparently Pinker or his agent has offered it widely. I would like to know so as not to make a fool of myself offering it to people who have already seen it" (letter of December 14, 1900, from Paul R. Reynolds to Cora Crane, in the Butler Library Crane Collection).

[120] The Revolutionary War novel on which Methuen had already paid Crane an advance of £100.

283. TO JAMES B. PINKER

Brede Place/[Thursday, March 9, 1899]

Dear Mr. Pinker:—/ The restrictions as to the serial publication of the novel [121] are that it shall be concluded before the 1st. of Nov. this year. As to price, I expect to get in the neighborhood of £600– for the American serial rights but I would not know at all what to say in regard to the English serial rights. Of course you will get as much as you can and that is all I can say. The buyers of the English serial rights would have to come in consultation with the buyers of the American serial rights but the American buyers would be very docile. Yours faithfully   S. *Crane*

284. TO JAMES B. PINKER

Brede Place/March 17th '99

Dear Pinker: As I wired you today, I can hold "God Rest Ye Merry Gentlemen" until May. Please tell me when Mr. Meldrum was kind enough to loosen his talons on the "Clan of No Name." I think my relations with the Blackwoods is about the most expensive friendship I have yet devised. Please let me know if the "Clan of No Name" is not sold by the 20th. Let me know by wire. In that case I shall come to London and wrestle with some newspaper friends.

I should think Black and White or the London Illustrated News are extremely likely people. I have myself sold them stories of much the same character without any trouble.

The novel [122] is now at 48000—words but the English market seems so stagnant and Reynolds is so successful that I have delayed sending you a copy of the first half of the book in order that I might get a copy off to Reynolds. I am confident that it will be the most successful book that I have ever published.[123]

If you can get £30. cash for both those stories *now*, I would rather have it than £50 next month, altho' they brought in America a trifle like £106. Yours faithfully   *Stephen Crane*

285. TO MR. COLLIS

March 18th '99

Dear Sir:— I have today recieved [*sic*] your cheque for £6. 12. 3 for

---

[121] *Active Service.*

[122] *Active Service.*

[123] It was apparently a psychological necessity for Crane to consider each new piece of work an improvement, financially as well as artistically, over the preceding one.

which this is my reciept [*sic*].[124] Yours Sin[cere]ly   *Stephen Crane*

286. JAMES B. PINKER TO STEPHEN CRANE

London, W.C. March 20, 1899

Dear Crane,/ As I telegraphed to you today, I have placed "The Clan of No Name" with Black & White, and they are to pay £15. 15 for it. Blackwoods returned it on the 9th inst.

I am glad the novel is going on, though I am afraid it looks as if the dates will get mixed.

You grumble at the English market, but it has not yet had a fair chance. It won't be sluggish when you give it what it wants and a reasonable time.

I will let you know about "God Rest Ye" as soon as possible. Sincerely yours,   *James B. Pinker*

287. CORA CRANE TO JAMES B. PINKER

Brede Place/April 25th [1899]

Dear Mr. Pinker: I send you 22 chapters of "Active Service." The balance you will get the end of this week.

Please do your very best to sell serially[125] and give editors to understand that two weeks is the limit to keep Mr. Crane's copy. Please make this your fast rule for all of Mr. Crane's work. Editors have always subscribed to this for me, when I have been disposing of Mr. Crane's stuff. Very truly yours   *Cora Crane*

287A. TO PAUL REVERE REYNOLDS

[Undated, but between May and November, 1899;
dictated to Cora, who wrote it, but signed by Crane]

Dear Reynolds: I enclose you a letter from the Saturday Evening Post.

As for "Active Service," Stokes and Company have, without my knowledge or permission, been attempting to sell it serially. I have told them that I wanted you to conduct that matter and in order to pervent [*sic*] confusion I send you word at the earliest possible moment. Yours faithfully   *S. Crane*

---

[124] Here ends dealings with Collis, who aided somewhat Crane's overdrawn exchequer.

[125] *Active Service* was copyrighted on July 21, 1899, by S. S. McClure for serial publication. Whether it was published serially is not known.

288. TO ELBERT HUBBARD

Brede Place/May 1st '99

My dear Hubbard:/ I wrote I think sometime in '97 suggesting that you reprint in the *Philistine* two little articles of mine which appeared here in the *Westminster Gazette*.[126] I have just been reading them again and I like them. I send you copies and if you are not a duffer you will consider them good and human enough even for your blinding *Philistine*. Send me the *Philistine* or I will set fire to East Aurora by cable.

I have been working up some grievances against you. I object strongly to your paragraphs about Rowan.[127] You are more wrong than is even common on our humble incompetant [*sic*] globe. He didn't do anything worthy at all. He received the praise of the general of the army and got to be made a lieutenant col. for a feat which about forty newspaper correspondents had already performed at the usual price of fifty dollars a week and expenses. Besides he is personally a chump and in Porto Rico where I met him he wore a yachting cap as part of his uniform which was damnable. When you want to monkey with some of our national heroes you had better ask me, because I know and your perspective is almost out of sight.

When I think of you I rejoice that there is one man in the world who can keep up a small independent monthly howler without either dying, going broke, or becoming an ass. Yours always   *Stephen Crane*

289. TO THOMAS HUTCHINSON [128]

Brede Place/May 1st. '99

Dear Sir:—/ I wish to thank you for your sympathetic letter but I am sorry to say that at present I find it impossible to do as you ask. Later, if you will send me the books, I will be glad to write in them whatever is in my head at the moment although I am sure that it will be of no interest.[129] Yours faithfully,   *S. Crane*

---

[126] They appeared under the title "With Greek and Turk" on June 14 and 18, 1897. Hubbard did not reprint them. The *Philistine* published two other Crane pieces this year: "Old Man Goes Wooing" (in July) and "Fishing Village" (in August).

[127] The sham hero whom Crane is ridiculing here is A. S. Rowan, author of "How I Carried the Message to Garcia."

This letter, reprinted from *Omnibus*, pp. 687–88, first appeared in the *New Colophon* of January, 1948.

[128] A book collector and autograph hunter of the nineties; he lived at Rugby and left a large library of inscribed volumes.

[129] Crane was never bashful about giving his autograph, whether to

290. COMMANDER J. C. COLWELL [130]
TO STEPHEN CRANE

United States Embassy./123 Victoria Street/
London, S.W. 27 May 1899

Dear Mr. Crane:/ I return the copy of the story of the "Adolphus" which I have read with much amusement and pleasure. You have hit off the local color of that sort of thing admirably and the unconscious humour of the actors on the little stage is quite true to life. . . .

I would suggest that (p. 1) the correspondents sit in the deck house or on a bench in the shade of the galley as the latter is a very crowded and uncomfortable place in small craft in hot weather and in 99 vessels out of 100 has no more room than is necessary for the cook and his pots.

The "Chancellorville" answers to the DETROIT, MARBLE-HEAD, MONTGOMERY class, and they are Commanders' commands.

"Flagship" is only used to describe a ship flying an Admiral's flag or a Commodore's board-pennant. In all other cases when two or more vessels are in company it is "Senior Officer's ship," or "S. O." or "S. O. P." "Senior Officer's pennant."

Lyda de Camp, who presided over a well-known sporting house in Jacksonville or to nine-year-old Lily Barrett, spending the winter with her parents at the St. James, in Jacksonville, who posted herself in the hotel lobby on the night Crane was brought in after the *Commodore* sinking. Catching sight of the child who had teased him for his autograph at inconvenient times earlier, he called out, "Where's that album?" and wrote opposite the signatures of William Jennings Bryan and John L. Sullivan: "Stephen Crane, able seaman, S. S. *Commodore.*" (This inscription first appeared in the *American Mercury* of June, 1934, under "Correspondence" addressed by Richmond Barrett of Newport, Rhode Island.) At another time and place unknown, on a folded sheet of paper undated and without the name of the recipient, Crane wrote: "May you never lack autographs./Stephen Crane." (This inscription first appeared in "Stephen Crane's Curious Conflagration," by John S. Mayfield, *American Book Collector,* December, 1956.)

[130] The U.S. Naval Attaché and his wife were weekend guests at Brede Place a few days before this letter was written. Crane must have shown him the manuscript of "The Revenge of the Adolphus," which Commander Colwell took away with him at Crane's request to make corrections in the use of nautical terms, ship's gear, etc. Crane was probably introduced to Colwell and others of the embassy circle through his friend and admirer, Lafayette Hoyt DeFriese.

"The Revenge of the Adolphus" was first published in the *Strand Magazine,* September, 1899, and in the United States in *Collier's Weekly,* October 28, 1899.

Chicken's captain (p. 9). Captain is a generic term afloat and means anything from the person commanding a canal boat to one commanding a battleship. Commander means a specific rank to which certain duties appertain.

P. 9. The boatswain would not remain in the cabin after the official business was finished, but after looking unhappy for a bit would slide out the door and hunt the more congenial company of his confrères, the warrant-officers mess. The executive officer would undoubtedly add himself to the gathering in the cabin and the four then there would probably be about the same age and with naval academy affinities.

P. 10. The crew of the natty gig of the yacht would probably pull a "steady stroke," but the "three men" in the heavy life boat of the tug would only wobble along.

P. 11. A cruiser of the "Chancellorville" class would have a couple of buglers on board and always go to "quarters" by bugle accompanied by the drum beat. The boatswain's whistle and call of the boatswain's mates is used in small craft with no bugles or drummers. I would suggest the opening of that chapter something like the following which is what would really happen: "Beat to quarters!" from Surrey.

The quick notes of a bugle and the sharp roll-rat-tat-tat-roll of a drum stirred the decks of the Chancellorville.

A quick patter of feet, a clanging of scuttle plates, rattle of ammunition hoists, and the energetic chug of breech-plugs followed as the guns were loaded and swung into extreme train ahead. Then everybody looked a little bored. Scarcely a word was spoken after the first order beyond the sharp repetition "shell-common" at each ammunition scuttle by the impatient carriers and the quiet "4000 yards" of the gun-division officers. The ship and her crew were ready &c &c. . . .

The "Adolphus" is a good story and will "go." Let me know when and where it is to appear. Very truly yours,   *J. C. Colwell*

291. TO AN UNKNOWN RECIPIENT

[Summer, 1899]

Yes, yes, I know that it has been wonderfully proven how that the doughboys and the Jackies know nothing of manorial architecture and Pierre Loti. They care not if the journal of the sisters De Goncourt is never published at all. Velasquez? No. Cervantes? No. United intellects of superior lands bade them be licked to the glory of Cervantes and Velasquez. I don't know why. I shall never know why. But there is an excellence of human conduct independent of Cervantes and

Velasquez.[131] The Spaniards who lay dead in El Caney knew something of it. Our men knew something of it. Mob-courage?—mob-courage. The mob has no courage. That is the chatter of clubs and writers. Pray go stand with your back to deadly fire from a painted drop for a pantomime and wave signals for half an hour without wincing and then talk of mob-courage.[132] Imperialism? All right. The White Man's Burden? What in hell did Private Jones and Seaman Smith know of it? Stop being sarcastic. A year hasn't diminished by one my respect for the men. I shall never see another war. I don't care if Buller drives all the Boers up Egypt's fattest pyramid. The men were all right.

292. TO JAMES B. PINKER

Brede/August 4 1899

Dear Pinker: I enclose a statement concerning the best American buyers. I shall write to some of the editors who lately [have] been asking me for stories.

I shall develope [sic] Lippincott's plan [133] as soon as I finish the war-stories.[134] The U.S. book-rts [rights] of the war-stories were promised to Stokes last year when I was in America. He is to advance $1000.

Lady Churchill has asked me to write for her Review.[135] I have consented of course. It is not a commercial transaction.

Thanks for the book and the cheque for £25.

Have you yet sold any of the stories?/Yours etc   S. Crane

131 Written when Crane was doing "War Memories" for Lady Randolph Churchill's magazine, The Anglo-Saxon Review, published there in December. "War Memories" makes reference to Velasquez and Cervantes, as does this letter (reprinted from Beer, pp. 353–54).

132 This is perhaps a reference to Crane's own exploit of acting as signalman between outpost units of the U.S. Marine Corps during a naval engagement in Guantánamo Bay, which earned him a citation for bravery from the War Department. (See report of Captain G. F. Elliott, U.S. Marine Corps, Commanding Company C, Lieut. Col. R. W. Huntington, Commanding Battalion—in the Butler Library Crane Collection.)

133 The plan for a book of battle sketches—Great Battles of the World, which Lippincott in the United States and Chapman & Hall in England published in 1901. Crane now resumed work on this series, persuaded by Pinker that there was money in it. Kate Frederic did the research for this book.

134 Wounds in the Rain, published in London by Methuen & Co. and in New York by Frederick A. Stokes, both in spring, 1900.

135 The Anglo-Saxon Review, founded by Lady Randolph Churchill as a new venture in magazine style and cultural ideals.

❋ ❋ ❋

Cora and Henry James

Crane this summer was living up to the nickname Robert Barr had given him, "Baron Brede." He took a party of friends to the Henley Regatta on July 4 and put them up at the local inn, and a few days later the party reassembled at Brede Place. It included Karl Harriman, a young chap from Ann Arbor, Michigan, and George Lynch, an old newspaper friend of Stephen, and A. E. W. Mason, the novelist.

In August, Henry James came over from Rye for the bazaar held in the Brede rectory garden for the benefit of the parish fund and for the District Nursing Association. Cora had a booth, Stephen lugged potted plants to waiting carriages, and George Lynch took snapshots at sixpence a shot. His camera caught Henry James with Cora. Another snapshot shows Henry James eating a doughnut Cora made (see the *Bookman*, October, 1932, p. 581). Cora sent James the snapshots, and James thanked her for the "strange images." With wit and gallantry he added: "But no, surely, it can't be any doughnut of yours that is making me make such a gruesome grimace. I look as if I had swallowed a wasp or a penny toy. And I tried to look so beautiful. I tried too hard, doubtless. But don't show it to anybody as H. J. trying." [136]

❋ ❋ ❋

293. TO THE SECRETARY OF THE NEW JERSEY HISTORICAL SOCIETY

[August 26, 1899]

Dear Sir: I am about to attempt a novel upon Revolutionary times in the Province of New Jersey,[137] and I would be very glad if you could

---

[136] Quoted in *Columbia Library Columns*, February, 1953. Snapshots of Cora and Henry James are in the Butler Library Crane Collection and the Syracuse University Library.

[137] Soon after his return to England Crane had signed a contract with Stokes and Methuen for a novel dealing with the American Revolution, arrangements being made by Pinker. Cora had cabled him about it when he was in Cuba, and so had Pinker. Since then he had done nothing about it, though Methuen & Co. had advanced him £100 against the new book. By August 26 Crane felt obliged to start work on it, but he abandoned the project; so he owed Methuen and Stokes a work in substitution. Crane then signed a new contract which Pinker explained in a letter of February 27, 1900 to Cora: "The terms of the contract with Stokes and Methuen are the terms which had been arranged for the other novel; that is to say, in Stokes' case the Irish

tell me the titles of some of the books on the manners and customs of the times in the Province. I am particularly interested in Elizabethtown, and I would be much obliged and gratified if you could give me the title of a good history of that city. / Faithfully yours,

Stephen Crane

294. *JOSEPH CONRAD TO CORA CRANE*

Pent Farm,/Stanford,/Near Hythe./27 Aug 99

Dear Mrs. Crane/ I am so sorry Stephen worried about the payment.[138] Thanks ever so much for the cheque—I've sent Hope yesterday £15 in Stephen's name. . . .

Could you come in September—second half? We are extremely sorry to suggest the delay of an event we have been looking forward to with eagerness and delight. Jessie's tearful. She sends her love and would write herself only she is bad with neuralgia. This is the second day of it. I am at work and doing very little as usual.

With affectionate regards from us both / Yours most faithfully

Jph Conrad

---

romance [*The O'Ruddy*] takes the place of the Revolutionary novel, and in Methuen's case, it takes the place of the novel the character of which was not specified."

An interesting sidelight on the abandoned project of the Revolutionary novel—and incidentally on Crane's habit, which Beer admits (p. 365), of neglecting to return books that he borrowed—is found in a letter to Cora from J. Garneson, Lippincott's London agent. Garneson wrote to remind her of a number of books procured from the United States "for Mr. Crane's use and which were to be returned when done with"; and in a second letter, March 25, 1901: "I am glad to know that you think you will be able to find the remainder of the books. The most important are the missing volumes of the *Proceedings of the New Jersey Historical Society*—as the set has cost eleven pounds—and in an imperfect form it would be worth comparatively little."

Crane's letter to the New Jersey Historical Society was first published in the New York *Sun* of June 10, 1900: "Stephen Crane, Jerseyman." The letter is dated as "written on Aug. 26, 1899, from Brede, in Sussex, England."

Pinker's letter and the two from Lippincott's agent, Garneson, are in the Butler Library Crane Collection.

[138] The £15 to Hope (Conrad's friend Capt. G. F. W. Hope) was probably toward Crane's share in the sailboat he and Conrad purchased from Hope earlier in the summer of 1899. Mrs. Conrad says in her memoirs, *Joseph Conrad and His Circle*, that Crane never paid his share (see also Letter 362).

295. CORA CRANE TO JAMES B. PINKER

Brede Place / [Thursday] Aug 31st '99

Dear Mr. Pinker:/ Mr. Crane says please let him know what you have done with the stories.[139] He is hastening to get the war book ready for the publisher and has 67000 words done now. When this is done he will have certain sums due from Stokes & Co. in America but in the meantime he is going to run very short. He has a wine dealer who threatens to serve papers tomorrow, if his bill for £35 is not paid at once. (today) Mr. Crane has a Whilomville story which you can have in three or four days. This is for Harper and of course means ready money to you. Can you send him a cheque for this at once?

This has nothing to do with my former request for £20—to enable Mr. Crane to take a few days holiday. This would be to take his niece to Lausanne where she is to go to school and to stay a few days there. Of course I don't know how Mr. Crane's account stands with you. But you will have this Harper story by Monday, of 4000 words which means £40—Please move—I was going to say Heaven & Earth but publishers is better to get every pennie [sic] you can. The wine man must be satisfied and Mr. Crane must have a change or I fear he will break down & we cant have that. / Sincerely yours   *Cora Crane*

295A. TO AN UNKNOWN RECIPIENT

[August, 1899]

I am, I think, sufficiently grateful to men who really did things for me and in particular to Mr. Garland who, as you know, gave me sound advice about 'The Red Badge.' But just what is it to the credit of A. and B. that they bought things from me? I mean, what is my obligation to them? They saw a profit to their papers in buying my stuff and we break even. If it comes to that sultry point, why shouldn't they be grateful to me? . . . It seems that I am the only person who had nothing to do with bringing myself before the public! . . . Why should I be grateful for an utterly bad piece of criticism that leaves out everything good in 'George's Mother' and mentions just the things I would like to write over again if that was honest? (Beer, pp. 376–77.) *

---

[139] Those comprising *Wounds in the Rain*.

* The legend that Crane would not rewrite (cf. Beer, p. 377) is refuted by the fact that Crane several times rewrote *The Red Badge* and revised *Maggie* after its first publication.

✿   ✿   ✿

Helen Howe Crane

William Howe Crane's eighteen-year-old daughter Helen sailed in
June for England with Wilbur, her uncle, and A. H. Peck, who claimed
to be a distant relative, and Mrs. Peck and their daughter. "Helen's
trip will, or ought to be, educational in its éffects and we expect it to
cost us something. . . . Her friends in Port Jervis think she is a very
lucky girl, to have an uncle and aunt in England to visit" (William to
Cora, July 12). Her father sent her away "to get her free from her
mother's influence. . . . It was because that she might easily become
reckless, that I sent her away,—at a venture" (William to Cora, August
14).

Helen committed a dishonest act, and her father wrote Cora:
"Your handling of the late episode, which must have been mortifying
as well as painful to you, left nothing undone. . . . It would not be
logical and, therefore would not be wise, to give Helen to understand
that she had squared the whole thing by a confession and an apology.
She is now on probation and the most she could ask from the most
generous and forgiving nature is that confidence shall be freely and
generously given to her as fast as she earns it." More important is the
postscript William added to this August 14 letter:

> I have no objection to your bringing influence to bear upon Helen
> to make her a Catholic. Of course, it would be unfortunate to
> make a bigot of her. But I do not think there is any danger of that
> because, for one reason, if you had been a bigot, you would not
> have married my brother Stephen. My own notion is that true
> religion is the essential and that the form, under which one wor-
> ships, is largely a matter of circumstance and is unimportant. I
> do not ask you to agree with this proposition. I am merely show-
> ing my position.   William.

Portions of this letter are quoted in Daniel G. Hoffman, *The Poetry
of Stephen Crane* (1957), pp. 114–15, Hoffman adding: "It is a strange
fruit of Crane's Methodist heritage that he should have passed as married to a woman of Roman Catholic faith." But there is no evidence
that Cora became a convert. She was also influenced by the Christian
Science practiced by Kate Frederic. Although Cora retained leanings
toward Roman Catholicism to the end of her life, she remained outside
any orthodox creed or church affiliation, exactly as Stephen did. It was

rather the discipline of the Roman Catholic Church that Cora favored for correcting Helen's laxities.

❀   ❀   ❀

296. WILLIAM HOWE CRANE TO CORA CRANE

Port Jervis, N.Y./September 3d, 1899

My Dear Cora: Your letter of August 25th reached me this morning. By this time, it is understood, of course, that Helen is to go to the school in Switzerland. I have sent in a letter to her thirty pounds in drafts to your order. I hope this is enough for present purposes, although, if it is not, I can send more. I shall be more flush the latter part of this month. I shall adopt all of your suggestions about Helen's money matters and shall send her an installment, as soon as she is there and I understand matters. My intention was to have you use the thirty pounds for clothing, books, traveling expenses etc., pay the balance to Madame Hubbe [140] and inform me how much more I should send to Madame Hubbe. This, of course, I shall send at once, as soon as I know the amount. I am worried lest Helen may get into trouble at the school and where there may be no good friend to protect her.

Do you think it might be wise for you to write to her a straightforward letter of advice, where you will call things by the right name and warn her that an indulgence in her indifference to the property rights of others might possibly land her in the police-court?

When a girl's character is in the formative state, she cannot have too many motives for doing right. You would, of course, write it in your tactful way; but it might be a point of view altogether new to her.

She will see the difference between being among strangers and among her friends. I leave this, however, entirely to your judgment.

If Helen has been guilty of such things before, I have never known it. She has always been more or less indifferent to the rights of our younger children; but she has made her appropriations openly and, in a measure, defiantly. I have arbitrated many of such matters.

I should be almost overwhelmed with this trouble, if I did not feel

---

[140] Mme Eytel-Hubbe, proprietress of the Rosemont-Dézaley School at Lausanne. It was at the suggestion of Mabel Barr and her younger sister, Edith Richie, both of whom had received part of their education at the same school, that Helen Crane was to be sent there (see Edith R. Jones, "Stephen Crane at Brede," *Atlantic Monthly,* June, 1954).

that you were bearing my burdens for me and managing everything
so well. . . .

Give my love to Helen, if she is with you yet, when this arrives,
and also to Stephen.

Mr. and Mrs. Peck [141] were greatly impressed with their visit at
Brede Place and are very busy telling Port Jervis about it. We don't
have to say a word. Your affectionate brother,   *Wm. H. Crane*

297. *TO EDMUND CLARENCE STEDMAN* [142]

Brede Place/Sep. 4th-'99

Dear Mr. Stedman: The two little books—"The Black Riders" and
"War is Kind" contain every line which I've written outside of prose
form.[143] I hope you are now entirely recovered from your illness and I
hope that the new book will be the success which its distinguished
author has the right to exact. Pray give my regards to your son Mr.
Arthur Stedman, and believe me to be with the most pleasant remembrance. Yours faithfully   *Stephen Crane*

298. *CORA CRANE TO JAMES B. PINKER*

Brede Place / Monday [September 4, 1899]

Dear Mr. Pinker:/ Mr. Crane begs that you will send *at once* to my
account [144] at Oxted £35—as today I have had to draw that for one of
his accounts & I'm overdrawn now. Please do not fail with this.

---

[141] Remote cousins of Stephen Crane's, whose mother was Mary Helen
Peck.

[142] The only editor to anthologize Crane's poetry during Crane's lifetime. *War Is Kind* was published 1899 by Stokes in New York.

[143] These volumes lack two dozen poems not published in his lifetime
(see Daniel G. Hoffman, *The Poetry of Stephen Crane* [1957]).
Stedman's *An American Anthology 1787–1900* (Houghton Mifflin Com-
pany, 1900) published from *The Black Riders* Nos. I, XXII, XXV, XXVII,
LXV; and from *War Is Kind* Nos. VI, XIII, XVIII. They are not among
Crane's best poems, with the exception of *The Black Riders* No. XXVII ("A
youth in apparel that glittered") and *War Is Kind* No. XIII ("The wayfarer").
Omnibus, pp. 565–75, summarizes the composition of *The Black Riders*, influ-
ences on Crane's poetry, and the structural formula of the typical Crane poem.
Hoffman's excellent study traces in considerable detail various influences on
Crane's poetry.

[144] The Cranes were continually taking from the right hand to give to
the left, transferring funds from Cora's accounts to Stephen's to pay debts.

The Battle of *"Badajos"* [145] the second one for Lippincott, you shall have by Friday morning. Yours Sincerely   *Cora Crane*

299. JOSEPH CONRAD TO STEPHEN CRANE

Pent Farm/Stanford/Near Hythe/
Sunday [September 10? 1899]

Dear Old Pard./ Right, Bully for you. You are the greatest of the boys —and you are as good as I want you so you needn't trouble to apologise.

Could you come? You would make me happy. And will you pardon me for not writing to you. Dear Stephen I am like a dammed paralyzed mud turtle. I can't move. I can't write. I can't do anything. But I can be wretched, and, by God! I am!

Jess sends her love to the whole house. Give my affectionate regards and compliments. Let me know *the day before* when you are coming. You are a dear old chap. Ever yours,   *Conrad*

300. TO JAMES B. PINKER

Brede / Thursday [September 14? 1899]

My dear Pinker: I send you a Whilomville story—3230 words—for which Harper's should pay $160—

If you can send £15 to c/o "Cora Crane, Lloyd's Bank, New Oxted"?

I am getting serious about the Transvaal.[146] See if you can work it up. Hurriedly   *C* [147]

---

[145] This story, retitled "The Storming of Badajos," was published in *Lippincott's Magazine*, April, 1900. It was included in the posthumously published *Great Battles of the World* (1901).

[146] As always, when the pressures increased, Crane began to think of flight. Unlike the youth Henry Fleming, Crane ran not away from battle fronts but *toward* them. The war in the Transvaal was getting into full swing, and many of Crane's old newspaper friends were already there. But Pinker must have thrown ice on the idea; for Cora, panic-stricken, wrote near the end of September: "I am glad you wrote him *not* to go to the Transvaal. His health is not fit for it. He had a return of Cuban fever while we were in Paris and he is in no physical condition to stand a campaign no matter how short it may be. Then he has settled down to his work so well and ought not to leave home before Jan. or Feb. at least." She added a postscript, "Please dont let Mr. Crane know I've said a word against the Transvaal."

[147] The signature C stands for Crane. That he is under time pressures is indicated by the signatures of his letters, varying from Stephen Crane to

301. TO JAMES B. PINKER

Brede Place / Sep. 22nd '99

Dear Pinker:—/ I enclose the signed contract [148] which I apprehend they are going to use as a sort of spear to prod me up. I can't send a complete list of books but from time to time I shall send requests.

In your financial statement to me I note that you do not include "The Reluctant Voyagers." [149] Should it be in?

Thank you very much for paying Mrs. Burke. [150]

I am just finishing a Harper story. I am under the impression that they the Harpers, do not count very well. One of the late stories "The Carriage Lamps" or maybe "The Knife" [151] was, I think, exactly 4500 words whereas the marked price for "The Knife" was only £37:16:0–. And for "The Carriage Lamps" it is only £36:15:0–. This looks as if they may have got away with £3– or £4– of ours.

Also in regard to the statement there will be some later credits from the English Illustrated Magazine?

I know that you are amused by my telegram of yesterday. The fact is that I am anxious to get the 80000 words ready for Stokes and your letter recieved [sic] in Paris [152] filled me with an idea that I had missed a few thousand words—in short that I had written a story and then absolutely forgotten it as I often do.

S. Crane to S. C. and now in 1899 letters more frequently C, as here, "Hurriedly / C."

[148] With Frederick A. Stokes, probably for *The O'Ruddy* (see Letter 304).

[149] "The Reluctant Voyagers" was sold to the Northern Newspaper Syndicate, a chain serving the counties of northern England, and appeared first in 1901 and then in *Last Words* (1902).

[150] Governess for Harold Frederic's children.

[151] These are "Whilomville stories." "The Carriage Lamps" was published in *Harper's Magazine*, February, 1900; "The Knife" in *Harper's*, March, 1900.

[152] In September Crane took his niece Helen to Lausanne, while Cora and Miss Edith Richie (the nineteen-year-old daughter of Crane's friends) stayed at the Hotel Louis le Grand. Their first overnight stop was at Folkstone, with Mr. and Mrs. H. G. Wells, the Brede Place coachman Pat—nicknamed Tolstoy because of his striking resemblance to the Russian writer—driving them in a big wagonette. There was music and fun after dinner, Catherine Wells accompanying Edith Richie on the piano. Stephen rejoined them two days later in Paris and there was a gay round of dinners, sightseeing, and theaters. Cora and Stephen wrote postal cards home to their dogs. Ill with malaria, Stephen shut himself in the hotel bedroom to write, as Stokes had put pressure on him to complete the volume of Cuban war sketches—*Wounds in the Rain*.

When can you come down? We are waiting to have you. Yours faithfully   *Stephen Crane*

301A. TO MARK BARR

Brede Place / Sept 29 [1899]

My dear Mark: Allow me to express barbarian applause. I am extremely glad of Philip and as I have ordered him a cheap mug—from me to him—you had better jolly well see that we understand his full and true name before the engraver gets a chance to write "Cassidy" or "Smefeldenheimer" on it—the mug, I mean.

You know me about writing letters. I cant do it. Your letter to me I *drank*. But—

Anyhow, it is all the boy now. The boy! May the time-of-his-life rock him gently in ease and may the cradle spill only enough to give him those shocks which inform men, inform men that everything is already well-combined for their destruction and that the simple honest defeated man is often a gentleman.

Rubbish—Salute for me our dear Mabel. Yours ever, my dear boy
S. Crane

302. TO JAMES B. PINKER

Brede Place / Sept 30 1899

My dear Pinker: I cannot express how worried I am over "Virtue in War" and "The Second Generation." [153] I can only remember writing one story and I would almost bet the two titles cover one story. We may be making a hideous blunder. Please find out. Yours etc   C

303. TO JAMES B. PINKER

Brede Place / Sept 31 [September 30, 1899]

Dear Pinker: Here is the first story [154] of a series which will deal with the struggles of the settlers in the Wyoming Valley (Pennsylvania) in

---

[153] "Virtue in War" appeared in *Leslie's Popular Monthly,* November, 1899, under the title "West Pointer and Volunteer"; "The Second Generation" in the *Saturday Evening Post,* December 2, 1899, and in the *Cornhill Magazine,* December, 1899.

[154] "Ol' Bennett and the Indians," published in *Cassell's Magazine,* December, 1900. Wilbur Crane, another of Stephen's brothers, had a daughter named Helen (not to be confused with William Howe Crane's daughter Helen), who was quoted in the Newark *Star-Eagle,* July 8, 1926: "Our family bookcases are full of tomes written by members of the family. . . . There is one fascinating one. . . . I believe it was written by my grand-

1776–79 against the Tories and Indians. Perhaps you had better hold it until I finish two or three more and then deal with some wealthy persons for the purchase of the lot, eh? For the U.S., they exactly fit Harper's Weekly, Phila Sat Evening Post, Youth's Companion (they pay *big*, once offered me £22 per 1000) or Lippincott's.

I am still nervous about Virtue in War and The Second Generation. Yours, etc   *S. C.*

304. ROBERT BARR TO STEPHEN CRANE

Hillhead, Oct. 2. 1899

My dear Stephen . . . / As I see myself as a boy in those incomparable boys stories you are writing for Harper's Mag. (no one has ever touched the innards of the actual boy until those stories were written) so I also see myself in every line of the letter you wrote to Stokes. The Lord gave me a rockier temper than you've got, as you very well know I having frequently displayed it at your own table, to my eternal disgrace, and I would have forgiven the Lord if he had compensated by giving me a chunk of your genius.

I have read both your letter and Stokes' over three or four times to get the hang of the thing, and this is my understanding of it.
1. Crane and Stokes. (Mutually agreeing.) £100 paid on receipt of copy.
2. Crane. (Cabling.) "Book finished. Will you cable money."
3. Stokes. (Cabling.) "Yes on receipt of complete MS."
4. S Crane. (Cabling.) "I withdraw the book."
5. Stokes (Writing.) "We stand by the London Convention of 1884."
6. BLOODY WAR.

Now it is quite plain that a misapprehension arose after No. 2. If the word "now" or "Today" had been added to your cablegramme there would have been no chance of a misunderstanding, but as the cable reads the mistake was liable to occur. The situation after No. 3. is that Stokes thinks he has acceded to your request, and I can imagine his amazement when you cable withdrawing the book.

I wouldn't break with Stokes on this, if I were you. He is a thoroughly honorable man, and the more I know of other publishers, the

father [The Reverend Jonathan Townley Crane]—it always stood next to his 'Arts of Intoxication' on the shelf. It is a history of the Wyoming valley in Pennsylvania, and recounts the wars of the early settlers with the Indians. It is graphically illustrated and several of the pictures are of a family of Myers, who in some way were relations of ours." "Ol' Bennett and the Indians" re-creates the substance of this book; the author, however, was not the Reverend Jonathan Townley Crane.

more I appreciate him. God Almighty, I should be glad if other publishers would keep to the letter of their agreement. . . . You were asking Stokes to do what they would not do for any other living man. They did it once for Frederic, but they refused to do it a second time, and they would have lost their money if they had. . . .

You are all right when you stick to the pen, and are apt to be all wrong when you meddle with business. You are too much like Edgar Allan Poe. Our friend Kipling never writes a business letter, and yet he gets into lawsuits, which is foolish of him.

You have got things on exactly the right basis now, in leaving Pinker to deal with editors and publishers. Write, write, write, anything but business letters.

I had dinner with Admiral Dewey down at Monte Carlo. He is one of the loveliest men that any fellow is privileged to meet. He admires two literary men, Stephen Crane and Rudyard Kipling. So *he's* all right, in every sense of the word. . . . Ever Yours   *Robert Barr*

305. CORA CRANE TO JAMES B. PINKER

Brede Place / Monday [October 9? 1899]

Dear Mr. Pinker: I send you another Whilomville Story.[155]

Please send to Oxted Bank £30 [156]—more than story is worth and Mr. Crane will be glad if you can send it at once.

There will be another Whilomville story for you in four days.

One of Lippincott's articles [157] is almost finished, also, but Mr. Crane finds difficulty in getting at it. However you will get it soon. Sincerely yours   *Cora Crane*

306. CORA CRANE TO C. W. KENT [158]

Brede Place / Oct. 14th '99

Mr. Stephen Crane regrets not having been in America to accept the

---

[155] Crane wrote these Whilomville sketches at a fast pace; by October 24 he had done eleven.

[156] Crane needed this £30 to get to Ireland, where he visited this month, taking with him Cora and Miss Edith Richie. Edith stayed with the Cranes all summer and into January, 1900. "One morning in October Stephen came down to breakfast and said, 'Edith has never been to Ireland. Let's go to Ireland.' Bless him! He was writing *The O'Ruddy* and he wanted some local color and I was a good excuse. So we packed our bags and off we went to London" (Edith R. Jones, "Stephen Crane at Brede," *Atlantic Monthly*, July, 1954).

[157] The *Great Battles* series.

[158] Writing Crane on behalf of the Poe Memorial Association, Cora

invitation of the Poe Memorial Association to be present at the unvailing [*sic*] of Folmay's bust of Edgar Allan Poe.

307. CORA CRANE TO JAMES B. PINKER

Brede Place / Saturday [October 21?, 1899]

Dear Mr. Pinker: We were much disappointed that you could not come to Brede Place today and hope that you will set an early date to come. Choose your own date.

Now to be quite frank, Mr. Crane must have this coming week £50. He simply must have it. I enclose a letter from our solicitor which will explain why this is imperative. Please return me the letter.

In looking over Mr. Crane's accounts with you, I find that you now have "Moonlight on the Snow" [159] and three "Wyoming Stories" [160] which mean, when sold, I judge £115. Against this you sent Mr. Crane £30 to Ireland.[161] Then there is *at least* £50 due from John Lane for the Lady Churchill article.[162] Of course we quite understand that you probably have advanced money to Mr. Crane that you have not yourself collected. Please do not think we do not quite appreciate this kindness, but you see Mr. Crane is now sending everything he writes to you and so cannot get any money from any other place on account of things written or to be written. It must be painful to you now but in the long run you will benefit as there *is* a market for anything Mr. Crane writes as you know. This is rather like promising golden streets to the good boy in a Sunday School class who wants the streets of mud today, but you are more certain of good results than the Sunday School lad.

Mr. Crane will send you another story by Tuesday and I mail today the first two chapters of the book Mr. Crane told you about.[163]

---

replying as his amanuensis. This letter indicates that Crane was highly thought of in Charlottesville, Virginia. The original holograph, brought to our attention by Thomas Mabbott, is in the Alderman Library of the University of Virginia.

[159] Published in *Leslie's Popular Monthly*, April, 1900.

[160] Wyoming Valley (Pennsylvania) tales: "Ol' Bennett and the Indians," first published in *Cassell's Magazine*, December, 1900, and "The Battle of Forty Fort" and "The Surrender of Forty Fort," published in *Last Words* (1902).

[161] Crane, Cora, and Miss Richie went to Ireland before Crane received the much-needed money from Pinker. By the fourteenth they were back at Brede Place.

[162] "War Memories."

[163] *The O'Ruddy.*

Let me know how you like them. I think it will make a popular success
& a *good play*.

Mr. Crane will just deluge you with stuff for the next two months.

Please let me know what you can do for us. Can't you manage to
send Mr. Crane £50 on receipt of this & go and make John Lane pay
you? I feel sure, now you see the urgent need you will not fail to help
us out. Very sincerely yours   *Cora Crane*

308. TO JAMES B. PINKER

Brede Place [October 24? 1899]

My dear Pinker: I enclose two copies of a story [164]—4000 words—
which is appropriate to the times. I would not take less than 60 guineas
for both U.S. and English rights. Yours   *C*

Over

By the Phila. Sat Evening Post printing "The Sergeant's Private
Mad-House" on Sept 30, the English copyright of it is lost of course.

309. JAMES B. PINKER TO STEPHEN CRANE

London, W. C. / [Tuesday] Oct. 24, 1899

Dear Crane,/ I have received the two mss [165] today, with your note,
and I also have to acknowledge a letter from Mrs. Crane. I confess that
you are becoming most alarming. You telegraphed on Friday for
£20; Mrs. Crane, on Monday, makes it £50; today comes your letter
making it £150, and I very much fear that your agent must be a
millionaire if he is to satisfy your necessities a week hence, at this rate.
Seriously, you pinch me rather tightly. Mrs. Crane says I have "probably advanced money to Mr. Crane that I have not myself yet collected." [166] As a matter of fact, this sum, at present, is £230. I mention
this to impress you less with an obligation to me than to yourself.
There is a risk of spoiling the market if we have to dump too many
short stories on it at once. The Whilomville tale that you sent me today
is the eleventh, so that one more will complete that series, unless
Harpers think of extending it. Why do you not do the battle articles
for Lippincotts? [167]

I suppose the twenty folios you sent me are the beginning of the

---

[164] The Whilomville story Pinker mentions in Letter 309.
[165] The two chapters mentioned in Letter 307.
[166] Quoting Letter 307.
[167] *Great Battles of the World.*

novel which will be for Methuen here and Stokes in America.[168] Is that so? Have you another copy for me to send to Stokes, or am I to get one made.

I will do my best to try to manage *something* during the next ten days or a fortnight.[169] Yours ever,   *James B. Pinker*

310. CORA CRANE TO JAMES B. PINKER
Brede Place/Thursday ꞌA.M. [October 26, 1899]

Dear Mr. Pinker: The matter is so very urgent and important that I am sending this reply to your letter by train.

First, as the Whilomville stories are cash—they have always been paid for on delivery of the ms. by the New York office—I am *begging that you will send today* the amount due for one you received yesterday ("The Light")[170] £40 to Oxted Bank to my credit. Please *send it directly to my account*. The enclosed note from C. Hayles will explain the need. If this cheque[171] for £32.14.6 is not paid these people will issue writ—at once—and give us no end of trouble.

Please send cheque on receipt of the second "Whilomville" story, which will go to you tomorrow also immediately to my account. In this way we can pull matters through until you can see your way, "within the next ten days or a fortnight", to send every possible pennie. [*sic*]

Now Mr. Pinker, how could you say to Mr. Crane not to dump too many short stories upon the market for fear of spoiling it?[172] This is a fatal thing to say to a writing man. Particularly to Stephen Crane. And how can you think so with an utterly unspoiled and vast American market? Harpers and the Saturday Evening Post and one story to McClures are the only things sold in America *now* and you could sell a thousand short stories of Mr. Crane's there if you had them.

You say you have advanced £230 which you have not collected.

---

[168] *The O'Ruddy*, published in 1903 by Stokes in New York, and in 1904 by Methuen in London.

[169] On October 26 Pinker sent Scribner's three manuscripts, the first of a planned series of eight stories, and pointed out that "for the series at present appearing in *Harper's Magazine* Mr. Crane is receiving £10.10/– per thousand words for the serial rights, and he suggests a similar rate of payment in the present case." Pinker begs for an early decision. *Scribner's Magazine* had published "The Open Boat" in 1897, but did not accept these manuscripts and published nothing more of Crane's until 1937, when "The Open Boat" was reprinted. (Pinker's letter to Charles Scribner's Sons is in the Scribner files.)

[170] "The Light" was not printed, at least not by that title.

[171] By "cheque" Cora means bill.

[172] See Letter 309.

This is very good of you and our need is proof of our appreciation but why dont you make these publishers pay cash for Mr. Crane's stories. They have *always had* to pay cash before this.

You will have the first of the articles for Lippincotts [173] by Nov. 10th. You must understand the great time it takes to get detail for these things.

The first two chapters of the New Novel Mr. Crane says for you to try to have Stokes accept. If you will refer to his contract with them you will see that it calls for "the next novel which is to be on the American Revolution." Mr. Crane says to have a copy made & send to them asking if they will take it, "Romance" [174] on same terms as the Rev. novel. If they won't do this, Mr. Crane will write the Rev. novel first & will sell this "Romance" to come out serially at any time & in book form *after* the Rev. novel.[175]

Will you see from Harpers if they want eighteen "Whilomville" stories.[176] I believe this was the number named at one time. At present they will not make a very large book and Mr. Crane wants to make it larger than it now is.

Have you tried the American "Youth Companion" for the Early Settlers [177] stories? I think they might like them.

Now please wire me on receipt of this "all right," if you have sent £40 to my account at Oxted so that I may be sure that this troublesome cheque is paid.

If there is any doubt of your being able to get the amount that Mr. Crane must have, £150, will you write me and I will come up and see what I can do borrowing some on some of his stuff. Mr. Crane is now engaged in fighting his last creditors and they can be fought only with money.

Again thanking you for your help I am / Very sincerely yours

Cora Crane

311. TO JAMES B. PINKER

Brede Place/Nov. 4th '99

My dear Pinker:—/ I am enclosing a double extra special good thing.

---

[173] Cora means the first in the series of battle sketches, chronologically —"The Battle of Bunker Hill," printed in *Lippincott's Magazine*, June, 1900.

[174] *The O'Ruddy.*

[175] American Revolution novel.

[176] By now Crane had written a dozen "Whilomville Stories." *Whilomville Stories*, containing thirteen sketches, was published by Harper's in New York and London in 1900.

[177] The Wyoming Valley tales.

At the same time I am sending a copy to Forbes Robertson in an attempt to make him see that in a thirty minute sketch on the stage he could so curdle the blood of the British public that it would be the sensation of the year, of the time.[178] As soon as I get word from Robertson I will communicate the word to you but I suppose there is no intermediate reason against sending the story out to magazines since we can always prevent calamity by refusing their terms. These remarks of course apply merely to some difficulty over the copyright in America which would have to be protected in case of a possible rendering by Forbes Robertson appearing before the story was published in America.

I will not disguise from you that I am wonderfully keen on this small bit of 1500 words. It is so good—for me—that I would almost sacrifice it to the best magazine in England rather than see it appear in the best paying magazine. I suppose many men stir you with tumultuous sentiments concerning work which they have just completed but—anyhow you take a copy of this story home with you and read it and let me know your opinion. This is something which you do not always do. I can go all over the place and write fiction about almost anything and if you give me a racing tip from time to time it is extremely handy.

I received your cheque for £50 much to my gratification and I hope that you will manage the other cheque for £50 as soon as possible. I am sorry that the collections are so slow. I can do nothing save to continue to turn out the best work in my power and turn it out as fast as possible. Your remark upon the possibility of over loading the market struck me as being extremely wrong. I have been aware for some years that I have been allowing over half of my real market to languish without any of Stephen Crane's stories. I mean "The Century" "Scribners," "Youth's Companion" and a lot of newspaper syndicates in America which have made me personal requests to help fill their pages.

Please write me at some length about various stories and in particular always gladden my heart when you have news of a sale. For instance the information that you had sold "The Second Generation" [179] to the Cornhill magazine was conveyed to me when I recieved [sic]

---

[178] If this is "The Upturned Face," misnamed "The Burial" in Cora's Letter 313, Crane is right in being "wonderfully keen" on it, as it is one of his masterpieces. This letter brings to light for the first time Crane's intention that this story should be dramatized. Sir Johnston Forbes-Robertson, the actor, turned down Crane's proposal.

[179] *Cornhill Magazine,* December, 1899, and the *Saturday Evening Post,* December 2, 1899.

the proofs. It is only a matter of a few pounds but anyhow it was pleasant to know it and I might have had the pleasure earlier.

I have collected about a ton of information on the Battle of New Orleans [180] and the article is now a mere matter of putting together these voluminous notes in their most dramatic form and this I shall manage within a few days. Yours etc   *S. C.*

312. WILLIAM HOWE CRANE TO STEPHEN AND CORA CRANE

Port Jervis, N.Y./November 7th, 1899

My dear Stephen and Cora: Your letters were received yesterday, as was also a letter from Helen. I feel chagrined to read in Helen's letter that the Madame [181] had asked her to write you for money. Her (the Madame's) first letter to me was so indefinite on the money question that I did not know how much to send in order to square up the first term's bill. So, I wrote asking if anything had been paid. . . .

If Helen were not so crude, we would not be troubling you with her. This same Heidenthal's sister told some one, so that it came to us, that Helen had written to him; and I wrote her about it, asking her if she was keeping her promise to me not to correspond with any man without my knowledge and consent. He is as crude as a setter pup, with as little harm in him. But Helen lowers herself to even notice him. You are mistaken, if you think that Helen does not care for you. I am sure she is devoted to her Aunt Cora. I shall leave the matter of Helen's allowance entirely to Cora. She knows how much Helen has had (I sent her a pound) and I shall not send her any more at all. Cora can decide how long it ought to last. Will you send to Helen and charge to me a copy of Addison's Spectator? I do not know of any reading that inculcates a love of truth more effectively, unless it may be "The Deerslayer." . . .

I spent the night with George [182] at Newark a few days ago and I asked him about The Historical Collections of New Jersey. He says you are welcome to the book which he has, but the name is different. I have forgotten the name by this time and I'll write and get it and then write you again. George is doing well. Ed's [183] coal business is

---

[180] "Brief Campaign Against New Orleans," published in *Lippincott's Magazine*, March, 1900, and in *Great Battles of the World* (1901).

[181] Mme. Eytel-Hubbe, in whose school Helen, William Crane's daughter, was enrolled at Lausanne.

[182] George Crane, an older brother.

[183] Edmund Crane, Stephen's brother.

prospering. He leaves Hartwood this week. Bert [184] still lives at Bing-hamton and has Townley [185] boarding with him. Townley is helpless and in need of constant care and attention. Our Agnes [186] is taller than her mother and than Helen. She is a lovely girl. She and one or two others take turns in being at the head of the class at school. We are all well. Cornelia [187] sends love.   Yours affectionately,   *Wm. H. Crane*

313. CORA CRANE TO JAMES B. PINKER

Brede Place,/Tuesday [November 7? 1899]

Dear Mr. Pinker: I send you Chapter XLV of Romance.[188] 36800 words in all, of which I've sent you four copies. We were in hopes by today to hear from you that you had made some arrangement with Stokes & Co.

Mr. Crane says: to offer "The Wyoming Stories"—if the Youth's Companion don't want them, to *Harpers* young people. And to offer to the New Magazine in New York both the "Burial" [189] and "And if He Wills We Must Die."

Please let us know to whom you are offering the serial rights of the Romance. Have you tried the Cosmopolitan in America?

We hope to hear that Lippincotts cheque and one from Stokes will come soon. Yours very sincerely   *Cora Crane*

314. TO WILLIS B. CLARKE [190]

[Brede Place, November, 1899]

. . . My mother was a very religious woman but I don't think that she was as narrow as most of her friends or her family. . . . My brothers

---

[184] Bert is Wilbur Crane, Stephen's brother. He lost caste with the other Cranes when he married a housemaid.

[185] Townley, one of Stephen's older brothers. The two oldest brothers were Townley and George.

[186] Edmund Crane's daughter.

[187] William's wife.

[188] *The O'Ruddy.*

[189] "The Upturned Face," published in *Ainslee's Magazine*, March, 1900, and posthumously in *Last Words* (1902). "The Upturned Face" represents Crane at his best. "And if He Wills We Must Die" was printed in the *Illustrated London News*, July 28, 1900, in *Frank Leslie's Popular Monthly*, October, 1900, and reprinted in *Last Words*.

[190] A young admirer who visited Crane in November, 1899, and took down in shorthand these notes. Reprinted from Beer (pp. 239, 245–46), portions being here pieced together from Beer's quotations. (Other short-hand notes were used throughout Beer's biography.) "In 1903 Mr. Clarke

tell me that she got herself into trouble before I was old enough to follow proceedings by taking care of a girl who had an accidental baby. Inopportune babies are not part of Methodist ritual but mother was always more of a Christian than a Methodist and she kept this girl at our house in Asbury until she found a home somewhere. Mother's friends were mostly women and they had the famous feminine aversion to that kind of baby. It is funny that women's interest in babies trickles clean off the mat if they have never met papa socially. . . . After my father died, mother lived in and for religion. We had very little money. Mother wrote articles for Methodist papers and reported for the [New York] *Tribune* and the [Philadelphia] *Press*. Every August she went down to Ocean Grove and reported proceedings at the Methodist holy show there. . . . My brother Will used to try to argue with her on religious subjects such as hell but he always gave it up. Don't understand that mother was bitter or mean but it hurt her that any of us should be slipping from Grace and giving up eternal damnation or salvation or those things. You could argue just as well with a wave. . . . She was always starting off when she felt well enough to some big prayer meeting or experience meeting and she spoke very well. Her voice was something like Ellen Terry's but deeper. She spoke as slowly as a big clock ticks and her effects were impromptu.[191] . . . It is in me to think that she did some good work for the public schools. One of my sisters was a teacher [192] and mother tried for years to get women placed on the school boards and to see that whisky was not sold to boys under age. . . . I used to like church and prayer meetings when I was a kid but that cooled off and when I was thirteen or about that, my brother Will told me not to believe in Hell after my uncle had been boring me about the lake of fire and the rest of the sideshows. . . . Once when I was fourteen an organ grinder on the beach at Asbury gave me a nice long drink out of a nice red bottle for picking up his hat for him. I felt ecstatic walking home and then I was an Emperor and some Rajahs and Baron de Blowitz all at the same time. I had been sulky all morning and now I was perfectly willing to go to a prayer meeting and Mother was tickled to death. [193]

---

began to collect copies of letters and facts for a life of Stephen Crane, but was so baffled by conflicting statements that he dropped the work" (p. 387). Beer unfortunately failed to preserve any of the letters Clarke loaned him.

[191] Crane, who himself worked against time, describes his mother in terms of a clock.

[192] Agnes, who was fifteen years older than Stephen.

[193] For Crane's imaginative reconstruction of this personal incident see *George's Mother.*

And, mind you, all because this nefarious Florentine gave me a red drink out of a bottle. I have frequently wondered how much mothers ever know about their sons, after all. She would not have found it much of a joke. . . . They tell me that I got through two grades in six weeks which sounds like the lie of a fond mother at a tea party but I do remember that I got ahead very fast and that father was pleased with me. He used to take me driving with him to little places near Port Jervis where he was going to preach or bury somebody. Once we got mixed up in an Irish funeral near a place named Slate Hill. Everybody was drunk and father was scandalized. . . . He was so simple and good that I often think he didn't know much of anything about humanity. Will, one of my brothers, gave me a toy gun and I tried to shoot a cow with it over at Middletown when father was preaching there and that upset him wonderfully.[194] He liked all kinds of animals and never drove a horse faster than two yards an hour even if some Christian was dying elsewhere. But it is a big job to be presiding elder in a Methodist Conference. He worked himself to death, my people thought.

315. TO H. B. MARRIOTT-WATSON [195]

Brede Place   November 15th, 1899

Dear Mr. Marriott Watson:/ We of Brede Place are giving a free play to the villagers at Christmas time in the school-house and I have written some awful rubbish which our friends will on that night speak out to the parish.

But to make the thing historic, I have hit upon a plan of making the programmes choice by printing thereon a terrible list of authors of the comedy and to that end I have asked Henry James, Robert Barr, Joseph Conrad, A. E. W. Mason, H. G. Wells, Edwin Pugh, George Gissing, Rider Haggard and yourself to write a mere word—any word "it," "they," "you,"—any word and thus identify themselves with this crime.

Would you be so lenient as to give me the word in your hand writing and thus appear in print on the programme with this distinguished rabble. Yours faithfully,   *Stephen Crane*

---

[194] This incident reappears in Crane's story "Lynx Hunting." The original episode is retold by Helen R. Crane in "My Uncle, Stephen Crane," *American Mercury,* January, 1934.

[195] Author of *Heart of Miranda* and other works. This is a typewritten letter signed by Crane.

✿   ✿   ✿

"The Ghost" at Brede Place

The Cranes prepared for a most unusual Christmas party with three dozen guests at Brede Place to witness or participate in "The Ghost," a play written by ten collaborators and presented on December 28 at the schoolhouse in Brede village. Legend created Brede Place as a haunted house, and "The Ghost" exploited the legend. The ten collaborators were Henry James, Robert Barr, George Gissing, Rider Haggard, Joseph Conrad, H. B. Marriott-Watson, H. G. Wells, Edwin Pugh, A. E. W. Mason, and Stephen Crane. "The Ghost" has been called "a literary curiosity unrivaled," but it is unrivaled only in its authorship.

As Mason had had experience as an actor, he took the part of the ghost. (Later he turned to writing novels, one of which is burlesqued in Hemingway's *The Sun Also Rises*.) He was the only one of the ten collaborators to participate in the play. Mrs. H. G. Wells provided piano music appropriate to the occasion (see Appendix 27).

Crane had a program printed to distribute to his guests and the Brede village audience. (A copy of this program is in the Berg Collection of the New York Public Library; a signed copy is in the Butler Library Crane Collection.) The cast of the characters in "The Ghost" included Rufus Coleman, lifted from Crane's *Active Service;* Doctor Moreau, deriving from H. G. Wells's *Island of Doctor Moreau;* Peter Moreau (the doctor's son), deriving from Henry James's *Turn of the Screw; Suburbia,* deriving from Pugh's first success, *Street in Suburbia;* Miranda, perhaps echoing A. E. W. Mason's *Miranda of the Balcony* or H. B. Marriott-Watson's *Heart of Miranda.* Gilbert and Sullivan's *Mikado* provided the source of Three Little Maids from Rye (Holly, Buttercup, and Mistletoe).[196]

The occasion of "The Ghost" caused a stir in local newspapers and in the Manchester *Guardian* (January 13, 1900):

A remarkable piece of literary patchwork has lately been allowed to waste its sweetness on the Sussex air. This is the play which has been written for an amateur performance by a string of our most

---

[196] "The Ghost at Brede Place," by John D. Gordan, *Bulletin of the New York Public Library* LVI (December, 1952), 591–95. Beer and Berryman mention the play but give no detailed account of it. The affair is discussed by H. G. Wells in *Experiment in Autobiography* (1934), by C. Lewis Hind in *Authors and I* (1921), and by Edith Richie Jones in the *Atlantic Monthly,* July, 1954.

popular novelists. . . . One is deeply sorry that it is not to be published. . . . When the London theatres are so devoid of good plays as is the present case, it seems unkind to deprive managers of such an opportunity. The expense of scenery could hardly be an objection, for both acts passed in the same locality—an "empty room in Brede Place."

The Sussex *Express* (January 5, 1900) reported that Stephen Crane paid all the expenses incurred in the production, and the *South Eastern Advertiser* (January 5, 1900) described the play as a combination of farce, comedy, opera, and burlesque.

The plot, as summarized by the *Advertiser,* was as follows:

The ghost *first introduces himself to the audience, the inference being that he appears on special occasions at midnight for the special delectation of the antiquary or tourist, the latter of whom is held in abomination by the said ghost. A couple of tourists then appear, followed by "three little maids from Rye," Holly, Buttercup, and Mistletoe, and these ladies [Mrs. Mark Barr, Miss Bowen, and Miss Edith Richie] were rapturously encored for their rendering of the selection, "Three Little Maids from Rye," which bore a suspicious resemblance to an air from a popular opera. Miss [Florence] Bray, in the capacity of caretaker, gave one the impression that the greater part of her life had been spent in showing visitors over the place. Miranda [Miss Sylvia Bowen] delighted the audience with a castanet dance, which she was compelled to repeat. A poem was then recited by Suburbia [Miss Ethel Bowen] which convulsed the audience, and so moved one of the party he wiped away tears with his ample whiskers. A very amusing chorus, "We'll be there," was rendered, Miss Richie singing the chorus capitally.*

In the next act Rufus Coleman [Mr. Cyril Frewer, son of the rector of Brede village] appears in the haunted room at 11:30, and whilst waiting for the apparition Mistletoe enters and unbosoms her sorrow to Rufus in an original up-to-date song, "The Sussex Volunteers," which depicts the call to arms of "The Absent-Minded Beggar," and the forlorn condition of the girl he left behind him. . . . As the hour of midnight approaches Doctor Moreau [Mr. F. L. Bowen] gives a correct imitation of cock-crowing, followed by "Simon the Cellarer," and a pleasing selection by Miss Bowen. At midnight the company are paralysed by the sudden appearance of the ghost from apparently nowhere, and he commences his weird history, but reminds himself that he can relate it better with soft musical accompaniment, and this is accorded him. He states that in the year 1531 he was sitting in that very same room, consuming six little Brede boys, and washed down his meal with an appropriate quantity of beer. This overcame him, and whilst in a stupor four courageous Brede men enter, and saw him asunder. . . . The caretaker constantly corrects the ghost during the time he is making his statement, and she emphatically denies that it was beer he was drinking. She said he knew it should be "sack," and that he will get the "sack" from his post if he commits such glaring historical errors again. At this juncture the ghost makes a speedy exit, and reappears partially divested of his ghostly raiment, when he causes laughter by going round with his hat, his fee to each batch of tourists being two "bob." A grand chorus and dance, taken part in by the ghost and tourists, concluded the piece. (The time of the play is 1950.)

Crane, the *Advertiser* adds, not only defrayed expenses of the production but paid also for an addition to the stage, which he presented to the school. Mr. Mason, whose representation of the ghost was very realistic, also performed the duties of stage manager in a very satisfactory manner.[197]

MANUSCRIPT PAGE OF "THE GHOST" [198]

The ghost: *"I am the ghost. I dont admit this because I am proud. I admit it because it is necessary that my indentity [sic] should be established. My identity has been desputed [sic] for many centuries—how many, I forget—anyhow, it was some time ago. It is difficult to be a ghost here. I would like to have an easier place. Tourists come here and they never give me a penny although I had my last pipe of 'baccy two hundred years ago and I drank my last pint of bitter [beer] in '53. . . . Ha, a noise— Perhaps some terrible tourist— Will I fly? No; despite my constitutional timidity, I will stand my ground.*

[197] Another account of the plot of "The Ghost," drawn from the Sussex *Express*, is given in Gordan's article (see preceding note). The above quotations from the *Guardian* and the *Advertiser* ("Theatricals at Brede") are drawn from copies of the originals presented to us by Roger M. Frewen of Brede Place and are reproduced here for the first time.

[198] This page, in Crane's handwriting, is reproduced for the first time. The original is owned by Roger M. Frewen of Brede Place. In the Butler Library Crane Collection are five pages of "The Ghost," of which page 2 is typewritten and page 3 is in Cora's hand. Typescript of seven pages is in the Berg Collection of the New York Public Library (see *Stephen Crane: An Exhibition* [Columbia Libraries, 1956]).

(*Enter tourist with white whiskers and his wife.*)

Tourist with white whiskers: "*Now, you see, my dear, there is no such things* [sic] *as ghost. Really there is not. It is all a superstition. There is no such thing as a ghost.*

The Ghost: (*approaching unnoticed.*) "*Aw* — — *pardon?*"

Tourist with w w (*jumping*) *Beg pardon?*

Ghost *Oh, nothing. Only I thought I heard you denying the existence of ghosts.*

T. with w. w. (*excitedly*) *Well, you did. I can prove to you mathematically that it is impossible———*"

Ghost (*holding up his hand*) *Don't. I couldn't bear to hear that*

✿   ✿   ✿

316. CORA CRANE TO JAMES B. PINKER

Brede Place [Mid-November? 1899]

Dear Mr. Pinker: My husband says that he does not at all approve of the idea of a Xmas story for Tillotson's. He says that he has never written Xmas stories of the kind which seems to be specified and declared that he will not begin now.

Last year, Mr. Crane's stories appeared in seven or eight Xmas numbers—as you may well know—and not one of them by any possibility could have even rang [*sic*] in the house "Xmas." If Tillotsons want a story to publish in their Xmas program, they can easily get it but my husband will not write a "seasonable" story.[199]

I enclose Chapter XXI of Romance.[200] Chapter XXII is written but not all typed. Yours sincerely   *Cora Crane*

317. CORA CRANE TO JAMES B. PINKER

Brede Place/Dec. 7th '99

Dear Mr. Pinker:/ Mr. McClure is just playing the "artful" to keep from paying up. There is £5–against Mr. Crane's credit in his office. I have written Mr. Robert McClure asking him to let you have cheque for the last story.

Thanks for the £20–Sent to my account at Oxted. Please send

---

[199] By such formulas Crane could persuade himself that he was not prostituting his genius by writing stories "to order." Pleased at being asked to write something for Lady Randolph Churchill's magazine, and yet more pleased with the £50 he was paid, he had told Pinker that this was "not a commercial transaction" (Letter 292).

[200] Chap. xiv of *The O'Ruddy*, Crane's satirical romance of old Ireland, was sent Pinker in mid-October, 1899.

another £20, as I am £39 over-drawn. Make McClure's pay you. They are scotch!! Very Sincerely yours   *Cora Crane.*

P.S. Mr. Crane says that he has not time now to stop & do a story of 7500 words for which he will have to wait some weeks for return. So he will put this story aside now as he did the "Irish Romance," and return to short stuff which will bring in money at once. After the holidays, perhaps he can settle and do them both.

I must have misunderstood Mr. Crane about the play.[201] He now wishes me to say that he wants your opinion as to whether there is any one in London who would do an American Military Play and who? Let him know if there is any chance for it here, to be produced.

I'm sending you a second copy of the short story. You got my word about selling "The Upturned Face?"   *C. C.*

318. CORA CRANE TO JAMES B. PINKER

Brede Place/Dec. 12th [1899]

Dear Mr. Pinker: Mr. Crane asks if you will send, *at once* upon receipt of this letter, £18. to Mr. Plant[202]—18 Bedford Row Greys [sic] Inn. London? It is *absolutely necessary* that he has it without delay.

Mr. Crane will be in town and come to see you toward the week's end. He will bring you the first article[203] for Lippincott. Yours Sincerely   *Cora Crane*

319. WILLIAM HOWE CRANE TO CORA CRANE

Port Jervis, N.Y./December 22d, 1899

My Dear Cora: Pardon my long silence. We in Port Jervis have been having our hands full of trouble lately. Lew Goldsmith, whom Stephen knows, robbed our bank of a large sum of money, large enough to force it to close its doors. The town will almost be bankrupt, if outstanding claims are pressed while the money is tied up in the bank.

---

[201] Based on the Cuban War, a play Crane began while living on board the correspondents' tug *Three Friends* in 1898, and of which he finished two acts. Reynolds wrote Crane on January 9, 1900, that he had offered the play to Nat Goodwin, the New York actor, but that Goodwin returned it "saying that he does not think the play suitable for the kind of part he could play." And William Gillette, to whom Reynolds at Crane's urging also sent the manuscript copy, took a similar viewpoint.

[202] Alfred Plant, solicitor.

[203] "The Battle of Bunker Hill," the first—chronologically—in the *Great Battles* series.

I am not embarassed [*sic*] by the failure; but it has made so much work and the town is so agitated that we have all had our hands and hearts full. I owe you an explanation. I paid Stephen's debt to Madame Hubbe because she wrote that Stephen had borrowed it through Helen. She wrote me in about these words—"He not only left her without any pocket-money, but borrowed from me through his niece the sum of thirty francs, which he has not repaid."[204] I haven't said anything to Helen about it. . . .

I hardly think I can afford to send Agnes[205] to Lausanne next year. Besides, she is doing very nicely in school here and is always at or near the head of her classes. You may be surprised to hear it; but it is a fact that we have very good schools here. They have been revolutionized in their methods and standards during the last few years. Helen did not begin to avail herself of the advantages that even Port Jervis offered her when she was here. Please allow me to say that there is a false quantity in some of your letters, copies of which you sent me, that you had written to Helen, when you say to her that Port Jervis could not teach her this or that. The fault is with her, or rather, was with her. The superintendent of our schools is a finished scholar and gentleman and a scientific educator. But Helen was so indolent in her studies, careless in her choice of associates and so persistent in her ways, that your invitation came as a god-send. She needed a tremendous moral and intellectual awakening and I think she is getting it. I am not defending Port Jervis. I am telling you facts, in order that you may fully understand Helen's case. I appreciate your goodness to her. In her last letter, she shamed her mother by contrasting her mother's irregularity in letter-writing with your punctuality. She said she always knew when to expect a letter from you. We sent some photographs to Helen at Lausanne. Are there some that you would like us to send to you. We'll do it. My clerk breaks in at this point and asks me to get him one of Stephen's autographs. Will you kindly enclose one in your next?

I do not know how "Active Service" is selling. We have it in our public library and I see it occasionally upon private tables; and it is very much liked. I have not chanced to see very much printed comment upon it. Ed's wife gets the newspaper cuttings about Stephen and his works. I'll ask her to send some of the latest to you.

I take the Journal, because, among the N.Y. Papers, it comes the

---

[204] Helen's version was that her Uncle Stephen had departed without leaving her any pocket money; also that Stephen had borrowed 30 Swiss francs from her.

[205] Edmund Crane's daughter.

nearest to representing my politics. I never bother with the murder stories and I feel very sure that the children do not.

I shall keep your hint in mind, however. After all, the only live questions of today are economic questions and I would not like to have, for a steady diet, the papers that are always systematically and stubbornly wrong. By the way, I should like to know what Stephen's views are over the Transvaal matter. We are almost all pro-Boer here. I have looked in vain for your name among the American women who are fitting out the hospital-ship.[206] I hope Stephen's health is improved. We are all well and send love. I do not know whether I shall be able to afford a European trip next year or not. I'm coming, if I can afford it. Yours affectionately,   *Wm. H. Crane*

320. TO MR. AND MRS. WILLIS BROOKS HAWKINS

Brede Place, Christmas, 1899

MR. and MRS. STEPHEN CRANE / send / CHRISTMAS GREETINGS, and / GOOD WISHES for your / HEALTH and HAPPINESS in 1900.[207]

320A. TO THOMAS HUTCHINSON[?]

[1899]

I am not carnivorous about living writers. I have not read any of the books that you ask me to criticize except that of Mr. Howells, and it has disappointed me. My tastes? I do not know of any living author whose works I have wholly read. I like what I know of Anatole France,

---

[206] The hospital ship *Maine*, christened in honor of the American battleship sunk in Havana Harbor. The bold idea of equipping a hospital ship to be sent to the Transvaal with funds jointly subscribed in England and the United States was launched by Lady Randolph Churchill as a symbol cementing the ties between the two countries.

Crane gave his views on the Transvaal at an afternoon gathering at Lamb House, Mrs. Humphry Ward doing the honors at the tea table. "People tell me that the South Africans and the Japanese can shoot like the devil and then tell me a couple of Guard regiments could whip them in a week. When a Yankee says such things he is bragging but I guess an Englishman is just lugging the truth from some dark cave."

[207] The front leaf of this printed Christmas card, designed with ivy leaves, gives this message: "Friendship, like. . . / . . . the Ivy clings/ to Olden Memories,/ . . . Ways and Things." One surmises that Cora composed the verse. The envelope, postmarked December 11, is addressed in Cora's hand. That the Cranes had not kept in touch with Hawkins is indicated by their ignorance of his new address, the greeting being forwarded from the old address of 141 East 25th Street, New York City.

Henry James, George Moore, and several others. I deeply admire some
short stories by Mr. Bierce, Mr. Kipling, and Mr. White.* Mr. Hardy,
since you especially inquire about his work, impresses me as a gigantic
writer who 'overtreats' his subjects. I do not care for the long novels of
Mr. Clemens, for the same reason. Four hundred pages of humour is
a little bit too much for me. My judgment in the case is not worth
burning straw, but I give it as portentously as if kingdoms toppled
while awaiting it under anxious skies (Berryman, pp. 248–49).

---

* This may refer either to Stewart Edward White, then a coming young
American author and friend of Robert Barr, or William Hale White, English novelist (1831–1913), who wrote under the pseudonym of Mark Rutherford.

5

1900

THE YEAR BEGINS with Cora writing to Pinker on January 2: "Mr. Crane is ill again—in bed but is still keeping at his work."

The house party, lasting three days, concluded with a ball on the night following the performance of "The Ghost," and after the musicians had packed up their instruments and departed Crane collapsed with a hemorrhage of the lungs—the beginning of the end. Cora in alarm appealed to H. G. Wells, who himself had had tuberculosis as a young man; Wells mounted a bicycle and rode off in the dawn to call a doctor from Rye.

Gossip smoked and blazed fitfully. On January 24 Robert Barr wrote to an American:

> *Mrs. Crane is so incensed by the nonsense talked about the New Year party at Brede that Stevie is taking her home. England has been kind to Stevie in many ways but some of his cherished friends have said things too carelessly about his most generous but not too formal hospitality and I have heard some gossip that must wound him deeply. His skin is very thin and he is subject to a kind of jealousy that knows how to hurt him worst. His present plan is to take some land in Texas and live in the open air but, between ourselves, it is all over with the boy. He may last two years but I can not bring myself to hope for more than that. . . . He sails on the first of the month* (Beer, pp. 383–84).

But if Crane ever seriously intended quitting England at this time, Alfred Plant, the solicitor, must have been the one to nip any such plan. Plant could hardly have failed to point out that Crane would lay himself open to the charge of running out on his creditors if he left the country then. And so the year begins with Cora pleading with Pinker for more advances against an already overdrawn account. Always she counts on payments for stories and books not yet contracted for or not yet published, and always she writes checks against an overdrawn bank account to pay bills long overdue and begs poor Pinker to make good the checks that bounce.

Cora went to Paris to buy some clothes for Helen Crane, and during her absence Stephen had two more severe hemorrhages on April 1–2; his ill-health had reached a crisis. These 1900 letters from January to June stress the panic of his closing life—the panic of his hopeless finances and the panic of his hopeless prospects for survival. These themes are counterpointed one against the other, as in Cora's letter to Pinker (No. 339). Cora knew that Stephen was dying and denounced herself for allowing so much entertainment at Brede Place, but she kept up a cheerful front and hopefully expected the impossible. Her letters to Pinker document the pathos of her plight.

William Crane, unable financially to aid his dying brother, sent Stephen *A Consumptive's Struggle for Life,* written by one of their father's old friends, Dr. Buckley (Letter 349). H. G. Wells offered Crane spurious encouragement mixed with grim realities (Letter 350). "I am so anxious about him," Cora replied to Wells (No. 354). Crane's physicians decided that the Black Forest might save him. Their fee for this advice was fifty guineas each, and Cora beseeched Pinker once more (Letter 358). So Crane left England, with Conrad and other friends seeing him off at Dover (Letter 365).

"I always fancied," Robert Barr wrote Karl Harriman after Crane's death, "that Edgar Allan Poe revisited in the earth as S. Crane, trying again, succeeding again, failing again, and dying ten years sooner than he did on the other occasion of his stay on earth" (Letter 370).

Crane's stay on earth was short. He survives as artist.

✿   ✿   ✿

321. CORA CRANE TO JAMES B. PINKER

[Brede Place] Tuesday [January 2, 1900]

Dear Mr. Pinker: Mr. Crane is ill again—in bed but is still keeping at his work. The pressing of his creditors is so distressing. Now I simply loathe bothering you again, but I can't help it. There is some money, I feel sure, due from Stokes and Co. on "Active Service." Did you ask them for a statement? And is there any news of their wanting the Romance? Of course they want it but I can understand they are dragging things out through the mail to make better terms. If these large sums, which ought to come from Stokes and for the serial rights of story could be gotten in, it would put Mr. Crane straight. But as it is we have to keep begging you to put cheques in bank all the time. I don't know what Mr. Crane would do without your kind help through these long days of trying to get straight, but I'm sure you feel that in the long run he will prove his appreciation of your simply saving him from going smash. Again I have to beg for £20—to be placed *at once* to my credit at Brown & Shipleys.[1] I am obliged to draw against it for things which can't be put off.

Please let me know by wire what Stokes says. Every moment saved means so much less worry for Mr. Crane. And will you let us know by letter to whom you have offered the Romance serially? It ought to bring a good round sum.

You will have two or three more chapters of the book by the end of the week.

Above all things; please do not get out of patience with these constant requests for money *"at once."* If you can only get a whacking good price for serial of book it would put Mr. Crane straight. Very Sincerely yours   *Cora Crane*

322. CORA CRANE TO JAMES B. PINKER

[Brede Place] Thursday [January 4, 1900]

Dear Mr. Pinker: I enclose you a bit more of the Battle article. The rest goes to you tomorrow as well as another chapter of Romance.[2]

It is now 4.30 P.M. and your promised wire has not come. However, I hope that you have managed to do as I asked you yesterday. It is so important. Miss [Helen] Crane ought to have her money for ticket today as she leaves either tomorrow night or on Saturday morning for Paris. She *can't* leave until money reaches her. Then, as I explained if the money is not deposited with Brown & Shipley, & cheques are returned again, they may ask me to close my account.

Please *wire* Mr. Crane at once if you know either the American or British serial rights of novel are sold. Every moment [of] suspense saved him means better work. Yours Sincerely   *Cora Crane*

322A. TO MRS. EDWARD PEASE

[Inscribed in a copy of The Monster, January 4, 1900]

Dear Mrs. Pease: I am rejoicing in the Russian raiment[3] and I am

---

[1] London bankers.

[2] *The O'Ruddy.*

[3] Mrs. Pease, according to David Garnett in *The Golden Echo*, had a

sure nobody but you would have thought of it. It is the very kind of thing I like. A long 20th century to you and yours   *Stephen Crane*

323. *TO CURTIS BROWN*

[Inscribed in a copy of *Active Service*] Brede Place/Sussex/Jan 6, 1900

To Curtis Brown/ from Stephen Crane/ with the highest assurances of regard and esteem, and wishes for continual good-luck

324. *CORA CRANE TO JAMES B. PINKER*

[Brede Place] Saturday [January 6, 1900]

Dear Mr. Pinker: Your letter with copy of "Badajos" [4] received. The cheque for £20—also. Mr. Crane will send corrected copy by tonight's post, and he asks you to send *without fail* on Monday £30—to Oxted Bank. He simply must have it, so please do not fail. It is to meet cheques that have once been returned and credit is gone here if they are not paid this time. Mr. Crane is now working hard & will keep you busy this month with stories.

Can you get Methuen to make advance upon the next story they are to have. The Irish story.[5] Please move London to have cheque at Oxted Bank before it closes on Monday. It means endless worry, upsetting Mr. Crane for work and goodness only knows what if cheques are returned again. This Lippincott article is worth £35—is it not? & there will be another before weeks [*sic*] out. Yours Sincerely

Cora Crane

325. *CORA CRANE TO THOMAS PARKIN* [6]

Brede Place,/Sunday [January 7? 1900]

Dear Mr. Parkin: I am sending you a few letters of authors well

---

fondness for Turkish trousers and "odd attire"; but the "Russian raiment" may have come originally from some one of the numerous exiles who in the nineties found asylum from czarist tyranny in the neighborhood of Limpsfield. Cora at the end of the year sent her friend and former neighbor an inscribed copy of *Great Battles of the World:* "To my dear friend Mrs. Pease with every wish for a Happy 1901. CC." This copy of *Great Battles* is owned by Nicolas Pease, of Limpsfield; the inscribed copy of *The Monster* is now in the George Arents Collection at Syracuse University.

[4] "The Storming of Badajos," published in *Lippincott's Magazine,* April, 1900.

[5] *The O'Ruddy.*

[6] County magistrate and book collector who had a home at Hastings, nine miles from Brede Place. He wrote to Cora Crane saying he had a dupli-

know[n] today. Henry James, Edwin Pugh, A. E. W. Mason, H. B. Marriott-Watson, Robert Barr, H. G. Wells, Joseph Conrad (whose real name is Korzeniowski.) I also send you a program of the "Ghost." It's a unique program. My husband sends you a copy of "George's Mother." [7] You may like it as you appreciated "Maggie."

We enjoyed our afternoon so much at your house and we hope it will not be long before you come to Brede Place. Very Sincerely yours
                                                          Cora Crane

326. CORA CRANE TO JAMES B. PINKER

[Brede Place/January 7, 1900]

Dear Mr. Pinker: Your telegram just received. Mr. Crane intended no threat and will keep all engagements made with you. He does not understand what your telegram means and it has quite upset his days work. The facts are that he must have a lot of money this month. At least £150—and he is trying to earn it, and had no doubt that you would not help him, until your telegram came which neither of us can quite understand.

I've wired you to please deposit the £30 to my credit at Brown Shipley & Co. Founders Court London and I pray that it is done by the time this reaches you. It's a matter of saving credit which it seems absurd to lose. Please write us fully that we may depend upon you to raise the money needed if you get the stuff to sell.

I mailed you this morning a little story—"The Tale of a dark-brown Dog." [8]

Please let us know just what you have of Mr. Crane's unsold, and

---

cate copy of *The Oxenbridges of Brede Place*, and asking if she would accept it as a gift. Sir Goddard Oxenbridge, who died in 1531, was (according to legend) an ogre who ate a small child for his dinner every night and was finally sawed in half by the children of the neighborhood; his bloody shade ever afterward haunted Brede Place. Parkin asked if there was a chance that the play, "The Ghost," would be published. If so, he would like a copy; he considered the piece "a real literary curiosity" on account of the names attached to it. Parkin presently arranged a luncheon at his home in Crane's honor. The theatrical program of "The Ghost" is reproduced in *Bulletin of the New York Public Library*, December, 1952. Another copy is owned by Roger M. Frewen.

[7] The inscribed copy reads simply: "To Thomas Parkin/From Stephen Crane/Jan 4, 1900/Brede." This copy and Cora's letter to Parkin are in the Berg Collection of the New York Public Library.

[8] "Dark Brown Dog," published in *Cosmopolitan*, March, 1901.

how matters stand with you. And *please* do not fail to deposit today
£30 to credit of *Cora Crane* with *Brown Shipley & Co.* Yours Sincerely

Cora Crane

327. JAMES B. PINKER TO CORA CRANE

London, W. C./Jan. 9th, 1900

Dear Mrs. Crane,/ I have just received your letter of yesterday, and
also the short story from Mr. Crane.

I have this morning paid in to your credit with Messrs Brown,
Shipley, & Co. a cheque for £30. I am sure it is not necessary for me
to tell you that you and Mr. Crane may always count on all the help I
can give, but as you know, the demands on my help have been greater
in extent and persistency than was ever contemplated, and I was therefore very much surprised to receive Mr. Crane's letter of the 5th.[9] As
you and he think I misinterpreted it, let me repeat what he said:—

"I must have the money. I cannot get on without it. If you cannot
send £50 by the next mail, I will have to find a man who can. I know
this is abrupt and unfair, but self-preservation forces my game with
you precisely as it did with Reynolds."

If this did not mean what I took it to mean, I am at a loss to understand it. However, I am glad to have your assurance that Mr. Crane
did not threaten any breach of our Agreement.

I enclose a statement showing how Mr. Crane's account stands.
Of unsold MSS. I have "Moonlight on the Snow," 6,000 words; three
"Wyoming" tales, making together 6,700 words,[10] three "Spitzbergen"
tales;[11] making together 7,800 words (the British serial rights of the
first has been sold, as you will see from the account); "Manacled," 1,500

---

[9] This letter has not been found. Crane replied on this same day in
softened tone (see Letter 328).

[10] Pinker sold "Moonlight on the Snow" to *Frank Leslie's Popular
Monthly,* where it appeared in April, 1900. Cora sold the Wyoming tales
after Crane's death, the money being paid into Crane's estate.

[11] Spitzbergen tales: "The Kicking Twelfth," published in *Pall Mall
Gazette,* February, 1900, and in *Ainslee's Magazine,* August, 1900; "The
Shrapnel of Their Friends," published in *Ainslee's Magazine,* May, 1900;
"And if He Wills, We Must Die," appearing also under the title "The End
of the Battle," published in the *Illustrated London News,* July 28, 1900,
and in *Leslie's,* October, 1900, and "The Upturned Face," published in
Ainslee's Magazine, March, 1900. All these tales were collected in *Last
Words* (London: Digby, Long & Co., 1902). The best one, "The Upturned
Face," was not yet placed in August, when Black & White rejected it.

words;[12] "An Illusion of Red and White," 2,000;[13] and the story received this morning, 2,500.

The quickest way to get return would be to complete the Battle articles,[14] and I hope that this is what Mr. Crane is doing.

Have you a copy of the story written for Lady Randolph Churchill for me to send to Stokes? It is, as you know, included in the book,[15] and I have no copy here. I think probably Methuens will take plates from Stokes. I suggested it to them some months ago. We also want the title for the book. Yours sincerely,   *James B. Pinker*

Can you let me have another copy of the second Spitzbergen story, "The Shrapnel of Their Friends"?

328. *TO JAMES B. PINKER*

Brede/Jan 9 [1900]

My dear Pinker: My wife's account in the bank is some pounds overdrawn already if the note for £31 has been presented. Plant is kicking for £10 and Her Majesty calls tomorrow for my income tax. Please send £20 to Brown Shipley. I am trying to get off the Chapter XII [16] simultaneous [*sic*] with this interesting note.

I am enclosing you a letter from the editor of The New Magazine.[17] They have plenty of money anyhow and at any rate. It might be another good place for the Spitzbergen Stories.

I hardly know what to say further save that you are a BENIFIT [*sic*]. Yours etc.   *S. Crane*

329. *CORA CRANE TO JAMES B. PINKER*

[Brede Place] Tuesday A.M. [January 9, 1900]

Dear Mr. Pinker: Both your letter to me saying that you had sent £30.

---

[12] First published in *Argosy*, August, 1900; apparently not sold serially in England. Reprinted in *The Monster & Other Stories* (1901).

[13] Published in the New York *World*, May 20, 1900; apparently not sold serially in England. Reprinted in *The Monster*.

[14] The series called *Great Battles of the World* (1901): "Vittoria"; "The Siege of Plevna"; "The Storming of Burkersdorf Heights"; "A Swede's Campaign in Germany: I. Leipzig, II. Lutzen"; "The Storming of Badajos"; "The Brief Campaign Against New Orleans"; "The Battle of Solferino"; and "The Battle of Bunker Hill."

[15] This refers to "War Memories," which Lady Randolph Churchill published in December, 1899, in the *Anglo-Saxon Review*. (Beer is mistaken in saying that Crane wrote "War Memories" in January, 1900.) The book referred to is *Wounds in the Rain*, published in September, 1900.

[16] Of *The O'Ruddy*.

[17] An American publication, with a representative in London.

to Brown Shipley & Co to my credit, for which I thank you very much, and your letter to Mr. Crane, reached us this morning's Post. Mr. Crane says he had no idea of putting any of his work in other hands than yours and cannot understand why you should have received any such impression. He would be glad if you would send him back his letter to let him see what could have misled you.[18] Mr. Crane is very faithful to any agreement and he appreciates the fact that you have advanced money upon stories before you received payment for them yourself.

Now, as I wrote you, Mr. Crane is in immediate need of £150— Would Methuen *advance* upon "The Irish Romance?" Of course though there is no contract Mr. Crane wants them (Methuen) to have this book. But we cannot lose sight of the fact that *if* Methuen does not care to make an immediate advance there is someone else who will. By Friday several more chapters of the story will be finished. Shall I come up on Friday morning reaching your office about 2.30 P.M. and bring what is then finished of the novel? Or can *you* see Methuen and say that now they have or can get at any time the ms. for war stories. And ask them if they will advance £100—at once on this (Irish) story? If they will do this they can send contract for Mr. Crane to sign for this book—and for the *next one* for which they are to pay £200.[19] But please find out from them tomorrow what they will do in the matter. I don't want Mr. Crane to come up personally as it [will] mean several days gone from his work. And I don't want to come up myself if I can help it as I'm not well and dread the journey, only if I can be of any use to you in raising the money for Mr. Crane please let me know. If you think it would do any good for *me* to see Methuen for Mr. Crane, please write or wire & I will come up whenever you say. Mr. Curtis Brown, who is an old friend of Mr. Crane's, and of whom doubtless you know, is anxious to buy a book from him and says that he will give a bigger price than anyone. His address is 11, Park Road. Regents Park.

Will you advise if you think it would be better for Mr. Crane to drop "The Irish Romance" and do short stories in order to raise this money. But do your best to get Methuen to advance £100. Mr. Crane must have £150—and almost immediately—that fact remains. Please answer by return and advise. Yours Very Sincerely   *Cora Crane*

---

[18] Pinker evidently returned Crane's January 5 letter as it was not among the group of Crane letters Pinker preserved.

[19] Perhaps the novel on the American Revolution, which Crane abandoned.

330. CORA CRANE TO JAMES B. PINKER

Brede Place,/Jan 10th 1900

Dear Mr. Pinker: Your letter and statement received. Stokes and Co. have a copy of the article in Lady Churchill's magazine.[20] I sent it to them.

About the Lippincott articles. They were to pay £200 for 18000 words, in six (6) articles.[21] They seem now to be paying at the rate of £30—each. That will make them pay £50 for the sixth article. Is this right? The £54 credited against "Battle of Bajados" [Badajos] I suppose means for New Orleans [22] as well. Hastily & Sincerely yours

Cora Crane

331. TO JAMES B. PINKER

Brede/Feb 5 [1900]

Dear Pinker: Thank you for £20. Please let me know about the £50 by telegraph. The note came due today and it will soon be back on my hands.

Shall I write you a short story for it or shall I continue on the Romance? [23] Yours etc

S. C.

---

[20] *The Anglo-Saxon Review.*

[21] The series was later extended to nine articles, all of which ran serially in *Lippincott's Magazine* before being published in book form as *Great Battles of the World* (1901).

[22] "The Brief Campaign Against New Orleans," published in *Lippincott's Magazine,* March, 1900.

[23] This letter and the following one to Pinker, written on the same day, are poles apart; they disclose Crane's unpredictable emotional gyrations in this period of illness and ever-present anxieties.

An English newspaper dated June 16, 1900, commenting on Crane's death, reported a correspondent as having said that months before it was easy to see that Stephen Crane's years, if not months, were already numbered. "In February last I met him at the house of a friend—bibliophile, ornithologist, and amateur artist—living at Hastings [Thomas Parkin]. Painful was the contrast between the young author of the 'Red Badge of Courage' and the other guests, all of whom were in good health and spirits. Poor Stephen had that white, worn-out, restless look betokening complete nervous exhaustion. He took no tea, and did not join in general conversation, but moved about uneasily as if in search of something he could not find. Among the guests present was 'that sombre genius,' as 'Shirley' has called the author of 'Mark Rutherford' [William Hale White]. But although the two men spent an hour in each other's company, they did not exchange so much as a syllable!"

332. *TO JAMES B. PINKER*

Brede Place./Feb. 5th 1900

Dear Mr. Pinker: I spent two months trying to find an effective title to the book of War Stories. I decided upon *"Wounds in the Rain."* This seemed to me *very effective.*

Dominick's [24] views are of no account to me whatever and I am surprised that Methuen found occasion to agree with him on any point.

The sub-title—the books on the Cuban War have for more than a year terrified the Stokes firm and they have not the slightest idea that they are now in possession of the only fairly decent book on the Cuban War which has yet been written—the sub-title, I say, can be dispenced [sic] with for America and become this: "A collection of War Stories." [25] As for Methuen, he can adopt the same sub-title if he likes.

But as for the premier title, "Wounds in the Rain," I shall not change that unless I am *compelled* to do so. Yours faithfully

Stephen Crane

333. *TO JAMES B. PINKER*

Brede/Thursday [February 8, 1900]

Dear Pinker: I *am sending* you "Vittoria" for Lippincotts.[26]

There are 6000 words or more. The XIX Chapter of the Romance I have thought best to make wait in the typing since a Lippincott article is such sure quick money. Please send £15 pounds to my wife's credit at Brown Shipleys and credit the remainder to my a/c.

Remember the 12th. I must have a good sum on the morning of that day. I rec'd your letter this morning re Lippincott's provisional acceptance. I can send the articles at the rate of one per week. This makes the fifth. Let me know on Saturday what can be done on the 12th. On that date the XIX Chapter of the Romance will reach you.

---

[24] London representative of Frederick A. Stokes & Co., New York, who published *Wounds in the Rain* in September, while Methuen this same month published it in England.

[25] The American edition by Stokes did not carry this sub-title but simply *War Tales*. The title Crane suggested was used by Methuen in the English edition: *A Collection of Stories Relating to the Spanish-American War of 1898.*

Pinker wrote Crane on February 1: "He thinks so long a title as the one you have chosen would seriously affect the sale of the volume, and he tells me that in view of the glut of books on the Cuban war which has appeared in America he thinks it is unwise to proclaim in your title that your book deals with the same subject." Dominick won the argument.

[26] Published in *Lippincott's Magazine,* July, 1900.

Please wire me on Friday night but state the words rather ambiguously because my post-master is my grocer.[27] Yours   C.

334. TO JAMES B. PINKER

Brede/Saturday [February 10, 1900]

Dear Pinker: I rec'd your letter acknowledging arrival of Vittoria but you were silent on the question of the £15 which I asked you to deposit.

I enclose Chapter XIX of the Romance.[28] Chapter XX may be able to reach you at the same time. I hope to have the thing done soon.

The next battle for Lippincotts is "Lützen."[29] It should reach you within ten days. This article will be the one for which £50 is to be paid.

Please stretch yourself on Monday. There will be £30 due from Stokes on the Romance, £30 from Lippincott on Vittoria which with Lippincotts £100 makes £160. I would like to have £100 on Monday. Yours faithfully   S. Crane

335. CORA CRANE TO JAMES B. PINKER

Brede Place/Feb. 14th 1900

Dear Mr. Pinker: Your letter of Feb. 13th at hand. I thank you for attending to my request.

Mr. Crane says to try to get £100 from Lippincott for American book rights and to get it *now,* telling them that's the reason they get it so cheap. Please do your best to get a cheque from them *at once* and if you do, please deposit it to my credit with Brown and Shipley & let us know about it. Yours Sincerely   Cora Crane

P.S. Can't you sell the English bookrights of this book?

336. TO JAMES B. PINKER

Brede Place,/March 24th [1900]

Dear Pinker: Please send a cheque to A. T. Plant, 18 Bedford Row, Grey's Inn for £22 before Wednesday or a bailiff will be here and also

---

[27] Obviously Crane owed money to the grocer and no doubt also to the other Brede merchants. The grocer as postmaster would know when Crane received money and by the telegram what sum.

[28] *The O'Ruddy.*

[29] "Lützen," one of the *Great Battles* series, is not listed in *Bibliography* and perhaps was not printed in any journal; Crane finished writing it by March 24 (see Letter 336).

deposit £20 to my wife's a/c at Brown Shipley, and send the enclosed wire. This does not include the £15 which I asked from you today. "Lützen (£50) is finished today but the typing will require tomorrow. It will reach you by special stamps. The XXIV Chapter of the novel is finished but not yet typed. It will reach you on Tuesday.

The novel stands at 61000 but I am extremely doubtful about my prudence in writing it at this time.

Would you take my note for £100? But as to the £22 and the £20 answer by enclosed telegraph form.

I expect the "Romance" to pull me out much more than even. I only question the wisdom of my abandoning my lucrative short story game for this long thing which doesn't pay (much) until the end. Yours sincerely   S. Crane

P.S. Cheques to the amount of £16 have been sent back from the bank and I must almost meet my little weekly grocer and butcher bill.

337. TO JAMES B. PINKER

[Brede Place,/March 31, 1900] [30]

Dear Pinker: I enclose Chapters XXIV and XXV (4000 wds) of the Romance for typing and also the remainder of the "A Swede's Campaign in Germany" [31] article.

I understand you did not manage the cheque for £30. I sent my wife off to Paris with the money that my brother had sent to buy some clothes for my niece in Paris and my wife *must* get a draft on Monday. Cannot you send her by cable a draft for £20 on the Parisian correspondents of your bankers in London, and also send £10 to her a/c at Brown Shipley & Co.? The poor things may be left high and dry in Paris.

My wife's address is "Hotel St. Petersbourg, Paris." I enclose a wire which I hope—I beg you to be able to send early Monday A. M.

---

[30] This letter is reprinted from *Love Letters to Nellie Crouse* (1954), p. 81, where it is misdated 1899. Stephen had wired Cora in Paris asking her to call on his old friend from the Art Students' League days, Corwin Knapp Linson. But before she could do so, Cora was called home by a wire from her housekeeper with news of Stephen's sudden collapse from hemorrhages. In September, after her return to England from the United States, where she had taken Crane's body for burial, she wrote Linson these details (see Appendix 11), giving March 31 as the date of her departure for Paris where she was to meet Helen Crane coming from Lausanne.

[31] Another of the *Great Battles* series, of which one part was "Leipsic" and the other "Lützen."

The Romance will run very little beyond the 80000 words. Chap
XXVI may reach you Tuesday. Yours etc.   S. *Crane.*

✿   ✿   ✿

Crane's Ill-Health Reaches a Crisis

On March 31 Cora set out from Brede Place for Paris, where she expected to meet Helen Crane coming from Lausanne. They planned to
go shopping. Cora had a discriminating knowledge of fashions and
clothes, and Judge William Crane, an indulgent father, had written
Cora asking her to get for his daughter whatever she needed with
the money he sent. On April 2 Cora in Paris received a telegram from
her housekeeper and cook, Vernall, saying Crane had had two severe
hemorrhages; the wire was sent without his knowledge, as Stephen
would not have wished Cora to be upset. Cora immediately sent off
wires to Moreton Frewen and Hoyt De Friese telling them what had
happened, begging her friend Mrs. De Friese to obtain from the American Embassy the name of the most eminent lung specialist in London
and to arrange for him to go at once to examine Stephen. Mrs. De
Friese was given a special note of introduction from the embassy,
where Crane's illness was considered a matter of international concern, to Dr. J. T. Maclagen. With a further loan of the embassy's good
offices, she also managed to procure two trained nurses who went
down to Brede Place on the same train with the physician. Cora and
Helen caught the night boat from Calais and reached home April 3.

✿   ✿   ✿

338. *CORA CRANE TO JAMES B. PINKER*

[Brede Place] Friday night [April 6, 1900]

Dear Mr. Pinker: Mr. Crane is ill. I have had a Specialist down from
London & *had to give him a cheque for* £50. He was so encouraging
that I am glad. I have a battle article—"Solferino" [32]—I will have it up
to you in a few days time, it's partly typed. I enclose a note to Lippincott, but it will be quicker to post it direct, asking them to send you a
cheque or to deposit it at Brown & Shipley to my credit to meet the
cheque given to Doctor Maclagen of 9 Cadogan Place. I don't think
they will hesitate as it was a matter of saving Stephen Crane's life. I

---

[32] "The Battle of Solferino," published in *Lippincott's Magazine,* October, 1900.

was recalled from Paris. I will try to write you more fully tomorrow.
The draft you sent to Paris has not reached me yet. I've not slept once
[since] Tuesday except short naps & so I'm dead tired. Please write
Lippincott. Yours sincerely   *Cora Crane*

339. CORA CRANE TO JAMES B. PINKER

[Brede Place] Saturday [April 7, 1900]

Dear Mr. Pinker: Please don't let any consideration prevent your sending £50. to Brown & Shipley Monday before bank hours to meet the
cheque I paid the London specialist. It may be the cause of saving Mr.
Crane's life. The report is favorable.

Your draft to Paris never reached me so I suppose it has been returned to you.

I've written Lippincott. Let me know if Serial is sold. If Mr. Crane
should die I have notes of end of novel so it could be finished & no
one will lose—if that thought should occur.[33] Please let me hear from
you. Very Sincerely yours   *Cora Crane*

340. WILLIAM HOWE CRANE TO CORA CRANE

Port Jervis, N.Y./April 7/1900

My dear Cora:— We are greatly alarmed and grieved over Stephen's
condition. We await further news with anxiety. I fear that I can't help
you with money at present. My bank account is very much depleted.
I am just leaving for Supreme Court session this morning. We all send
love to Stephen, Helen and yourself. Please send news often. Yours
affectionately,   *Will.*

---

[33] Here Cora's panic betrays her into admitting what she must until
now have firmly refused to see. Crane had told Nellie Crouse he did not
care to live beyond thirty-five; to Karl Harriman he made it thirty-one; and
to the young American, Willis Clarke, who visited him in November, 1899,
he had said, "I'm just a dry twig on the edge of the bonfire." After his visit
to the Trudeau sanitarium his stubborn refusals to see doctors or to heed
their advice must have terrified Cora. Somebody, remarking on Crane's
health, frightened her, and Crane wrote a note: "Please have the kindness
to keep your mouth shut about my health in front of Mrs. Crane hereafter.
She can do nothing for me and I am too old to be nursed. It's all up with me
but I will not have her scared. For some funny woman's reason, she likes
me. Mind this" (Berryman, p. 248).

When Sanford Bennett hurried over from France after Crane's collapse,
he found a desperate woman pacing the floor "lashing her skirt with one of
his [Crane's] riding crops. She broke into frantic denunciation of herself for
allowing so much entertainment at Brede. It was a ghastly quarter of an

341. *JOHN BASS* [34] *TO STEPHEN CRANE*

Peking [China], April 10th 1900

My dear Crane/ One morning in this far away land Mrs Bass and I awoke to find a New Year Greeting from Mrs Crane and yourself. It was good of you to think of us after these years.

Since I saw you we have had rather good luck. If you remember Mrs. Bass was very ill in Greece [35] and she had hardly recovered when the Spanish American war broke out. The boy was strong and in good health. We left him on a farm with his grandfather in New England and Mrs Bass and I started for the Philippines representing Harper Bros.

When the Insurrection broke out [36] the [New York] Herald being discontented with their man took me on. The double work for the Herald and Harpers in a tropical country was more than I could stand. Without the help of Mrs. Bass I could not have done it. She broke down and went home returning six months after with the boy. Then as I was full of malarial bugs we started for the Paris exposition via Suez. Bennett [37] stopped us asking if I would go to China for six months. Ergo, here we are in the midst of filth, chinamen and court intrigues, trying to get a little light on the future of China, the prospective war between Japan & Russia. We want to return at the end of six months once more to civilization where we hope to have a flat in Paris.

Although pretty well out of touch with the Western world we have from time to time caught one of your notes, now a war article, now a "Whilomville" peace story.

---

hour. She finally sank into a chair, sobbing. . . . She had no real hope of his recovery. But she showed her courage, and cheered him up. It may be that he had married her from chivalry, but he had grown very fond of her indeed. There was something very fine about her" (Thomas Beer, "Mrs. Stephen Crane," *American Mercury* (March, 1934), pp. 289–95).

[34] War correspondent with Crane in Greece.

[35] Mrs. Bass was stricken with typhoid fever in Athens during her pregnancy. A day or two later the Cranes left Athens. Later, at Oxted, Stephen received news of her condition from Eben Alexander, the American Minister to Greece. He himself lost a son from the same disease a few months after he returned to the United States; his wife also nearly succumbed. (Alexander's letters to the Cranes are in the Butler Library Crane Collection.)

[36] The Filipinos revolted first against Spain and later against the United States. The Filipinos revolted against the United States when the peace treaty ending the Spanish-American War gave the Philippines to the United States. The insurrection Bass refers to is the Aguinaldo Insurrection.

[37] James Gordon Bennett, owner and publisher of the New York *Herald*.

That was sad about Harold Frederic. How a man of his intelligence could have left two little girls in the plight he did without providing for them in any way, I cant see. I suppose that he was always in debt. Do you know what has become of the children, and if they are in need I should be glad to help with my small subscription if there be need.

I should be glad to hear from you whenever you feel inclined to write.

Mrs. Bass is writing a note to Mrs. Crane; so I will not speak for her.

I am looking forward to hunting you up when I return from the Orient to have a good chat on our hardships, trials and experiences of the Greek campaign.

Are you at work at some "magnus opus." As for myself I am plodding along with unbounded ambition but limited expectation.

Hoping that Mrs Crane and you are in the best of health. Yours truly   *John F. Bass*

342. CORA CRANE TO JAMES B. PINKER

[Brede Place] Wednesday [April 11, 1900]

Dear Mr. Pinker: I am glad to tell you that my husband seems a little better today. He had a quiet day and night with no hemorrhage, and takes his nourishment well. His illness will be a long one and I shall be under great expense. I hope that the American & British Serial rights of the Romance will be sold and will pay for these expenses. Please do your very best and let me know. Ready money is an absolute necessity in illness. I have two nurses who cost £2.4.6 each per week beside their expenses. Then there are medicines and living expenses— so do your best to get serial money in. My niece is typing the battle article [38] which you shall have this week. I hope my husband will be able to dictate the remainder of the last one from notes soon so that I can get the £100 from Lippincott.

Now Mr. Pinker, It was a matter of life & death to have the Specialist down. I could not leave any stone unturned. *You* might not have gone to office on Saturday or Friday. I *had* to write to Lippincott at the same time & I wrote you.[39] One cannot stand upon ceremony

---

[38] "The Battle of Solferino."

[39] "I dont think they [Lippincott] will hesitate as it was a matter of saving Stephen Crane's life" (No. 338). Pinker evidently saw it in a different light and was not at all agreeable to Cora going over his head in writing Lippincott's representative, Garneson.

at such a moment, and indeed I was almost distracted. Pray forgive
any seeming lack of courtesy to yourself. Very Sincerely   *Cora Crane*

343. WILLIAM HOWE CRANE TO STEPHEN CRANE

Port Jervis, N.Y./April 13/1900

My dear Stephen:—/ We are very anxious over your sickness. There
is in our morning paper every day a London dispatch, giving the latest
news from you. We find this unsatisfactory, and are awaiting anxiously
for letters. If your trouble is tubercular, we think you ought to leave
the English climate and come to America. You and your wife will be
welcome at our house, as long as you choose to stay.

It is pleasant here, excepting in the winter, and then you can, if
you choose, flit southward with the birds.

I hope this will find you in improved health. Your affectionate
brother,   *William*

344. CORA CRANE TO H. G. WELLS

Brede Place,/Sunday [April 15, 1900]

Dear Mr. Wells: Stephen was taken with hemorrhages [40] on the 31st
March, two hours after I had started to go to Paris to meet Miss Crane,
who was leaving school. I was recalled on Tuesday the 3rd April by
wire & crossed that night. I found him in a very dangerous state when
I got here. Sent for trained nurses at once & got the best lung specialist
the U.S. Embassy knew about, down from London. He gave us hope.
There has been no hemorrhage now since Monday last [*i.e.*, since
April 9]. The doctors say if he pulls through until next Thursday
[April 19]—ten days—that he will be out of danger. Then the future
plans will have to be made. I fear that we shall have to give up Brede
Place & go to a more bracing place, on the sea.

Thank you for your kind letter. Stephen sees his letters today for
the first time. He is much better & very cheerful.

Please give Miss Crane's and my own love to your wife.[41]

With kindest regards   Yours sincerely   *Cora Crane*

---

[40] Word had leaked out already of Crane's illness. Reading of it in the
London *Academy*, Wells wrote Cora on April 13 asking for news of his condition, and he wrote Stephen a week later.

[41] The Cranes, Helen, and Edith Richie had stayed overnight with Mr.
and Mrs. Wells at their house near Folkestone at the time when Crane
escorted his niece from Paris to the school at Lausanne.

345. CORA CRANE TO JAMES B. PINKER

[Brede Place. About April 15, 1900]

Dear Mr. Pinker: This is just a line to say that the doctors think Mr. Crane much better. They say if he can pull through to Thursday [April 19]—ten days—he will be out of danger. The doctor said to him today—"In three weeks you can work." As soon as he is strong enough, we will (the doctor & I) take him up to London for another consultation as to the best way to care for his health in future. I shall have to take him to some sea-side place for a few weeks from there. I think that I can send one nurse away in another week. The wonderfully good care he has had has pulled him through. Dr. Skinner [42] says that the trouble seems only superficial; not deeply rooted.

Please send the last two Chapters (ms) of the Romance down. Mr. Crane sent them to you to be typed on March 31st.

I hope you will see your way to selling the serial rights so that no money worries need retard Mr. Crane's recovery. Please let me hear from you. Very Sincerely yours   *Cora Crane*

346. CORA CRANE TO JAMES B. PINKER

[Brede Place] Monday [April 16, 1900]

Dear Mr. Pinker: I thank you for letters telling me that you had deposited £25—to my credit.

Mr. Crane says that Lippincotts owe £110—so he makes it. I am sending you a typed copy corrected of last battle article on Tuesday P.M. or Wednesday. Mr. Crane asks if it is possible, if you will send £100—of the Lippincott money. We want to get him to Bournemouth [43] if possible among the pines for a time. Please send cheque immediately. This is such a critical time now—every post delay will make his temperature fly up—so please do your very best.

---

[42] Dr. Ernest B. Skinner, the physician whom H. G. Wells had summoned from Rye after Crane's first collapse in late December, was also one of the witnesses to Crane's will (dated from Brede Place, April 21, 1900).

[43] Bournemouth, where the shade of Robert Louis Stevenson still lingered in a yellow-brick house on the edge of Alum Chyne. Crane's abomination of Stevenson is well known.

Stevenson lived fourteen years with tuberculosis, the disease brought so far under control in the favorable climate of the South Seas that he found it possible to ride horseback, exert himself in heavy outdoor labor, and in the end he did not die of tuberculosis. It seems at least conceivable that Crane, but for his stubborn refusal to see doctors and to accept the discipline of a rigorous health routine, might similarly have prolonged his own life.

Have you gotten Tillotson's[44] Romance rights yet? Mr. Crane says if they don't answer this week to take it away from them and try some one else. "The New Magazine" of New York. Very Sincerely yours   *Cora Crane*

347. CORA CRANE TO JAMES B. PINKER

[Brede Place] Tuesday [April 17, 1900]

Dear Mr. Pinker: I send you the battle article for Lippincott. Please ask them to send Mr. Crane the Feb. number of magazine also to send *proofs. Always* to send proofs![45] Please say the mistake in the New Orleans battle could have been mended by the turn of a pen if the proof had been sent. Please let me know just how we stand now with Lippincott. Today the doctor said that Mr. Crane would be better for work in two or three weeks time, that it would divert his mind so the other and last battle article can be finished then.

I am thinking of renting Brede Place,[46] furniture linen, servants, horses carriage etc. If you hear of any one who might want it tell them to write to me. Do you think this a good plan? Write what you think of this on a seperate [*sic*] paper. Mr. Crane sees letters now but nothing that could possibly worry him. Very Sincerely yours   *Cora Crane*

348. JAMES B. PINKER TO CORA CRANE

[April 20? 1900]

Dear Mrs. Crane/ Thank you for your letter enclosing the Battle

---

[44] "Tillotson's Newspaper Literature," an English syndicate "For Supplying the Newspaper Press with Special Articles and the Works of Popular Novelists."

[45] Cora seems to have been more scrupulous about proofreading Crane's manuscripts than either his publishers or his agent. To Pinker she raged (August 15): "Please make Methuen understand that their contract is with *me* now & that when I ask for proofs to be sent me of book, I intend to have them. . . . Please tell them to send proof of *Wounds in the Rain.* I've always done my late husband's work of that kind as you know. I also want to see the dedication page so that *I* may be sure that there is no mistake." And to G. H. Perris, to whom she presently turned after consultation with Plant, in a move to wrest funds for living expenses from the estate, she complained (October 20), as to "The Squire's Madness," the "mistakes are simply endless!" Earlier reminders to Perris to obtain proofs for this story from *Crampton's Magazine* had gone unheeded.

[46] Cora must have consulted Moreton Frewen in regard to subletting Brede Place. Appeals had been passed along to numerous friends to keep on the lookout for a likely tenant.

article.[47] There is one more to come to complete the series. I have asked Lippincotts to be sure & send proofs, and for a copy of the February number.

I am so glad to hear Mr. Crane is better, and I will not fail to send you at once any news likely to cheer him. Very sincerely yours

349. WILLIAM HOWE CRANE TO CORA CRANE

Port Jervis, N.Y., Apr. 21st, 1900

My dear Cora:—/ We have received your letter, and two from Helen, within a day or two, and were delighted to learn that Stephen is improving.

Of course, we feel that the letters are always a little belated, when they relate to a question of life and death; but, as long as they are not contradicted by the newspaper dispatches, we take a great deal of comfort out of them. I wish you or Helen [48] would write almost every day, as we are very anxious. We also have many inquiries from his friends in Port Jervis and elsewhere.

---

[47] "The Battle of Solferino." The manuscript was typed by Helen Crane at Brede Place.

[48] Helen Crane, whose peccadilloes had been a sore problem, was now lending needed support and comfort in this critical period of Crane's illness, relieving her Aunt Cora of much of the load of correspondence with anxious friends. But Will Crane's peremptory demand for daily bulletins contrasts with the more sympathetic understanding of Eben Alexander: "You were very good to let me know about Stephen, when you must have been busy every moment and almost wild with anxiety." Alexander now had a professorship at Chapel Hill, "a restful place" where the mountain air was beneficial to consumptives. Another young man, a correspondent friend of Crane also known to Alexander, had been cured of the same disease on going to live for some months near Asheville. Writing to Cora (May 17) Alexander opened his own home to the Cranes to "come and live with us just as long as you will." Evidently with some knowledge of Crane's debts, he added: "There is absolutely nothing that either of you will have to spend a cent for. . . . Now it stands to reason that, with money coming in from books already published, and with practically no expenses, he can get on his feet in time, so far as money is concerned.

"We live in utmost simplicity, but I don't think either of you will mind that. If I had money, I would send enough in two minutes to relieve any present bother on that score. But I have only my salary. You two would add practically nothing to our living expenses. I do hope you will come, if you and Stephen think it would be good for him. We shall be as glad to have you as if you were our own children."

But it was not to be. Before Cora received this letter, Crane was dead.

My brother, George, has asked the Drew Theological Seminary if they would like to have father's Theological books. For my part I am willing to donate the books to the Institution, but I would like to have Stephen's consent; as, in mother's will, his interest in the library is larger than the interest of any of the rest of us.[49]

I did not give you the invitation to Port Jervis lightly, and we hold ourselves in readiness to do the best we can for you and Stephen, if you come here. I shall try to get and send to Stephen a book, written by Dr. Buckley, one of father's old friends, on "A Consumptive's Struggle for Life." He had hemorrhages when he was a young man and began the use of Dr. Howe's breathing tube, which Stephen knows about. He recommends it very highly, and also makes some valuable suggestions about climate. Stephen can tell you that I have blown on Dr. Howe's tube over twenty years, and I am sure that it has done me great good.

The people of Port Jervis take a certain pride in Stephen and they are very much concerned about his health. I hope you will write often. There is no special family news. We are all well, the relatives are also in good health. Did I write Stephen that Uncle Luther [50] had died and was buried early in April? He died practically of old age, although a slight cold, which ran into pneumonia, was the immediate cause of his death. I was one of the pallbearers.

We all send love to you, Stephen and Helen, from Your Affection-ate Brother,   *William*

I dictated this to my girl. She is responsible for the punctuation &c. I think you may have missed my point about Janice Meredith.[51] It is a story of the Revolutionary War and the venue is laid in N. Jersey: and I understood that Stephen was writing or was about to write just such a book.   *Will.*

350. H. G. WELLS TO STEPHEN CRANE [52]

April 22. 1900

My dear Crane,/ I have just heard through Pinker that you are still

---

[49] Crane's mother took note of his literary preoccupations by leaving to him the major portion of his father's library. Stephen's interest in it was described in William H. Crane's "Accounting of Proceedings" as American executor of his brother's will as "of only nominal value."

[50] Uncle Luther was the classical scholar of the Peck side of the family.

[51] *Janice Meredith* (1899) was an extremely popular historical romance by Paul Leicester Ford.

[52] For Cora's reply see Letter 354.

getting better and I rejoice mightily thereat. I was hugely surprised to hear of your haemorrhaging for you're not at all the hectic sort of person who does that with a serious end in view.

As an expert in haemorrhages I would be prepared to bet you any reasonable sum—I'll bet an even halo only I am afraid of putting you on that high mettle of yours—that haemorrhages aren't the way you will take out of this terrestrial Tumult.

From any point of view it's a bloody way of dying, and just about when you get thirsty and it bubbles difficult and they inject you with morphia, I know few, more infernally disagreeable.

And confound it! what business have you in the Valley? It isn't midday yet and Your Day's Work handsomely started I admit, is still only practically started. The sooner you come out of that Valley again and stop being absolutely irrelevant to your work, the better!

Please remember us very kindly to Mrs. Crane. Yours Ever

H. G. Wells

351. CORA CRANE TO JAMES B. PINKER

[Brede Place] Monday [April 23? 1900]

Dear Mr. Pinker: I enclose you the dedication [53] to be put on the first page of the *"War Stories"* both in the American edition which Stokes & Co are bringing out and in the English Edition which Methuen is bringing out. . . .

I thank you for your letter of 20th April. Please do your best to hurry up the sale of the Serial rights of Romance. Mr. Crane wants to know to whom you have shown it in English and who has it now.

Can you arrange to deposit £30—to my credit this week? I want to send one nurse away at end of week (Thursday). We are bringing Mr. Crane to a room on ground floor today, so he·can be taken out in the sunshine every day. The doctor will let me [word missing] with next week. He has had an abscess which has given great pain and which is still not finished with. Otherwise he is getting on wonderfully well. Yours Sincerely   *Cora Crane*

P.S. I hope that you can manage the £30 I ask for.   *C. C.*

---

[53] The dedication of *Wounds in the Rain* reads:

BREDE PLACE, SUSSEX, April, 1900.
To / MORETON FREWEN / THIS SMALL TOKEN OF THINGS /
WELL REMEMBERED BY / HIS FRIEND / STEPHEN CRANE

Wounds in the Rain was published in New York in September by Frederick A. Stokes & Co. and in England by Methuen & Co. (Cf. *Stephen Crane: A Bibliography* [1948], pp. 50–52.)

352. CORA CRANE TO JAMES B. PINKER

[Brede Place] Tuesday [April 24, 1900]

Dear Mr. Pinker: Please *send* by return Chapter XXIV and XXV of the Romance. Mr. Crane sent them to you to be typed when I was away.

The doctors say that a sea voyage is the thing for Mr. Crane. Is *there* any way in which you can raise money for him? Can you get Methuen or Stokes to make an advance? Please do your best and as *quickly* as you can.

Mr. Crane was moved down stairs yesterday. And will be carried out in the sunshine today. The Abscess keeps him back a little as it is so painful but the danger from hemorrhage is quite over. Can you get some English newspaper to pay expenses for Mr. Crane & myself to St. Helena [54] & back & a month there? He can send them some interesting letters & interview Group.

Will you also tell any one likely to want Brede Place, servants, horses, etc.—that they can have it at reasonable figure. Sincerely yours
                                                                 Cora Crane

P.S. *Please* let me know by return just how we stand with Lippincott, & how much they have to pay on delivery of the next battle.   *C. C.*

353. JAMES B. PINKER TO CORA CRANE

[Late April? 1900]

Dear Mrs. Crane/ I will do my best, but it is very difficult in the circumstances to get further advances. I thought you were going to utilize the Lippincott money to take Mr. Crane to Bournemouth.[55]   *Pinker*

---

[54] A Boer camp, where most of the prisoners taken in the South African war were interned, had been established on St. Helena. Crane had concocted a scheme of going there to write for the New York *Journal*, the London *Daily Chronicle*, and the *Morning Post* a series of articles based on interviews with prisoners. Cora and Helen Crane would go with him.

[55] Dr. Skinner, who had earlier reassured Cora that "the trouble seems only superficial," had by now "given Crane up"; he advised an immediate change to a seaside resort, such as Bournemouth, or a sea voyage. Maclagen, the London specialist, thought the patient should not be moved "for at least two months." A change, he thought, "may be advisable later." On May 2 he wrote to Cora: "I am very sorry to have had such a bad report of Mr. Crane. I would not readily take a hopeless view of his case."

St. Helena was now out of the question; friends urged removal to a sanitarium somewhere on the Continent. The choice lay between the cure at Davos in the Swiss high Alps (where R. L. Stevenson had been a patient some fifteen years before, and Thomas Mann was to become one about the

354. CORA CRANE TO H. G. WELLS

Brede Place, / April 25th 1900

Dear Mr. Wells: Stephen is not up to letter writing so I am answering your very cheerful letter to him. I am so anxious about him. The lung trouble seems over! The doctor today, after an examination, said that the right lung was entirely un-affected. The trouble is that this dreadful abscess which seems to open from time to time in the bowels —or rectum, makes him suffer the most awful agony. And it takes away his strength in an alarming fashion. The abscess seems to have upset the bowels too. So he is very weak. Then the *fever* (Cuban fever) comes for an hour or two each day. The chills seems to have stopped the past week. And he hopes within three or four weeks to go on a sea voyage. Write to him when you can. Sick people have fancies that their friends neglect them and wonder at small number of letters, etc. Of course, I have up to date read all letters first and there are many which I think best he should not see—you understand.

Please accept our united kindest regards for yourself and wife. I hope she is well. Very Sincerely yours   *Cora Crane*

355. WILLIAM HOWE CRANE TO CORA CRANE

Port Jervis, N.Y.
April 30/1900

My dear Cora:—/ I shall be glad to have Helen go with you to St. Helena. The only question is one of expense. If it will only cost about what it would have cost to continue her at school, I shall be satisfied.

It has been rather a severe drain. But we wish her to have some advantages and we have not begrudged the expense.

Stephen paid me $500 on account of $1250 which he was to pay me for a one-eighth interest in Hartwood. He has no deed and even hasn't a contract—which, however, makes no difference.[56] Now, if he

---

same number of years later) and the celebrated "Nordracht treatment" in the German Black Forest area. The Duchess of Manchester, an intimate friend of the Frewens, was strongly in favor of Davos. She had lost two daughters by tuberculosis. Sometime in April she wrote: "My dear Cora: I think Mr. Crane would be very comfortable at Davos. It is the Nordracht cure without the brutality. You could not get anyone in at Nordracht, under six-eight months. I am not even sure Dr. Doughty has a vacancy as his limit is sixty in the Sanitarium—but if you decide I will write and bring the case before him. Affectionately yours, C." (The duchess was the Cuban-born Consuelo Yznaga, known as "the American Duchess.")

[56] Stephen wrote William Crane on October 29, 1897: "I am a wanderer

does not wish to complete the transaction, the situation is about like this:—I credit him with $500; I charge him with various items, including the 100£ which I sent him in March, 1899,[57] and he is still in my debt 155^{27}/_{100}$, at this date.

Of course, I do not expect him to pay this, until he gets ready. I am merely setting forth the business situation of the Hartwood transaction. If he is able to think of business matters, kindly show him this letter and I think he'll concur. We are overjoyed to hear of Stephen's improvement. He'll have to seek a drier climate. Fred Lawrence,[58] an old friend of Stephen's, says that New Mexico is one of the three best places in the world for lung troubles.

We all are well and send love to you all. Yours affectionate brother,   *William*

Can you give me some idea what the trip to St. Helena will cost?

356. *TO HIS NAMESAKE* [59]

[Brede Place, / April, 1900]

My dear Stephen:/ I need not say to you that I welcomed your advent with joy. You and I will struggle on with the name together and do as best we may. In the meantime, I would remind you to grow up, as much as possible, like your gentle, kindly, lovable father, and please do not repeat the vices and mistakes of   Your devoted uncle,

Stephen Crane

357. *TO A BOOK REVIEWER*

[Brede Place. / Early 1900?]

. . . No thanks. If the Whilomville stories [60] seem like Little Lord

---

now . . . but—afterwards—I think of P. J. and Hartwood" (Letter 201). Edmund Crane had moved from Hartwood to Port Jervis, and William had taken over Edmund's equity in the 3,500-acre estate.

[57] Evidently a loan made to Stephen when his creditors were threatening him with bankruptcy proceedings.

[58] Dr. Frederic M. Lawrence, with whom Crane roomed during his New York City days (1893–1894), wrote Thomas Beer in 1923 some reminiscences (see Appendix 21, 22).

[59] Stephen, son of Edmund, Crane's brother, then living in Port Jervis, New York. Stephen, a twin, died in the spring of 1921. In his will Crane left him one-half of his estate. Cora saw little Stephen when she visited Edmund's house in June, 1900.

This letter, reprinted from *Omnibus*, first appeared in the Introduction and Notes to *The Red Badge of Courage*, ed. Max J. Herzberg (1926), p. xxx.

[60] Crane's Whilomville stories, starting in August, 1899, ran for one

Fauntleroy to you you are demented and I know that you are joking, besides. See here, my friend, no kid except a sick little girl would like Lord Fauntleroy unless to look at Birch's pictures for it. The pictures are all right.

358. CORA CRANE TO JAMES B. PINKER

[Brede Place] Tuesday [May 8? 1900]

Dear Mr. Pinker: I thank you for your letter. The doctors, there is another consultation tomorrow—which means fifty guineas each. You see how far £10. goes with two nurses at £2.2- a week each. A valuable life can't be saved by saving pennies or pounds.

The doctors say that Mr. Crane's *life* can be saved and that perhaps a cure can be made by his going to the Black Forest for the "Nordracht" treatment. Now I give you an outline of what has to be done. He is carried on an air bed on a stretcher to *Rye*. There an invalid carriage will take him, the nurses one doctor and myself, to Dover. Here we rest for one or perhaps two weeks at the Lord Warden Hotel to have sea air & rest then a deck cabin to Calais & there an invalid carriage awaits us. *It* costs *sixteen* first class fares and there is no change to the Black Forest. The expense, so Cook's people say is as follows—

Invalid carriage to Dover, holding every one—four first class fares.
10/ each on steamer & 20/ extra for cabin.
Calais to Black Forest—£60—

With expenses at the Hotel at Dover it will mean £100—to get there and I must have this within the week. Now you know the situation.[61]

---

year in *Harper's Magazine*, a story an issue to August, 1900, inclusive. The collection, in the press at the time of Crane's death in June, appeared in mid-August, 1900.

[61] This included innumerable other debts. Alfred Plant, Moreton Frewen's solicitor, wrote to Cora on May 7: "I am in receipt of your letter of the 5th inst. and can only say it was at Mr. Frewen's express wish that I asked you for the list of debts, as he was most anxious that this trouble should be, if possible, removed. . . . I believe he has written direct to Dr. Skinner, and am certain that he is doing all in his power to help you." Moreton Frewen, who knew a great many influential people, had already approached the American banker and art collector, J. P. Morgan, on Crane's behalf; and Morgan replied, May 18, that he would be "very glad" to see Frewen "about Mr. Crane at any time," either at his home or his office. Crane reached Dover on May 15. (The Morgan letter and Plant's letter to Cora are in the Butler Library Crane Collection.)

Try to get someone to take Brede if you can even if they pay running expenses only for two months until I can pull matters together again.

This is a matter of life or death so please do your best. The lung has healed over and he has a chance to get well & live for years if we can get him out of England. Yours Sincerely   *Cora Crane*

359. WILLIAM HOWE CRANE TO CORA CRANE

Port Jervis, N.Y.
May 10/1900

My dear Cora:—/ I have received your telegram and also a letter from Dr. Skinner. We are grieving over the situation; but I really cannot send money, in any amount to make it worth while, at present. It has been years since I have been so hardly pressed as I am now.

It looks as if it might be best for Helen to come home.

Dr. Clement Cleveland and wife, good friends of mine, went to Europe on Howard Gould's yacht a day or two ago; and will leave Liverpool June 30th on the Campania. If, when this reaches you, you think it best that Helen return, I wish you would write to the S. S. Co. and engage passage for Helen for that trip, asking that she be put as near Dr. Cleveland as possible. Then put the S. S. Co. in communication with me and I'll send the necessary funds. . . .   *Wm. H. Crane*

360. JOSEPH CONRAD TO CORA CRANE

10th May 1900

My dear Mrs. Crane/ Your letter distresses me beyond measure and confirms my fears as to your material situation. It has been the object of my anxiety and of many sad thoughts. You may imagine that had it been in my power to render you any sort of service I would not have waited for any sort of appeal.[62] I've kept quiet because I feel myself powerless. I am a man without connections, without influence and without means. The daily subsistence is a matter of anxious thought for me. What can I do? I am already in debt to my two publishers, in arrears with my work, and know no one who could be of the slightest use. It is not even in my power to jeopardize my own future to serve you. If it had been, such is my affection for Stephen and my admira-

---

[62] Cora made no such appeal to Henry James. But James, with his extraordinary sensitiveness must have guessed her need or else he learned of it from others, for on June 5, the day Stephen died at Badenweiler, James sent Cora £50, begging her to view it as a convenience "and dedicate it to whatever service it may best render my stricken young friend. It meagerly represents my tender benediction to him."

tion of his genius, that I would do so without hesitation, to save him. But my future, such as it is, is already pawned. You can't imagine how much I suffer in writing thus to you. I have been almost distracted since I had your letter. Won't Stephen's relations come forward.[63]

Pardon me for not saying more. I feel too unhappy. Always yours

Jph. Conrad

PS I am writing to Mr. B———.[64]

361. *CORA CRANE TO JAMES B. PINKER*

[Brede Place] Saturday [May 12? 1900]

Dear Mr. Pinker: The doctors say that for Mr. Crane to recover he *must* get out of England. The *Black Forest* first. Now this means, an expensive move within the week. Can you manage an advance in some way? Mr. Crane is no worse & the right lung holds out, only this change must be made without delay. We will go to some small Inn in the Black Forest & Rent Brede Place as it stands. I shall have to take nurse & the Doctor will go with us. It's a *very* expensive journey but it's a matter of life or death and it must be done. Please advise me. Can you cable Stokes to advance or get Methuen to advance or How about Serial? Please reply at once. This climate seems simply death. . . . Very Sincerely Yours   *Cora Crane*

362. *JOSEPH CONRAD TO CORA CRANE*

Sunday [May 13? 1900]

Dear Mrs. Crane—/ What awful news you are giving us! And yet people given up by the doctors have been known to live for years.

Of course I will take the boat over.[65] I didn't offer to come near your place knowing myself powerless to help you, not wishing to bring

---

[63] Crane's relatives did not come forward (see Letter 359).

[64] Blackwood, publisher of *Blackwood's Edinburgh Magazine*.

[65] The sailboat jointly owned by Conrad and Crane, of which Mrs. Conrad writes in *Joseph Conrad and His Circle:* "We had bought the boat, *La Reine*, from Mr. Hope on the understanding that Stephen and my husband were to be joint owners, and half the time we kept her in Folkestone and the other half of the time Stephen had her in Rye. But he had never paid his half-share and his wife's proposition was that she should allow their local wood merchant to take her over in payment for their wood account."

Cora's "proposition" certainly appears one-sided. But Crane had paid something down on the boat (see Letter 294), and David Garnett's testimony (in *The Golden Echo*) that Mrs. Conrad's tendency to exaggeration was very like Ford Madox Ford's, balances the picture here.

my barren sympathy and my helpless sorrow only to hinder you who
are fighting the battle.

Believe our hearts are with you. May heaven give you strength
and the supreme consolation of faith. I can't give you an idea how unhappy I am since I have received your letter. Always yours

Jph. Conrad

☙ ☙ ☙

Stephen Crane at Dover,
En Route to the Black Forest

Robert Barr went to Dover to see Crane and gave his promise to finish
The O'Ruddy from notes that Stephen was even then dictating to Cora.
Henry James had intended going, but found himself unexpectedly confronted with a mound of proofs that his publishers demanded back
within an impossibly narrow time limit, so he wrote to Cora at Badenweiler. He had bicycled over to Brede with two friends soon after the
Cranes' departure "to show them the face of the old house; but the
melancholy of it was quite heart-breaking. So will it, I fear, always be
to me." Conrad, ill himself, "dragged to Dover" to spend twenty
minutes with his dying friend—long enough to stamp on his memory
the wasted figure on the bed "with his wonderful eyes fixed on the
ships that showed through his open window, the feeble voice, and the
stretcher on which he was to make this final journey."

On the crossing to Calais on May 24 en route to the Black Forest,
the Cranes were accompanied by a physician—probably Dr. Bruce—
two trained nurses, Crane's niece Helen, and his favorite dog Sponge.
The party stayed eight days in Dover before Stephen could be moved.
Mrs. Conrad writes that in order to save money Cora had the nurses
fed outside the hotel, a building of tarnished splendor in the Second
Empire style, "but I know that the wife often went without."

☙ ☙ ☙

363. TO SANFORD BENNETT [66]

[Brede Place, May 14]

. . . My condition is probably known to you. . . . I have Conrad on
my mind very much just now. Garnett does not think it likely that his
writing will ever be popular outside the ring of men who write. He is

---

[66] Reprinted from Berryman (p. 259), this is Crane's last letter.

poor and a gentleman and proud. His wife is not strong and they have a kid. If Garnett should ask you to help pull wires for a place on the Civil List for Conrad please do me the last favor. . . . I am sure you will.

364. CORA CRANE TO H. G. WELLS

Lord Warden Hotel/Dover/May 15th, 1900

Dear Mr. Wells:/ We got Stephen safely here today. We rest here one week and then if I can arrange it and all goes well, I take him on to the Black Forest.[67] Dr. Mitchel Bruce said one lung is all right so far and that there is the chance of recovery—I should say, the chance of *life*! The doctor and two nurses have to go with us. The wound needs constant care. I've done all mortal can do and I hope! I wish I could have seen you and the dear wife before going—My best love to you both. Sincerely yours ever,   *Cora Crane*

P.S. I've a sore hand so can't write properly.   *C. C.*

365. CORA CRANE TO H. G. WELLS

Lord Warden Hotel,/Dover. Sunday [May 20, 1900]

Dear Mr. Wells:/ Nurses think best for Stephen not to see any one before starting. Best for him to be quite alone tomorrow, so I must ask you not to come & I *am* sorry. I will write you of our journey. Love from us all to your wife. Faithfully yours,   *Cora Crane*

If ever a good book or magazine turns up send it to us in the wood.[68]

---

[67] In a letter to John Galsworthy, May 17, Conrad wrote: "The Frewens pay *all his* [Crane's] transit to the Black Forest,—rather more than £ 100" (see *Joseph Conrad: Life and Letters,* ed. G. Jean-Aubry [Doubleday, Page & Co., 1927], I, 294–95, where it is misdated May 7).

Moreton Frewen's generosity to the Cranes is on record, and he undoubtedly contributed to the expenses of the Black Forest journey. But Conrad is probably here repeating gossip. For though he made and lost fortunes, Frewen was by no means a wealthy man, and one finds no evidence to support this statement. Alfred Plant wired Cora at Badenweiler June 7: "Frewen strongly objects to removal. It will utterly ruin prospect of fund [Cora had applied for help from the Royal General Literary Fund, of which J. M. Barrie was one of the trustees] and cannot be paid for otherwise." (Telegram in the Butler Library Crane Collection.)

[68] The Black Forest.

366. CORA CRANE TO JAMES B. PINKER

Lord Warden Hotel,/Dover Sunday [May 20, 1900]

Dear Mr. Pinker:/ Mr. Crane wants this dedication put in "The O'Ruddy" book.[69] He wants it dated from Brede Place.

I've wired you to telegraph price offered for serial. Mr. Crane wants Robert Barr to finish it & perhaps Mr. Kipling may edit (don't mention this yet). You should get big serial price. Hastily yours

Cora Crane

Write! Please, Wyoming Tales should bring big prices. It will be a long time before there are more.

May—1900/Brede Place/Sussex/England/
To/My Wife/Stephen Crane

367. CORA CRANE TO JAMES B. PINKER

Lord Warden Hotel,/Dover May 23rd [1900]

Dear Mr. Pinker:/ We are crossing tomorrow to Calais and from there have a Salon carriage to *Bâle*.[70] Address there at *Hotel Trois Rois* until later address comes. I thank you for your letter. Mr. Robert Barr will call to see you and will explain our wishes about Romance. Please *register* all contracts you have to *Bâle* for Mr. Crane to see. He asks you to please do this at once. Yours truly   *Cora Crane*

368. CORA CRANE TO JAMES B. PINKER

Villa Eberhardt/Badenweiler/Schwartz Wald/Germany
May 29th [1900]

Dear Mr. Pinker:/ I enclose proof—Please let me know what has been done about serial rights? Who is your man in U.S.? Why don't you put it in Mr. Reynolds hands to sell? Have you seen Robert Barr? Now this is a matter that must be attended to. *I* can sell the American serial

---

[69] When *The O'Ruddy* was finally published (1903), neither the English nor American edition carried this dedication.

[70] After the Channel crossing on May 24, the journey to the Black Forest was resumed with a pause of two or three days for recuperation at the Swiss border town of Basel (Bâle). Reaching Basel on May 25 would have meant arrival at Badenweiler, in the Bavarian Alps, May 27 or May 28. The Villa Eberhardt, where Crane occupied a room on the second floor, was one of the houses belonging to the sanitarium, and remains today, unchanged since Crane's time. To tourists of Badenweiler it is pointed out as a literary landmark, the death-place of a famous American author.

rights myself and I simply must have money for Mr. Crane.[71] Please send a typed copy of the ms—to Robert Barr at once. He will explain & please let me hear from you *what* is being done. I'm sure Mr. Reynolds could sell the Wyoming stories in U.S.[72] Do try him with them. Very Sincerely yours *Cora Crane*

369. WILLIAM HOWE CRANE TO CORA CRANE

June 8/1900

My dear Cora:—/ Several times I have taken up my pen to write you, but have halted because I could not think of anything to write that would fit the situation. We are simply benumbed by this calamity which has fallen upon you and upon us. I engaged passage upon a steamer sailing yesterday, but canceled it upon the receipt of your telegram. Port Jervis is in mourning.

So many people here knew him, that the village claimed him as one of her sons and always felt pride in his achievements.

I suppose Stephen's wish was to be buried in our family plot at Elizabeth, New Jersey.[73]

Write or wire me such arrangements as you would like to have made and I'll look after them. Of course, I do not know the particulars of your plans. If it is thought best that Helen should come home with Dr. Cleveland, you can get in communication with him by writing c/o J. P. Morgan & Co., London. . . . Your affectionate brother, *William*

370. ROBERT BARR TO KARL EDWIN HARRIMAN

Hillhead, Woldingham/Surrey/June 8, 1900

I was delighted to hear from you, and was much interested to see the article on S. Crane you sent me. It seems to me the harsh judgment of an unappreciative commonplace person on a man of genius. Stephen had many qualities which lent themselves to misapprehension, but at the core he was the finest of men, generous to a fault, with something of the old time recklessness which used to gather in the ancient literary taverns of London. I always fancied that Edgar Allan Poe revisited in the earth as S. Crane, trying again, succeeding again,

---

[71] The frantic tone of this communication reflects Cora's acute emotional disturbance as well as her need. In declaring that she, independently, could sell American serial rights to *The O'Ruddy* she no doubt had in mind Curtis Brown's previous offer to buy a novel of Crane at "higher prices" than anyone else would pay.

[72] Cora sold the Wyoming stories when Pinker failed to place them.

[73] Stephen's grave is at Hillside, New Jersey, now a separate township.

failing again, and dying ten years sooner than he did on the other occasion of his stay on earth.

When your letter came I had just returned from Dover, where I stayed four days to see Crane off for the Black Forest. There was a thin thread of hope that he might recover, but to me he looked like a man already dead. When he spoke or rather whispered, there was all the accustomed humor in his sayings. I said to him that I would go over to the Schwarzwald in a few weeks, when he was getting better, and that we would take some convalescent rambles together. As his wife was listening he said faintly. "I'll look forward to that," but he smiled at me and winked slowly, as much as to say, "You damned humbug, you know I'll take no more rambles in this world." Then, as if the train of thought suggested what was looked on before as the crisis of his illness, he murmured, "Robert, when you come to the hedge—that we must all go over—it isn't bad. You feel sleepy—and—you don't care. Just a little dreamy curiosity—which world you're really in—that's all."

Tomorrow, Saturday, the 9th, I go again to Dover to meet his body. He will rest for a little while in England, a country that was always good to him, then to America, and his journey will be ended.

I've got the unfinished manuscript of his last novel here beside me, a rollicking Irish tale, different from anything he ever wrote before. Stephen thought I was the only person who could finish it, and he was too ill for me to refuse. I don't know what to do about the matter, for I never could work up another man's ideas. . . .

From the window beside which I write this I can see down in the valley Ravensbrook House, where Crane used to live and where Harold Frederic, he, and I spent many a merry night together. . . . Stephen died at three in the morning, the same sinister hour that carried away our friend Frederic nineteen months before. . . .[74]

I feel rather like the last of the Three Musketeers the other two gone down in their duel with death. I am wondering if, within the next two years, I also will get the challenge.[75] If so, I shall go to the competing ground the more cheerfully that two such good fellows await the outcome on the other side.   *Robert Barr*

371. ANNOUNCEMENT

Queen Anne's Mansions / St. James Park. [About June 11, 1900]

Mrs. Stephen Crane has arranged that friends of her late husband's

---

[74] Curiously enough, three o'clock in the morning marked the death of another American author, F. Scott Fitzgerald.

[75] Barr did not die until 1912.

may see him to say goodbye, at The Mortuary, 82 Baker St. on Thursday between the hours of 3 and 5 o'clock.

❀ ❀ ❀

Epilogue

Crane died on Tuesday, June 5. Friends—especially Moreton Frewen, Mason, and Plant—strongly opposed removal of the body from Germany for burial; they considered the cost, transit difficulties, and so forth, prohibitive. But Cora was not to be dissuaded. The idea of leaving Stephen to lie in an uncared-for grave on alien soil was unthinkable to her.

So Crane's body was taken to a London mortuary and the announcement of the lying in state was sent to his friends (No. 371). It is in Helen Crane's handwriting, prepared, no doubt, at Cora's request, possibly dictated by her.

Cora probably spent several days at Queen Anne's Mansions, a family hotel in London, where she had friends and had frequently stayed on her trips to town. Among the many condolences she received was a letter from Henry James, expressing his sorrow on the "miserable news," which he learned through the newspapers: "What a brutal needless extinction—what an unmitigated unredeemed catastrophe! I think of him with such a sense of possibilities & powers." [76]

On June 17, accompanied by Helen Crane and two of the Brede dogs, Sponge and Powder-Puff, Cora sailed from Southampton on the North German Lloyd liner *Bremen* with Crane's body. There was a service at the Metropolitan Temple in New York City, followed by interment in the Crane family plot at Hillside, New Jersey.

Cora remained almost a month in the United States, visiting the William Cranes at Port Jervis, and the Edmund Cranes, who were spending the summer in the little town of Rio in Sullivan County. On July 19, with her friend Mrs. Brotherton, she sailed for England, to take up life again and begin the task of packing up and clearing out personal belongings from Brede Place. After the move to London, she and Mrs. Brotherton took temporary lodgings at 47 Gower Street. In September they moved to a small house in South Kensington, The Boltons, at 6 Milborne Grove, where Cora had hopes of cashing in on the flourishing tourist trade toward payment of the £70-a-year rental.

---

[76] Letter dated June 7, 1900, in the Butler Library Crane Collection.

She planned to let one floor to an American couple, or a single man, with pension—a plan that never materialized. (See Cora's letters in the Appendix, Nos. 8, 10, 11, 13, 14.)

      ❀   ❀   ❀

APPENDIX

THE LETTERS in this section,[1] some of which represent the most interesting ones in this book, bring together for the first time reminiscences of Stephen Crane by his many friends, ranging from Irving Bacheller's letter to Cora on July 13, 1900 (No. 4) to A. E. W. Mason's letter to Vincent Starrett on October 4, 1945 (No. 27). Most of them are printed for the first time.

Cora's letters trace the poignancy of her loss, her attempt to carry on Stephen's literary career by recasting his unfinished manuscripts and also her attempt to initiate a literary career of her own by writing for the pulps, and then the collapse from hopes and illusions to the grim realities—she ends in Jacksonville, Florida, as madam of The Court.[2] She was fated to end where she began, in the same situation

---

[1] Drawn from an extraordinarily large collection in the Butler Library Crane Collection at Columbia University, the Hamlin Garland Collection at the University of Southern California, the papers of Thomas Beer, and from other sources specified in the acknowledgment pages.

[2] In "Cora Comes Back" (concluding chapter of *The St. Johns: A Paradise of Diversities* ["Rivers of America series"; New York: Farrar & Rinehart, 1943]), James Branch Cabell and A. J. Hanna spread the legend that The Court was built as an architectural imitation of Brede Place. But it bore not the slightest resemblance to the English house, as is evidenced by a photograph in the Butler Library Crane Collection. It is to the unique honor of Hanna that he did not subscribe to all of the fairy tales put forth in "Cora Comes Back," and that he opposed, though unsuccessfully, inclusion of this chapter in the book. This note corrects the unfounded version circulated in *The St. Johns,* and unfortunately repeated in *Omnibus* (p. xx), and in the Modern Library edition of *The Red Badge of Courage* (1951; introduction, p. v.). A detailed analysis tracing sources of this and other misrepresentations found in "Cora Comes Back," is given in a special Appendix to Lillian

and plight she endured when first she met Stephen Crane. A young friend of Cora in England wrote years afterwards, when she was then familiar with all the gossip about Stephen's wife, "I do not know how she lived and do not care. She was 'on the level.' She was plucky and gay and kind."

The section contains a notable Conrad find, the letter to Peter F. Somerville (No. 16), discovered recently in The Library of Congress. "I hardly meet anyone now who knows or remembers anything of him," Conrad wrote Somerville a decade after Stephen's death. "Mere literary excellence won't save a man's memory." Conrad, however, was mistaken. Both Crane and Conrad remain remembered today because of their literary excellence.

Irving Bacheller's letters (Nos. 4, 17) recapitulate what he later wrote about Crane in his *Coming Up the Road* (1928), but his letters reveal intimately his personal charm and Christian charity.

The spirited letter of John Northern Hilliard (No. 18) gives us a portrait of Crane as he knew him: "Crane was a big man as well as a big writer—the biggest writer, to my mind, this country has produced." (Hilliard conveniently ignores Hawthorne, Melville, Twain, and Henry James.)

The portrait of Crane by Frederic C. Gordon (No. 20) stands at odds with that of Hilliard: "He was all that we used to mean by the word *gentleman*." Perhaps so, but Gordon saw Crane only in the daylight and knew him not at all in his "night wanderings." Hilliard knew the night side of Crane, and so too did E. W. McCready (No. 25). As Dr. Frederic M. Lawrence (No. 21) puts it: "Every man has as many reputations as he has acquaintances."

That Crane was self-conscious of his literary stature is indicated by Frank Noxon's reported remark: "Oh, Stevie is just making biography for himself," as reported in Lawrence's letter to Beer (No. 21), whose biography of Crane, says Lawrence, misses "much of the real Stephen Crane." Lawrence's letter touches on many events rendered in the text of this volume. In the fall of 1896 Crane wired Theodore Roosevelt, then Commissioner of Police, to defend himself against charges made by policeman Charles Becker versus one Dora Clark, accused of soliciting and defended by Crane as innocent. On Crane's protest and evidence Magistrate Brann released Dora Clark. That Crane, "in spite of his devotion to realism in literature, was incurably romantic about women" is remarked on by Lawrence.

Frank Noxon's letter (No. 24), reproduced here from the original typed manuscript in the Newark Public Library, deals mainly with

Gilkes' biography, *CORA CRANE* (Indiana University Press, 1959).

Crane's days at Syracuse University and with the banquet given Crane by the Society of the Philistines. Noxon is not the only person to claim that *Maggie,* "at least in its early form, was wholly or in part written at Syracuse." To establish precisely where Crane wrote this or that is no easy task. The success of *The Red Badge* flushed out numerous Crane friends to claim that it was written in their attic, room, or studio.

McCready's letter (No. 25) recalls Cora Taylor's Hotel de Dream in Jacksonville, Florida, where Crane first met Cora in November, 1896.

Ericson's letter (No. 26) to Ames W. Williams, bibliographer of Crane's works, recalls their acquaintance during Ericson's Art Students' League days on East 23d Street, New York, Crane writing there portions of *The Red Badge.* "He wrote slowly. It amazed me how he could keep the story in mind while he was slowly forming the letters. This I thought the most extraordinary thing I had ever seen. . . . I felt an awe for him when I saw how naturally his imagination worked through his hand as though he really lived in another world."

❊   ❊   ❊

1. THE WORK OF STEPHEN CRANE

[A transcript of Crane's handwritten copy of an article signed "Holland," appearing in the Philadelphia *Press,* December 4, 1894, reproduced here for the first time.]

The editorial comment published in "The Press" this morning upon the fiction of Stephen Crane justified what was said of that young author some months ago in this correspondence [April 15, 1894]. Then it was predicted that Crane if he was careful of his powers, subjected them to thorough discipline, would surely make a name for himself in American literature. He was a shy, almost nervous young man when I saw him and talked with him about the first of his works of fiction which had been published only a few days [*Maggie,* 1893].

It contained the evidences of great power, of real imagination, and a sort of poetic quality as well which would be sure to take him out of the list of the perfunctory realists. At that time I saw the manuscript of the story that is now running in "The Press" as a serial. Then Mr. Crane had some purpose of publishing it in the first instance complete in book form. A hasty reading of the story very greatly impressed me. Here was a young man not born until long after the war days had closed who nevertheless by power of imagination, by a capacity intuitively to understand the impulses which prevailed in war days, had been able to write a story perhaps the most graphic and truthful in its suggestion of some of the phases of that epoch which has ever appeared in print.

If Mr. Crane is careful, is true to his best impulses, follows his intuitions and pays no heed to those who write this or that about American fiction, he is quite likely to gain recognition before very long as the most powerful of American tellers of tales.

2. ARTICLE IN THE PORT JERVIS (N.Y.) UNION, NOVEMBER, 1895

AN EXTRAORDINARY WORK

STEPHEN CRANE'S TALENT RECOGNIZED BY
THE REVIEWS AND NEWSPAPERS OF THE
UNITED STATES

Some months ago the *Union* announced the publication of a work from the pen of Mr. Stephen Crane, entitled "Red Badge of Courage." This work deals with the events of a single battle, the battle of Chancellorsville and describes in a style of the most powerful realism the experience of a raw New England youth, who received his baptism of fire in that sanguinary contest. The work is a departure from the ordinary method of treating military subjects in the graphic and powerful manner in which the horrors of war are described. The talent evinced in the work is of a high order and has [had?] reviews of [from all over?] the United States. Quotations from a few of the favorable notices are given below.

In view of the fact that the 124th Regiment, recruited from Orange county, bore an honorable and important part in this battle, checking the advance of Stonewall Jackson's impetuous troopers after the extreme right of the Union line had been driven back and disorganized by their unexpected onset, the work will have a special interest in this locality. Here are a few of the quotations:

The Home Journal, Boston, Oct. 19.:—"The Red Badge of Courage is a story of wonderful power, in character not like unto anything concerning our late struggle that we have ever read and in point of intensity of interest standing unsurpassed."

The Transcript, Boston, Oct. 26.:—"The Red Badge of Courage is a book with a mighty theme. It is designated on the title page as merely 'an episode of the civil war,' but it is something more than this. It is a tremendous grasping of the glory and carnage of all war; it is the rendering, in phrases that reveal like lightning flashes, of the raw fighter's emotions, the blind magnificent courage and the cowardice equally blind of a youth first possessed by the red sickness of battle."

Free Press, Detroit, Oct. 7.:—"Stephen Crane describes in a style that reminds one of Victor Hugo in its terse brief sentences, its aptness of comparison and its strength of scene painting, what men feel and see in war."

Globe, St. Paul, Minn., Oct. 20.:—"In substance the book is one which both Mr. Howells and Andrew Lang might enjoy. This is equivalent to say[ing] that Mr. Crane has performed a feat compared to which the pasturing of the lion and lamb in company is a mere bagatelle."

Post, Chicago, Oct. 26.:—"The action of the story throughout is splendid and all aglow with color, movement and vim. The style is as keen and bright as a sword-blade and Kipling has done nothing better in this line. The rank and file has its historian at last and we have had nothing finer since the 'Retreat of the Ten Thousand.'"

Plain-Dealer, Cleveland, Oct. 27.:—"It is perfectly apparent that the experiences described were those of the author."

Times, Minneapolis, Oct. 13.:—"The battle descriptions are intensely real and the whole book is full of superb word painting."

News, Providence, R.I., Oct. 9.:—"This is a book to be read at a single sitting—or two sittings at most. It is the story of a single battle in the American Civil War, a realism and impression that carries the reader from first chapter to last, almost irresistibly in the telling."

Beacon, Boston, Oct. 12.:—"Mr. Crane narrates with a depth of comprehension and a pitiless sincerity that are nothing less than fascinating. To read the book is like looking upon a painting of Verestchagin." [3]

3. TO ELBERT HUBBARD

[1896 or 1897] [4]

What?
You define me God with these trinkets?
Can my misery meal on an ordered walking
Of surpliced numbskulls?

---

[3] Russian artist, 1842–1904, best known for his military paintings.

[4] Crane sent Hubbard for his Philistine a poem sometime in 1896 or 1897. The holograph manuscript, in Syracuse University Library, published as No. IV in War Is Kind, includes the postscript given below. Hubbard did not print the poem, but the back wrapper of his April 1898 number of the Philistine carried these three lines:

You tell me this is God?
I tell you this is a printed list,
A burning candle, and an ass.

And a fanfare of lights?
Or even upon the measured pulpiting
Of the familiar and true?
Is this God?
Where, then, is hell?
Show me some bastard mushroom
Sprung from a pollution of blood.
It is better.

Where is God?/ Stephen Crane

Oh, Hubbard, mark this well. Mark it well! If it is over-balancing your
discretion, inform me.   S. C.

4. IRVING BACHELLER TO CORA CRANE

Canton St. Law Co. N.Y., July 13, 1900

My Dear Madame: Your husband, whom I loved and whose death
was my sorrow as well as that of many, came into my office—a frail boy
of unusual modesty—one day in '93 or '94.[5] I had heard of him; I had
not seen him before then. He said he had written a story; he didn't
know whether it was good or not; Mr. Howells had read it and thought
well of it; he wished me to read it and see if [it] were of any use to
me; he needed money, he had enough of praise. I took it home with me
that night—a bulky manuscript. It was the Red Badge of Courage. My
wife and I read it through together and with great delight. I bought
the story for my newspapers. It made a hit. Editorials appeared in
many papers praising it. Mr. Talcott Williams of the Phila. Press wrote
of it with enthusiasm. When Stevey—that was what we called him
those days—went to the Press office all the editors and reporters
thronged about him eager for a word. The book came out and they
began to talk of him beyond the seas; a light had risen. The editor of
a great magazine invited Steve and me to visit him one morning. I
went to introduce the new comer. They were all sending for him those
days—men who would not have wiped their old shoes on him before
then—precieuses of literature.

In *War Is Kind* (1899) this passage concludes No. IV: "A little ink
more or less!" The opening portion of No. IV, consisting of six lines, is missing in the holograph manuscript. Crane might have written the opening part
after sending Hubbard the above version.

[5] It was 1894. See "The Original Manuscripts of *The Red Badge of
Courage*," their history and Crane's creative process described, in *Omnibus*,
pp. 201–24 and pp. 213 ff. on Bacheller's first sight of the manuscript.

Bacheller, an extraordinarily kind and gentle person, replied here to

"Why did you not give us a chance at the Red Badge of Courage?" said the editor.

Stephen made some evasive answer but coming away he told me laughing that he had sent it there and got it back "with thanks."

He wrote many short tales for me—I do not remember the titles and my books are all in N.Y. He went to Mexico for me—was it in the fall of '94 or '95?[6] I cannot tell here and now. Wrote many delightful sketches of the country and came back with the longest revolver I ever saw.[7] If I can do more let me know. You have my sympathy. I have thought of him and of you often. Yours sincerely   *Irving Bacheller*

5. STEPHEN CRANE: A SOLDIER OF FORTUNE [8]

By Hamlin Garland

The death of Stephen Crane, far away in the mountains of Bavaria, seems to me at this moment a very sorrowful thing. He should have continued to be one of our most distinctive literary workers for many

---

Cora's request for reminiscences of Stephen to use for the biography she planned to write. The contents of this letter square with Bacheller's account of Crane in Bacheller's *Coming Up the Road* (1928). Cora, treasuring this letter, pasted it into a book marked in her hand: "This book belongs to / Mrs. Stephen Crane / 6, Milborne Grove / The Boltons / South Kensington[.] See also the other Bacheller letter, Appendix 17.

[6] Crane started his western trip for the Bacheller syndicate in the first week of February, 1895.

[7] Crane had this revolver with him at Ravensbrook, where he astonished Ford Madox Ford and Harold Frederic with exhibitions of his marksmanship.

[8] First published in *The Saturday Evening Post*, July 28, 1900; later in *Book-Lover*, II (Autumn, 1900), under the title "Stephen Crane." Another version, silently contradicting the facts given in this first appearance of Garland's reminiscences, was published by Garland in the *Yale Review*, April, 1914: "Stephen Crane as I Knew Him." A third variant account is given in Garland's *Roadside Meetings* (1930). See also Garland's "Stephen Crane the Bohemian," *Bookman*, January, 1930.

Of the several essays on Crane published during the year of his death we have selected the two best, this and the critical appraisal by H. G. Wells (see Appendix 9). Karl Harriman's "A Romantic Idealist—Mr. Stephen Crane" was published before Crane died, in April, 1900, in the Boston *Literary Review*. R. G. Vosburgh's "The Darkest Hour in the Life of Stephen Crane" was not published until summer, 1901, in *Book-Lover*, and Corwin Linson's reminiscences of his friend did not appear until 1903, in the *Saturday Evening Post*, April 11: "Little Stories of Stephen Crane." Beginning June 5, 1900, dozens of obituaries appeared on both sides of the Atlantic.

years to come. And yet I cannot say I am surprised. His was not the physical organization that runs to old age. He was old at twenty.

It happened that I knew Crane when he was a boy and have had some years exceptional opportunities for studying him. In the summer of 1888 or 1889 I was lecturing for a seaside assembly at Avon, New Jersey. The report of my first lecture (on "The Local Novelists," by the way) was exceedingly well done in the "Tribune," and I asked for the name of the reporter. "He is a mere boy," was the reply of Mr. Albert, the manager of the assembly, "and his name is Stephen Crane."

Crane came to see me the following evening, and turned out to be a reticent young fellow, with a big German pipe in his mouth. He was small, sallow and inclined to stoop, but sinewy and athletic for all that —for we fell to talk of sports, and he consented to practice baseball pitching with me. I considered him at this time a very good reporter, and a capital catcher of curved balls—no more, and I said goodby to him two weeks later with no expectation of ever seeing him again.

In the summer of '91, if I do not mistake, I was visiting Mr. and Mrs. Albert at their school in New York City, when a curious book came to me by mail.[9] It was a small yellow-covered volume, hardly more than a pamphlet, without a publisher's imprint. The author's name was Johnston Smith. The story was called "Maggie, a Girl of the Streets," and the first paragraph described the battle of some street urchins with so much insight and with such unusual and vivid use of English that I became very much excited about it. Next day I mailed the book to Mr. Howells, in order that he might share the discovery with me. The author had the genius which makes an old world new.

On that very afternoon Crane called upon me and confessed that he had written the book and had not been able to get any one to publish it. Even the firm of printers that put it together refused to place their imprint upon it. He said that the bulk of the edition remained unsold, and that he had sent the book to a number of critics and also to several ministers. On the cover of each copy (as on mine) was written, in diagonal lines, these words or their substance in Crane's beautiful script: "The reader of this story must inevitably be shocked, but let him persist, and in the end he will find this story to be moral." I cannot remember exactly the quaint terms of this admonition, but these words give the idea.

I said to him: "I hardly dare tell you how good that story is. I have sent it to Mr. Howells as a 'find.' Go and see him when he has read it. I am sure he will like it."

He then told me that he had been discharged from the staff of the

---

[9] *Maggie* was first published in 1893, not 1891.

"Tribune." He seemed to be greatly encouraged by our conversation, and when he went away I talked with his friends about the book, which appealed to me with great power. I have it still. This desperate attempt of a young author to get a hearing is amusing to an outsider, but it was serious business with Crane then.

I did not see him again until the autumn of 1892, when I went to New York to spend the winter. He wrote occasionally, saying, "Things go pretty slow with me, but I manage to live."

My brother Franklin was in Mr. Herne's Shore Acres Company in those days, and as they were playing an all-season engagement at Daly's theater we decided to take a little flat and camp together for the winter. Our flat was on One Hundred and Fifth street, and there Crane visited us two or three times a week. He was always hungry and a little gloomy when he came, but my brother made a point of having an extra chop or steak ready for a visitor and Crane often chirped like a bird when he had finished dinner. We often smiled over it then, but it is a pleasure to us now to think we were able to cheer him when he needed it most.

He was living at this time with a group of artists—"Indians," he called them—in the old studio building on East Twenty-third street. I never called to see him there, but he often set forth their doings with grim humor. Most of them slept on the floor and painted on towels, according to his report. Sometimes they ate, but they all smoked most villainous tobacco, for Crane smelled so powerfully of their "smoke-talks" that he filled our rooms with the odor. His fingers were yellow with cigarette reek, and he looked like a man badly nourished.

This crowd of artists, according to his story, spent their days in sleep and their nights in "pow-wows" around a big table where they beat and clamored and assaulted each other under a canopy of tobacco smoke. They hated the world. They were infuriated with all hanging committees and art editors, and each man believed religiously in his own genius. Linson was one of those Crane mentioned, and Vosburg[h] and Green. Together they covenanted to go out some bleak day and slay all the editors and art critics of the city.

Crane at this time wore a light check suit and over it a long gray ulster which had seen much service. His habitual expression was a grim sort of smile. One day he appeared in my study with his outside pockets bulging with two rolls of manuscript. As he entered he turned ostentatiously to put down his hat, and so managed to convey to my mind an impression that he was concealing something. His manner was embarrassed, as if he had come to do a thing and was sorry about it.

"Come now, out with it," I said. "What is the roll I see in your pocket?"

With a sheepish look he took out a fat roll of legal cap paper and handed it to me with a careless, boyish gesture.

"There's another," I insisted, and he still more abruptly delivered himself of another but smaller parcel.

I unrolled the first package, and found it to be a sheaf of poems. I can see the initial poem now, exactly as it was then written, without a blot or erasure—almost without punctuation—in blue ink. It was beautifully legible and clean of outline.

It was the poem which begins thus:

"God fashioned the ship of the world carefully."

I read this with delight and amazement. I rushed through the others, some thirty in all, with growing wonder. I could not believe they were the work of the pale, reticent boy moving restlessly about the room.

"Have you any more?" I asked.

"I've got five or six all in a little row up here," he quaintly replied, pointing to his temple. "That's the way they come—in little rows, all made up, ready to be put down on paper."

"When did you write these?"

"Oh! I've been writing five or six every day. I wrote nine yesterday. I wanted to write some more last night, but those 'Indians' wouldn't let me do it. They howled over the other verses so loud they nearly cracked my ears. You see, we all live in a box together, and I've no place to write, except in the general squabble. They think my lines are funny. They make a circus of me." All this with a note of exaggeration, of course.

"Never you mind," I replied; "don't you do a thing till you put all these verses down on paper."

"I've got to eat," he said, and his smile was not pleasant.

"Well, let's consider. Can't we get some work for you to do? Some of these press syndicate men have just been after me to do short stories for them. Can't you do something there?"

"I'll try," he said, without much resolution. "I don't seem to be the kind of writer they want. The newspapers can't see me at all."

"Well, now, let's see what can be done. I'll give you a letter to Mr. Flower, of the 'Arena,' and one to Mr. Howells. And I want to take these poems to Mr. Howells to-morrow; I'm sure he'll help you. He's kind to all who struggle."

Later in the meal I said: "Why don't you go down and do a study of this midnight bread distribution which the papers are making so much of? Mr. Howells suggested it to me, but it isn't my field. It is yours. You could do it beyond anybody."

"I might do that," he said; "it interests me."

"Come to-morrow to luncheon," I said, as he went away visibly happier. "Perhaps I'll have something to report."

I must confess I took the lines seriously. If they were direct output of this unaccountable boy, then America had produced another genius, singular as Poe. I went with them at once to Mr. Howells, whose wide reading I knew and relied upon. He read them with great interest, and immediately said:

"They do not seem to relate directly to the work of any other writer. They seem to be the work of a singularly creative mind. Of course they reflect the author's reading and sympathies, but they are not imitations."

When Crane came next day he brought the first part of a war story which was at that time without a name. The first page of this was as original as the verses, and it passed at once to the description of a great battle. Such mastery of details of war was sufficiently startling in a youth of twenty-one who had never smelled any more carnage than a firecracker holds, but the seeing was so keen, the phrases so graphic, so fresh, so newly coined, that I dared not express to the boy's face my admiration. I asked him to leave the story with me. I said:

"Did you do any more 'lines'?"

He looked away bashfully.

"Only six."

"Let me see them."

As he handed them to me he said: "Got three more waiting in line. I could do one now."

"Sit down and try," I said, glad of his offer, for I could not relate the man to his work.

He took a seat and began to write steadily, composedly, without hesitation or blot or interlineation, and so produced in my presence one of his most powerful verses. It flowed from his pen as smooth as oil.

The next day I asked for the other half of the novel. "We must get it published at once," I said. "It is a wonderful study. A mysterious product for you to have in hand. Where is the other part?"

He looked very much embarrassed. "It's in 'hock,'" he said.

"To whom?"

"To the typewriter."

We all laughed, but it was serious business to him. He could see the humor of the situation, but there was a bitter rebellion in his voice.

"How much is it 'hung up' for?"

"Fifteen dollars."

I looked at my brother. "I guess we can spare that, don't you think?"

So Crane went away joyously and brought the last half of "The Red Badge of Courage," still unnamed at the time. He told us that the coming of that story was just as mysterious as in the case of the verses, and I can believe it. It literally came of its own accord like sap flowing from a tree.

I gave him such words of encouragement as I could. "Your future is secure. A man who can write 'The Red Badge of Courage' can not be forever a lodger in a bare studio."

He replied: "That may be, but if I had some money to buy a new suit of clothes I'd feel my grip tighten on the future."

"You'll laugh at all this—we all go through it," said I.

"It's ridiculous, but it doesn't make me laugh," he said, soberly.

My predictions of his immediate success did not come true. "The Red Badge of Courage" and "Maggie" were put through the Syndicate with very slight success. They left Crane almost as poor as before.

In one of his letters, in April, he wrote: "I have not been up to see you because of various strange conditions—notably my toes coming through one shoe, and I have not been going out into society as much as I might. I mail you last Sunday's 'Press.' I've moved now—live in a flat. People can come to see me now. They come in shoals, and say I am a great writer. Counting five that are sold, four that are unsold and six that are mapped out, I have fifteen short stories in my head and out of it. They'll make a book. The 'Press' people pied some of 'Maggie,' as you will note."

I saw little of him during '93 and '94, but a letter written in May, '94, revealed his condition:

"I have not written you because there has been little to tell of late. I am plodding along on the 'Press' in a quiet and effective way. We now eat with charming regularity at least two times a day. I am content and am now writing another novel which is a bird. . . . I am getting lots of free advertising. Everything is coming along nicely now. I have got the poetic spout so that I can turn it on and off. I wrote a Decoration Day thing for the 'Press' which aroused them to enthusiasm. They said in about a minute, though, that I was firing over the heads of the soldiers."

His allusion to free advertising means that the critics were wrangling over "The Black Riders" and "Maggie." But the public was not interested. I had given him a letter to a Syndicate Press Company, and with them he had left the manuscript of his war novel. In a letter written in November, 1894, he makes sad mention of his lack of success:

"My Dear Friend: So much of my row with the world has to be silence and endurance that sometimes I wear the appearance of having forgotten my best friends, those to whom I am indebted for everything. As a matter of fact, I have just crawled out of the fifty-third ditch into which I have been cast, and now I feel that I can write you a letter which will not make you ill. ———— put me in one of the ditches. He kept 'The Red Badge' six months until I was near mad. Oh, yes—he was going to use it but— Finally I took it to B. They use it in January in a shortened form. I have just completed a New York book that leaves 'Maggie' at the post. It is my best thing. Since you are not here I am going to see if Mr. Howells will not read it. I am still working for the 'Press.'"

At this point his affairs took a sudden turn, and he was made the figure I had hoped to see him two years before. The English critics spoke in highest praise of "The Red Badge," and the book became the critical bone of contention between military objectors and literary enthusiasts here at home, and Crane became the talk of the day. He was accepted as a very remarkable literary man of genius.

He was too brilliant, too fickle, too erratic to last. Men cannot go on doing stories like "The Red Badge of Courage." The danger with such highly individual work lies in this—the words which astonish, the phrases which excite wonder and admiration, come eventually to seem like tricks. They lose force with repetition, and come at last to be absolutely distasteful. "The Red Badge of Courage" was marvelous, but manifestly Crane could not go on doing such work. If he wrote in conventional phrase, his power lessened. If he continued to write in his own phrases he came under the charge of repeating himself.

It seems now that he was destined from the first to be a sort of present-day Poe. His was a singular and daring soul, as irresponsible as the wind. He was a man to be called a genius, for we call that power genius which we do not easily understand or measure. I have never known a man whose source of power was so unaccounted for.

The fact of the matter seems to be this. Crane's mind was more largely subconscious in its workings than that of most men. He did not understand his own mental processes or resources. When he put pen to paper he found marvelous words, images, sentences, pictures already [sic] to be drawn off and fixed upon paper. His pen was "a spout," as he says. The farther he got from his own field, his own inborn tendency, the weaker he became. Such a man cannot afford to enter the white-hot public thoroughfare, for his genius is of the lonely and the solitary shadow-land.

✧   ✧   ✧

6. WILLIAM DEAN HOWELLS TO CORA CRANE [10]

Annisquam, Mass.,/July 29, 1900

Dear Mrs. Crane:/ I would so willingly help you about words for
your husband's monument [11] if I were good for anything in that way.
But I am not, as I find once more after trying in this case. You know
how I valued him who is gone so untimely, and how I prized what he
did. I think it was nearly all of it very great work, and if he could have
lived what he did would have been nothing to what he could have
done.

Hamlin Garland first told me of "Maggie," which your husband
then sent me. I was slow in getting at it, and he wrote me a heart-
breaking note to the effect that he saw I did not care for his book. On
this I read it and found that I did care for it immensely. I asked him
to come to me, and he came to tea and stayed far into the evening,
talking about his work, and the stress there was on him to put in the
profanities which I thought would shock the public from him, and
about the semi-savage poor, whose types he had studied in that book.
He spoke wisely and kindly about them, and especially about the
Tough, who was tough because, as he said, he felt that "Everything
was on him." He came several times afterwards, but not at all oftener
than I wished, or half so often; and I knew he was holding off from
modesty. He never came without leaving behind him some light on the
poor, sad life he knew so well in New York, so that I saw it more truly
than ever before. He had thought wisely and maturely about it, but he
had no plan for it, perhaps not even any hope without a plan. He was
the great artist which he was because he was in nowise a sentimental-
ist. Of course I was struck almost as much by his presence as by his
mind, and admired his strange, melancholy beauty, in which there was
already the forecast of his early death. His voice charmed me, and the
sensitive lips from which it came, with their intelligent and ironical
smile, and his mystical, clouded eyes. Inevitably there was the barrier
between his youth and my age, that the years make, and I could not
reach him where he lived as a young man might. I cannot boast that I
understood him fully; a man of power before he comes to its full expression is hard to understand; it is doubtful if he is quite in the secret
of himself; but I was always aware of *his* power, and nothing good

[10] Published in the *Academy*, August 18, 1900.

[11] William Crane wrote to Cora in 1901 for her approval of the inscription he selected for Stephen's tombstone: "Stephen Crane, Poet—Author/
1871–1900."

that he did surprised me. He came to see me last just before he sailed for England the last time, and then he showed the restlessness of the malarial fever that was preying on him; he spoke of having got it in Cuba. But even then, with the sense that we were getting at each other less than ever, I felt his rare quality. I do not think America has produced a more distinctive and vital talent. Yours sincerely,

W. D. Howells

7. FRANK SMALLEY [12] TO CORA CRANE

Syracuse, N.Y., Aug. 2, 1900

Dear Mrs. Crane:/ Your letter making inquiries about Mr. Crane's connection with Syracuse University has just reached me. Our records show that he entered the University in 1890 as a member of the Class of '94. I do not think he remained the first year [13] through although he may have done so, the records do not show that, nor do they show that he came to us from Lafayette College which I remember he did. He doubtless left Syracuse in the Spring of 1891. I knew him well. I have been a member of the Faculty here since 1874 and being a ΔY and a brother brought him to my residence one evening soon after he entered and I conversed with him a long time. He was not inclined to be very studious and I find he has credit in only one subject and in that he has our highest mark, of course that study is English literature. He devoted himself to athletic sports with ardor, especially base-ball and was our finest player. His mother felt considerable anxiety about him and wrote me several letters. We looked upon him as an exceedingly bright young man, of large capacity. He would not be cramped by following a course of study he did not care for. That is the secret of his few credits on the books.

We are proud of his connection with this University. I was not surprised to learn of his great work and that he had won for himself imperishable fame, and I read his writings with a feeling of almost paternal pride.

I suggest the following names of persons who remember him and doubtless can give you facts of interest: [14] Prof. C. J. Little, Evanston,

---

[12] Professor Smalley was Crane's Latin teacher at Syracuse.

[13] Crane enrolled for the spring, 1891, term; he was at Lafayette College the fall, 1890, term. He was at Syracuse only one semester.

[14] Cora wrote Smalley for reminiscences of Stephen for her biography of him. Before she abandoned this project, she wrote many of his friends, including Irving Bacheller (see Appendix 4), William Dean Howells (see Appendix 6), Hamlin Garland (see Appendix 10), and Louis C. Senger (see Appendix 14).

Ill.–Prof. of history when Mr. Crane was here. Prof. J. Scott Clark, Evanston, Ill.–Prof. of English here in '90. Principal W. H. Perry, Lowville, N.Y., who first brought him to my residence. George H. Bond, Syracuse, N.Y. who knows his athletic record. These, perhaps, can suggest others.

We have given in our Alumni Record some space to Mr. Crane.

Write me freely if I can be of further service to you. Sincerely,

Frank Smalley/Latin

8. *CORA CRANE TO HAMLIN GARLAND*

[London] Aug. 8th 1900

Dear Mr. Hamlin Garland:/ I want to thank you for the appreciative article which you wrote of my late husband, for the Saturday Evening Post.[15] So very few people understood Stephen or even knew him. I want you to read his books still to come out and if *you* could review them, particularly "Wounds in the Rain" it would mean so much to make his work live. I feel sure that *you* will see how much better work there is in this book than in the "Red Badge of Courage." Then,–"The O'Ruddy" which is to be published later on–is really splendid work. I feel sure that my husband's *best* work was done the last year of his life. *He* thought so.[16]

It was a great disappointment that you did not come to Brede Place to see us. Stephen said that he supposed you had reason to believe that he had neglected you and so did not care to reply.[17]

Cora was the first to attempt a biography of Crane. Louis Senger never succeeded at the same intention, and Willis Clarke gave up on finding himself bewildered by his source material. Crane resisted all attempts at being biographed until Thomas Beer, drawing heavily from Willis Clarke's preparatory material, recast Crane in the image approved by the Crane family. Thomas L. Raymond's *Stephen Crane* (Carteret Book Club, 1923), is the first Crane biography. It is, however, no more than a sketch. John Berryman's *Stephen Crane* (1951) is a version of Beer, modernized by its Freudian interpretation. A documented chronology has yet to be written.

[15] See Appendix 5.

[16] Psychologically it was as necessary for Cora to think so as it had been for Crane.

[17] Garland felt slighted by Crane's neglect, but both were increasingly conscious of an unbridgeable gulf opening between them with the passage of time. Garland had strongly disapproved of Crane's transplanting himself to England, and in the years after Crane's death his later estimate of his talent came to be more and more affected by moral disapproval of both his early bohemianism and the style of living at Brede Place. "There was something essentially unwholesome about his philosophy," Garland wrote in 1914

It is my hope to write a little book of Stephen's life. It will have little commercial value; no value at all except, perhaps, to those who knew his work. May I use any of the facts named in your article? Or will you tell me of anything of interest?

It is my hope to settle in a tiny house in London. But ways and means are a puzzle just now. Will you address me care of my solicitor, Alfred T. Plant Esq. 21, Bedford Row, Greys Inn—as now I'm in lodgings and I don't know for how long a time.[18] Faithfully yours

Cora Crane/Mrs. Stephen Crane

9. STEPHEN CRANE FROM AN ENGLISH STANDPOINT [19]

By H. G. Wells

The untimely death at thirty of Stephen Crane robs English literature of an interesting and significant figure, and the little world of those who write, of a stout friend and a pleasant comrade. For a year and more he had been ailing. The bitter hardships of his Cuban expedition had set its mark upon mind and body alike, and the slow darkling of the shadow upon him must have been evident to all who were not blinded by their confidence in what he was yet to do. Altogether, I knew Crane for less than a year, and I saw him for the last time hardly more than seven weeks ago. He was then in a hotel at Dover, lying still and comfortably wrapped about, before an open window and the calm and spacious sea. If you would figure him as I saw him, you must think of him as a face of a type very typically American, long and spare, with very straight hair and straight features and long, quiet hands and hollow eyes, moving slowly, smiling and speaking slowly, with that deliberate New Jersey manner he had, and lapsing from speech again into a quiet contemplation of his ancient

---

in the *Yale Review.* "He was not born for long life and he was not born for development. His work did not change except for the worse. It remained fragmentary and severe."

[18] Cora and her friend, Mrs. Brotherton, were in lodgings at 47 Gower Street. In September they moved to a small house at 6 Milborne Grove, The Boltons, South Kensington. She lived there until her final return to the United States on April 28, 1901, where she spent several weeks with her Aunt Mary Holder in New York City. She was next in Owensboro, Kentucky, with friends, while undergoing a breakdown which lasted some six to eight months; again, a short time in New Orleans, then back to Owensboro, and finally to Jacksonville to build The Court, which she operated until her death, on September 4, 1910, of a cerebral hemorrhage at the age of forty-five.

[19] First published in the *North American Review,* August, 1900. The footnotes are ours.

enemy. For it was the sea that had taken his strength, the same sea that now shone, level waters beyond level waters, with here and there a minute, shining ship, warm and tranquil beneath the tranquil evening sky. Yet I felt scarcely a suspicion then that this was a last meeting. One might have seen it all, perhaps. He was thin and gaunt and wasted, too weak for more than a remembered jest and a greeting and good wishes. It did not seem to me in any way credible that he would reach his refuge in the Black Forest only to die at the journey's end. It will be a long time yet before I can fully realize that he is no longer a contemporary of mine; that the last I saw of him was, indeed, final and complete.

Though my personal acquaintance with Crane was so soon truncated, I have followed his work for all the four years it has been known in England. I have always been proud, and now I am glad, that, however obscurely, I also was in the first chorus of welcome that met his coming. It is, perhaps, no great distinction for me; he was abundantly praised; but, at least, I was early and willing to praise him when I was wont to be youthfully jealous of my praises. His success in England began with the *Red Badge of Courage,* which did, indeed, more completely than any other book has done for many years, take the reading public by storm. Its freshness of method, its vigor of imagination, its force of color and its essential freedom from many traditions that dominate this side of the Atlantic, came—in spite of the previous shock of Mr. Kipling—with a positive effect of impact. It was a new thing, in a new school. When one looked for sources, one thought at once of Tolstoy; but, though it was clear that Tolstoy had exerted a powerful influence upon the conception, if not the actual writing, of the book, there still remained something entirely original and novel. To a certain extent, of course, that was the new man as an individual; but, to at least an equal extent, it was the new man as a typical young American, free at last, as no generation of Americans have been free before, of any regard for English criticism, comment, or tradition, and applying to literary work the conception and theories of the cosmopolitan studio with a quite American directness and vigor. For the great influence of the studio on Crane cannot be ignored; in the persistent selection of the essential elements of an impression, in the ruthless exclusion of mere information, in the direct vigor with which the selected points are made, there is Whistler even more than there is Tolstoy in the *Red Badge of Courage.* And witness this, taken almost haphazard:

> *At nightfall the column broke into regimental pieces, and the fragments went into the fields to camp. Tents sprang up like*

strange plants. Camp fires, like red, peculiar blossoms, dotted the
night. . . . From this little distance the many fires, with the black
forms of men passing to and fro before the crimson rays, made
weird and satanic effects.

And here again; consider the daring departure from all academic
requirements in this void countenance:

A warm and strong hand clasped the youth's languid fingers
for an instant, and then he heard a cheerful and audacious whis-
tling as the man strode away. As he who had so befriended him
was thus passing out of his life, it suddenly occurred to the youth
that he had not once seen his face.

I do not propose to add anything here to the mass of criticism
upon this remarkable book. Like everything else which has been
abundantly praised, it has occasionally been praised "all wrong"; and
I suppose that it must have been said hundreds of times that this book
is a subjective study of the typical soldier in war. But Mr. George
Wyndham, himself a soldier of experience, has pointed out in an admirable preface to a reissue of this and other of Crane's war studies [20]
that the hero of the *Red Badge* is, and is intended to be, altogether a
more sensitive and imaginative person than the ordinary man. He is
the idealist, the dreamer of boastful things brought suddenly to the
test of danger and swift occasions and the presence of death. To this
theme Crane returned several times, and particularly in a story called
Death and the Child [21] that was written after the Greek war. That
story is considered by very many of Crane's admirers as absolutely his
best. I have carefully reread it in deference to opinions I am bound to
respect, but I still find it inferior to the earlier work. The generalized
application is, to my taste, a little too evidently underlined; there is
just that touch of insistence that prevails so painfully at times in Victor
Hugo's work, as of a writer not sure of his reader, not happy in his
reader, and seeking to drive his implication (of which also he is not
quite sure) home. The child is not a natural child; there is no happy
touch to make it personally alive; it is THE CHILD, something un-
falteringly big; a large, pink, generalized thing. I cannot help but see
it, after the fashion of a Vatican cherub. The fugitive runs panting to

[20] In *Pictures of War* (Heinemann, 1898).
[21] In *Harper's Weekly*, March 19, 26, 1898; and in *The Open Boat and*
Other Stories (Heinemann, 1898; Doubleday & McClure, 1898; Doubleday
and McClure, 1905).

where, all innocent of the battle about it, it plays; and he falls down breathless to be asked, "Are you a man?" One sees the intention clearly enough; but in the later story it seems to me there is a new ingredient that is absent from the earlier stories, an ingredient imposed on Crane's natural genius from without—a concession to the demands of a criticism it had been wiser, if less modest, in him to disregard—criticism that missed this quality of generalization and demanded it, even though it had to be artificially and deliberately introduced.

Following hard upon the appearance of the *Red Badge of Courage* in England came reprints of two books, *Maggie* and *George's Mother*, that had already appeared in America six years earlier.[22] Their reception gave Crane his first taste of the peculiarities of the new public he had come upon. These stories seem to me in no way inferior to the *Red Badge;* and at times there are passages, the lament of Maggie's mother at the end of *Maggie*, for example, that it would be hard to beat by any passage from the later book. But on all hands came discouragement or tepid praise. The fact of it is, there had been almost an orgy of praise—for England, that is; and ideas and adjectives and phrases were exhausted. To write further long reviews on works displaying the same qualities as had been already amply discussed in the notices of the *Red Badge* would be difficult and laborious; while to admit an equal excellence and deny an equal prominence would be absurd. But to treat these stories as early work, to find them immature, dismiss them and proceed to fresher topics, was obvious and convenient. So it was, I uncharitably imagine, that these two tales have been overshadowed and are still comparatively unknown. Yet they are absolutely essential to a just understanding of Crane. In these stories, and in these alone, he achieved tenderness and a compulsion of sympathy for other than vehement emotions, qualities that the readers of *The Third Violet* and *On Active Service* [*sic*] his later love stories, might well imagine beyond his reach. . . .

And since Crane had demonstrated, beyond all cavil, that he could sit at home and, with nothing but his wonderful brain and his wonderful induction from recorded things, build up the truest and most convincing picture of war; since he was a fastidious and careful worker, intensely subjective in his mental habit; since he was a man of fragile physique and of that unreasonable courage that will wreck the

---

[22] Not six years earlier but three, as *Maggie* was published in England by Heinemann in 1896 and was first printed in the United States in 1893. Nor was *George's Mother* reprinted, as Wells puts it; *George's Mother* was published for the first time in 1896 by Edward Arnold almost simultaneously in the United States and England.

strongest physique; and since, moreover, he was habitually a bad traveler, losing trains and luggage and missing connections even in the orderly circumstances of peace, it was clearly the most reasonable thing in the world to propose, it was received with the applause of two hemispheres as a most right and proper thing, that he should go as a war correspondent, first to Greece and then to Cuba. Thereby, and for nothing but disappointment and bitterness, he utterly wrecked his health. He came into comparison with men as entirely his masters in this work as he was the master of all men in his own; and I read even in the most punctual of his obituary notices the admission of his journalistic failure. I have read, too, that he brought back nothing from these expeditions. But, indeed, even not counting his death, he brought back much. On his way home from Cuba he was wrecked,[23] and he wrote the story of the nights and days that followed the sinking of the ship with a simplicity and vigor that even he cannot rival elsewhere.

The Open Boat is to my mind, beyond all question, the crown of all his work. It has all the stark power of the earlier stories, with a new element of restraint; the color is as full and strong as ever, fuller and stronger, indeed; but those chromatic splashes that at times deafen and confuse in the *Red Badge,* those images that astonish rather than enlighten, are disciplined and controlled. "That and *Flanagan,*"[24] he told me, with a philosophical laugh, "was all I got out of Cuba." I cannot say whether they were worth the price, but I am convinced that these two things are as immortal as any work of any living man. And the way *The Open Boat* begins, no stress, plain—even a little gray and flattish:

> *None of them knew the color of the sky. Their eyes glanced level, and were fastened upon the waves that swept toward them. These waves were of the hue of slate, save for the tops, which were of foaming white, and all of the men knew the color of the sea. The horizon narrowed and widened, and dipped and rose, and at all times its edge was jagged with waves that seemed thrust up in points like rocks.*
>
> > *Many a man ought to have a bathtub larger than the boat which here rode upon the sea. These waves were most wrongfully*

---

[23] It was on his way to Cuba that he was wrecked, on New Year's Day, 1897.

[24] "Flanagan and His Short Filibustering Adventure," *McClure's Magazine,* October, 1897; *Illustrated London News,* August, 1897.

*and barbarously abrupt and tall, and each froth top was a problem
in small-boat navigation.*

From that beginning, the story mounts and mounts over the
waves, wave frothing after wave, each wave a threat, and the men toil
and toil and toil again; by insensible degrees the day lights the waves
to green and olive, and the foam grows dazzling. . . .

The Open Boat gives its title to a volume containing, in addition
to that and *Flanagan,* certain short pieces. One of these others, at least,
is also to my mind a perfect thing, *The Wise Men.* It tells of the race
between two bartenders in the city of Mexico, and I cannot imagine
how it could possibly have been better told. And in this volume, too,
is that other masterpiece—the one I deny—*Death and the Child.*

Now I do not know how Crane took the reception of this book,
for he was not the man to babble of his wrongs; but I cannot conceive
how it could have been anything but a grave disappointment to him.
To use the silly phrase of the literary shopman, "the vogue of the short
story" was already over; rubbish, pure rubbish, provided only it was
lengthy, had resumed its former precedence again in the reviews, in
the publishers' advertisements, and on the library and booksellers'
counters. The book was taken as a trivial by-product, its author was
exhorted to abandon this production of "brilliant fragments"—anything
less than fifty thousand words is a fragment to the writer of literary
columns—and to make that "sustained effort," that architectural undertaking, that alone impresses the commercial mind. Of course, the man
who can call *The Open Boat* a brilliant fragment would reproach
Rodin for not completing the edifice his brilliant fragments of statuary
are presumably intended to adorn, and would sigh, with the late Mr.
Ruskin, for the day when Mr. Whistler would "finish" his pictures.
Moreover, he was strongly advised—just as they have advised Mr.
Kipling—to embark upon a novel. And from other quarters, where a
finer wisdom might have been displayed, he learned that the things
he had written were not "short stories" at all; they were "sketches"
perhaps, "anecdotes"—just as they call Mr. Kipling's short stories "anecdotes"; and it was insinuated that for him also the true, the ineffable
"short story" was beyond his reach. I think it is indisputable that the
quality of this reception, which a more self-satisfied or less sensitive
man than Crane might have ignored, did react very unfavorably upon
his work. They put him out of conceit with these brief intense efforts
in which his peculiar strength was displayed.

It was probably such influence that led him to write *The Third
Violet.* I do not know certainly, but I imagine, that the book was to be
a demonstration, and it is not a successful demonstration, that Crane

could write a charming love story. It is the very simple affair of an art student and a summer boarder, with the more superficial incidents of their petty encounters set forth in a forcible, objective manner that is curiously hard and unsympathetic. The characters act, and on reflection one admits they act, *true*, but the play of their emotions goes on behind the curtain of the style, and all the enrichments of imaginative appeal that make love beautiful are omitted. Yet, though the story as a whole fails to satisfy, there are many isolated portions of altogether happy effectiveness, a certain ride behind an ox cart, for example. Much more surely is *On Active Service* an effort, and in places a painful effort, to fit his peculiar gift to the uncongenial conditions of popular acceptance. It is the least capable and least satisfactory of all Crane's work.

While these later books were appearing, and right up to his last fatal illness, Crane continued to produce fresh war pictures that show little or no falling off in vigor of imagination and handling; and, in addition, he was experimenting with verse. In that little stone-blue volume, *War Is Kind*, and in the earlier *Black Riders*, the reader will find a series of acute and vivid impressions and many of the finer qualities of Crane's descriptive prose, but he will not find any novel delights of melody or cadence or any fresh aspects of Crane's personality. There remain some children's stories to be published and an unfinished romance. With that the tale of his published work ends, and the career of one of the most brilliant, most significant, and most distinctively American of all English writers comes to its unanticipated *finis*.

It would be absurd, here and now, to attempt to apportion any relativity of importance to Crane, to say that he was greater than A or less important than B. That class-list business is, indeed, best left forever to the newspaper plebiscite and the library statistician; among artists, whose sole, just claim to recognition and whose sole title to immortality must necessarily be the possession of unique qualities, that is to say, of unclassifiable factors, these gradations are absurd. Suffice it that, even before his death, Crane's right to be counted in the hierarchy of those who have made a permanent addition to the great and growing fabric of English letters was not only assured, but conceded. To define his position in time, however, and in relation to periods and modes of writing will be a more reasonable undertaking; and it seems to me that, when at last the true proportions can be seen, Crane will be found to occupy a position singularly cardinal. He was a New Englander of Puritan lineage,[25] and the son of a long tradition of

---

[25] He was not a New Englander; he was born in Newark, New Jersey, and his family was old in the state.

literature. There had been many Cranes who wrote before him. He has shown me a shelf of books, for the most part the pious and theological works of various antecedent Stephen Cranes.[26] He had been at some pains to gather together these alien products of his kin. For the most part they seemed little, insignificant books, and one opened them to read the beaten *clichés,* the battered, outworn phrases, of a movement that has ebbed. Their very size and binding suggested a dying impulse, that very same impulse that in its prime had carried the magnificence of Milton's imagery and the pomp and splendors of Milton's prose. In Crane that impulse was altogether dead. He began stark—I find all through this brief notice I have been repeating that in a dozen disguises, "freedom from tradition," "absolute directness," and the like— as though he came into the world of letters without ever a predecessor. In style, in method, and in all that is distinctively *not* found in his books, he is sharply defined, the expression in literary art of certain enormous repudiations. Was ever a man before who wrote of battles so abundantly as he has done, and never had a word, never a word from first to last, of the purpose and justification of the war? And of the God of Battles, no more than the battered name; "Hully Gee!"—the lingering trace of the Deity! And of the sensuousness and tenderness of love, so much as one can find in *The Third Violet!* Any richness of allusion, any melody or balance of phrase, the half quotation that refracts and softens and enriches the statement, the momentary digression that opens like a window upon beautiful or distant things, are not merely absent, but obviously and sedulously avoided. It is as if the racial thought and tradition had been razed from his mind and its site plowed and salted. He is more than himself in this; he is the first expression of the opening mind of a new period, or, at least, the early emphatic phase of a new initiative—beginning, as a growing mind must needs begin, with the record of impressions, a record of a vigor and intensity beyond all precedent.

10. CORA CRANE TO HAMLIN GARLAND

6, Milborne Grove/The Boltons/South Kensington/
London S.W./Sep. 17th 1900

Dear Mr. Hamlin Garland:/ It is very good of you to allow me to use your article in my little book of Stephens [*sic*] life. I thank you very much. As yet, I have not worked much upon it as I want to give it my entire strength. I've been trying to write short stories but they are woe-

---

[26] The theological books of his father, for instance, included *The Arts of Intoxication* (1870), and *Holiness the Birthright of All God's Children* (1874). Another book on Crane's shelf at Brede Place was *What Must I*

fully bad,[27] though I have sold two. I am of the opinion that it is criminal for people to write who know nothing about it—but one must live, and I must work to live.

I have taken this small house and will rent one floor, sitting-room, bedroom and bath. It is very quiet and open. If you hear of any one coming to London will you tell them of this? In this way, also, I shall add to my small income I hope.

Please thank your wife for her kind sympathy. No one can realize how great my loss is or how difficult it is to fight for an existence which I don't want. But my faith bids me believe that we shall be together again. Our life was too beautiful, too full of work and sunshine not to be continued, under new conditions perhaps, but still I am sure that I shall be with him again.

When this reaches you, Stephen's book "Wounds in the Rain," (Stokes & Co.,) will be out. I hope that you will like it.

With my kindest regards to your wife and yourself believe me,
Faithfully yours   *C. H. Crane*[28]/*Mrs. Stephen Crane*

Do to be Saved? (1858), by the Methodist Bishop Jesse T. Peck, uncle of Crane's mother. For the influence of these books on Crane's poetry see Daniel G. Hoffman, *The Poetry of Stephen Crane* (1957), ch. iii. Cora Crane's "List of Books, Brede Place" is in the Butler Library Crane Collection (cf. Hoffman, pp. 31–32).

[27] She had written several stories: "José and the Saints," which the *Graphic* considered "good and powerful," but which it dared not print. Cora remarked to Perris: "Rubbish, the public can't want all love and milksop!" Her story was found to be "too gruesome for the present editorial frame of mind on this side of the Atlantic." Another piece was "The Lavender Trousers," whose subject was the "Angel child" of Crane's Whilomville stories. Neither of these was published, but "The Red Chimneys" was sold to a Chicago syndicate and the Northern Newspaper Syndicate bought "Cowardice." Not sold were "Elbridge Carter's Dream" and "An Old World Courtship." "What Hell Might Be," a bitter confession of disillusionment which Cora had composed in 1898 during Stephen's rumored desertion in Havana, was bought by *Smart Set*. The magazine *Truth* asked to see more of her work. Not sold were two nonfiction reportage pieces: "Arundel Castle" and "The Seventeenth Regiment of Light Dragoons." The latter was a historical account of an Irish cavalry troop that fought on the side of the British in the American Revolution. Cora's writing it perhaps stemmed from the novel on the American Revolution which Stephen never got around to writing.

[28] Cora's letters during this period were written on black-bordered stationery monographed "C C." She signed her name C. H. Crane (Cora Howorth Crane).

11. CORA CRANE TO CORWIN KNAPP LINSON [29]

6, Milborne Grove,/London S.W./Sep. 28th 1900

Dear Mr. Linson:/ On April 1st last I was in Paris to meet Helen Crane who was coming from school at Lausanne. My dear husband wired me on that day, your address and to go and see you or send you my card. Think of it! He had had two horrible hemorrhages then! I left him on March 31st seemingly quite well and as he would not tell me himself or allow servants to wire me, I knew nothing of his illness until my housekeeper telegraphed without his knowledge on April 2nd when I hurried back with Miss Crane, by the night boat. And so I never sent you my card but now I write to say, that if you come to London I shall be very glad to see you. I am settled in this little house working very hard trying to write woefully bad stories—pot boilers! Stephen does not seem lost to me; only gone upon a journey which I will take one day, so that we may be together again to work & live under the new conditions. Very sincerely yours

C. H. Crane/(Mrs. Stephen Crane)

12. LOUIS C. SENGER [30] *TO HAMLIN GARLAND*

Port Jervis, N.Y./October 9, 1900

Mr. Hamlin Garland/ My dear Sir./ Just before Stephen Crane went to Cuba he told me to write to you in case anything happened to him down there. It did not impress me much at the time, but like much else that Crane said I have thought of it since.

There was no particular message for you, for you know that what Crane would have them think he himself left with his friends. But if you do not already know it, I believe he would have me assure you that the appreciation shown for his early work by yourself and Mr. Howells was the first of that particular success which he so much craved. It was not enough like the stuff they had been brought up on to please most people, and I have always felt an enormous impatience with people who would measure either himself or his work by ordinary standards. I read your article in the *Post* [31] and liked it much, but Crane's force was entirely in himself, I think, and entirely natural. Crane has always been described as abnormal, but it occurs to me that his was the real sensitive child's mind, and that it is the rest of us who

[29] Linson was then in Paris (see Appendix 19).

[30] A boyhood friend, Senger lived in Port Jervis.

[31] See Appendix 5.

are a little run down. Crane was capable of seeing the ordinary and familiar with first eyes.

I'm sure I do not know why he should have showed me so much of his work, and God knows I must have hurt him. I read *Maggie* from chapter to chapter in a house over on the far east side, where he lived with a crowd of irresponsibles.[32] I brought Linson, who is my cousin, and Crane together and we were the first to read his *Lines*.[33] One day he told me he was going to write a war story and later he showed me some chapters of the *Red Badge*. "I deliberately started in to do a pot-boiler," he told me then, "something that would take the boarding-school element—you know the kind. Well, I got interested in the thing in spite of myself, and I couldn't, I couldn't. I *had* to do it my own way." This was the first and only time I ever knew Crane's courage to falter in the least, and this was after five years of it, and he was writing then on the paper the meat came home in.[34]

I saw Crane only once after the Cuban affair. He was sick and joked mirthlessly that they had not got him yet. You know that Stephen Crane was essentially a soldier. Sometimes the thought has come to me that he would have elected to die in battle rather than wait for the slower death of which I believe he had a prophetic knowledge.

He spoke of you often, and always with a sense of blame for himself lest you should think him ungrateful. He was never that. Sincerely Yours,   *Louis C. Senger*

13. CORA CRANE TO CORWIN KNAPP LINSON

6 Milborne Grove/[London],/Oct. 18th 1900

Dear Mr. Linson:/ I thank you very much for your letter of Oct 12th. As you say, what we need is to be in touch with material things, & I feel sure that your friendship for my dear one is a material thing, & so I want it. It will help to keep tighter the bonds which his going into the beyond before me cannot alter.

In the spring I shall try to let my little house for the season for enough money to pay the rent and to pay my expenses, perhaps at Badenweiler or some little place in the Zimmerwald. If I am able to do this I shall stop a day in Paris to see you, and your wife. It will be such a delight to hear you tell of the early days when you lived—on potato salad, was it not? Stephen always made me shudder at the idea

---

[32] Probably the Pendennis Club.

[33] Poems—*The Black Riders.*

[34] This incident was reported in the *Book Buyer* in 1896.

of potato salad for *breakfast*! How I wish you could have seen him as the Squire at Brede Place. I used to call him "The Duke." The old house would have delighted you. Stephen was so very happy there. I could not drag him to town or indeed off the Place. We had a little park of 100 acres, and Stephen would take his morning ride within the fence, over the turf. It is such a joy to me now to remember that his last years here were so filled with comfort; with comfort bought by work. His life was so filled with good. We had the two children of Harold Frederic you know, and there was always some poor-in-luck or health chap staying with us. Sometime I hope to tell you about Stephen's charity—and no one, not even himself felt it to be charity. His character the last year was wonderful! He could see all things clearly. His mind was too wonderful to stay here, and that is why God took him. On this subject I cannot write quite coherently. Yes, Helen Crane was Stephen's niece from Port Jervis. She was with us over a year, but spent part of the time at school at Lausanne. She may come to visit me in the Spring & go on the continent with me.[35]

Stephen only got your address from McClures, after I had gone to Paris in April, and wired it to me. He had asked for it some time before but you were then in the East, he heard.

With my kindest regards to yourself & wife, believe me. Very sincerely yours   *C. H. Crane*

14. CORA CRANE TO LOUIS C. SENGER

6, Milborne Grove,/London S.W./Oct. 22nd 1900

Dear Mr. Sanger [*sic*]:/ My difficulties and duties have been so many that I have not been able to settle to the work I long so to do, Stephen's Life. Of course I want to put in the work the best that is in me and you can appreciate how difficult that is, when my mind is worried by the lack of £. s. d. However, that is only a temporary matter. I am writing some woefully bad short stories and also a series of papers on the British regiments that served in the war of the American Revolution.[36] By Xmas I hope to have this work ended.

All sorts of information comes to me of Stephen's struggle before the "Red Badge" success.

Will you write me about this work we want to do?[37] I wish that

---

[35] This plan did not materialize; Cora's relations with William Crane later became strained to the breaking point.

[36] "The Seventeenth Regiment of Light Dragoons."

[37] Senger had offered to help Cora with the projected biography of Stephen. Decades later Senger still intended to write some memoirs of Crane, but he never did (see also Appendix 12).

it were possible for you to come to London in the spring, for us to revise and finish the book together. Helen said something about your
visiting Mr. Linson in Paris.

This address will find me for years to come, I trust and I shall be
glad to hear from you.

I'm sure that it will interest you to know that Stephen's last book
out here,—and in the U.S. too—is having a success. It is in the second
edition already, and artistically its success is as great as the "Red
Badge." Have you read it? "Wounds in the Rain." What do the Americans say about it, or do they say anything?

With kindest regards believe me   Very sincerely yours
                                C. H. Crane/(Mrs. Stephen Crane)

15. JOSEPH CONRAD TO CORA CRANE

Someries./Luton, Beds. [Bedfordshire]/27 Ap. 1908

My dear Cora/ I can not sufficiently thank you for the memento of
poor Stephen. I had for him a very deep affection; hardly a day passes
without my thoughts turning to that genius so soon lost to the world.
I am deeply grateful for this proof of your continued friendship for
us both.

Jessie will be writing to you soon. Borys [38] sends his love. Believe
me my dear Cora always your very affectionate friend and servant
                                                        J. Conrad

16. JOSEPH CONRAD TO PETER F. SOMERVILLE [39]

Capel House,/Orlestone,/N^r. Ashford. [1912?]

Dear Sir,/ Many thanks for your friendly and flattering letter.

Poor Crane was at one time 'puffed,' but he was never properly
appreciated. We were great friends from the first, after his arrival in
England. The lower part of his face was rather weak but he had the
forehead and eyes of genius.

Believe me my dear Sir no paper, no review, would look at anything that I or anybody else could write about Crane. They would
laugh at the suggestion. Crane? Who's Crane? Who cares for Crane?
I assure you from personal knowledge that the English Review is
smothered under MSS—good stuff about actualities, about new work,
about coming men; about things in which the public is interested.

[38] One of Conrad's two sons.
[39] Not yet identified. He lived at Orlestone during 1910–1918. The
original of this letter is in The Library of Congress.

Nowadays when one is dead one is dead for good. Mere literary excellence won't save a man's memory. In fifty years' time some curious literary critic (of the professional scribbler kind) will perhaps rediscover him as a curiosity and write a short paper in order to earn five guineas.

Sad but true. I hardly meet anyone now who knows or remembers anything of him. For the younger oncoming writers he does not exist, simply. One or two have heard of the Red Badge and asked me "what sort of thing it is." "Is it worth looking at."—And the earth is scarcely dry over his grave over there in New York State [40] where a lot of literary humbugs encouraged him halfheartedly and disparaged him (as 'mere journalist') behind his back. There too a most unworthy lot of scribblers (some with great reputations) crowded round him flattering him, patronising him, advising him—and slandering him. I had to look at all this, powerless. Poor Crane was such a good fellow that it was almost impossible to persuade him that everybody was not as straight as he was himself.

Well this is an old story now and hardly worth talking about.
Yours faithfully   J. Conrad

17. IRVING BACHELLER TO WILLIAM HAMILTON OSBORNE [41]

Nov. 2, '21

Dear Mr. Osborne: Introduced Stephen Crane to the public. He came into my office with a rather worn and dirty manuscript. He was a thin, slender, dark skinned youth of about twenty-one. He had been camping about in artists studios in the vicinity of Washington Square—if I remember rightly. He had come down from up the Hudson to N.Y. with the cheery confidence of youth and some manuscripts. He had made friends of insight who loved the things that he loved and who soon began to love him. They had been doing what they could to help him over the hard going which is in the way of most young authors.

---

[40] Conrad's error; should be New Jersey.

[41] The Newark Schoolmen's Club, November 7, 1921, placed on the front of the Newark Public Library building in memory of the fiftieth anniversary of Stephen Crane's birth a tablet "inscribed to the memory of Stephen Crane, born in Newark, November 1, 1871," and commemorating Crane's achievements as a writer whose work "anticipated strong later tendencies in American literature." The tablet was unveiled by Stephen's niece, Helen Crane. William Hamilton Osborne was one of the organizers of this "celebration," referred to in Bacheller's letter. See Thomas L. Raymond, *Stephen Crane* (Carteret Book Club, 1923).

He came to me modestly with this bundle of manuscript. He said that it had been in the hands of Hamlin Garland and Mr. Howells and that it had seemed to interest them. I think he said that Mr. Garland had made some suggestion regarding the development of the tale. He wished me to read it and if I thought it worth while, to publish it in the syndicate of newspapers I represented. I took the manuscript with no idea, of course, that I had found one of the great treasures of the century, altho I had heard of Stephen and his talents. It was The Red Badge of Courage. I read it that night and felt its power. We published it. While it was running, the editor of the Phila. Press wrote and asked me to bring Stephen over to meet the editors and the city staff of the Press. We went. Editors, reporters, proof readers, compositors came to shake his hand. They had seen the new light and under its illumination the real soldier in Battle and down under his feet and Blouse. They knew, too, that the truth had never been told before. I saw that day what was coming to Steve.

I saw him every day after that for a time and chiefly at the Sign O' the Lanthorne, a little bohemian club of newspaper writers. I sent him to Mexico where he wrote many quaint and vivid sketches the best of which was I think "The Ass and the Mountain"[42] and a tale of town life published in The Lanthorne Book the title of which I do not remember.[43] Then came the Spanish war. I sent him to Jacksonville with seven hundred dollars in Spanish gold and a belt in which to carry it. He was to get over to Cuba as soon as possible. I never saw him again. I did not hear from him until the manuscript of the Open Boat arrived in my office. In that adventure the belt of gold had gone to the bottom of the sea. I could not afford to send another; so he hired to another editor and went on.

I wish that I could come to your celebration. I was fond of Stephen and I feel that these things I know of him should be a part of the record of his life in which you and his fellow citizens have a just pride and particularly I wish you to know that with many faults he had a high spirit, loving justice and honor and beauty and loyalty and courage. Sincerely yours   *Irving Bacheller*

---

[42] "How the Donkey Lifted the Hills," published in *Pocket Magazine*, June, 1897. The best thing Crane wrote from his western trip was "The Bride Comes to Yellow Sky," published in *McClure's Magazine*, February, 1898.

[43] Crane's contribution to *The Lanthorn Book: Being a Small Collection of Tales and Verses Read at The Sign o' the Lanthorn 126 William Street, New York* (1898) was "The Wise Men."

18. JOHN NORTHERN HILLIARD [44] *TO THOMAS BEER*

Carmel, [California] February 1, 1922

My dear Mr. Beer:— . . . You see, I knew Crane in the first days of his coming to New York; he had written little else than sport correspondence from Hudson, N.Y., where he had gone to the Academy, for the New York papers. This was before the days of Maggie and the Red Badge, and the Black Riders. He was writing the Red Badge when I left New York, and I did not see him again until the Cuban campaign, though I had a great many letters from him between the years 1895 and 1900. And this brings me to the subject of letters. I have back in the East about 150 letters of Crane's and a bunch of his manuscripts—fragments. I left Rochester, N.Y. in 1911, where I had been managing editor of The Post Express, to devote the rest of my life to freelancing. I packed up all my household goods as well as the lares and penates. And my books—a library of 3,500 volumes. These are stored away. Included among this domestic litter of years are all of my Crane books—all first editions, with inscriptions by Crane, manuscripts of his, and his letters. If I could only get them, there might be material in them that you could use. . . . As to your data on Mrs. Crane, I can't help you there. I never met the lady; and in such few letters as I received from Crane after his marriage, and in the latter years of his life in England, he never mentioned his wife or referred to personal matters. I have a recollection of about as many conflicting and unreliable statements concerning her as has been your misfortune. Do you know if she is still alive? As to the silence of Crane's relatives, I suppose that they are not particularly enamored of the way he looked at life and lived it, though it is difficult to think this in this age.[45] But they were ministerial folk. Crane lived the life of the bohemian in those days—a bit too feverishly, perhaps, for his own good, that is to say, for his physical health. He drank and he smoked and like Robert Louis Stevenson he had a hankering after the women. He took up with many a drab, and was not overly particular as to her age, race or color. Many a time I have heard him say that he would have to go out and get a nigger wench "to change his luck." Time and again he would bring a lady from the streets to his room. He had no eye for

---

[44] Editor of the Rochester *Union and Advertiser* and of the *Post Express,* Hilliard published some of Crane's letters.

[45] The Crane family, shocked at rumors about Cora's past, disbelieved them, and Beer kept silent about Crane's affair with Cora and about her past in order not to offend the Crane family. Of four slight references to Cora in Beer's *Stephen Crane,* two occur in the Appendix.

women of his own class or station.[46] He preferred the other kind. I
can understand this. Women of his own class could have given him
nothing. In the slums he got life. He got the real thing, and that was
what he was always looking for—the real, naked facts of life. And in
seeking them, in living them, he was tolerant and absolutely un-
ashamed. This was because he was big. He knew nothing about cant;
he was no more of the Pharisee than the animal seeking food and answering the call of the female. And young as he was in those years, he
had a fine and great contempt for the conventional hypocrisy of his
fellows. He never minced matters in his speech. He spoke right out as
nakedly as he wrote the Black Riders. And he tried no more to hide
his relations with the women of the underworld than an animal would.
So I can understand that he must have shocked his relatives. . . .
Crane was a big man as well as a big writer—the biggest writer, to my
mind, this country has produced. He lived his own life, a free, un-
trammeled life; he had great courage (he was the most utterly fearless
man I have ever known); he faced poverty blithely, and he wrote absolutely to please himself. And always he had a gay spirit, even when, as
often happened in those days, we sat together in Union Square and
speculated on the flapjacks and coffee we would eat and drink if we
would eat and drink if we had two-bits between us. And then, when
the gods were kind, and a newspaper editor gave us a check, it was ho!
for fleshpots and an all-night session at poker. It is those days, those
play times that remain freshest in my memory, for Crane was always
playing. He played all his life. He was the Playboy of the Western
World.[47] He was always imagining himself something, from Hell-Devil
Dick of the Deadwood Range to the Red Rover of the Spanish Main.
He was exactly as he delineated Jimmy Trescott in the Whilomville
Stories. He was Jimmy Trescott. That book comes pretty near to being
autobiography. . . . Mr. Conrad, I believe, has put the seal of authority on the Open Boat story,[48] as one of the greatest sea stories in literature. In my humble opinion, the short story, The Bride Comes to
Yellow Sky, in the same volume,[49] is one of the finest things Crane ever
did. I have been over that country a great deal, and for atmosphere
that one little yarn has all the short stories and novels of the Southwest
beaten to a frazzle. It is Texas. . . .

One thing before closing, do please, take a fall out of that non-

---

[46] That Hilliard is mistaken is shown by Crane's love affairs with Helen
Trent, Lily Brandon Munroe, Nellie Crouse, and also with Cora Taylor.

[47] The title of Synge's now-famous play.

[48] Conrad in his introduction to Beer's biography.

[49] In *The Open Boat and Other Stories* (1898).

sensical Ford Maddox Heuffer stuff he wrote about Crane in the New York Evening Post Literary Review.[50] He meant well, but he has no humor. And no one without at least a modicum of humor ought to write about Crane, for Crane was bubbling over with fun and, as I said, was always playing. He didn't have wit, but he had a great gift of fun and a sardonic humor. . . . But I know he was a big man and a big writer and when you tell me that professors of letters refer to him as in the "Richard Carvel" class, it makes me feel like gnawing chunks out of the furniture.[51] So you may count on me to do anything it is humanly possible. And here's skol! to your work.

Always sincerely yours,   *John Northern Hilliard*

19. CORWIN KNAPP LINSON TO THOMAS BEER

Salamagundi Club/Forty-Seven Fifth Avenue/New York
27 Hooper Ave/Atlantic Highlands/N.J./April 30/1923

Thomas Beer, Esq./ Yonkers, N.Y.
Dear sir:/ . . . The last time I saw Steve was in New York just previous to his departure for England. That must have been in 1898 as he had just returned from Greece, where I had been in '96, and just before I myself went over again in Nov. '98.[52] We went to a small hotel on 23rd St. and 4th Ave.—or Lexington—and had a farewell dinner. He then told me that he was intending to marry a girl and go to England, giving me to understand that she had suffered from unfortunate circumstances, just what I do not now remember; and he of course did not detail, nor did I inquire into. It was none of my affair except to listen, and when he asked my opinion, I told him that as far as I could understand the situation I would do the same thing were I in his place. Youth is somewhat Quixotic anyway, and we were just boys. He was satisfied with that and the subject was not again alluded to—and that is all I know about that phase of his career. That he did the right thing I am sure. At the time of his death, I received a letter from Mrs. Crane (Sept. 28, 1900) and it was just such a letter as any lady would write.

---

[50] "Two Americans," by Ford Madox Ford, New York *Evening Post Literary Review,* March 26, 1921.

[51] As Daniel G. Hoffman suggests, Crane's sexual drives were probably compulsive. But the note of exaggeration is strong in Hilliard's interpretation (cf. Hoffman, *The Poetry of Stephen Crane,* for an entirely different reading of Crane).

[52] Linson has mistaken the dates and sequence of events. Crane, on his way to cover the Greco-Turkish War, returned to England from Greece, not to the United States. The girl he planned to marry was of course Cora Taylor.

As to Doris Watts,[53] I never heard of her before, and so I am glad to be among the exceptional "friends in New York" who did not assist in the construction of that "mountain of lies" he complained of.

Steve was always to me just a genius of a boy, self-willed at times, sensitive in the extreme, but loyal and lovable. I could have quarreled with him more than once if I had followed his lead,—I did once, or rather, I shot back at him a retort which he provoked, and which he resented to the extent of several months' absence from my society— but when we met again it was in the old spirit of camaraderie and without a reference to the disagreement.

I do not believe for a moment any such yarn as you quote from the said McCumer.[54] I am glad to hear that Davis [55] walloped him for it, and I would have done the same—providing always the ability!

Crane was no more a "dope fiend" than I in my belief, and I never got the slightest inkling that he was the subject of gossip in New York. Everything that he ever said about women to me or in my hearing was admirable. His was a fine nature, and his appreciation of the charm and frankness of true womanhood, and the innocence of young girl-hood, was chivalry itself.

As to his going to England, I do know that he went there because the "atmosphere" suited him[,] the publishers friendly or better, which all meant that his work was valued at its worth, and this fellowship and appreciation was meat and drink to him. If there was any gossip in New York of which I was aware, it was the frequent slams he got from those who could not understand him, and the jeers which he laughed at to me but which rankled plainly enough. He wasn't happy in New York, and he *was* happy in England—voila tout. Why not? With Conrad and Robert Barr and all the rest, and his horse and house. I think that if he had not been a writer he would have been a mounted policeman! He would almost rather ride a horse than play ball, and he almost punched a rib in once when I met him at the home

---

[53] Also known as Mrs. Bowen, wife or mistress of one of Crane's friends. Crane gave her $150, and she pursued him for more, threatening to come to Hartwood. Crane went to New York City to settle the situation (1896). In a note written in November, 1899, he recalled: "I leaned on the door and told her to drop this nonsense. There was one of those horrors called Turkish corners in the room with a shield stuck full of knives. She lost her temper and grabbed a knife from the shield. It flew over my shoulder and stuck into the wood beside my ear and quivered so that I can still hear the noise" (Beer, p. 309).

[54] Thomas McCumber, a photographer and barfly gossip, who spread the calumny that Crane took morphine.

[55] Richard Harding Davis (cf. Berryman, pp. 233-34).

base at the end of a stiff run! His arm with the hard ball at the end of it was some catapult! with me furnishing the impetus.

Now, finally, I never knew of his love of certain colors except as "crimson oaths" and similar emphasis in word pictures. I do remember that the sketches of mine that he liked were notes in *gray* blues and yellows (not bright color).[56]

I got only one letter from him on his southern trip, of date (can't find it just now, but will come across it and send to you). It was only a trifle, written in a bantering spirit, and I am using it in my book [57] —which by the way threatens to remain a unique specimen of typewriting!—Steve was not a voluminous correspondent, and was too busy anyway, with cowboys and rurales. I do not think he wrote much more to my cousin.[58] . . .

Now you might think that my testimony, on a witness stand, would be thrown out as partial. But although I used sometimes to think that Steve was perhaps the most complete example of a self-absorbed ego that was ever carried on two feet, and as irresponsible— sometimes—as a goat, yet these shortcomings would no sooner be apparent than they would be at once wiped off the slate by his very charm of personality and sturdy honesty of intent. And as to all the rest, there is plenty of petty meanness in the world to account for it. I give him a clean bill of health on that score. . . . Yours very sincerely   *Corwin Knapp Linson*

By now, May 6th./Delay unavoidable.

20. FREDERICK C. GORDON TO THOMAS BEER

High Orchard, Westfield, N.J./May 25, 23

Dear Mr. Beer:/ I am afraid I can be of little use to you in the matter of dates, which never interested me. The few letters I had from Crane have disappeared. I think it was the fall of '92 [1894] and the winter following that he lived with me. I know it was the year that Tammany was defeated after the Lexow investigation, for Steve and I pushed through the excited crowds on election night, picking up material for an article he was to write for the next morning's World.[59] If Edward

---

[56] On Crane's concept of color in literature see Frank Noxon's letter to Max Herzberg (Appendix 24).

[57] Linson's memoirs of Crane, *My Stephen Crane,* written almost thirty years ago, were published by Syracuse University Press in 1958.

[58] Louis C. Senger (see Appendix 12, 14).

[59] "Heard on the Street Election Night" was published in the New York *Press* (1894), as is indicated by a clipping of this article in the Butler Library

Marshall, who was editor of the World at that time, is still alive he should be able to help a lot, for he believed in Crane's future, and gave him all the commissions he could. Hamlin Garland was also greatly interested in him then.

He had spent the previous summer [1894] camping in the wilds of Sullivan county, where he wrote a large part of the Red Badge of Courage.[60] On his return in October he took a little room near my place, and began to hunt for a job. Toward the end of a black, cold rainy day he came in to see me, soaking wet, shivering and coughing—utterly done up. He had been down to see Marshall, who had refused to take him on the World staff, because he believed the hectic newspaper work would ruin his genius for imaginative writing, but offered to buy special articles from him. Steve hadn't a nickle for car fare—too proud to mention it to Marshall—so he tramped in the cold downpour from the World building to 23rd street—no overcoat, and literally on his uppers. He was ripe for pneumonia. I got him into an extra bed I had, and in a week he was up, nearly as good as new. My shop was so big that he might just as well stay, and so he finished the Red Badge there [fall of 1894], and wrote a lot of other things.

The memory of that time is really precious to me. Crane was a delightful and stimulating companion, with no faint resemblance to the vicious portrait of him you so rightly refuse to accept. Whatever his conduct may have been at times (and I have no knowledge of anything wrong there) his ideals were fine, his sense of honor high, and his faith in mankind unshaken. He was all that we used to mean by the word gentleman.[61] I never saw him even slightly intoxicated. True, I did

Crane Collection and which is listed in Stephen Crane: An Exhibition (1956). This appeared simultaneously with "Stephen Crane: Some New Stories," by R. W. Stallman, in the Bulletin of the New York Public Library (September, 1956), where the manuscript version is reproduced from Crane's pocket notebook: "Election Night: New York 1894." In this election rout Tammany Hall candidates went down before the Republican onslaught.

[60] In the summer of 1894 Crane camped out at Twin Lakes, Pennsylvania, with Dr. Frederic M. Lawrence and his wife, Louis Senger and his cousin Corwin Linson, Wickham Young, and other friends; while there at Camp Interlaken, Crane and Senger printed a newspaper, Pike County Puzzle, reporting on camp "activities" with horseplay wit and in burlesque style. One column, for example, reported the meeting of the "Enlightened Brothers of Anarchy," electing for president "Wicked Wickham." An advertisement lists "Stephen Crane / Drink Mixer / Whiskey Sours and Hot Slings a Speciality / Reference: Dr. Burt."

[61] Though Gordon's specific facts are probably true enough (Crane was a gentleman in his chivalric manners with women), to make Crane out a

not go out with him much on his night wanderings. Daylight was necessary for my work, and so I slept religiously at night, while night was usually his best time for the studies he wished to make. Then he associated with those of the underworld, with an intense curiosity to understand their point of view. He never could have been really drunk when he returned, or I should have known it.

I wish you could have known that old shack of a studio building. It had been the home of the Art Students' League. There were three street entrances, and it had been remodeled and twisted about so much at various times, to suit the growing needs of the League, that it took an expert pilot to guide a stranger through its mysteries. The upper floors were filled with artists, musicians and writers, young men and women, decent people all, who were glad of the low rents and really congenial atmosphere. The landlord was an artist, and as considerate of our financial difficulties as he could be in reason. Our life there was free, gay, hard working—and *decent*. I had one of the biggest studios, and naturally people gathered there a good deal. Smoking, talking, and sometimes a little cards. There was no money going—no one had any—but I remember some game that required the loser to go out and fetch a can of beer. Once he failed to come back, and a search party with lamps (the hall lights went out at 11) found him comfortable on a remote stairway, but the can was empty! He explained that he had lost himself in the labyrinth, but was not worrying so long as the beer lasted.

And there you see the sum of Crane's sins while he was with me—so far as I know.

I can recall no party I gave in a restaurant, but do remember one in my studio. . . .

As for the restaurants, those were the lean days, and we generally fed at the cheapest places we could find. On rare occasions we would blow ourselves to a real 50 center, *with wine!* They could be had then. A favorite place for that was the Hotel Griffon on West 9th Street, the original of the Casa Napoleon of Thomas Janvier's stories. I suppose it is gone now. But we were not often enough at any of those "expensive" places to be known there.

As for the knife throwing incident,[62] I know nothing of that. I

"gentleman" seems forced and one-sided in view of the facts that contradict any such label. If Crane was often the gentleman, he was also often the conceited and irresponsible heel.

[62] This incident is described by Beer in his *Stephen Crane* (p. 309), and is mentioned in Corwin Linson's letter to Beer (see Appendix 19, n. 53).

have a vague memory of having heard something about it, but I fancy I didn't believe it, and so the tale made little impression. . . . Very Sincerely yours   *Frederick C. Gordon*

21. DR. FREDERIC M. LAWRENCE [63] TO THOMAS BEER

Dr. Frederic M. Lawrence/1520 Spruce Street/Philadelphia/
Nov. 8, 1923

Mr. Thomas Beer,/New York,

My dear Mr. Beer:—/ Unlike Mr. Conrad, my wonder is that a biography of Stephen Crane has been so long delayed. I would have expected such a work to appear almost immediately after his death, when his striking personality stood out clearly and countless anecdotes were fresh in the minds of his friends. I am sure Crane himself would have expected it—in fact, I recall Noxon's [64] comment after some particularly startling occurrence: "Oh, Stevie is just making biography for himself."

I like your book, and yet it seems to me that it misses much of the real Stephen Crane. Of course every man has as many reputations as he has acquaintances. Crane and I were inseparable in Syracuse, we loafed our summers away in Port Jervis, we lived together in our so-called "Pendennis Club" on Avenue A while I was more or less intermittently studying medicine, and he was writing "Maggie" (and publishing it at his own expense under the *nom de plume* of "Johnston Smith" and then couldn't sell a copy). He also wrote "George's Mother," both books being drawn from our own observations and adventures. He had a great admiration for Hamlin Garland, and through the latter was one evening invited to call on W. D. Howells. That was the beginning of recognition for Crane's work.

---

[63] Lawrence, a fraternity brother of Crane at Syracuse University, was a close friend: "There was scarcely a day or evening which we did not spend together. When I went to New York to study medicine Crane went along. . . . We occupied the principal room on the second floor overlooking the East River and distant Brooklyn, and it was there that Crane did most of his earlier work. In addition to ourselves there were perhaps half a dozen other medical students in the boarding house, and at Crane's suggestion we assumed the title of the 'Pendennis Club' " (*Stephen Crane's Love Letters to Nellie Crouse* [1954], p. 5).

[64] Frank W. Noxon, of the Class of '94 at Syracuse and a fraternity brother of Crane, published reminiscences of his famous classmate: "The Real Stephen Crane," *Step Ladder* (Chicago), January, 1928; see also Appendix 24.

He continued to spend much of his time with me after I came to Philadelphia in 1895, and I recall how I went out with him one morning to send a telegram to Theodore Roosevelt, then Police Commissioner, saying that he, Crane, was coming over to prefer charges against a certain policeman—was his name Becker? [65] with the result that an aroused and resentful police department bent all its unscrupulous energies to discrediting Crane and making New York too hot for him to live in.

I remember also his first trip to Fredericksburg and other Virginia towns his delight in the reminiscences of the old soldiers whom he met there and his determination to write a real story of the Civil War; [66] and particularly I recall the day on which the "Red Badge" was put on sale in Wanamakers, how Crane bought a copy and, sitting in the old Rathskeller here, inscribed it to me. Talcott Williams [67] did a great deal to make the book known. I wish that you could have the impressions of the Crane of that period that Irving Bacheller, Ralph Paine and E. J. Edwards could furnish.[68] Paine was with him in Jacksonville during the long wait to get away to Cuba on the "Commodore" and could give you a lot of stories apropos of that tragic episode.

After that came England and Greece and only occasional letters, then the long-impending yet sudden breakdown, the hurried but hope-

---

[65] Detective Charles Becker had threatened to arrest Crane when he protested the innocence of Dora Clark, arrested for soliciting. Brought into court, she was released on Crane's testimony. "Stephen Crane as Brave as His Hero/ Showed the 'Badge of Courage' in a New York Police Court" ran the headline in the New York *Journal*, September 17, 1896.

This same Becker, later Lieutenant Becker, was indicted in 1912 for the murder of Herman Rosenthal (murdered in reprisal for squealing on police and gambling house graft). Convicted twice, he lost his appeal to the higher courts and went to the electric chair in 1915. He was the first New York City policeman ever sentenced to death. The Becker-Rosenthal case, prolonged and sensational, swept the nation and brought about investigations into police department corruption throughout the country.

[66] The only evidence that Crane visited Fredericksburg and the battlefields there in 1893 is this single statement (cf. Berryman, p. 71). Crane went there in the spring of 1896 (see Letters 120, 128).

[67] Talcott Williams was on the staff of the Philadelphia *Press*, where *The Red Badge* appeared in shortened newspaper version in December, 1894. In 1896 Williams reviewed Crane's "The Little Regiment," in *Book News*.

[68] Irving Bacheller wrote reminiscences of Crane in *Coming Up the Road* (1928), and Ralph Paine in *Roads of Adventure* (1922). E. J. Edwards was probably a newspaper reporter. He gave Crane a bed occasionally at his place on West 217th Street (see Letter 162).

less journey to the Black Forest, and not so long afterward the cold, blustery day when we left all that remained of Stephen Crane in the cemetery in Elizabeth.[69] It is difficult to realize that nearly twenty five years have passed since then. . . .

With best wishes for the success of your book, I am   Very truly yours,   *Frederic M. Lawrence*

22. DR. FREDERIC M. LAWRENCE TO THOMAS BEER

Dr. Frederic M. Lawrence/1520 Spruce Street/Philadelphia/
Nov. 20, 1923

My dear Mr. Beer:/ . . . I am amused and yet not a little disgusted at the attitude of some of Crane's old friends. The plain truth is that Crane, in spite of his devotion to realism in literature, was incurably romantic about women, and this extended even to the girl of the streets. Many unkind things said about him were justifiable, for he was absolutely irresponsible in money matters; but whatever the stories about women, you can always find in Crane's behavior a curious trace of chivalry. If you know the real story of "Mrs." Crane, you will find it there—but I can readily understand why no biography came from her hand. Crane lived with Mayhew [70] the year after I left New York, and that was, I fancy, his wildest period. I knew a few of the old "N.A.D." [71] building crowd, and am very glad that you have located Linson [72]—I have lost track of him for years. Crane's first magazine article, a description of a coal mine, was done in collaboration with Linson. It appeared in McClures about 1892.[73] I can remember the two of them turning up in Port Jervis on their return from Scranton with a miner's lamp as a souvenir. . . .

In anticipation of our better acquaintance I remain/Very truly yours,   *F. M. Lawrence*

---

[69] Hillside, New Jersey.

[70] A 23d Street tough and bar-fighter, Eddie Mayhew (cf. Berryman, p. 99).

[71] The Needham Building on East 23d Street, housing the Art Students' League, where Crane shared rooms in 1893 and 1894 with R. G. Vosburgh, an illustrator, Frederick Gordon, also an illustrator (he did the drawings for *The Black Riders*), and other friends, including David Ericson (see Appendix 26).

[72] Corwin Linson, who illustrated some of Crane's sketches (see Appendix 19).

[73] "In the Depths of a Coal Mine," *McClure's Magazine*, August, 1894. Linson illustrated it. However, it was not Crane's first published piece.

23. HAMLIN GARLAND INSCRIPTION

New York/Mar 18/1924

[Inscribed in a copy of *The Black Riders*] [74]

I saw Crane set down some of these lines while sitting at my desk. Evidently they were composed subconsciously and (as he said) needed only to be drawn off [by] way of his pen's point.   *Hamlin Garland*

24. FRANK W. NOXON TO MAX J. HERZBERG [75]

706 Otis Bldg.,/Washington, D.C./Dec. 7, 1926

My dear Mr. Herzberg:—/ One of Stephen Crane's characteristics was a haunting solicitude for the comfort and welfare of other people, especially those of narrow means. He thought about it as one thinks about an art or craft, developing a style and inventing original methods.

My acquaintance with him began at Syracuse University, where we were in the Class of '94 and in the Delta Upsilon Fraternity, which Crane had joined at Lafayette earlier in the year. The earliest thing I remember concerning him was an essay which he read one night in chapter meeting on some serious political subject related to Russia. I saw the manuscript and in conversation later exclaimed at its exquisite legibility. This astonished me in a daily newspaper reporter such as Crane had already been. He replied that from the outset of his writing he had kept in mind the compositor, whose earnings depended upon the amount he could set, and this in turn upon the time it took to read the copy.

Among his favorite objects of solicitude were dogs. He loved them and was beloved by them. He embraced without question the well-known theory, which I had then never heard before, that the instinctive attitude of a dog toward a new human acquaintance was an

---

[74] Garland wrote this note on the dedication page; the book is dedicated to Garland.

[75] Frank W. Noxon published "The Real Stephen Crane" in *Step-Ladder* (Chicago, January, 1928). This letter is important for his dating of the first draft of *Maggie*, his note on Crane's concept of color in literature, and his reminiscences of the dinner tendered Crane by the Society of the Philistines (December 19, 1895).

Max J. Herzberg, Newark high school principal and editorial writer for the Newark *News*, was president of the Stephen Crane Association in Newark, which obtained possession in 1929 of the house at 14 Mulberry Place, Newark, where Stephen was born. He edited several editions of *The Red Badge* and wrote the biography of Crane in the *Encyclopaedia Britannica*. He died in 1958.

infallible test of character, and that no man who felt repugnance or even indifference toward canines, familiar or casual, could be wholly trusted for a kind heart toward those of his own species. Crane wrote of a dog named Jack; and I distinctly recall the fondness he showed for a story about this Jack,[76] which he let me read. The St. Nicholas magazine returned it, explaining that too many good dog stories were already in hand, but speaking in complimentary terms. I got the impression that Stephen regarded this as friendly not only to him but to the dog; and his gratitude in literary defeat had a note of affectionate pride.

No doubt some of our acquaintances in those days as well as critics and readers since had ascribed Crane's interest in unfortunate women to another instinct than sympathy and compassion. Nobody can be sure. But knowing him pretty well and seeing him a good deal in the company of girls, toward whom he showed respect and deference, I have no difficulty in believing that when he wrote about scarlet sisters or vehemently defended one as later he did in a New York police court,[77] the dominant impulse was a desire to serve the helpless. "Maggie, a Girl of the Streets," at least in its early form, was wholly or in part written at Syracuse.[78] With typical carelessness the author left the sheets lying about in the front corner room which he shared with Clarence Norton Goodwin. Some of those pages were picked up and read by droppers-in. The other day a '93 man whom I had not seen for many years asked me what I thought of Crane as a man at the time, knowing that he was writing that sort of thing. Had it been my observation, as it had been his, that Crane's own conduct seemed to contrast with his choice of literary themes? In 1926 this sounds primitive. It was 1890, and it was a Syracuse much more Methodist and very much more "divinity" than now. By the way, in after years Crane told me about the publication of "Maggie." He had vainly peddled it among the publishers, though to his delight the gentle realist, Howells, reading it for somebody [Harpers?] had written an enthusiastic

---

[76] "Jack," a dog story extant in three unfinished manuscripts belonging to the Barrett Collection, is described in "Stephen Crane: Some New Stories," ed. R. W. Stallman, *Bulletin of the New York Public Library,* LXI (January, 1957), 38.

[77] Crane's police encounters were reported in the New York *Journal,* September 17, 1896 ("Stephen Crane as Brave as His Hero"), in the New York *Tribune,* September 17, 1896 ("Saved from a Fine by Stephen Crane; Novelist Testifies in Behalf of a Woman Accused of Soliciting"), and in the Brooklyn *Daily Eagle,* October 17, 1896 ("Mr. Crane and the Police").

[78] See Introduction to Bowery Tales; pp. 3 ff., *Omnibus,* for an account of the composition and history of *Maggie.*

memorandum. Finally he paid for bringing it out himself, using the pseudonym "Johnston Smith." The cover was yellow paper with the title in large black letters. Four men were hired to sit all day one in front of another in New York elevated trains, reading intently and holding up the volume so that passengers would think the metropolis was "Maggie"-mad.

With his catholic taste in people Crane in our day combined considerable sense of social form. At the fraternity house one function was an annual party to which every co-ed on the hill was invited, the requisite number of partners being recruited from our chapters at other Central New York colleges. For the party[,] in Crane's one winter with us, after getting into his own evening dress he went about the house with a box of shirt studs and a punch, detecting local brethren whose well starched bosoms were innocent both of studs and of holes and rectifying the deficiency.

Crane was brave, physically, morally and socially. Nothing would do, therefore, but he must pity the coward and try to understand him. So we got "The Red Badge of Courage." Incidentally, the use of the word "Red" in this title was part of a program. After the book appeared he and I had somewhere a talk about color in literature.[79] He told me that a passage in Goethe analyzed the effect which the several colors have upon the human mind. Upon Crane this had made a profound impression and he had utilized the idea to produce his effects. Do you remember the colors of the burning chemicals in "The Monster"? There you had them all at once.

Most of us were surprised, though we needn't have been, when this lover of his kind got into a war. It is well remembered how the description of Chancellorsville in "The Red Badge," written by a youth not born until 1871, stirred the Civil War veterans and singled out the author as the one sure-fire war correspondent should war come. War came—with Spain; and Mr. Hearst's people annexed Crane for Cuba. The next fall, driving in a "hack" from Boston to Cambridge, where

---

[79] *"Crane's style is prose pointilism.* It is composed of disconnected images, which coalesce like the blobs of color in French impressionist paintings, every word-group having a cross-reference relationship, every seemingly disconnected detail having interrelationship to the configurated whole. The intensity of a Crane work is owing to this patterned coalescence of disconnected things, everything at once fluid and precise. A striking analogy is established between Crane's use of colors and the method employed by the impressionists and the neo-impressionists or divisionists, and it is as if he had known about their theory of contrasts and had composed his own prose paintings by the same principle." *Omnibus,* p. 185. On Crane and French impressionist painters, see pp. 185–187.

he was reporting a foot-ball game,[80] Crane in the intervals between those harrowing coughs which got him in the end told me about Santiago. He said he was of no use whatever. The moment the fighting began Crane started carrying buckets of water to the wounded and paid no attention whatever to the observation necessary for writing newspaper despatches.

Not even Crane, love him as most men did, was always able to command from others that tolerance which he diffused so infinitely. At our era, security against nicotine was still a hope to which a he-man might aspire. The heating system in the chapter house carried smoke from one room to another. Whether the brethren (assaying then pretty high in divinity students) were more annoyed and alarmed at having to inhale attenuated whiffs so penetrating to their castles, or concerned for the salvation of the smokers, the iron heel descended, and an unregenerate group captained by the grinning Crane and consisting of Goodwin, Congdon, and perhaps others (I never smoked until I was 50 but often went along) were translated to the cupola, where on freezing days in ulsters, ear-laps, mittens and arctics they exhaled the fumes unsmelt to heaven. Some years ago in Northampton, Mass., I visited F. K. Congdon, who was, and I suppose is, superintendent of schools there. Congdon with a Sherlock Holmes air wanted to know whether in 1907 I was an editorial writer on the Boston Herald. I was, and his clue had been an article on Crane mentioning the cupola smoker, which Congdon said no other newspaper man could have known about.

If you go to East Aurora you will see an exhibition [of] handwriting and other souvenirs of Crane, but Crane was one of the series who were driven from Elbert Hubbard by what they believed was Hubbard's abuse of them. In 1893 or thereabouts, soon after I went to Boston, Hubbard ended by his and the Dean's mutual consent his short sojourn at Harvard, leaving behind him among other things an unexpired rental on a Cambridge post-office box, to which subscriptions and contributions might be sent for a new magazine called The Philistine. It seems that one Bickford and one Taber (with the latter of whom I became intimate and enjoy to this day quinquennial re-unions) for a brief while in Denver, where they worked on the Times, published a Philistine. When Hubbard quit the soap business for literature he did not instantly acquire either that classic appearance or that con-

---

[80] In Cambridge on November 7, 1896, Princeton played Harvard, and Crane reported the game in the New York *Journal*. If he was again reporting a Harvard football game when this conversation with Noxon allegedly took place, it must have been in November 1898, after his return from Cuba.

fidence in his pen which subsequently amazed all the continents, so he took on a series of editors, of whom Taber was first. Taber proposed the revival of the Philistine. Not knowing these worthies, but dwelling in Boston and noting the Cambridge address, which made them seem near, although already they were in fact far away in East Aurora, I sent them some piece of nonsense about a character named Clanging-harp, which was published, and an acquaintance began by mail with both Taber and Hubbard. Presently Crane appeared likewise among the contributors. A by-law of the Society of the Philistines published on the magazine cover prescribed a duty of members to attend the annual dinner. Some years went by without the first annual dinner, but about 1895 it was announced that the annual dinner was coming off with Crane as guest of honor. Borrowing money and probably clothes, I made the journey to Buffalo, where the feed was held at the Genesee House. There must have been 15 or 20 there, most of us freaks or near-freaks, and on the menu were scriptures by others who couldn't come but admired the guest. Hubbard, still timid, sat at the foot of the table and Taber at the head; Crane on Taber's right; Claude Fayette Brag-don [81] (who these days without the Fayette designs scenic and costume investiture for theatrical productions) on his left, with me next; and on Crane's right, Willis W. Hawkins, Editor then of Brains [publishing house]. Hawkins borrowed cuff links of me which I never got back.

After dinner Taber rose and began his speech. "Probably," he said, "the most unique———." That was as far as he got. A voice somewhere down toward Hubbard called out "Can 'unique' be compared?" This was the signal. It determined the tone of the festivities. In the best Clover and Gridiron manner Taber and all the other speakers were guyed and ragged from start to finish. Crane, having the time of his life, was called up, and they had as much fun with him as with the others.

When Crane sat down up rose Claude Bragdon. After 31 years I can still hear the sound of his voice and see the look on his face. "I came here," he said, "to do honor to Stephen Crane, not to ridicule him. I regret to take this step, but I cannot longer remain in the room." The door was on the far side of the table. To get out, Bragdon had to walk around behind Taber and Crane. Hawkins stood and blocked him. "One moment," he said. "I am the oldest man in this room. I know Stephen Crane better than anyone else here. I have slept with him, eaten with him, starved with him, ridden with him, swum with him.

---

[81] See pp. 85–86, 120 for Bragdon's account of the Philistine Society affair.

I know him through and through, every mood. I have come here, like our friend, to do honor to Stephen Crane. I have taken part in all that has occurred, and he knows I love him and admire him. He knows that you all do. I assure you he feels more complimented by the spirit of this meeting than he would have been by all the solemn eulogies that could be pronounced." Crane was nodding his head off. Everybody applauded.

"I am sorry," said Bragdon, "if I have made a mistake. I ask your pardon."

"Pardon is granted you," Hawkins answered, "on one condition."

Bragdon looked up inquiringly.

"That condition," said Hawkins, "is that you turn around and take your seat."

And Bragdon did it.

I never knew the particular circumstances under which in Crane's case the author, like so many others, fell out with Hubbard, but have always assumed that it was the Fra's democratic prejudice against royalties. Whatever the reason, the inevitable assault appeared in the Philistine, and in Crane's case it was no less than a serious and circumstantial narrative of his having been "drowned in the Irish Sea," though Crane considerably survived this obituary. Yours truly,

Frank W. Noxon

25. E. W. McCREADY TO B. J. R. STOLPER [82]

Hammond River,/New Brunswick, Canada/Jan. 22, 1934

Dear Mr. Stolper: . . . I encountered the lady [Cora Taylor], along with Paine,[83] one wild night in our filibustering days. The house was on the outskirts of Jacksonville. There was a semi-circular sign of generous size over the door, bearing in great letters of gold the inviting legend "Hotel de Dream." It was hers. She was hostess—in the later euphemism. The non-coms & privates [84] numbered some 12 or 15—

---

[82] Ernest W. McCready, correspondent of the New York *Herald*, was a shipmate of Crane and Ralph D. Paine on *The Three Friends* during the Spanish-American War. B. J. R. Stolper compiled *Stephen Crane: A List of His Writings and Articles About Him* (1930).

[83] Ralph Paine, newspaper correspondent; he dedicated his *Roads of Adventure* (1922) to Crane and McCready.

[84] McCready's reference to "non-coms and privates" is purposefully ambiguous. It could apply equally well to young men, habitues of the Hotel de Dream, or to the girls they brought with them. There were no girls boarded on the premises.

of unusual comeliness and youth—especially, considering Jacksonville of 1897. The lady was handsome, of some real refinement, aloof to most —to all, indeed, until Steve and Cap. [Captain] Murphy [85] arrived— newly come from death and the sea, eager for drink, and drowsy ease. . . . Paine and I were in one section of the house and did not that night encounter Crane—whom Paine already knew [86]—but only heard distantly the Murphy party. But we returned some nights later— Christmas Eve—sojourned—and sat in at the "family" board next day for *Christmas dinner*—Paine carving the noble bird. . . . However, P[aine] learned then & thereafter, between sessions at the roulette wheel, that our Mr. Crane had discovered the lady reading his book.[87] Murphy & Crane were thinly incog. [incognito]. Presently, as the skipper hoisted a few more and a few more [drinks] he revealed his friend's identity. The news pierced the lady's very liver. *Paine told me* he heard of the subsequent exodus or hegira, after the Porto Rican campaign, I think, to London & the society of Harold Frederic et al of the Bohemian literary set in London & Surrey or Sussex. There they were in a country house.[88] My impression of the Dame aux Camellias (or whatever it is) is still vivid. Fact is, she was a cut above us in several ways, notably poise and surety of command of herself & others. If she had any false notes I was then all too unskilled in recognizing authentic "class," or lack of it, to detect any. One carries gold in war time or on campaign, and there was drink a-plenty, of course. Yet even before we knew that Crane had not only staked the claim but that there was instantaneous mutual attraction (I'm no bio-chemist, you'll guess) we never proposed to her that a little love interlude would be profitable to her and quite irresistible to us. Why? It was after all, the "Hotel de Dream." I'll have to go to one of De Maupassant's yarns to match my reflections on this encounter as reviewed from this distance— say 37 or 38 years along the road. Stephen took her in his stride—and, as it turned out, in some very solid respects, the gray mare proved to be the best horse. . . .

---

[85] Of the *Commodore*, the steamship that sank off the Florida coast on New Year's Day, 1897. McCready has confused the chronology here, for the Christmas dinner he describes took place before the *Commodore* disaster. Crane met Cora in early November. The dinner McCready describes seems more likely to have taken place on Thanksgiving Day, 1896.

[86] Paine had known Crane at Asbury Park when Crane was writing shore news there during summer vacations.

[87] *George's Mother*, which Crane inscribed "To an unnamed sweetheart on November 4, 1896" (see No. 177).

[88] First at Oxted in Surrey and then at Brede Place in Sussex.

26. *DAVID ERICSON TO AMES W. WILLIAMS* [89]

Provincetown/Nov 4th, 1942

Dear Mr. Williams:/ About the year 1893 Steven [*sic*] Crane drifted
into my studio in the old Needham building, East 23d St. The Art Students League [90] had just moved up town to the new quarters on 57th St.;
my studio was one of the many occupied by painters, and illustrators.
We were all poor struggling for means of existence. He was at that
time writing "The Red Badge of Courage." I remember one time when
he was lying in a hammock of his saying "That is great!" It shocked me
for the moment. I thought how conceited he is. But when he read me
the passage, I realized at once how wonderfully real it was, and said
that the writer had that advantage over us painters in that he could
make his men talk, walk and think. Where as a painter can only depict
a man in one position at a time. He seemed very pleased with this
compliment. That was a week or so before I painted his sweetheart's
portrait.[91] After that he gave me a copy of the "Black Riders" which
he promised to sign, but which he never did. We both forgot about it.
About that time he went down to the slums with an artist by the name
of Carrol. They were gone about a week. That was when he was writing "Maggie." Steve said nothing, but Carrol told me it was a horrible
experience. Crane only smiled about it, for to him it was the cream of
life. He got what he was after. He would drift away for days, and then
come back some times staying with me, and some times with the other
fellows. He went about a good deal with a young man by the name
of Vosburgh, an illustrator from Chicago. Vosburgh would sometimes
lie a bed all day and when asked why he didn't get up? Answered that
he had had nothing to eat. So of course we would go out together and
have something. One time after Steven Crane had been with me for
several days he said, Well! Dave let's go out to lunch. It is my treat
now. I got my pay today. (Seven dollars a week, from the New York
Tribune) So we went to one of the little cheap restaurants on East
23rd St., where we sat down at a table for two. He immediately pulled
out his pad and pencil, and began to write as usual. Then we ate

[89] David Ericson is a professor at Columbia University; Ames W. Williams is a Crane scholar and cobibliographer (with Vincent Starrett) of
Stephen Crane: A Bibliography (1948).

[90] At 143–147 East 23d Street, where Crane lived for over a half year
in the studio of R. G. Vosburgh during 1893 and in the studio of Frederick
Gordon in 1894. Vosburgh did some drawings for some of Crane's journalistic articles, and Gordon illustrated *The Black Riders*.

[91] Of Lily Brandon Munroe, a sketch Ericson never finished and which
has been lost.

silently or talked very little. I think I ate no more than usual but anyway when we had finished, he walked out. So it was my turn again as
usual. I enjoyed it very much for I could see how completely he had
forgotten his promise. (It was the real Bohemian) He was absolutely
indifferent to comfort or discomfort. I can remember so well how when
he came down from the country he would come in and put his little
hand bag down in the middle of the Studio floor, sit down on a little
sketching stool, pull out his pad, pen, and a bottle of ink, and begin to
write with only a few words of greetings. I do not remember that he
ever erased or changed anything. His writing was clean and round
with a ring around his periods. He wrote slowly. It amazed me how
he could keep the story in mind while he was slowly forming the
letters. This I thought the most extra-ordinary thing I had ever seen.
I do not think that any one ever noticed it. I felt an awe for him when
I saw how naturally his imagination worked through his hand as
though he really lived in another world. It seemed as though his con-
centration of ideas of what he had seen, and heard with a certain
artistic perception enabled him to draw his characters so vividly. "The
Beefsteak Club" entertained him once and they began to guy him
when he got up to speak. So he told them all to go to Hell! He was
sometimes sarcastic about people's thoughtlessness, and felt that life
was an accident. I can not remember any of our conversation. I was
very busy with my painting and classes at that time. He was slender,
youthful, mild and his voice was soft. His complexion was sallow, gray
eyes, and light brown hair. Howells, and Garland appreciated him
more than any one else. I am afraid that this will not be very useful to
you. But it is all that I can remember. With best wishes for your success. I am yours very sincerely.   *David Ericson*

27. A. E. W. MASON TO VINCENT STARRETT

51 South Street,/London, W.1./4th October, 1945

Dear Mr. Starrett,/ I cannot remember when I first met Stephen
Crane, but I became friendly with him and went down to stay for a
week at Christmas with Cora and himself at Brede Place, six or seven
miles from Rye, which the Cranes had taken from Moreton Frewen;
in fact, Clare Sheridan, the sculptress, who is living there now, is
Frewen's daughter.[92] There was a large party of us that Christmas.

---

[92] Brede Place is now owned by Roger M. Frewen. A portrait of Moreton Frewen is given in *The Remarkable Mr. Jerome*, by Anita Leslie, and
the history of Brede Place is given in *My Crowded Sanctuary*, by Clare
Sheridan.

The house, which frankly was not in a state to be occupied, was sketchily furnished and I think there was arranged a dormitory in which six or seven men slept. I know that I was given a room to myself but warned not to open, except very cautiously, two great doors which enclosed one side of it. There was no electric light and naturally enough I opened very carefully the two doors. I found that if I had taken one step forward, I should have stepped down about thirty feet into the chapel, this being the private pew or box of the owners of the house. We had, I remember, rushes on the floor instead of carpets, and there were other disadvantages which meant nothing to us, for we were all of us young.

One of the conditions of our visit was that we should each write a line for a pantomime which he proposed to produce in the village hall on one of the evenings: and, with one rehearsal, we did it and, apparently, to my infinite astonishment, with much laughter and success.

Crane gave a ball on one night, to which he had invited the leading figures of the country-side, but there was a tremendous fall of snow, and this being the day before motors, hardly a local resident turned up. This was, perhaps, just as well for H. G. Wells arrived with his wife and he invented a game of racing on broomsticks over the polished floor, which I think would have staggered the local gentry if they had turned up.

Beyond Wells and a man who is now a most important Solicitor and a dramatic critic, I have not one idea of the people who were staying there, but I do remember being greeted by Henry James, who was standing at the gate of his garden at Rye as I drove past him, and being warned by him that I might find an actress or two in the party and should be careful not to get caught.

After this, and fairly soon after, Stephen got ill. I can't remember what year this was [1899] but it was a year during which he had written twenty accounts of battles in various magazines (I think chiefly in The Cornhill),[93] and got £100 for each article. You, of course,

---

[93] In the *Cornhill Magazine* the following stories were printed in 1899: "Second Generation," "Self-Made Man," "God Rest Ye, Merry Gentlemen." One Whilomville story, "His New Mittens," was printed in 1898. Most of his battle sketches appeared in 1900 in *Lippincott's Magazine*; others in *Ainslee's Magazine, Cassell's Magazine,* and *Frank Leslie's Popular Monthly* (1900). But as to the number of these battle pieces and prices received for them, Mason's memory has indeed "played him very false," or he is simply repeating the legend of Crane's high prices. There were nine battle articles in all—not twenty—for which Crane got £30–£50 each, not £100 (see Letter 330).

will have details. I think it was the Christmas before he died, unless my memory has played me very false.

From that time, I began to see a good deal of Stephen and went down fairly often to Brede Place. It wasn't really fit for him and he told me finally that he had been coughing up blood, which Cora wouldn't stand. Some time that last spring I have a recollection of seeing him in bed in the open air, under the shelter of a corner of Brede Place, and that he was looking forward—or pretending to look forward—to getting well in the Black Forest. The doctor had very little hope of his recovery and said that he should never have stayed in that house which had no proper plumbing or furniture.[94] I remember that bats flew about my ceiling and walls until the candle was put out and they settled down then to share the room with me.

As to *The O'Ruddy*, during that last spring he asked me to read it. He told me its history. He had begun it, scoffing at some of us who were writing that sort of romantic tale, but, as he went on with it, he got bitten by the theme and the treatment and the period, and was enjoying himself writing it. I read it very carefully. I think there must have been, even at that time, a suggestion or hint that if he did not come back, I should finish it, but of that I can't be sure.[95] Certainly I read it carefully and inclined to realize that this was not his pigeon at all. However, I think I told him that he must get well and finish it himself. After he died, Cora wrote to me and asked me to undertake it. I didn't, for although I guessed that Stephen's affairs were not very flourishing, I did not think that *The O'Ruddy* would add either to his estate or his reputation. It was a little time afterwards that Barr finished the book and justified my reluctance. Stephen had left nothing whatever to guide you as to how the story was going to run. I think he was letting it go its own way.

I think that's all that I remember. I liked Stephen very much. He was a great enthusiast and if he had been a little less 'Early English,'

---

[94] Mason's impressions of Brede Place echo those of Ford Madox Ford (see p. 202). It seems to have dropped out of memory, forty-five years later, that English country houses at the turn of the century were without central heating, plumbing, or electricity.

[95] Nothing in the record indicates that Crane ever asked or wanted Mason to finish the book. His choice was Robert Barr. When Barr backed out, Cora then turned to Marriott-Watson and finally Mason; and when Mason either could not or would not get on with the job, the matter was settled only by Stokes, the publishers, taking it into their own hands two and a half years after Crane's death and persuading Robert Barr to undertake the completion (see Lillian Gilkes and Joan H. Baum, "Stephen Crane's Last Novel: *The O'Ruddy*," *Columbia Library Columns*, February, 1957).

just to suit Brede Place, it is possible that he might have lived longer. But that I don't know. You couldn't heat the place and the winter could be pretty harsh. I think it is likely, from what I remember, that when he was alone, he was not out enough in the open air.

However, I see that I am beginning to guess; so I fall back upon a certainty, which is that I have a new Hanaud novel called "The House in Lordship Lane" coming out next year. Yours sincerely,

A. E. W. Mason

Catalogue

The following catalogue identifies the sources for the letters in this volume. The number refers to the numbered sequence of the letters in the text. Not included in this tabulation are letters reproduced or quoted from in the editorial notes and footnotes, as usually such sources are identified in the notes themselves. The editorial notes and footnotes contain a considerable number of letters reproduced or quoted from, including letters of Bernard Shaw, Henry James, some Stephen Crane inscriptions, and so forth; these items are not included in the List of Letters. Not included in this collection is the correspondence of Amy Leslie and Willis Brooks Hawkins, pertaining to the loan she made Stephen Crane, these letters belonging to the Dartmouth College Library. Also not included is a set of some thirty letters of James B. Pinker belonging to the Clifton Waller Barrett Collection.

I

Letters and autograph inscriptions belonging to the Clifton Waller Barrett Collection now in the Alderman Library of the University of Virginia, published by permission of Clifton Waller Barrett: Nos. 30, 41, 43, 45, 47, 48, 53, 55, 56, 57, 59, 65, 70, 72, 78, 79, 81, 83, 84, 85, 86, 87, 90, 92, 93, 94, 95, 96, 97, 98, 99, 100 (copy in the Syracuse University Library), 102, 103 (copy in the possession of Melvin H. Schoberlin), 104, 105, 106, 108, 109, 110, 114, 116, 117, 120, 121, 128, 134, 135, 136, 146, 148, 155, 157 (also the Crane notes 1 and 2 quoted in the footnote to No. 157), 175, 179, 181, 189, 194, 195, 196, 204, 269, 320, 323.

Also belonging to the Barrett Collection, acquisitions added as the manuscript was being prepared for the press: Nos. 173, 240, 241, 244, 246, 252, 253, 259, 236A, 287A.

Letters belonging to the Thomas Beer papers in the possession of Miss Alice Beer, published by her permission: No. 289; Appendixes 18–22.

Letter 59, belonging to the Boston Public Library, published by permission.

Letters and autograph inscriptions belonging to the Berg Collection of the New York Public Library, published by permission: Nos. 50, 60, 61, 64, 66, 80, 82, 91, 118, 119, 133, 138, 140, 142, 143, 145, 149, 152, 153, 154, 156, 160, 161, 192, 315, 325 (and the Crane inscription quoted in the footnote to No. 325), 371; also the letter quoted on p. 263.

Letters and autograph inscriptions belonging to the Butler Library Stephen Crane Collection, Columbia University, published by permission: Nos. 22, 24, 27, 33, 36, 37, 38, 40, 44, 71, 73, 101, 112, 113, 115, 130, 168, 170, 171, 176, 182, 183, 184, 185, 186, 187, 188, 190, 191, 197, 202, 205, 210, 215, 218, 220, 221, 222, 223, 225, 226, 227, 229, 230, 232, 237, 239, 248, 249, 251, 254, 256, 257, 258, 260, 262, 264, 276, 280, 282, 286, 290, 294, 296, 299, 304, 309, 312, 319, 327, 340, 341, 349, 350, 355, 359, 360, 362, 369. Also the William Howe Crane letters quoted from in the editorial note on p. 215; also Appendixes 4, 6, 15, and 25.

Letters and autograph inscriptions belonging to the Dartmouth College Library, published by permission: Nos. 68, 147, 162, 173, 177, 198, 201, 228; also Appendix 23.

Letter 6, belonging to the Delta Upsilon Fraternity at Syracuse University, published by permission of Odell S. Hathaway.

Letter 107, belonging to Elliot B. Hague, M.D., of Buffalo, New York, published by his permission.

Letters belonging to Odell S. Hathaway, published by his permission: Nos. 2, 3, 4, 5, 11, 15, 42, 69, 88, 89.

Letter belonging to the Historical Society of Pennsylvania, published by permission: No. 297.

Letters and autograph inscription belonging to the Houghton Library, published by permission of Harvard College: Nos. 23, 26, 124, 132, 164, 169, 172.

Letter belonging to the Huntington Library, published by permission of the Henry E. Huntington Library and Art Gallery: No. 13; also Crane inscription in footnote to No. 94, and Appendixes 8, 10.

Letters belonging to the Josiah K. Lilly Collection of Indiana University Library, published by permission of Josiah K. Lilly: Nos. 17, 54, 74.

Letter belonging to Waring Jones, of Minneapolis, Minnesota, published by permission of Miss Helen Hilliard: No. 125.

Letter belonging to Roger M. Frewen, published by his permission: No. 236.

Crane inscription belonging to Lafayette College Library, published by permission: No. 163.

Letter belonging to Phillip M. Barr, published by permission: No. 301A.

Letters belonging to The Library of Congress, published by permission: No. 16; Appendix 16.

Letter belonging to the Newark Public Library, published by permission: Appendix 24.

Letters belonging to Melvin H. Schoberlin, published by his permission: Nos. 100, 103, 271; also Appendix 14.

Letters belonging to Frederick B. Smillie, of Norristown, Pa., published by his permission: Nos. 28, 29, 34, 75, 234.

Letters belonging to R. W. Stallman (the gift of Vincent Starrett): Nos. 273, 279, 285; also Appendix 27.

Letters belonging to the George Arents Collection of Syracuse University Library, published by permission of Syracuse University Library: Nos. 5, 14, 51, 52, 63, 77, 90, 122, 127, 129, 131, 139, 144, 150, 151, 266, 267, 270, 272, 274, 275, 277, 278, 281, 283, 284, 287, 292, 295, 298, 300, 301, 302, 303, 305, 307, 308, 310, 311, 313, 316, 317, 318, 321, 322, 324, 326, 328–339, 342, 345, 346, 347, 348, 351, 352, 353, 358, 361, 366, 367, 368; also Appendixes 11, 13.

Letters belonging to the H. G. Wells Collection of the Library of the University of Illinois, published by permission of the University of Illinois Library: Nos. 344, 354, 364, 365.

Letters and autograph inscription belonging to the University of Southern California Library, published by permission of the University of Southern California Library: Nos. 35, 39, 46, 76, 165, 166, 167, 207; also Appendixes 8, 10, 12.

Letter belonging to the Alderman Library of the University of Virginia, published by permission of the University of Virginia Library: No. 306.

Letter belonging to Ames W. Williams, published by permission of David Ericson: Appendix 26.

Letters belonging to Yale University Library, published by permission of Yale University Library: Nos. 206, 261, 263, 265, 268.

II

Letters and inscriptions published here for the first time: Nos. 21, 23, 26, 28, 29, 30, 34, 36, 37, 38, 40, 59, 71, 93, 94, 95, 98, 101, 105, 107, 113, 115, 116, 120, 125, 128, 130, 132, 135, 136, 163, 164, 169, 171, 172, 175, 182, 183, 184, 185, 186, 187, 188, 191, 202, 207, 225, 236, 239, 240, 241, 244, 246, 252, 253, 254, 257, 259, 260, 261, 263, 265, 266, 267, 269, 270, 271, 272, 273, 274, 275, 277, 278, 279, 280, 281, 282, 283, 284, 285, 286, 287, 289, 290, 292, 295, 296, 297, 298, 300, 301, 301A, 302, 303, 304, 305, 306, 307, 308, 309, 310, 311, 312, 313, 316, 317, 318, 319, 320, 321, 322, 323, 324 (and the Crane inscription in footnote to No. 325), 326, 327, 328, 329, 330, 331, 332, 333, 334, 335, 336, 337, 338, 339, 340, 341, 342, 343, 344, 345, 346, 347, 348, 349, 350, 351, 352, 353, 354, 355, 358, 359, 360, 361. Also the Crane notes in footnotes to No. 157, 289, and Cora's note in footnote to No. 300. Also Appendixes 4, 8, 10, 11, 12, 13, 14, 16, 17, 18, 19, 20, 21, 22, 23, 24, 25, 26, 27.

Letter reprinted from *Contacts,* by Curtis Brown (Harper, 1935), p. 262: No. 123.

Letter reprinted from *Joseph Conrad: Life and Letters,* ed. G. Jean-Aubry (Doubleday, Page, 1927), I, 211–12: No. 213.

Letter reprinted from *Life and Letters of William Dean Howells,* ed. Mildred Howells (Doubleday, Doran & Company, Inc., 1928), II, 44: No. 124.

Letters reprinted from *Paul Revere Reynolds,* by Frederick Lewis Allen (privately printed, 1944): Nos. 200, 214, 219, 224, 243, 245, 247, 250.

Letters reprinted from *Stephen Crane,* by Thomas Beer (Alfred A. Knopf, 1923); in *Hanna, Crane, and the Mauve Decade,* by Thomas Beer (Alfred A. Knopf, 1941): Nos. 1, 7, 8, 9, 10, 12, 20, 25, 31, 49, 67, 158, 178, 180, 199, 208, 209, 211, 212, 217, 231, 233, 235, 238, 291, 314, 357.

Letters reprinted from *Stephen Crane,* by John Berryman (William Sloane Associates; Methuen, 1950): Nos. 62, 208, 255, 320A, 363.

Letters reprinted from *Stephen Crane's Love Letters to Nellie Crouse,* Edwin H. Cady and Lester G. Wells, eds. (Syracuse University Press, 1954): Nos. 3, 6, 14, 51, 52, 63, 77, 90, 100, 103, 122, 127, 129, 131, 139, 144, 150, 151, 268, 329; also Appendixes 7 and 24.

Letters reprinted from *Stephen Crane,* by Thomas L. Raymond (Carteret Book Club, 1923): No. 193; also the Joseph Conrad letter quoted on p. xxx.

Letters reprinted from *Stephen Crane: An Omnibus,* selected and edited, with critical introductions and notes, by Robert Wooster Stallman (Alfred A. Knopf, 1952; William Heinemann, Ltd., 1954): Nos. 2, 4, 5, 6, 8, 9, 10, 11, 13, 14, 15, 16, 17, 18, 19, 25, 28, 31, 32, 34, 35, 39, 41, 42, 43, 45, 46, 47, 48, 49, 53, 54, 55, 56, 57, 58, 62, 67, 68, 69, 70, 72, 74, 75, 76, 78, 79, 80, 81, 83, 84, 85, 86, 87, 88, 89, 92, 102, 103, 104, 106, 108, 109, 110, 111, 114, 117, 121, 123, 124, 134, 137, 146, 147, 148, 155, 157, 158, 159, 162, 165, 166, 174, 178, 179, 181, 189, 194, 195, 196, 198, 199, 200, 201, 203, 204, 206, 212, 214, 216, 217, 219, 224, 228, 231, 233, 238, 243, 245, 247, 250, 255, 268, 288, 356, 357, 363.

Letter reprinted from *A Stephen Crane Collection,* by Herbert Faulkner West (Dartmouth College Library, 1948), p. 14: Nos. 147, 162 (inscription).

Letter reprinted from *Stephen Crane: A Bibliography,* by Ames W. Williams and Vincent Starrett (John Valentine, 1948), p. 13: No. 16.

Letters reprinted from *Roadside Meetings,* by Hamlin Garland (Macmillan, 1930): Nos. 35, 46, 76, 165, 166.

Letter reprinted from introduction and notes to *The Red Badge of Courage,* by Max J. Herzberg (D. Appleton Company, 1926): No. 356.

Letter reprinted from *23 Books: The Stories Behind Them,* by John T. Winterich (Books Art Club, 1938; Lippincott, 1939), p. 124: No. 18.

Letters reprinted from *Two Letters from Stephen Crane to Joseph Conrad* (First Editions Club, 1926): Nos. 203, 228.

Letters reprinted from *My Stephen Crane,* by Corwin Knapp Linson, ed. Edwin H. Cady (Syracuse University Press, 1958): No. 126; also Crane to Linson letters, Nos. 29A, 46A.

INDEX

References are to pages. Boldface indicates letters, telegrams, inscriptions, and other written communications to or from the person referred to.